Rick Steves'
SPAIN &
PORTUGAL
2001

Other ATP travel guidebooks by Rick Steves

Rick Steves' Europe 101: History and Art for the Traveler (with Gene Openshaw)
Rick Steves' Postcards from Europe
Rick Steves' Europe Through the Back Door
Rick Steves' Mona Winks: Self-Guided Tours of Europe's Top Museums
  (with Gene Openshaw)
Rick Steves' Best of Europe
Rick Steves' France, Belgium & the Netherlands (with Steve Smith)
Rick Steves' Germany, Austria & Switzerland
Rick Steves' Great Britain & Ireland
Rick Steves' Italy
Rick Steves' London (with Gene Openshaw)
Rick Steves' Paris (with Steve Smith and Gene Openshaw)
Rick Steves' Rome (with Gene Openshaw)
Rick Steves' Scandinavia
Rick Steves' Spain & Portugal
Rick Steves' Phrase Books: German, Italian, French,
  Spanish/Portuguese, and French/Italian/German
Asia Through the Back Door (with Bob Effertz)

Copyright © 2000, 1999, 1998, 1997, 1996 by Rick Steves
Cover © 2000 Avalon Travel Publishing,
  © 1999, 1998 by John Muir Publications

All rights reserved.
Printed in the United States of America

Second printing March 2001.

For the latest on Rick Steves' lectures, guidebooks, tours, and
public-television series, contact Europe Through the Back Door,
Box 2009, Edmonds, WA 98020, tel. 425/771-8303, fax 425/771-0833,
www.ricksteves.com, or e-mail: rick@ricksteves.com.

ISBN 1-56691-234-2
ISSN 1084-4414

Europe Through the Back Door Editors: Risa Laib, Jacquie Maupin
Avalon Travel Publishing Editor: Kate Willis
Copy Editor: Chris Hayhurst
Research Assistance Brent A. Hurd, Tooraj Fooladi
Production & Typesetting Kathleen Sparkes, White Hart Design
Design Linda Braun
Cover Design Janine Lehmann
Maps David C. Hoerlein
Printer Banta Company
Cover Photo Giralda Tower and Cathedral, Sevilla, Spain;
copyright © Blaine Harrington III

Distributed to the book trade by Publishers Group West, Berkeley, California

CONTENTS

Top Destinations in Spain and Portugal

INTRODUCTION

Like a grandpa bouncing a baby on his knee, Iberia is a mix of old and new, modern and traditional. Spain and Portugal can fill your travel days with world-class art treasures, folk life, exotic foods, sunshine, friendly people, and castles where the winds of the past still howl. And, in spite of its recent economic boom, Iberia (particularly Portugal) remains Europe's bargain basement. Tourism is huge here. Spain, with 40 million inhabitants, entertains 50 million visitors annually. Iberia is very popular — and you're about to learn why.

This book breaks Spain and Portugal into their top big-city, small-town, and rural destinations. It then gives you all the information and opinions necessary to wring the maximum value out of your limited time and money in each of these destinations. If you plan a month or less in Iberia, this lean and mean little book is all you need.

Experiencing Spain and Portugal's culture, people, and natural wonders economically and hassle-free has been my goal for 25 years of traveling, tour guiding, and writing. With this book, I pass on to you the lessons I've learned, updated for 2001.

Rick Steves' Spain & Portugal is a tour guide in your pocket, with a balanced, comfortable mix of exciting cities and cozy towns topped off with an exotic dollop of Morocco. It covers the predictable biggies and stirs in a healthy dose of Back Door intimacy. Along with seeing a bullfight, the Prado, and flamenco, you'll buy cookies from cloistered nuns in a sun-parched Andalusian town and recharge your solar cells in an Algarve fishing village. You'll eat barnacles with green wine in village Portugal and scramble the ramparts of an ancient Moorish castle. I've been selective, including only the most exciting sights and experiences. For example, there are countless whitewashed Andalusian hill towns; I recommend the best two.

The best is, of course, only my opinion. But after two busy decades of travel writing, lecturing, and tour guiding, I've developed a sixth sense of what tickles the traveler's fancy.

This Information Is Accurate and Up-to-Date

This book is updated every year. Most publishers of guidebooks that cover a region from top to bottom can afford an update only every two or three years, and then the research is often by letter. Since this book is selective, covering only the places I think make the best month or so in Iberia, it can be personally updated each summer. Even with annual updates, things change. But if you're traveling with the current edition of this book, I guarantee you're using the most up-to-date information available. Trust me, you'll regret trying to save a few bucks by traveling with old information. If you're packing an old book, you'll quickly learn the seriousness of your mistake ...in Europe. Your trip costs about $10 per waking hour. Your time is valuable. This guidebook saves lots of time.

Planning Your Trip

This book is organized by destinations. Each destination is covered as a mini-vacation on its own, filled with exciting sights and homey, affordable places to stay. In each chapter, you'll find the following:

Planning Your Time, a suggested schedule with thoughts on how best to use your limited time.

Orientation, including tourist information, city transportation, and an easy-to-read map designed to make the text clear and your arrival smooth.

Sights with ratings: ▲▲▲—Don't miss; ▲▲—Try hard to see; ▲—Worthwhile if you can make it; no rating—Worth knowing about.

Sleeping and **Eating**, with addresses and phone numbers of my favorite budget hotels and restaurants.

Transportation Connections to nearby destinations by train, bus, or car, with recommended roadside attractions for drivers.

The **appendix** is a traveler's tool kit, with telephone tips, a climate chart, a list of festivals, and cultural background.

Browse through this book, choose your favorite destinations, and link them up. Then have a great trip! You'll travel as a temporary local, getting the absolute most out of every mile, minute, and dollar. You won't waste time on mediocre sights because, unlike other guidebooks, this one covers only the best. Since your major financial pitfall is lousy, expensive hotels, I've worked hard to assemble the best accommodations values for each stop. And, as you travel the route I know and love, I'm happy you'll be meeting some of my favorite Spanish and Portuguese people.

Trip Costs

Five components make up your trip cost: airfare, surface transportation, room and board, sightseeing/entertainment, and shopping/miscellany.

Airfare: Don't try to sort through the mess yourself. Get and use a good travel agent. A basic round-trip flight from the United States to Madrid or Lisbon should cost $700 to $1,000, depending on where you fly from and when. Always consider saving time and money by flying "open-jaw" (into one city and out of another, e.g. into Barcelona and out of Lisbon).

Surface Transportation: For a three-week whirlwind trip linking all of my recommended destinations, allow $350 per person for second-class trains and buses ($500 for first-class trains) or $500 per person (based on 2 people sharing) for a three-week car rental, tolls, gas, and insurance. Car rental is cheapest to arrange from home in the United States. Train passes, easily purchased outside of Europe, are also available at some of the larger European train stations. You may save money, however, by simply buying tickets as you go (see "Transportation," below).

Room and Board: While most will spend more (because they've got it and it's fun), you can thrive in Iberia on $50 a day per person for room and board. A $50-a-day budget allows $5 for lunch, $15 for dinner, and $30 for lodging (based on 2 people splitting the cost of a $60 double room that includes breakfast). That's doable. Students and tightwads will do it on $30 ($15 per bed, $15 for meals and snacks). But budget sleeping and eating require the skills and information covered below (or more extensively in *Rick Steves' Europe Through the Back Door*).

Sightseeing and Entertainment: In big cities, figure $3 to $4 per major sight (Prado, Picasso Museum), $2 for minor ones (climbing church towers), and $25 for splurge experiences (flamenco, bullfights). An overall average of $10 a day works for most. Don't skimp here. After all, this category directly powers most of the experiences all the other expenses are designed to make possible.

Shopping and Miscellany: Figure $1 per coffee, beer, ice-cream cone, and postcard. Shopping can vary in cost from nearly nothing to a small fortune. Good budget travelers find that this category has little to do with assembling a trip full of lifelong and wonderful memories.

Exchange Rates

I list prices in pesetas and escudos throughout the book.

```
180 Spanish pesetas (ptas) = about $1;
   100 ptas = about 55 cents.
220 Portuguese escudos = about $1;
   100 escudos = about 45 cents.
```

The Portuguese use a dollar sign after the number of escudos (e.g., 180 escudos is 180$00 or 180$). To convert prices into dollars, think of pesetas and escudos as pennies and cut 50 percent in either country (Spain: 3,000 ptas = roughly $15, actually $16.50; Portugal: 5,000$00 = roughly $25, actually $23).

Euros: The euro, adopted as a currency by 11 European countries (including Spain and Portugal), won't materialize into actual bills and coins until 2002. For travelers in 2001, it's not an issue.

Prices, Times, and Discounts

The prices, hours, and telephone numbers in this book are accurate as of mid-2000. Iberia is always changing, and I know you'll understand that this, like any other guidebook, starts to yellow even before it's printed.

In Europe—and in this book—you'll be using the 24-hour clock. After 12:00 noon, keep going—13:00, 14:00, and so on. For anything over 12, subtract 12 and add p.m. (14:00 is 2:00 p.m.).

This book lists peak-season hours for sightseeing attractions. Off-season, roughly October through April, expect shorter hours, more lunchtime breaks, and fewer activities. Confirm your sightseeing plans locally, especially when traveling off-season.

Portuguese time is usually one hour earlier than Spanish time (due to daylight saving time). Morocco time can be up to two hours earlier than Spanish time.

While discounts for sightseeing and transportation are not listed in this book, seniors (60 and over), students (with International Student Identity Cards), and youths (under 18) often get discounts—but only if they ask.

When to Go

Spring and fall offer the best combination of good weather, light crowds, long days, and plenty of tourist and cultural activities. Summer and winter travel both have their predictable pros and cons. July and August are most crowded and expensive in coastal areas, less crowded but uncomfortably hot and dusty in the interior. For weather specifics, see the climate chart in the appendix. Whenever you anticipate crowds, particularly in July and August, call hotels in advance (call from one hotel to the next, with the help of your fluent receptionist) and try to arrive early in the day.

Sightseeing Priorities

Depending on the length of your trip, here are my recommended priorities.

3 days:	Madrid, Toledo
5 days, add:	Barcelona
7 days, add:	Lisbon
10 days, add:	Andalucía, Sevilla
14 days, add:	Granada, Algarve
17 days, add:	Costa del Sol, Morocco
20 days, add:	Coimbra, Nazaré
22 days, add:	Salamanca, Segovia

Red Tape, Business Hours, and Banking

You currently need a passport but no visa and no shots to travel in Spain, Portugal, and Morocco.

For visitors, Iberia is a land of strange and frustrating schedules. Most businesses respect the afternoon siesta. When it's 100 degrees in the shade, you'll understand why.

Generally shops are open from 9:00 to 13:00 and from 15:00 or 16:00 to 19:00 or 20:00, longer in touristy places. On Saturday, shops often open only in the morning and are closed Sunday. The biggest museums stay open all day. Smaller ones often close for a siesta.

Banking: Bring a Visa or MasterCard with a four-digit PIN so you can use the same card to withdraw cash from ATMs and to charge any expensive items. Both Spain and Portugal have easily available, easy-to-use 24-hour ATMs with English instructions. They'll save you time and money (on commission fees). I traveled painlessly throughout Spain and Portugal in 2000 with my Visa debit card. Get details at your bank and bring an extra copy of your card just in case it gets demagnetized or gobbled up by a machine. Bring some cash or a few traveler's checks as a backup. If you are planning on getting cash advances from your regular credit card, be sure to ask the card company about fees before you leave.

Banks are generally open Monday through Friday from 9:00 to 14:00 in Spain and 8:30 to 15:00 in Portugal (often with a lunch break).

Spanish banks charge acceptable commissions for changing traveler's checks. American Express offices (found only in big cities) have a slightly less-favorable rate but change any type of traveler's check without a commission. Portugal's banks charge outrageous, unregulated commissions ($8–15). Shop around. Sometimes the hole-in-the-wall exchange offices offer better deals than the bank. Look for the rare American Express office. Better yet, have an ATM card handy.

Language Barrier

For me, nowhere in Europe is the language barrier more frustrating than in Iberia. Learn the key phrases. Here, a phrase book comes in handy, particularly if you want to interact with local people. You'll find that doors open quicker and with more smiles when you can speak a few words of the language.

Spanish is easier than Portuguese to learn and pronounce. Try to learn the pleasantries. Fortunately, in Portugal's big cities and along the Algarve, people in the tourist business generally speak English. Otherwise, Spanish, French, or sign language come in handy.

My Spanish and Portuguese phrase book, which includes a traveler's dictionary, will help you hurdle the language barrier. You'll find the Survival Phrases in the appendix of this book helpful as well.

Travel Smart

Reread this book as you travel and visit local tourist information offices. Buy a phone card and use it for reservations and confirmations. Use taxis in the big cities, bring along a water bottle, and linger in the shade. Connect with the cultures. Set up your own quest for the best cream cake, cloister, fish soup, or whatever.

Enjoy the friendliness of the local people. Ask questions. Most locals are eager to point you in their idea of the right direction. Wear your money belt, pack a pocket-size notepad to organize your thoughts, and practice the virtue of simplicity. Those who expect to travel smart, do.

Whirlwind Three-Week Tour

Design an itinerary that enables you to hit the festivals, bull-fights, and museums on the right days. As you read this book, note the problem days: Mondays, when many museums are closed, and Sundays, when public transportation is meager. Treat Saturdays as weekdays.

Plan ahead for banking, laundry, post-office chores, and pic-nics. Maximize rootedness by minimizing one-night stands. Mix intense and relaxed periods. Every trip (and every traveler) needs at least a few slack days. Pace yourself. Assume you will return.

Warning: Tourists are targeted by thieves throughout Spain and Portugal, especially in Barcelona, Madrid, Sevilla, and Lisbon. While hotel rooms are generally safe and I've never heard of a tourist being mugged, cars are commonly broken into, purses are snatched, and pockets are picked. Be on guard, wear a money belt, and treat any commotion around you as a smoke screen for theft. Don't believe any "police officers" looking for counterfeit bills. Drivers should park carefully and leave nothing of value in the car; locals leave their cars empty and unlocked. When traveling by train, keep your rucksack in sight and get a *couchette* (bed in an attendant-monitored sleeping car) for safety on overnight trips.

Spain & Portugal's Best Three-Week Trip

Day	Plan	Sleep in
1	Arrive in Madrid	Madrid
2	Madrid	Madrid
3	El Escorial, Valley of Fallen, Segovia	Segovia
4	Segovia and Salamanca	Salamanca
5	Salamanca, Coimbra	Coimbra
6	Coimbra, Batalha, Fatima, Nazaré	Nazaré
7	Beach day in Nazaré, Alcobaça side trip	Nazaré
8	Nazaré, Lisbon	Lisbon
9	Lisbon	Lisbon
10	Lisbon side trip to Belém and Sintra	Lisbon
11	Lisbon to the Algarve	Salema
12	Free beach day, Sagres	Salema
13	Across Algarve, Sevilla	Sevilla
14	Sevilla	Sevilla
15	Andalucía's Route of White Villages	Arcos
16	Arcos, Jerez, Tarifa	Tarifa
17	A day in Morocco	Tarifa
18	Gibraltar, Costa del Sol	Nerja
19	Nerja to Granada	Granada
20	Granada	Granada
21	Through La Mancha to Toledo	Toledo
22	Toledo	Toledo/Madrid/fly

While this itinerary is designed to be done by car, it can be done by train and bus (7–8 bus days and 4–5 train days). For three weeks without a car, I'd modify it to start in Barcelona and finish in Lisbon. From Barcelona, fly or take the night train to Madrid (see Toledo, Segovia, El Escorial); take the night train to Granada; bus along Costa del Sol to Tarifa (see Morocco); bus to Arcos, Sevilla, and Algarve; and take the train to Lisbon. This skips Coimbra and Salamanca and assumes you'll fly open-jaw into Barcelona and fly out of Lisbon. If you're catching the train from Lisbon back to Madrid, you can sightsee your way in three days (via Coimbra and Salamanca) or simply catch the night train to Madrid. Note that transportation connections are better from Coimbra to Salamanca than vice versa.

Tourist Information

Your best first stop in a new city is the Turismo (tourist information office). Get a city map and advice on public transportation (including bus and train schedules), special events, and recommendations for nightlife. Many Turismos have information on the entire country. When you visit a Turismo (abbreviated TI in this book), try to pick up maps for towns you'll be visiting later in your trip.

While the TI has listings of all lodgings and is eager to book you a room, use their room-finding service only as a last resort (bloated prices, fees, no opinions, and they take a cut from your host). You'll get a far better value by using the listings in this book and going direct.

The national tourist offices in the United States are a wealth of information. Before your trip, get their free general information packet and request any specific information you want, such as city maps and schedules of upcoming festivals.

Spanish National Tourist Offices: For general information, call 888/OKSPAIN (www.okspain.org, www.tourspain.es).

In New York: 666 Fifth Ave., 35th floor, New York, NY 10103, tel. 212/265-8822, fax 212/265-8864, e-mail: nyork @tourspain.es.

In Illinois: 845 N. Michigan Ave., Suite 915E, Chicago, IL 60611, tel. 312/642-1992, fax 312/642-9817, e-mail: chicago @tourspain.es.

In Florida: 1221 Brickell Ave. #1850, Miami, FL 33131, tel. 305/358-1992, fax 305/358-8223, e-mail: miami@tourspain.es.

In California: 8383 Wilshire Blvd. #960, Beverly Hills, CA 90211, tel. 323/658-7188, fax 323/658-1061, e-mail: losangeles @tourspain.es.

Portuguese National Tourist Office: 590 Fifth Ave., fourth floor, New York, NY 10036, tel. 800/PORTUGAL or 212/354-4403, fax 212/764-6137, www.portugal.org, e-mail: tourism @portugal.org.

Moroccan National Tourist Office: 20 E. 46th St. #1201, New York, NY 10017, tel. 212/557-2520, fax 212/949-8148, www.tourism-in-morocco.com.

Gibraltar Information Bureau: 1156 15th St. N.W., Suite 1100, Washington, D.C. 20005, tel. 202/452-1108, fax 202/452-1109.

Recommended Guidebooks

You may want some supplemental travel guidebooks, especially if you are traveling beyond my recommended destinations. When you consider the improvement it will make in your $3,000 vacation, $25 or $35 for extra maps and books is money well spent. For several people traveling by car, the extra weight and expense of a small trip library are negligible.

Lonely Planet's guides to Spain and Portugal are thorough, well-researched, and packed with good maps and hotel recommendations for low- to moderate-budget travelers, but they're not updated annually. Students and vagabonds will like the hip *Rough Guide: Spain* and *Rough Guide: Portugal* (written by insightful British researchers, but not updated annually) and the highly opinionated *Let's Go: Spain and Portugal* (by Harvard students, thorough hostel listings, updated annually, includes Morocco). *Let's Go* is best for backpackers with a train pass interested in the youth and night scene. Older travelers enjoy Frommer's Spain/Morocco and Portugal guides even though they, like the Fodor guides, ignore alternatives that enable travelers to save money by dirtying their fingers in the local culture. The popular, skinny Michelin Green Guides to Spain and Portugal are excellent, especially if you're driving. They're known for their city and sightseeing maps, dry but concise and helpful information on all major sights, and good cultural and historical background. English editions are sold in Iberia. The well-written and thoughtful Cadogan guides to Spain and Portugal are excellent for "A" students on the road. The encyclopedic Blue Guides to Spain and Portugal are dry as the plains in Spain but just right for some.

The Eyewitness series has editions covering Spain, Barcelona, Madrid, Sevilla/Andalucía, Portugal, and Lisbon (published by Dorling Kindersley, sold in the United States or Iberia). It's extremely popular for its fine graphics, 3-D cutaways of buildings, aerial-view maps of historic neighborhoods, and cultural background. I use and like them, but if you pull out the art, the print that's left is pretty skimpy.

Juan Lalaguna's *Spain: A Traveler's History* provides a readable background on this country's tumultuous history. John Hopper's *The New Spaniards* provides an interesting look at Spain today.

Rick Steves' Books and Videos

Rick Steves' Europe Through the Back Door 2001 gives you budget travel tips on minimizing jet lag, packing light, planning your itinerary, traveling by car or train, finding beds without reservations, changing money, outsmarting thieves, avoiding rip-offs, hurdling the language barrier, staying healthy, taking great photographs, using your bidet, and much more. The book also includes chapters on 35 of my favorite "Back Doors," three of which are in Iberia.

My **Country Guides**, a series of seven guidebooks including this book, cover the Best of Europe; Great Britain/Ireland; France/Belgium/Netherlands; Italy; Scandinavia; and Germany/Austria/Switzerland. All are updated annually and come out in December.

My **City Guides** cover London, Paris, and Rome. Updated annually (and available in January), these practical guides offer in-depth coverage of the sights, hotels, restaurants, and night-life in these grand cities along with illustrated tours of the great museums.

Rick Steves' Europe 101: History and Art for the Traveler (with Gene Openshaw, 2000) tells the story of Europe's peoples, history, and art, with a chapter on Iberia. Written for smart people who were sleeping in their history and art classes before they knew they were going to Europe, *101* really helps Europe's sights come alive.

Rick Steves' Mona Winks (with Gene Openshaw, 1998) provides fun, easy-to-follow, self-guided tours of Europe's top 20 museums in London, Paris, Rome, Venice, Florence, and Madrid. Madrid's Prado is the thickest tour in the book.

Rick Steves' Spanish & Portuguese Phrase Book gives you the words and survival phrases necessary to communicate your way through a smooth and inexpensive trip.

My television series, *Travels in Europe with Rick Steves*, includes six half-hour shows on Spain and Portugal. A new series of 16 shows, called *Rick Steves' Europe*, includes a show on Lisbon and airs in 2001. The 52 earlier shows still air on both public television and the Travel Channel. These are also available in information-packed home videos, along with my two-hour slide-show lecture on Spain and Portugal (call us at 425/771-8303 for our free newsletter/catalog).

Rick Steves' Postcards from Europe, my autobiographical book, packs 25 years of travel anecdotes and insights into the ultimate 3,000-mile European adventure. Through my guidebooks I share my favorite European discoveries with you. *Postcards* introduces you to my favorite European friends.

All of my books are published by Avalon Travel Publishing (www.travelmatters.com).

Maps

The maps in this book, drawn by Dave Hoerlein, are concise and simple. Dave, who is well-traveled in Spain and Portugal, has designed the maps to help you locate recommended places and get to the TIs, where you'll find more in-depth, free maps of the cities or regions.

Don't skimp on maps. For an overall Europe trip, consider my new Europe Planning Map, geared for the traveler with sight-seeing destinations prominent (call us at 425/771-8303 for our free newsletter/catalog). Excellent Michelin maps are available—and cheaper than in the United States—throughout Iberia in bookstores, newsstands, and gas stations. Train travelers can do fine with a simple rail map (such as the one that comes with your train pass) and city maps from the TIs. Drivers should invest in good 1:400,000 maps and learn the keys to maximize the sight-seeing value.

Tours of Spain and Portugal
Travel agents can tell you about all the normal tours, but they won't tell you about ours.

At Europe Through the Back Door, we offer 20-day tours of Spain and Portugal featuring most of the highlights in this book (departures April–Oct, 26 people on a big bus with two great guides and lots of empty seats). For details, see www.ricksteves.com or call 425/771-8303.

Transportation
By Car or Train?
Cars are best for three or more traveling together (especially families with small kids), those packing heavy, and those scouring the countryside. Trains and buses are best for solo travelers, blitz tourists, and city-to-city travelers.

Traveling by Bus and Train
Public transportation in Spain is becoming as slick, modern, and efficient as in northern Europe. Portugal is straggling in train service but offers excellent bus transportation. The best public transportation option is to mix bus and train travel. Always verify bus or train schedules before your departure. Never leave a bus or train station without your next day's schedule options in hand. To study ahead, see http://bahn.hafas.de/english.html, www.renfe.es (Spain), or www.cp.pt (Portugal).

Trains: While you could save money by purchasing tickets as you go, you may find the convenience of a railpass worth the extra cost. Iberia, Spain, and Portugal offer "flexi" railpasses that allow travel for a given number of days over a longer period of time. Spain also offers a rail-and-drive pass, which, if used thoughtfully, gives you the ease of big-city train hops and the flexibility of a car for rural areas such as the Andalusian hill towns. Spain's train passes come with a fine-print extra that many travelers overlook: It's good on overnight Talgo trains from Madrid to Paris or Lisbon and from Barcelona to Paris, Milan, and Zurich (though a supplement is charged). A Eurailpass pays for itself only if you're traveling to Spain from the north (Paris to Madrid costs $135 second class). Remember, you'll be making a lot of connections by buses, which are not covered by Eurail. Travelers under age 26 can buy cheap tickets in Wasteels offices (in most major train stations).

If you're on a budget, avoid the pricey overnight hotel trains from France or Italy into Spain; cheaper options exist (and involve a transfer at the Spanish border). If you can easily afford to take a hotel train, consider flying instead to save time.

The long second-class train rides from Madrid to Barcelona,

Cost of Public Transportation

My free *Rick Steves' Guide to European Railpasses* has the latest on 2001 prices. To get the railpass guide, call us at 425/771-8303 or visit www.ricksteves.com/rail (you can order most passes online).

SPAIN FLEXIPASS (2000)

	1st class	2nd class
Any 3 days in 2 months	$200	$155
Extra rail days (max. 7)	35	30

Spain & Iberic Flexipass holders pay a supplement (included w/reservation) for the fast Talgo and AVE trains. For $45-$200, take a "Night Talgo" sleeper train from Madrid or Barcelona to Lisbon, Paris, Zurich, or Milan.

SPAIN RAIL & DRIVE PASS (2000)

Any 3 rail days and 2 car days in 2 months.

	1st class	extra car day
Economy car	$255	$49
Compact car	269	65
Intermediate car	279	75
Compact automatic	290	85

Prices are approximate per person for 2 traveling together. Solo travelers pay about $75 extra. 3rd and 4th persons sharing car buy only the railpass. Extra rail days (2 max.) cost $39. To order Rail & Drive passes, call DER at 800/549-3737 or Rail Europe at 800/438-7245.

IBERIC FLEXIPASS (SPAIN/PORTUGAL)

1st class: Any 3 days in 2 months for $205. Extra rail days (7 max.): $45.

PORTUGUESE FLEXIPASS

1st class: Any 4 days out of 15 for $105.

Iberia: Map shows approximate point-to-point one-way 2nd class rail fares in $US. Add up fares for your itinerary to see whether a railpass will save you money.

New in 2001: The Eurail Selectpass will allow you to create a flexipass for any 3 countries directly connected by rail or ferry. See our Railpass Guide for details.

Lisbon, Sevilla, and Granada cost about $50 each. First class costs 50 percent more (often as much as a domestic flight). If you're buying point-to-point tickets, note that roundtrip tickets are 20 percent cheaper than two one-way tickets.

Most overnight trains have berths and beds that you can rent (not included in the cost of your train ticket or railpass). Sleeping berths (*litera*) cost $15. A *coche-cama*, or bed in a classy quad compartment, costs $20; and a bed in a double costs $25. For long trips I go overnight on the train or fly (domestic shuttle flights are generally under $100). Even if you have a train pass, reservations (for 600 ptas) are required on long Spanish train rides (over 3 hours). Reserve a seat for your departure as soon as you arrive in a town, either at the train station or at a RENFE office (see below) in big city centers. Travelers with first-class reservations are entitled to the use of comfortable "Intercity" lounges in train stations in Spain's major cities.

RENFE (the acronym for the Spanish national train system) used to be "Relatively Exasperating, and Not For Everyone," but it is getting better. To save time in Spain, consider buying tickets or reservations at the RENFE offices located in over 100 city centers. These are more central and less crowded/confusing than the train

Public Transportation Routes

station. Or, for information and reservations, dial RENFE's national number (tel. 90-224-0202) from anywhere in Spain. I buy my train tickets in Spain, but if you want to order RENFE tickets before your trip, contact Rail Europe (tel. 800/438-7245, www.raileurope .com) or DER (tel. 800/549-3737, www.dertravel.com).

Spain categorizes trains this way:

The high-speed train called the **AVE (Alta Velocidad Española)** whisks travelers between Madrid and Sevilla in less than three hours. AVE is now 85 percent covered by the Eurailpass (Madrid to Sevilla costs Eurailers about $9). Franco left Spain a train system that didn't fit Europe's gauge. AVE trains run on European-gauge tracks.

The **Talgo** is fast, air-conditioned, and expensive. Talgo 200 is a train designed to run on AVE rails. **Intercity** and **Electro** trains fall just behind Talgo in speed, comfort, and expense. **Rapido**, **Tranvia**, **Semi-directo**, and **Expreso** trains are generally slower. **Cercania** are commuter trains for big-city workers and small-town tourists. **Regional** and **Correo** trains are slow, small-town milk runs. Trains get more expensive as they pick up speed, but all are cheaper per mile than their northern European counterparts.

In Spain, *salidas* means "departures" and *llegadas* is "arrivals"; in Portugal, *partidas* and *chegadas* are departures and arrivals, respectively. To decipher Portuguese train schedules, *diario* means "daily," *mudanca de comboio* means "change trains," *so* means "only," and *não* means "not." This is a typical qualifier: *"Não se efectua aos sabados, domingos, e feriados oficiais"* (not effective on Saturdays, Sundays, and official holidays). Or *"So se efectua aos ..."* ("only effective on ...").

In Spain, long-distance trains are priced differently according to their time of departure. Peak hours (*punta*) are most expensive, followed by *llano* and *valle* (quietest and cheapest times). Overnight trains (and buses) are usually less expensive than the daytime rides. On Spanish train schedules, "LMXJVSD" are the days of the week, starting with Monday. A train that runs "LMXJV-D" doesn't run on Saturdays. *Laborables* can mean Monday through Friday or Monday through Saturday. In either Spain or Portugal, to ask for a schedule at a ticket or information window, say *"Horario para _____–_____* [fill in names of cities], *por favor."* Most train stations have handy luggage lockers.

Buses: Always make reservations for long-distance buses ahead of time. Bus service on holidays, Saturdays, and especially Sundays can be dismal. Ask at the tourist office about travel agencies that sell bus tickets (and reserve seats) to save you time if the bus station is not central. Don't leave a bus station to explore a city without checking your departure options and making reservations if necessary. In the countryside, stop buses by waving. You can always stow your luggage under the bus.

Portugal has mostly slow milk-run trains and an occasional Expreso. Off the main Lisbon–Porto–Coimbra train lines, buses are usually a better bet. In cases where buses and trains serve the same destination, the bus is often more efficient.

Bus schedules in Portugal are clearly posted at each major station. Look for *"Partidas"* (departures), not *"Chegadas"* (arrivals). They follow this standard format:

Destino	Partida	Chegada	Preço
Lisboa	14.15	16.35 (1)	1,200$

If you see this schedule in Coimbra, your bus leaves Coimbra at 14:15 and arrives in Lisboa at 16:35. The times are listed with periods instead of colons. Exceptions are noted with a numeral. For instance, the "(1)" means you should look for a list of definitions at the end of the schedule. (1) could be: *"Excepto sabados e domingos"* (Except Saturdays and Sundays). More key Portuguese "fine-print" words: Both *as* and *aos* mean "on." *De* means "from," as in "from this date to that date." *Feriado* means "holiday." *Directo* is "direct." *Ruta* buses make many stops. The posted schedules list most, but not all, destinations. If your intended destination isn't listed, check at the ticket/info window for the most complete schedule information. For longer trips your ticket may include an assigned seat.

Spain's bus system is more confusing than Portugal's because of its many different bus companies (though they're usually clustered within one building). The larger stations have an information desk with all the schedules. In smaller stations, check the destinations and schedules posted on each office window.

Iberian drivers and station personnel rarely speak English. Buses, even direct ones, often stop at stations for up to 30 minutes. In either Spain or Portugal, ask the driver "How many minutes here?" ("*¿Cuantos minutos aquí?*") so you can get out for a break. Some buses are entirely nonsmoking; others are nonsmoking only in the front. When you buy your ticket, ask for nonsmoking (*no fumadores* in Spanish, *não fumador* in Portuguese). It's usually pointless, since passengers ignore the signs, but it's a statement. Radios, taped music, and videos will accompany your ride. Bring earplugs for silence. Buses rarely have WCs but stop every two hours or so. Bus stations have WCs (rarely with toilet paper) and cafés offering quick and cheap food.

Taxis

Most taxis are reliable and cheap. Drivers generally respond kindly to the request, "How much is it to ____, more or less?" (Spanish: "*¿Cuanto cuesta a ____, mas o menos?*" Portuguese: "*Quanto cuesta a ____, mais o menos?*"). Spanish taxis have more extra add-ons (luggage, nighttime, Sundays, train-station pickup, and so on). Rounding the fare up to the nearest 50 pesetas or escudos is adequate for a tip. City rides cost $2 to $4. Keep a map in your hand so the cabby knows (or thinks) you know where you're going. Big cities have plenty of taxis. In many cases, couples travel by cab for little more than two bus or subway tickets.

Car Rental

It's cheapest to rent a car through your travel agent well before your departure. You'll want a weekly rate with unlimited mileage. Figure about $200 a week. For three weeks or longer, it's cheaper to lease; you'll save money on taxes and insurance.

Comparison shop through your agent. Beware of cheap weekly rates followed by very expensive daily costs. Remember, you can turn in your car at any office on any day (normally with credit for early turn-in or extra charge for extension). Also remember that rental offices usually close midday Saturday until Monday.

I normally rent a small economy model. For peace of mind, I splurge for the CDW insurance (Collision Damage Waiver, about $15 a day). A few "gold" credit cards cover CDW insurance; quiz your credit-card company on the worst-case scenario. Travel Guard offers CDW for $6 a day (U.S. tel. 800/826-1300). With

Standard European Road Signs

the luxury of CDW you'll enjoy Iberia's highways, knowing you can bring back the car in an unrecognizable shambles and just say, "S-s-s-sorry."

Driving

Driving in Iberia is great—sparse traffic and generally good roads. While the International Driver's License is officially required (cheap and easy to obtain from AAA; bring two photos and $10), I drive in Iberia with only my U.S. driver's license. (The Spanish version of AAA is the Real Automobil Club; Portugal's is the Automobil Clube de Portugal.)

Good maps are available and inexpensive throughout Iberia. Freeways in Spain and Portugal come with tolls (about $4 per hour) but save huge amounts of time. On freeways, navigate by direction (*norte, oeste, sur, este*). Also, since road numbers can be confusing and inconsistent, navigate by city names.

Drive defensively. If you're involved in an accident, you will be blamed and in for a monumental headache. Seat belts are required by law. Expect to be stopped for a routine check by the police (be sure your car-insurance form is up to date). There are plenty of speed traps. Tickets are issued and paid for on the spot. Portugal is statistically one of Europe's most dangerous places to drive. You'll see lots of ambulances on the road.

Gas and diesel prices are controlled and the same everywhere—around $3.50 a gallon for gas, less for diesel. *Gasolina* is either normal or super; unleaded is now widely available. Note that diesel is called *gasoleo*.

Get used to metric. A liter is about a quart, four to a gallon; a kilometer is six-tenths of a mile. Convert kilometers to miles by cutting them in half and adding back 10 percent of the original (120 km: 60 + 12 = about 72 miles; 300 km: 150 + 30 = about 180 miles).

If possible, make a copy of your key for safety and convenience. Choose parking places carefully. Leave valuables in the trunk during the day and leave nothing worth stealing in the car overnight. While you should avoid parking lots with twinkly asphalt, thieves break car windows anywhere, even at stoplights. Police recommend leaving the glove compartment open and your car unlocked at night. If it's a hatchback, take the trunk cover off at night so thieves can look in without breaking in. Parking attendants all over Spain holler, "*Nada en el coche*" ("Nothing in the car"). And they mean it. Ask at your hotel for advice on parking. In cities you can park safely but expensively in guarded lots.

Telephones, Mail, and E-mail

You cannot travel smartly in Iberia without using the telephones. A few tips will minimize frustration.

Coin-operated phones are rapidly being replaced by card-operated phones, making long-distance calling a breeze. Phone cards, sold at post offices, newsstands, and tobacco (*tobaco*) shops, work only in the country they're purchased in. Upon entering Spain or Portugal, buy a phone card (*tarjeta telefónica* in Spanish, *cartão telefónico* in Portuguese). I buy the biggest-value card and blow any remaining credit on a phone call home before leaving the country (about 50 cents/minute from any phone booth to the United States). Use your card to reserve hotels, confirm sightseeing plans, and call home. To use the card, simply insert it into the slot on the phone, wait for a dial tone and digital readout to show how much value remains on your card, and dial away—the cost of the call is automatically deducted from your card. Portuguese phone cards usually don't tell you your balance until after you dial, but they do beep for 15 seconds before dying. This gives you plenty of time to sign off or push the eject button (look at the directions on the phone beforehand) and slip in a new card.

Portuguese phones are even-tempered, but Spanish phones refuse to be rushed. After you "*inserta*" your "*tarjeta*" (phone card) into the Spanish phone, wait until the digital display says "*Marque numero*" and then dial. Dial slowly and deliberately. Push the square "R" button to get a dial tone for a new call.

Dialing Direct: All phone numbers in Spain and Portugal are nine-digit numbers (without area codes) that can be dialed direct throughout each country; for example, in Madrid you dial a nine-digit number whether you're calling Barcelona or across the street. To dial international calls direct, you'll need the international access codes and country codes (see the appendix). European time is six/nine hours ahead of the east/west coast of the United States. Midnight in Seattle is breakfast in Madrid. Remember that if you're calling to make hotel reservations from the United States.

USA Direct Services: Since direct-dialing rates have dropped, calling cards are no longer the good value they used to be. Still, calling the United States from any kind of phone (even your hotel room) is easy with a calling card. Each card company has a toll-free number in each European country that puts you in touch with an English-speaking operator who takes your card number and the number you want to call, puts you through, and bills your home phone number for the call (about $2 for the first minute, plus a $4 service charge and $2 per additional minute). Hanging up on an answering machine is a $6 mistake. First use a small-value coin or a Spanish or Portuguese phone card to call home for five seconds—long enough to say, "call me," or to make sure an answering machine is off so you can call back using your USA Direct number to connect with a person. For a list of AT&T, MCI, and Sprint calling-card operators, see the appendix. It's a rip-off to use USA Direct for calls between European countries.

Mail: To arrange for mail delivery, reserve a few hotels along your route in advance and give their addresses to friends or use American Express Company's mail services (available to anyone who has at least one American Express traveler's check). Allow 10 days for a letter to arrive. Phoning is so easy that I've dispensed with mail stops altogether.

E-mail: E-mail use among Iberian hoteliers is increasing. I've listed e-mail addresses when possible. Cybercafés are becoming popular in most cities, giving you reasonably inexpensive and easy Internet access.

Sleeping

In the interest of smart use of your time, I favor hotels (and restaurants) handy to your sightseeing activities. Rather than list hotels scattered throughout a city, I describe my favorite couple of neighborhoods and recommend the best accommodations values in each, from $10 bunks to $180 doubles.

Spain and Portugal offer some of the best accommodations values in Europe. Most places are government-regulated, with posted prices. While prices are low, street noise is high (Spaniards are notorious night owls). Always ask to see your room first. Check the price posted on the door, consider potential night-noise problems, ask for another room, or bargain down the price. You can request either *con vista* (with view) or *tranquilo* (*calado* in Portuguese). In most cases the view comes with street noise. Breakfast may or may not be included in your room cost. It is often used as a bargaining chip. Ask before accepting a room. Most of the year, prices are soft.

All rooms have sinks with hot and cold water. Rooms with private bathrooms are often bigger and renovated, while the cheaper rooms without bathrooms often will be dingier and/or on the top floor. Any room without a bathroom has access to a bathroom on the corridor. Towels aren't routinely replaced every day, so you should drip-dry and conserve.

It's officially prohibited for hotels to use central heat before November 1 and after April 1 (unless it's unusually cold); prepare for cool evenings if you travel in spring and fall. Summer can be extremely hot. Consider air-conditioning, fans, and noise (since you'll want your window open), and don't be shy about asking for

Sleep Code

To give maximum information in a minimum of space, I use this code to describe accommodations listed in this book. Prices listed are per room, not per person. When there is a range of prices in one category, the price will fluctuate with the season; these seasons are posted at the hotel desk. Especially in resort areas, prices go way up in July and August. A 6 or 7 percent tax (which is not included in listed prices) will often be added to your bill. Breakfast, while rarely included in Spain, is commonly included in Portugal.

S = Single room (or price for one person in a double).
D = Double or Twin. Double beds are usually big enough for nonromantic couples.
T = Triple (often a double bed with a single bed moved in).
Q = Quad (an extra child's bed is usually cheaper).
b = Private bathroom with toilet and shower or tub.
t = Private toilet only (the shower is down the hall).
s = Private shower or tub only (the toilet is down the hall).
CC = Accepts credit cards (**V**isa, **M**asterCard, **A**merican Express). If CC isn't mentioned, assume you'll need to pay cash.
SE = Speaks English. This code is used only when it seems predictable that you'll encounter English-speaking staff.
NSE = Does not speak English. Used only when it's unlikely you'll encounter English-speaking staff.

According to this code, a couple staying at a "Db-6,000 ptas, CC:V, SE" hotel would pay a total of 6,000 pesetas ($33) for a double room with a private bathroom. The hotel accepts Visa or Spanish cash in payment, and the staff speaks English.

ice. Many rooms come with mini-refrigerators (if noisy at night, unplug it).

Don't judge hotels by their bleak and dirty entryways. Landlords, stuck with rent control, often stand firmly in the way of hardworking hoteliers who'd like to brighten up their buildings.

Any regulated place will have a complaint book (*libro de reclamaciones* in Spanish and *livro de reclamações* in Portuguese). A request for this book will generally solve any problem you have in a jiffy.

Rooms in Private Homes: In both Spain and Portugal you'll find rooms in private homes, usually in touristy areas where locals decide to open up a spare room and make a little money on the side. Ask for a *cama, habitacion*, or *casa particulare* in Spain and a *quarto* in Portugal. They're cheap ($10–25 per bed without breakfast) and usually a good experience.

Historic Inns: Spain and Portugal also have luxurious, government-sponsored, historic inns. These *paradores* (Spain) and *pousadas* (Portugal) are often renovated castles, palaces, or monasteries, many with great views and stately atmospheres. While they can be a good value (doubles $80–200, reservations often necessary), I find many of them sterile, stuffy, and overly impressed with themselves, much like the tourists who stay there. I still list them where appropriate, as I enjoy wandering through them and having an occasional breakfast with real silver and too much service. But for a better value, sleep in what I call "poor-man's paradors"—elegant normal places that offer double the warmth and old-world intimacy for half the price.

Hostels and Campgrounds: Both Spain and Portugal have plenty of youth hostels and campgrounds, but considering the great bargains on other accommodations, I don't think they're worth the trouble and don't cover them in this book. Hotels and *pensiónes* are easy to find, inexpensive, and, when chosen properly, a fun part of the Spanish and Portuguese cultural experience. If you're on a starvation budget or just prefer camping or hosteling, plenty of information is available in the backpacker guidebooks, through the national tourist offices, and at local tourist information offices.

Making Reservations

Even though Easter, July, and August are often crowded, you can travel at any time of year without reservations. But given the high stakes, erratic accommodations values, and the quality of the gems I've found for this book, I'd highly recommend calling ahead for rooms. In peak times or for big cities, you can reserve long in advance. Otherwise, simply call several days in advance as you travel. For maximum flexibility, you might make a habit of calling between 9:00 and 10:00 on the day you plan to arrive, when the hotel knows who'll be checking out and just which rooms will be available. Use the telephone and the convenient phone cards. Most hotels listed are accustomed to English-only speakers. A hotel receptionist will trust you and hold a room until 16:00 without a deposit, though some will ask for a credit-card number. Honor (or cancel by phone) your reservations. Long distance is cheap and easy from public phone booths. Don't let these people down—I promised you'd call and cancel if for some reason you won't show up. Don't needlessly confirm rooms through the tourist office; they'll take a commission.

Those on a tight budget save piles of pesetas by traveling with no reservations and taking advantage of the discounted prices that hotels offer when it's clear they'll have empty rooms that day. Also, in the case of the places offering a 10 percent discount to those booking direct with this guidebook (as noted in hotel listings), remember to negotiate your best deal and only then claim the discount.

If you know exactly which dates you need and really want a particular place, reserve a room well in advance before you leave home. To reserve from home, call, fax, write, or e-mail the hotel. Simple English usually works. To fax, use the handy form in the appendix (online at www.ricksteves.com/reservation).

If you're writing, add the zip code and confirm the need and method for a deposit. A two-night stay in August would be "16/8/01 to 18/8/01" (Europeans write the date day/month/year, and hotel jargon uses your day of departure). You'll often receive a letter back requesting one night's deposit. A credit card will usually be accepted as a deposit. If your credit card is the deposit, you can pay with your card or cash when you arrive; if you don't show up, you'll be billed for one night. Reconfirm your reservations a day in advance for safety.

Eating in Spain

Spaniards eat to live, not vice versa. Their cuisine is hearty and served in big, inexpensive portions. You can get good $10 meals in restaurants.

Although not fancy, there is an endless variety of regional specialties. Two famous Spanish dishes are paella and gazpacho. Paella features saffron-flavored rice as a background for whatever the chef wants to mix in—seafood, sausage, chicken, peppers, and so on. Considered a heavy meal, it's usually served at midday rather than in the evening. Gazpacho, an Andalusian specialty, is a chilled soup of tomatoes, bread chunks, and spices—refreshing on a hot day and commonly available in the summer. Spanish cooks love garlic and olive oil.

Tipping is optional in Spanish restaurants, but many leave the coins or, if happy with the service, round the bill up to the next big bill (but not more than 5 percent).

The Spanish eating schedule frustrates many visitors. First off, many restaurants close during August. Secondly, when restaurants are open, they serve meals "late." Because most Spaniards work until 19:30, supper (*cena*) is usually served around 21:00 or 22:00. Lunch (*almuerzo*), also served late (13:00–16:00), is the largest meal of the day. Don't buck this system. Generally, no good restaurant serves meals at American hours.

The alternative to this late schedule, and my choice for a quick dinner, is to eat in tapas bars. Tapas are small portions, like appetizers, of all kinds of foods—seafood, salads, meat-filled pastries,

Tapas Tips

Here are some typical tapas:

aceitunas—olives
alinos—salads
bacalao—cod
boquerones—
    fresh anchovies
calamares fritos—
    fried squid rings
caracoles—snails
    (May–Sept)
chacinas—cold cuts
champinones—mushrooms
chorizo—spicy sausage
colo de toro or *rabo de toro*—
    bull-tail stew
ensaladilla—Russian salad
espinacas—spinach with
    chick peas
fritos—fried fish and meat
gambas—shrimp

gambas a la plancha—
    grilled shrimp
guiso—stew
jamón iberico—
    the best ham, from
    acorn-fed baby pigs
jamón serrano—cured ham
mejillones—mussels
pisto—mixed sautéed
    vegetables
pulpo—octopus
queso—cheese
queso manchego—
    sheep cheese
tabla serrana—could be a
    hearty plate of moun-
    tain meat and cheese.
tortilla española—Spanish
    potato omelette

deep-fried tasties, and on and on—normally displayed under glass at the bar (from about $1–10 for seafood). Confirm the price before you order (point and ask "*¿Quanto cuesta un tapa?*"). *Pinchos* are bite-size portions (not always available), tapas are snack-size, and *raciónes* are larger portions—half a meal. A *montadito* is a tiny open-faced sandwich (common at tapas bars; as in "*montadito de . . .*," meaning "little sandwiches of. . ."). *Bocadillos* (sandwiches) are cheap and basic. A ham sandwich is just that—ham on bread, period.

For a budget meal in a restaurant, try a *plato combinado* (combination plate), which usually includes portions of one or two main dishes, a vegetable, and bread for a reasonable price; or the *menu del día* (menu of the day), a substantial three- to four-course meal that usually comes with a carafe of house wine. Flan (caramel custard) is the standard dessert. *Helado* (ice cream) is popular, as is *blanco y negro*, a vanilla-ice-cream-and-coffee float.

Eating and drinking at a bar is usually cheapest if you eat or drink at the counter (*barra*). You may pay a little more to eat sitting at a table (*mesa*) and still more for an outdoor table (*terraza*). Locate the price list (posted in fine type on a wall somewhere) to know the menu options and price tiers. In the right place, a quiet coffee break on the town square is well worth the extra charge. But the cheapest seats sometimes get the best show. Sit at the bar and study your bartender—he's an artist.

When searching for a good bar, I look for the noisy places with piles of napkins and food debris on the floor, lots of locals, and the TV blaring. Popular television shows include bullfights and soccer games, American sitcoms, and Spanish interpretations of soaps and silly game shows (you'll see Vanna Blanco).

Spain produces some excellent wine, both red (*tinto*) and white (*blanco*). Major wine regions include Valdepeñas, Penedès, Rioja, and Ribera del Duero. Sherry, a fortified wine from the Jerez region, ranges from dry (*fino*) to sweet (*dulce*).—Spaniards drink the fino and export the *dulce*. *Cava* is Spain's answer to champagne. *Sangría* (red wine mixed with fruit juice) is popular and refreshing. To get a small draft beer, ask for a *caña*. Spain has good, cheap, boxed orange juice (*zumo de naranja*). For something completely different, try *horchata de chufa*, a sweet, milky beverage made from earth almonds.

For a quick and substantial breakfast, order *tortilla española* (potato omelet) with your *café solo* (black) or *café con leche* (with milk) in any café. The town market hall always has a colorful café filled with locals eating cheap breakfasts.

Eating in Portugal

The Portuguese meal schedule, while still late, is less cruel than Spain's. Lunch (*almoço*) is the big meal, served between noon and 14:00, while supper (*jantar*) is from 20:00 to 22:00. Tapas, there-fore, are not such a big deal. You'll eat well in restaurants for $8.

Eat seafood in Portugal. Fish soup (*sopa de peixe*) and shellfish soup (*sopa de mariscos*) are worth seeking out. *Caldo verde* is a popular vegetable soup. *Frango no churrasco* is roast chicken; ask for *piri-piri* sauce if you like it hot and spicy. *Porco a alentejana* is an interesting combination of pork and clams. As in Spain, garlic and olive oil are big. *Meia dose* means half portion, while *prato do dia* is the daily special. If appetizers (such as olives or bread) are brought to your table before you order, they are not free; you will pay if you consume. If you don't want the unordered food, ask to have it removed (if you eat even one olive, you'll pay for all the appetizers).

For a quick snack, remember that cafés are usually cheaper than bars. *Sandes* (sandwiches) are everywhere. The Portuguese breakfast (*pequeno almoço*) is just *café com leite* and a sweet roll, but due to the large ex-pat English community, a full British "fry" is available in most touristy areas. A standard, wonderful local pastry is the cream cake, *pastel de Nata* (called *pastel de Belém* in Lisbon).

Portuguese wines are cheap and decent. *Vinho da casa* is the house wine. *Vinho verde* is a young, light wine from the north that goes well with seafood. The Dão region produces the best red wines. And if you like port wine, what better place to sample it than its birthplace? Beer (*cerveja*) is also popular—for a small draft beer, ask for *uma imperial*. Freshly squeezed orange juice (*sumo de laranja*), mineral water (*agua mineral*), and soft drinks are widely available.

As in Spain, leaving the coins from your change is a nice touch. Rounding things up to the next big bill is considered generous.

Stranger in a Strange Land

We travel all the way to Europe to enjoy differences—to become temporary locals. You'll experience frustrations. Certain truths that we find "God-given" or "self-evident," like cold beer, ice in drinks, bottomless cups of coffee, hot showers, body odor smelling bad, and bigger being better, are suddenly not so true. One of the benefits of travel is the eye-opening realization that there are logical, civil, and even better alternatives. A willingness to go local ensures that you'll enjoy a full dose of European hospitality.

If there is a negative aspect to the European image of Americans, it is that we are big, loud, aggressive, impolite, rich, and a bit naive. While Europeans look bemusedly at some of our Yankee excesses—and worriedly at others—they nearly always afford us individual travelers all the warmth we deserve.

Back Door Manners

While updating this book, I heard over and over again that my readers are considerate and fun to have as guests. Thank you for traveling as temporary locals who are sensitive to the culture. It's fun to follow you in my travels.

Send Me a Postcard, Drop Me a Line

If you enjoy a successful trip with the help of this book and would like to share your discoveries, please fill out and send the survey at the end of this book to me at Europe Through the Back Door, Box 2009, Edmonds, WA 98020. I personally read and value all feedback.

For our latest travel information, visit www.ricksteves.com. For any updates to this book, check www.ricksteves.com/update. My e-mail address is rick@ricksteves.com. Anyone is welcome to request a free issue of our *Back Door* quarterly newsletter.

Judging from the happy postcards I receive from travelers, it's safe to assume you're on your way to a great, affordable vacation—with the finesse of an independent, experienced traveler. Thanks, and *buen viaje*!

BACK DOOR TRAVEL PHILOSOPHY
As Taught in *Rick Steves' Europe Through the Back Door*

Travel is intensified living—maximum thrills per minute and one of the last great sources of legal adventure. Travel is freedom. It's recess, and we need it.

Experiencing the real Europe requires catching it by surprise, going casual... "Through the Back Door."

Affording travel is a matter of priorities. (Make do with the old car.) You can travel—simply, safely, and comfortably—anywhere in Europe for $70 a day plus transportation costs. In many ways, spending more money only builds a thicker wall between you and what you came to see. Europe is a cultural carnival, and, time after time, you'll find that its best acts are free and the best seats are the cheap ones.

A tight budget forces you to travel close to the ground, meeting and communicating with the people, not relying on service with a purchased smile. Never sacrifice sleep, nutrition, safety, or cleanliness in the name of budget. Simply enjoy the local-style alternatives to expensive hotels and restaurants.

Extroverts have more fun. If your trip is low on magic moments, kick yourself and make things happen. If you don't enjoy a place, maybe you don't know enough about it. Seek the truth. Recognize tourist traps. Give a culture the benefit of your open mind. See things as different but not better or worse. Any culture has much to share.

Of course, travel, like the world, is a series of hills and valleys. Be fanatically positive and militantly optimistic. If something's not to your liking, change your liking. Travel is addictive. It can make you a happier American as well as a citizen of the world. Our Earth is home to 6 billion equally important people. It's humbling to travel and find that people don't envy Americans. They like us, but with all due respect, they wouldn't trade passports.

Globe-trotting destroys ethnocentricity. It helps you understand and appreciate different cultures. Travel changes people. It broadens perspectives and teaches new ways to measure quality of life. Many travelers toss aside their hometown blinders. Their prized souvenirs are the strands of different cultures they decide to knit into their own character. The world is a cultural yarn shop. And Back Door travelers are weaving the ultimate tapestry. Come on, join in!

BARCELONA

Barcelona is Spain's second city and the capital of the proud and distinct region of Catalunya. With Franco's fascism now history, Catalunyan flags wave once again. Language and culture are on a roll in Spain's most cosmopolitan and European corner.

Barcelona bubbles with life in its narrow Gothic Quarter alleys, along the grand boulevards, and throughout the chic, grid-planned new town. While Barcelona had an illustrious past as a Roman colony, Visigothic capital, 14th-century maritime power, and, in more modern times, a top Mediterranean trading and manufacturing center, it's most enjoyable to throw out the history books and just drift through the city. If you're in the mood to surrender to a city's charms, let it be in Barcelona.

Planning Your Time

Sandwich Barcelona between flights or overnight train rides. There's little of earth-shaking importance within eight hours by train. It's as easy to fly into Barcelona as into Madrid, Lisbon, or Paris for most travelers from the United States. Those renting a car can cleverly start here, sleep on the train or fly to Madrid, see Madrid and Toledo, and pick up the car as they leave Madrid.

On the shortest visit, Barcelona is worth one night, one day, and an overnight train out. The Ramblas is two different streets by day and by night. Stroll it from top to bottom at night and again the next morning, grabbing breakfast on a stool in a market café. Wander the Gothic Quarter, see the cathedral, and have lunch in Eixample (eye-SHAM-plah). The top two sights in town, Gaudí's Sacred Family Church and the Picasso Museum, are usually open until 20:00. The illuminated fountains (on Montjuïc, near Plaça Espanya) are a good finale for your day.

Barcelona

Of course, Barcelona in a day is insane. To better appreciate the city's ample charm, spread your visit over two or three days.

Orientation

Orient yourself mentally by locating these essentials on the map: Barri Gòtic/Ramblas (Old Town), Eixample (fashionable modern town), Montjuïc (hill covered with sights and parks), and Sants Station (train to Madrid). The soul of Barcelona is in its compact core—the Barri Gòtic (Gothic Quarter) and the Ramblas (main boulevard). This is your strolling, shopping, and people-watching nucleus. The city's sights are widely scattered, but with a map and a willingness to figure out the sleek subway system (or a few dollars for taxis), all is manageable.

Tourist Information

There are four useful TIs in Barcelona: at the airport (tel. 93-478-4704), at the Sants train station (near track 6), on Plaça de Catalunya (daily 9:00–21:00, on main square near my hotel recommendations, look for red sign, Gothic Quarter walking tours in English Sat–Sun at 10:00 from TI, 950 ptas, 2 hrs, call to reserve, tel. 93-304-3232; fair rates at TI exchange desk—open daily, room-finding service, half-price ticket booth from 3 hrs before show time), and at Paseo de Gàrcia 107—which covers all Catalunya (Mon–Sat 10:00–19:00, Sun 10:00–13:00, tel. 93-238-4000). Pick up the large city map, brochure on public transport, and the free quarterly "See Barcelona" guide with practical information (museum hours, restaurants, transportation, history, festivals, and so on).

Arrival in Barcelona

By Train: Although many international trains use the França Station, all domestic (and some international) trains use Sants Station. Both França and Sants have baggage lockers and subway stations: França's is "Barceloneta" (2 blocks away), and Sants' is "Sants Estacio" (under the station). Sants Station has a good TI, a world of handy shops and eateries, and a classy "Sala Euromed" lounge for travelers with first-class reservations (quiet, plush, TV, free drinks, study tables, coffee bar). Subway or taxi to your hotel. Most trains to/from France stop at the subway station Passeig de Gràcia, just a short walk from the center (Plaça de Catalunya, TI, hotels).

By Plane: Barcelona's El Prat de Llobregat Airport is 12 kilometers southwest of town and connected cheaply and quickly by Aerobus (immediately in front of arrivals lobby, 4/hrly until 24:00, 20 min to Plaça de Catalunya, buy 500-ptas ticket from driver, tel. 93-412-0000) or by RENFE train (walk the tunnel overpass from airport to station, 2/hrly at :13 and :43, 20 min to Sants Station and Plaça de Catalunya, 335 ptas). A taxi to or from the airport costs under 3,000 ptas. The airport has a post office, pharmacy, left luggage, and ATMs (far-left end of arrival hall as you face the street). Airport info: tel. 93-298-3838.

Getting around Barcelona

Subway: Barcelona's Metro, among Europe's best, connects just about every place you'll visit. It has five color-coded lines (L1 is red, L2 is lilac, L3 is green, L4 is yellow, L5 is blue). Rides cost 150 ptas. A T-1 Card gives you 10 tickets good for the bus or Metro for 825 ptas. Pick up the TI's guide to public transport. One, two, and five-day passes are available.

Hop-on hop-off bus: The handy Tourist Bus (*Bus Turistic*) offers two multi-stop circuits in colorful double decker buses (red route covers north Barcelona—most Gaudí sights, blue route covers south—Barri Gótic, Montjuïc) with multilingual guides (April–Dec

9:00–21:30, buses run every 10–20 min, buy tickets on bus). Ask for a brochure at the TI. The one-day (2,000 ptas) and two-day (2,500 ptas) tickets include discounts on the city's major sights.

Taxis: Barcelona is one of Europe's best taxi towns. Taxis are plentiful and honest (300-ptas drop charge, 110 ptas/km, extras posted in window). Save time by hopping a cab (Ramblas to Sants Station—600 ptas, luggage—100 ptas/piece).

Helpful Hints

Theft Alert: Barcelona feels safer than it did. Still, you're more likely to be pickpocketed here—especially on the Ramblas—than about anywhere in Europe. Be on guard. Leave valuables in your hotel. Keep no money in your pockets. If you stop for any show or commotion on the Ramblas, put your hands in your pockets before someone else does.

American Express: Amex offices are at Paseo de Gràcia 101 (Mon–Fri 9:30–18:00, Sat 10:00–12:00, tel. 93-415-2371, Metro: Diagonal) and at La Ramblas 74 opposite the Liceu Metro station (daily 9:00–24:00, tel. 93-301-1166).

U.S. Consulate: Passeig Reina Elisenda 23 (tel. 93-280-2227).

Emergency Phone Numbers: Police–092, Emergency–061.

Pharmacy: At the corner of Ramblas and Carrer de la Porta-ferrissa (daily 9:00–22:00, 24-hour info line: tel. 010).

Local Guides: The Barcelona Guide Bureau is a co-op with plenty of excellent local guides who give personalized four-hour tours for 25,000 ptas (Via Laietana 54, tel. 93-310-7778).

Internet Access: A handy choice among the many Internet cafés is Cybermundo Internet Center, a block off Plaça de Catalunya (daily 9:00–24:00, no line likely in morning, Carrer Bargara 3, tel. 93-317-7142).

Language: Although Spanish is understood here (and the basic survival words are the same), Barcelona speaks a different language—Catalan. (Most place-names in this chapter are listed in Catalan.) Here are the essential Catalunyan phrases:

Hello   *Hola*   (OH-lah)
Please   *Si us plau* (see oos plow)

Thank you	*Gracies*	(GRAH-see-es)
Goodbye	*Adeu*	(ah-DAY-oo)
Exit	*Sordida*	(sor-DEE-dah)
Long live Catalunya!	*Visca Catalunya!*	(BEE-skah . . .)

Introductory Walk: From Plaça de Catalunya down the Ramblas

A ▲▲▲ sight, Barcelona's central square and main drag exert a powerful pull as many visitors spend a major part of their time here doing laps on the Ramblas. Here's an orientation walk:

Plaça de Catalunya—This vast central square—littered with statues of Catalunyan heroes—divides old and new Barcelona and is the hub for the Metro, bus, airport shuttle, and both hop-on and hop-off buses (red/northern route leaves from El Corte Inglés, blue/southern route from west side of Plaça). The grass around its fountain is the best public place in town for serious necking. Overlooking the square, the huge El Corte Inglés department store offers everything from bonsai trees to a travel agency, plus one-hour photo developing, haircuts, and cheap souvenirs (Mon–Sat 10:00–21:30, closed Sun, supermarket in basement, ninth-floor terrace cafeteria with great city view—take elevator from near entrance, tel. 93-306-3800). Four great boulevards start here: the Ramblas, the fashionable Passeig de Gràcia, the cozier but still fashionable Rambla Catalunya, and the stubby, shop-filled, pedestrian-only Portal de L'Angel. Homesick Americans even have a Hard Rock Café. Locals traditionally start or end a downtown rendezvous at the venerable Café Zurich (cross street from café to reach . . .).

Ramblas Walk Stop #1: The top of the Ramblas—Begin your ramble 20 meters down at the ornate fountain (near #129). Grab a chair—a man will collect 50 ptas—and observe.

More than a Champs-Élysées, this grand boulevard takes you from rich at the top to rough at the port in a one-mile, 20-minute walk. You'll raft the river of Barcelonan life past a grand opera house, elegant cafés, plain prostitutes, pickpockets, con men, artists, street mimes, an outdoor bird market, great shopping, and people looking to charge more for a shoeshine than you paid for the shoes. When Hans Christian Andersen saw this street he wrote there's no doubt Barcelona is a great city.

Rambla means "stream" in Arabic. The Ramblas used to be a drainage ditch along the medieval wall that once defined what's now called the Gothic Quarter. The boulevard consists of five separately named segments, but address numbers treat it as a single mile-long street.

Open up your map and read some history into it: You're about to walk right across medieval Barcelona from Plaça de Catalunya to the harbor. Notice how the higgledy-piggledy street plan of the medieval town was contained within the old town walls—now gone but traced by a series of roads named Ronda (meaning "to go around"). Find the Roman town, occupying about 10 percent of what became the medieval town—with tighter roads yet around the cathedral. The sprawling modern grid plan beyond the Ronda roads is from the 19th century. Breaks in this urban waffle show where a little town was consumed by the growing city. The popular Passeig de Gràcia boulevard was literally the road to Gràcia (once a town, now a characteristic Barcelona neighborhood).

"Las Ramblas" is plural, a succession of streets. You're at Rambla Canaletes, named for the fountain. The black and gold Fountain of Canaletes is the beginning point for celebrations and demonstrations. All along the Ramblas you'll see newspaper stands (open 24 hours, selling phone cards) and ONCE booths (selling lottery tickets which support Spain's organization of the blind, a powerful advocate for the needs of disabled people).

Got some change? As you wander downhill, drop coins into the cans of the human statues (the money often kicks them into entertaining gear). Warning: Wherever people stop to gawk, pickpockets are at work.

Walk 100 yards downhill to #115 and...

Ramblas Walk Stop #2: Rambla of the Little Birds—Tradition-ally kids bring their parents here to buy pets (especially on Sundays). Apartment dwellers find birds, turtles, and fish easier to handle than dogs and cats. Balconies with flowers are generally living spaces, those with air-conditioning are generally offices. The Academy of Science's clock (#115) marks official Barcelona time—synchronize. The supermarket (#113) has cheap groceries and a handy deli with cooked food to go. Across the street, 50 meters behind the big modern Citadines Hotel, is a park with a newly discovered Roman necropolis (worth a look). Local apartment dwellers blew the whistle on local contractors who hoped they could finish their building before anyone noticed the antiquities they had unearthed. Imagine the tomb-lined road leading into the Roman city of Barcino 2,000 years ago.

Another hundred yards takes you to #109, Carrer del Carme, and...

Ramblas Walk Stop #3: Baroque Church—The big plain church lining the boulevard is Baroque, rare in Barcelona. While Barcelona's Gothic age was rich (with buildings to prove it), the Baroque age hardly left a mark (the city's importance dropped when New World discoveries shifted lucrative trade to ports on the Atlantic). The Bagues jewelry shop across Carrer del Carme from the church is known for its Art Nouveau jewelry (from the molds of Masriera, displayed in the window). At the shop's side entrance, step on the old-fashioned scales (free, in kilos) and head down the lane opposite (behind the church, 30 meters) to a place

From Plaça de Catalunya down the Ramblas

NOT TO SCALE-
PLAÇA DE CATALUNYA TO COLUMBUS
MONUMENT IS A 20 MIN. WALK

TO "STREET OF DISCORD"

PASSEIG DE GRACIA

PLAÇA DE CATALUNYA

EL CORTE INGLES

CAFE ZURICH

AEROBUS, BUS TURISTIC & TAXIS

CANALETES FOUNTAIN

SANTA ANNA

ACADEMY OF SCIENCE

BIRDS

CANUDA

BAROQUE CHURCH

CAFE GRANJA VIADER

CARME

PORTA.

CIGAR SHOP & EROTIC MUSEUM

LA BOQUERIA MARKET

FLOWERS

CARDENAL

"UMBRELLA" BLDG.

HOSPITAL

BARRIO

S. PAU

FERRAN

TO PLAÇA S. JAUME

MIRO MOSAIC

XINES

LICEU THEATER

PLAÇA REIAL

NOU RAMBLA

ESCUDELLERS

PALAU GUELL

MARITIME MUSEUM

COLUMBUS MONUMENT

PASSEIG COLOM

GOLONDRINAS

DCH

HARBOR

TO MARE MAGNUM

Ⓜ - METRO STATIONS

expert in making you heavier. Café Granja Viader (see "Eating," below) has specialized in baked and dairy delights since 1870.

Stroll through the Ramblas of Flowers to the subway stop marked by the red M (near #100), and...

Ramblas Walk Stop #4: La Boqueria—This lively produce market is an explosion of chicken legs, bags of live snails, stiff fish, delicious oranges, and sleeping dogs (#91, Mon–Sat 8:00–20:00, best mornings after 9:00, closed Sun). The Conserves shop sells 25 kinds of olives (straight in, near back on right, 100-gram minimum, 40–70 ptas). Full legs of ham (*jamón serrano*) abound; *Paleta Iberica de Bellota* are best and cost about 20,000 ptas ($110) each. Beware: *Huevos de toro* are bull testicles—surprisingly inexpensive...but oh so good. Drop by Mario and Alex's Café Central for an *espresso con leche* (far end of main aisle on left) or breakfast. Ask for Mario's "breakfast special" (potato omelet with whatever's fresh).

Further down the Ramblas at #83, the Art Nouveau Escriba Café—an ornate world of pastries, little sandwiches, and fine coffee—still looks like it did on opening day in 1906 (daily 8:30–21:00, indoor/outdoor seating, tel. 93-301-6027).

The Museum of Erotica (1,000 ptas, daily 10:00–24:00, across from market at #96) is your standard European sex museum—neat if you like nudes and a chance to hear phone ssssex in four languages.

At #100, Gimeno sells cigars (appreciate the dying art of cigar boxes). Go ahead...buy a Cuban cigar (singles from 100 ptas). Tobacco shops sell stamps.

Walk past Liceu Theater (reopened after a 1994 fire, tickets on sale 14:00–20:30, tel. 90-233-2211) to #46; turn left down an arcaded lane to a square filled with palm trees...

Rambla Walk Stop #5: Plaça Reial—This elegant neoclassical square comes complete with old-fashioned taverns, modern bars with patio seating, a Sunday coin and stamp market (10:00–14:00), Gaudi's first public works (the 2 helmeted lampposts), and characters who don't need the palm trees to be shady. Herbolari Ferran is a fine and aromatic shop of herbs, with fun souvenirs such as top-quality saffron or "safra" (Mon–Sat 9:30–14:00, 16:30–20:00, closed Sun, downstairs at #18 Placa Reial). The small streets stretching toward the water from the square are intriguing, seedy, and dangerous.

Back across the Ramblas, the **Palau Güell** offers an enjoyable look at a Gaudí interior (400 ptas, usually open Mon–Sat 10:00–13:00, 16:00–19:00, Carrer Nou de la Rambla 3–5, tel. 93-317-3974). If you'll see Casa Milà, skip the climb to this rooftop.

Farther downhill, on the right-hand side, is...

Ramblas Walk Stop #6: Chinatown—This is the world's only Chinatown with nothing even remotely Chinese in or near it. Named for the prejudiced notion that Chinese immigrants go hand in hand with poverty, prostitution, and drug dealing, the individual parts; Tue–Sun 9:00–18:00, shorter hours Oct–March; the 5-DM English guidebook does little to make the palace meaningful; U-1 direction: Westfriedhof to Rotkreuzplatz, then tram or bus #12 to Romanplatz and a 10-minute walk or tram #17 from downtown or the station direct; tel. 089/179-080).

BMW Museum—The BMW headquarters, located in a striking building across the street from the Olympic Grounds, offers a good museum popular with car buffs (5.50 DM, daily 9:00–18:00, last ticket sold at 17:00, closed much of Aug, U-3 to the end: Olympia-zentrum, tel. 089/3822-3307). BMW fans should ask about factory tours (often unreliable hours).

▲**Olympic Grounds**—Munich's great 1972 Olympic stadium and sports complex is now a lush park offering a tower (5 DM, commanding but so-high-it's-boring view from 820 feet, daily 9:00–24:00, last trip 23:30), an excellent swimming pool (5 DM, Fri–Wed 7:00–22:30, Thu 7:00–18:00), a virtual sports center where you can return Stefi Graf's serve, a good look at the center's striking "cobweb" style of architecture, and plenty of sun, grass, and picnic potential. Take U-3 to Olympia-zentrum direct from Marienplatz.

Tours of Munich: By Foot, Bike, and Bus

Walking Tours—Munich Walks offers two excellent walking tours: an introduction to the old town and "Infamous Third Reich Sites" (15 DM per tour, 3 hrs, tel. 0177-227-5901, www.berlinwalks.com). The old-town tour starts daily at 10:15 early April through October (also at 14:15 May–Aug, but not Sun). The Third Reich tour is offered at 10:15 on Monday, Thursday, and Saturday from June through early October (less in off-season). Both tours depart from the EurAide office (track 11) in the train station. There's no need to register—just show up. For transportation during the tour, bring any subway ticket (like a Kurzstrecke) or buy one from your guide.

Renate Suerbaum is a good local guide (170 DM for private two-hour walking tour, tel. 089/283-374).

City Bus Tour—Panorama Tours offers one-hour orientation bus tours (19 DM, daily April–Oct, on the hour from 10:00–16:00; Nov–March 10:00 and 14:30; guide speaks German and English; Arnulfstrasse 8, near train station; tel. 089/5490-7560).

Radius Tours offers "alternative" Munich tours on a party tram—you and your friends can rent out a cable car that whisks you along the city's public tram lines. Live music is optional (at the station in front of track 30, tel. 089/596-113).

Bike Tours—If you miss your fraternity, consider Mike's four-hour and seven-hour bike tours (4-hr tour: 36 DM, June–July daily 10:30, 11:30, 15:00, 16:00; April–May and Aug–Sept daily 11:30, 16:00; mid-March–March 31 and Oct 12:30 only; 7-hr

Barcelona's Gothic Quarter

To Block of Discord Casa Milà ❽

PASSEIG DE GRACIA

PLAÇA DE CATALUNYA

RONDA SANT PERE

❾ ❸

CATA-LUNYA

El Corte Ingles Dept. Store

300 YARDS

❿ ❷

❶❹ ❶❶ ❻ ❺

FONT.

AIRPORT BUS STOP

Ⓜ — METRO STATIONS

❶❽

BONSUCCES

C. SANTA ANNA

PALAU DE LA MUSICA

SANT PERE ALT

PINT FORT.

❹ ❶

❶❸

❷❷ ❶❾ ❷⓪ ❷❶

LICEU PORTAFERISSA

SANT PERE BAIX

SANTA CATERINA MARKET

SANT JOSEP MARKET "LA BOQUERIA"

PL. NOVA AV. CATEDRAL MAURA

CATEDRAL

❶❼ ❶❷

PLAÇA S.F. NERI

PAL-GEN.

PLAÇA DE L'ANGEL DE LA PRINCESA

GRAN TEATRE

CARRER DE FERRAN S. JAUME C. JAUME I

JAUME I

PICASSO MUSEUM

C. NOU RAMBLA

PLAÇA REIAL

CITY HALL

SANTA MARIA

PALAU GÜELL

C. ESCUDELLERS

❷❸

POST

FRANÇA STATION

❶❻

DRASSANES

AMPLE

PASS. ISABEL II

Ⓜ BARC.

MARITIME MUSEUM

CARRER MERCE

❷❹

CATALAN HISTORY MUSEUM

AV. D'ICARIA

COLUMBUS MONUMENT

MOLL DE LA FUSTA

PASSEIG DE COLOM

OLD PORT

TO BARCELONETA

TO MAREMAGNUM

❶ Hotel Allegro	❶❸	Quatre Gats
❷ Hotel Catalunya Plaza	❶❹	Meson Castilla
❸ Hotel Barcelona	❶❺	La Dolca Herminia
❹ Nouvel Hotel	❶❻	Restaurante Agut
❺ Hotel Toledano, Capitol & Cont.	❶❼	Rest. Egipte
❻ Hotel Lloret	❶❽	Self Naturista
❼ Hotel Jardi	❶❾	Bio Center
❽ Hotel Condes Barcelona	❷⓪	Citadines Ramblas Aparthotel
❾ Hotel Regente	❷❶	La Taverneta
❿ Hotel Duques Bergara	❷❷	Cafe Granja Viader
❶❶ Hosteria Grau	❷❸	La Fonda
❶❷ Taverna Basca Irati	❷❹	Tapas Street

on the building to the right are mostly Roman (wander inside for good Roman Wall views).

The colossal **cathedral**—started in about 1300—took 600 years to complete. Rather than stretching toward heaven, it makes a point to be simply massive (similar to the Gothic churches of Italy). The west front, while built according to the original plan, is only 100 years old (cathedral 8:00–13:30, 16:00–19:30; cloisters 9:00–13:00, 16:00–19:00; tel. 93-315-1554).

The spacious interior—characteristic of Catalunyan Gothic—was supported by buttresses. These provided walls for 28 richly ornamented chapels. While the main part of the church is fairly plain, the chapels—sponsored by local guilds—show great wealth. Located in the community's most high-profile space, they provided a kind of advertising to illiterate worshippers. Find logos and symbols of the various trades represented. The Indians Columbus brought to town were supposedly baptized in the first chapel on the left.

The **chapels** ring a finely carved 15th-century choir (*coro*). Pay 125 ptas for a close-up look (with the lights on) at the ornately carved stalls and the emblems representing the various Knights of the Golden Fleece who once sat here. The chairs were folded up, giving VIPs stools to lean on during the standing parts of the Mass. Each was creatively carved and—since you couldn't sit on sacred things—the artists were free to enjoy some secular fun here. Study the upper tier of carvings.

The **high altar** sits upon the tomb of Barcelona's patron saint, Eulalia. She was a 13-year-old local girl tortured 13 times by Romans for her faith and finally crucified on an X-shaped cross. Her X symbol is carved on the pews.

Ride the **elevator** to the roof and climb a tight spiral staircase up the spire for a commanding view (200 ptas, Mon–Fri 10:30–12:30, 16:30–18:30, start from chapel left of high altar).

Enter the **cloister** (through arch, right of high altar). In the cloister, look back at the arch, an impressive mix of Romanesque and Gothic. A tiny statue of St. George slaying the dragon stands in the garden. Jordi (George) is the patron saint of Catalunya and by far the most popular boy's name here. While cloisters are generally found in monasteries, this church added it to accommodate more chapels—good for business. Again, notice the symbols of the trades or guilds. Even the pavement is filled with symbols—similar to Americans getting their name on a brick for helping to pay for something.

Long ago the resident geese—there's always 13 in memory of Eulalia—functioned as a sophisticated alarm system. Any commotion would get them honking, alerting the monk in charge.

From St. Jordi, circle to the right (past a WC). The skippable little 100-ptas **museum** (far corner) is one plush room with a dozen

Barcelona's Cathedral

TO PLAÇA CATALUNYA

NOT TO SCALE

ARCS

ARCHITECT'S HOUSE

SARDANA DANCERS

BOTERS

PLAÇA NOVA

AVENIDA CATEDRAL

PALLA

"BARCINO"

TO RAMBLAS

CASA DE L'ARDIACA

PLAÇA DE LA SEU

MUSEU DIOCESÀ

❶

IRURITA

❽ ❼

CLOISTERS

GEESE

W C

❻

SHOP

❷

❸

COMTES

ROYAL

CORO

CATHEDRAL

PALACE

CARRER DEL BISBE

❹

❺

FRENERIA

PLAÇA DEL REI

CITY HISTORY MUSEUM

TO PLAÇA SANT JAUME

DCH

ROMAN TEMPLE

TO PICASSO MUSEUM

❶ Views of Roman Wall		❺ Elevator to spire	
❷ Baptistery		❻ St. Jordi	
❸ St. Mark's Chapel		❼ Museum	
❹ Tomb of St. Eulalia		❽ Chapel of St. Lucia	

old religious paintings. In the corner the dark, barrel-vaulted Romanesque Chapel of Santa Lucia was a small church predating the cathedral and built into the cloister. The candles outside were left by people hoping for good eyesight (Santa Lucia's specialty). Farther along, the Chapel of Santa Rita (in charge of impossible causes) usually has the most candles. Complete the circle and exit at the door just before the place you entered.

Walk uphill, following the church. From the end of the apse turn right 50 meters up Carrer del Paradis to the **Roman**

Temple (Temple Roma d' August). In the corner a sign above a millstone in the pavement marks "Mont Tabor, 16.9 meters." Step into the courtyard for a peek at a surviving corner of the imposing temple which once stood here on the city's highest hill, keeping a protective watch over Barcino (free, 10:00–14:00, 16:00–20:00).

Plaza del Rei—The Royal Palace sat on King's Square (a block from the cathedral) until Catalunya became part of Spain in the 15th century. Then it was the headquarters of the local inquisition. Columbus came here to show King Ferdinand his souvenirs from what he thought was India.

▲**City History Museum**—After a multimedia presentation on the history of the city, an elevator takes you down 20 meters (and 2,000 years) to walk the streets of Roman Barcelona. You'll see sewers, models of domestic life, and bits of an early Christian church. Nearly nothing remains of the Royal Palace (700 ptas, Tue–Sat 10:00–20:00, Sun 10:00–14:00, closed Mon and 14:00–16:00 off-season).

Frederic Mares Museum—This classy collection combines medieval religious art with a quirky bundle of more modern artifacts—old pipes, pinups, toys, and so on (Tue–Sun 10:00–15:00, closed Mon, between Plaza del Rei and cathedral).

▲**Sardana Dances**—The patriotic Sardana dances are held at the cathedral (often at 18:00 on Sat and most Sun at 12:00) and at Plaça de Sant Jaume (often at 18:00 Sun). Locals of all ages seem to spontaneously appear. They gather in circles after putting their things in the center—symbolic of community and sharing (and the ever-present risk of theft). Then they raise and hold hands as they hop and sway gracefully to the band. The band (*cobla*) consists of a long flute, tenor and soprano oboes, strange-looking brass instruments, and a tiny bongolike drum (*tambori*). The rest of Spain mocks this lazy circle dance, but it is a stirring display of local pride and patriotism.

Shoe Museum (Museu del Calcat)—Shoe lovers enjoy this two-room shoe museum (with a we-try-harder attendant) on the delightful Plaça Sant Felip Neri (200 ptas, Tue–Sun 11:00–14:00, closed Mon, 1 block beyond outside door of cathedral cloister, behind Plaça de G. Bachs). The huge shoe at the entry is designed to fit the foot of the Columbus memorial at the bottom of the Ramblas.

Plaça de Sant Jaume—On this stately central square of the Gothic Quarter, two of the top governmental buildings in Catalunya face each other: the Barcelona city hall (Ajuntament, free, Sat–Sun 10:00–14:00) and the seat of the autonomous government of Catalunya (Palau de la Generalitat). Sardana dances take place here many Sundays at 18:00 (see "Sardana Dances," above).

▲▲▲**Picasso Museum**—This is the best collection of Picasso's

(1881–1973) work in Spain, and the best collection of his early works anywhere. It's scattered through two Gothic palaces, six blocks from the cathedral.

Picasso's personal secretary, Sabartes, amassed a huge collection of his work and bequeathed it to the city. Picasso, happy to have a fine museum showing off his work in the city of his youth, added to the collection throughout his life. (Sadly, since Picasso vowed never to set foot in a fascist Spain, and he died 2 years before Franco, the artist never saw the museum.)

This is a great chance to see Picasso's earliest art and better understand his genius (725 ptas, Tue–Sat 10:00–20:00, Sun 10:00–15:00, closed Mon, free and required bag check, Montcada 15–19, Metro: Jaume, tel. 93-319-6310).

There's no English information inside but the art is presented chronologically. If you follow the rooms in numerical order and take this quick room-by-room tour, you can see Picasso's art evolve:

Room 4 (1895): With this earliest art, a budding genius emerges at age 12.

Room 6 (1896): Pablo moves to Barcelona and gets serious about art. The portraits (left as you enter, Padre del Artista) are of Pablo's first teacher, his father. The glass case is filled with what you do at art school. Every time Pablo starts breaking rules, he's sent back to the standard classic style.

Room 9 (1896)—reached through room 4: More school assignments. The goal: Sketch models to capture human anatomy accurately.

Room 10 (1896): On the left you see three self-portraits with a self-awareness of his genius showing in his eyes. The woman (Retrato de la Madre del Artista) is Pablo's mother. Fifteen-year-old Pablo is working on the fine details and gradients of white in her blouse. Pablo was closer to his mom than his dad. Spaniards keep both parents' surnames: Pablo Ruiz Picasso. Eventually he kept just his mom's name.

Room 11: During a short trip to Málaga, Picasso dabbles in Impressionism (unknown in Spain at the time).

Room 12: As a 15-year-old, Pablo does his first big painting for a fine-arts exhibition in Barcelona. While forced to show a religious subject (First Communion), Pablo uses it as an excuse to paint his family.

Room 13: *Science and Charity*, a prize-winning fine-arts exhibition piece, got Picasso the chance to study in Madrid. His little sister (perhaps portrayed in the arms of the nun) had just died. Here for the first time we see Picasso conveying real feeling. The doctor (Pablo's father) represents science. The nun represents charity and religion. But nothing can help and the woman is clearly dead (notice her face and lifeless hand). Pablo painted a little trick: Notice how the bed stretches and shrinks as you walk across the room. Four small studies for this painting hang in the back of the room.

Room 14: Fine-arts school in stuffy Madrid was boring. But Pablo enjoyed hanging out in the Prado Gallery and copying the masters (such as Velázquez' portrait of Phillip IV).

Room 15 (1900): Back in Barcelona, Art Nouveau is the rage. Upsetting his dad, Pablo quits art school and falls in with the avant-garde crowd. These bohemians congregate daily at the Four Cats (slang for "a few crazy people"—see "Eating," below). Declaring his artistic freedom, we see portraits of his new friends and nothing more of his family.

Room 17 (1900): Picasso goes to Paris, a city bursting with life, light, and love.

Room 18: Dropping the surname Ruiz, Pablo establishes his commercial brand name: "Picasso." Here we see the explorer Picasso befriending prostitutes and painting like Toulouse-Lautrec. La Espera (Margot)—with her bold outline and strong gaze—pops out from the Impressionistic background. Painting a dwarf (La Nana), Picasso, like Velázquez and Toulouse-Lautrec, sees "the beauty in ugliness."

Room 19 (1902): The bleak weather and poverty Picasso experienced in Paris leads to his "Blue Period." For three years he cranks out piles of blue art just to stay housed and fed. With blue—the coldest color—backgrounds and depressing subjects, this period was revolutionary in art history. Now the artist is painting not what he sees but what he feels.

Room 20 (1902)—across the hall, through two glass doors: Back home in Barcelona, Picasso paints his hometown at night from rooftops (Terrats de Barcelona). Still blue, here we see proto-cubism . . . five years before the first real cubist painting. The woman in pink (Retrato de la Sra. Canals), painted with classic "Spanish melancholy," finally lifts Picasso out of his funk, replacing the blue period with the happier pink period (of which this museum has only one painting).

Room 21 (1917): Jumping 15 years, we see Picasso is a painter of many styles. In the age of the camera, the cubist gives just the basics (a man with a bowl of fruit) and lets you finish it. We see a little post-Impressionistic Pointillism and a portrait looking like a classical statue (inspired by a trip to Rome). The chrome-framed painting of a spool of cable (between the information sheets on the wall) is remarkably realistic. The expressionist horse symbolizes to Spaniards the innocent victim. In bullfights, the horse—with blinders and pummeled by the bull—has nothing to do with the fight. Picasso used the horse—guts spilling out near the bull's horn—to show the suffering of war. (This shows up again in his future masterpiece, *Guernica*, which you can see in Madrid.)

Room 22 (1957): Notice the print of Velázquez' *Las Meninas* to the left of the doorway. Picasso, who had great respect for Velázquez, painted 60 interpretations of the painting many consider the greatest painting by anyone ever (it's in Madrid's Prado). In the big black-and-white canvas, Picasso plays with perspectives within the painting. The king and queen (reflected in the mirror in the back of the room) are hardly seen while the self-portrait of the painter towers above everyone. The two women of the court on the right look like they're in a tomb—but they're wearing party shoes. In this room and room 23, see the fun Picasso had playing paddleball with Velázquez' masterpiece.

Rooms 24 and 26 (1957): All his life Picasso said, "Paintings are like windows open to the world." Here we see the French Riviera. As a child, Picasso was forced to paint as an adult. Now, at age 60 (with little kids of his own and an also-childish artist Matisse for a friend), he paints like a child.

To exit, hike up the stairs through rooms 28 to 32 and lots of Picasso etchings and engravings, and out.

Textile and Garment Museum (Museu Textil i de la Indumentaria)—If fabrics from the 4th to 16th centuries leave you cold, have a *café con leche* on the museum's beautiful patio (museum, 400 ptas, Tue–Sat 10:00–20:00, Sun 10:00–15:00, closed Mon, patio is outside the museum but within the walls, 30 meters from Picasso Museum at Montcada 12–14).

▲▲Catalana Concert Hall (Palau de la Música Catalana)—This concert hall, finished in 1908, features the best moderniste interior in town. Inviting arches lead you into the 2,000-seat hall. A kaleidoscopic skylight features a choir singing around the sun while playful carvings and mosaics celebrate music and Catalunyan culture. Admission is by tour only, and starts with a relaxing 20-minute video (700 ptas, 1 hr, in English, daily on the hour 10:00–15:00, maybe later, tel. 93-268-1000). Ask about concerts (300 per year, inexpensive tickets).

Sights—Eixample

Uptown Barcelona is a unique variation on the common grid-plan city. Barcelona snipped off the building corners to create light and spacious eight-sided squares at every intersection. Wide sidewalks, hardy shade trees, chic shops, and plenty of Art Nouveau fun make the Eixample a refreshing break from the Old Town. For the best Eixample example, ramble Rambla Catalunya (unrelated to the more famous Ramblas) and pass through Passeig de Gràcia (described below, Metro: Passeig de Gràcia for Block of Discord or Diagonal for Casa Mila).

The 19th century was a boom time for Barcelona. By 1850 it was busting out of its medieval walls. A new town was planned to follow a gridlike layout. The intersection of three major thoroughfares—Gran Vía, Diagonal, and Meridiana—would shift the city's focus uptown.

The Eixample, or "Enlargement," was a progressive plan in which everything was accessible to everyone. Each 20-block-square district would have its own hospital and large park, each 10-block-square area would have its own market and general services, and each five-block-square grid would house its own schools and day-care centers. The hollow space found inside each "block" of apartments would form a neighborhood park.

While much of that vision never quite panned out, the Eixample was an urban success. Rich and artsy big shots bought plots along the grid. The richest landowners built as close to the center as possible. For this reason, the best buildings are near the Passeig de Gràcia. Adhering to the height, width, and depth limitations, they built as they pleased—often in the trendy new moderniste style.

Sights—Gaudí's Art and Architecture

Barcelona is an architectural scrapbook of the galloping gables and organic curves of hometown boy Antonio Gaudí. A devoted Catalan and Catholic, he immersed himself in each project, often living on-site. He called Parc Güell, La Pedrera, and the Sagrada Familia all home.

▲▲**Sagrada Familia (Sacred Family) Church**—Gaudí's most famous and persistent work is this unfinished landmark. He worked on the church from 1883 to 1926; your 800-ptas admis-sion helps pay for the ongoing construction (daily 9:00–20:00, off-season 9:00–18:00, Metro: Sagrada Familia, tel. 93-207-3031).

When finished, 12 100-meter spires (representing the apostles) will stand in groups of four and mark the three ends of the building. The center tower (honoring Jesus), reaching 170 meters up, will be flanked by 125-meter-tall towers of Mary and the four evangelists. A unique exterior ambulatory will circle the building like a cloister turned inside out.

The nativity facade really shows the vision of Gaudí. It was finished in 1904, before Gaudí's death, and shows scenes from the birth and childhood of Jesus along with angels playing musical instruments. (Because of ongoing construction, you may need to access this area—opposite the entrance, viewed from outside—by walking through the museum. Don't miss it.)

The little on-site museum displays physical models used for the church's construction. Gaudí lived on the site for more than a decade and is buried in the crypt. When he died in 1926, only the stubs of four spires stood above the building site. Judge for yourself how the controversial current work fits in with Gaudí's original formulation.

With the cranking cranes, rusty forests of rebar, and

Gaudí & Moderniste Sights

scaffolding requiring a powerful faith, the Sagrada Familia
Church offers a fun look at a living, growing, bigger-than-life
building. Take the lift (200 ptas) or the stairs (free but often
miserably congested) up to the dizzy lookout bridging two spires.
You'll get a great view of the city and a gargoyle's-eye perspective
of the loopy church. If there's any building on earth I'd like to
see, it's the Sagrada Familia...finished.

▲**Palau Güell**—This is a good chance to enjoy a Gaudí interior
(see "Introductory Tour," above). Curvy.

▲▲**Casa Milà (La Pedrera)**—This Gaudí exterior laughs down
on the crowds filling Passeig de Gràcia. Casa Milà, also called
La Pedrera (the Quarry), has a much-photographed roller coaster
of melting-ice-cream eaves. This is Barcelona's quintessential
moderniste building.

Visits come in three parts: apartment, attic, and rooftop. Buy

Modernista

The Renaixensa (Catalan cultural revival) gave birth to Modernista (Catalan Art Nouveau) at the end of the 19th century. Barcelona is the capital of Modernista. Meaning "a taste for what is modern," it lasted from 1888 to 1906. This free-flowing organic style broke with tradition and experimented with glass, tile, iron, and brick. Decoration became structural. It comes with three influences: nature, exotic (e.g., Chinese), and a fanciful Gothic twist to celebrate Catalan's medieval glory days. It was a way of life as Barcelona burst into the 20th century.

Antoni Gaudí is the most famous moderniste artist. From four generations of metalworkers, a lineage of which he was quite proud, he incorporated his ironwork into his architecture and came up with novel approaches to architectural structure and space.

Two other moderniste architects famous for their unique style are Lluís Domènech i Muntaner and Josep Puig i Cadafalch. You'll see their work on "The Block of Discord" (see below).

Barcelona's Eixample neighborhood shimmers with the colorful, leafy, flowing, blooming shapes of Modernista in doorways, entrances, facades, and ceilings.

the 1,000-ptas ticket to see all three. Starting with the apartment, an elevator whisks you to the *Life in Barcelona 1905–1929* exhibit (well-described in English). Then you walk through a sumptuously furnished Art Nouveau apartment. Upstairs in the attic, wander under brick arches—enjoying a multimedia exhibit of models, photos, and videos of Gaudí's works. From there a stairway leads to the fanciful rooftop where chimneys play volleyball with the clouds (daily 10:00–20:00—even on Mon, Passeig de Gràcia 92, Metro: Diagonal, tel. 93-484-5995, most days there are apartment tours in English at 16:30 and attic/rooftop tours at 18:00). At the ground level of Casa Milà is the original entrance courtyard for the Fundacio Caixa de Cataluyna, dreamily painted in pastels (free). The first floor hosts free art exhibits.

▲The Block of Discord—Four blocks from Casa Milà you can survey a noisy block of competing turn-of-the-century facades. Several of Barcelona's top moderniste mansions line Passeig de Gràcia (Metro: Passeig de Gràcia). Because the structures look as though they are trying to outdo each other in creative twists, locals nicknamed the block between Consell de Cent and Arago, "The Block of Discord." First (at #43) and most famous is Gaudí's

Casa Batllo, with skull-like balconies and a tile roof of cresting waves...or is it a dragon's back? (If you're tempted to frame your photos from the middle of the street, be careful—Gaudí died under a streetcar.) Next door, at Casa Amatller (#41, desk sells Moderniste Route combo tickets), check out architect Puig i Cadafalch's creative mix of Moorish and Gothic and iron grill-work. On the corner (at #35) is Casa Lleo Morera (by Lluís Domènechi Muntaner who did the Catalana Concert Hall— you'll see similarities). The perfume shop halfway down the street has a free and interesting little perfume museum in the back. The Hostal de Rita restaurant, just around the corner on Calle Arago, serves a fine three-course lunch for a great price at 13:00 (see "Eating," below).

Park Güell—Gaudí fans find the artist's magic in this colorful park (free, daily 9:00–20:00) and small Gaudí Museum (200 ptas, daily 10:00–20:00, closes off-season at 18:00, Metro: Vallcarca but easier by bus #24 from Plaça de Catalunya; 1,000 ptas by taxi). Gaudí intended this to be a planned garden city rather than a park. As a high-income housing project, it flopped. As a park...even after I reminded myself that Gaudí's work is a careful rhythm of color, shapes, and space, it was disappointing.

Modern Art Museum (Museu d'Art Modern)—East of the França train station in Parc de la Ciutadella, this manageable museum exhibits Catalunyan sculpture, painting, glass, and furniture by Gaudí, Casas, Llimona, and others (500 ptas, Tue– Sat 10:00–19:00, Sun 10:00–14:30, closed Mon).

Sights—Barcelona's Montjuïc

The Montjuïc (Mount of the Jews), overlooking Barcelona's hazy port, has always been a show-off. Ages ago it had the impressive fortress. In 1929 it hosted an international fair, from which most of today's sights originated. And in 1992 the Summer Olympics directed the world's attention to this pincushion of attractions.

There are many ways to reach Montjuïc: on the blue Bus Turistic route (see "Getting around Barcelona," above); bus #50 from the corner of Gran Vía and Passeig de Gràcia (150 ptas, every 10 min); subway to Metro: Parallel and catch the funicular (250 ptas one way, 375 ptas round-trip, daily 11:00–22:00, Sat–Sun only in winter); or taxi. The first three options leave you at the *teleférico* (cable car), which you can take to the Castle of Montjuïc (475 ptas one way, 675 ptas round-trip, daily 11:00–22:00, less off season, tel. 93-443-0859). Alternatively, from the same spot, you can walk uphill 20 minutes through the pleasant park. Only a taxi gets you doorstep delivery. From the port, the fastest and most scenic way to Montjuïc is via the 1929 Trasbordador Aereo (at tower in port, ride elevator up to catch dangling gondola, 1,200 ptas round-trip, 4/hrly, daily 10:30–19:00, tel. 93-443-0859).

Castle of Montjuïc—This offers great city views and a military museum (250 ptas, Tue–Sun 10:00–20:00, closed Mon). The seemingly endless museum houses a dull collection of guns, swords, and toy soldiers. An interesting section on the Spanish-American War covers Spain's valiant fight against American aggression (from its perspective). Unfortunately, there are no English descriptions. Those interested in Jewish history will find a fascinating collection of 9th-century Jewish tombstones.

▲**Fountains (Font Magica)**—Music, colored lights, and huge amounts of water make an artistic and coordinated splash on summer nights (Fri–Sun, 20-min shows start on the half-hour, 21:30–24:00, summer Thu eves also, from Metro: Plaça Espanya, walk toward towering National Palace).

Spanish Village (Poble Espanyol)—This tacky five-acre model village uses fake traditional architecture from all over Spain as a shell to contain gift shops. Craftspeople do their clichéd thing only in the morning (not worth your time or 950 ptas). After hours it becomes a popular local nightspot.

▲▲**Catalunyan Art Museum (Museo Nacional d'Art de Catalunya)**—Often called "the Prado of Romanesque art," this is a rare, world-class collection of Romanesque art taken mostly from remote Catalunyan village churches in the Pyrenees (saved from unscrupulous art dealers—many American).

The Romanesque wing features frescoes, painted wooden altar fronts, and ornate statuary. This classic Romanesque art—with flat 2-D scenes, each saint holding his symbol, and Jesus (easy to identify by the cross in his halo)—is impressively displayed on replicas of the original church ceilings.

In the Gothic wing, fresco murals give way to vivid 14th-century paintings of Bible stories on wood. A roomful of paintings by the Catalunyan master Jaume Huguet (1412–1492) deserves a close look.

Before you leave, ice skate under the huge dome over to the air-conditioned cafeteria. This was the prime ceremony room and dance hall for the 1929 International Exposition (museum-800 ptas, Tue–Sat 10:00–19:00, Sun 10:00–14:30, closed Mon, tel. 93-622-0375). The museum is in the massive National Palace building above the fountains, near Plaça Espanya (Metro: Plaça Espanya, then hike up or ride the bus; the Bus Turistic and bus #50 stop close by).

▲**Fundació Joan Miró**—For something more up-to-date, this museum showcases the modern-art talents of yet another Catalunyan artist and is considered the best collection of Joan Miró art anywhere. You'll also see works by other modern Spanish artists; don't miss the *Mercury Fountain* by Alexander Calder. This museum leaves those who don't like abstract art scratching their heads (800 ptas, Oct–June Tue–Sat 10:00–20:00, Thu until 21:30, Sun 10:00–14:30, closed Mon, July–Sept closes at 20:00).

Sleeping in Barcelona
(180 ptas = about $1, country code: 34)

Sleep Code: **S** = Single, **D** = Double/Twin, **T** = Triple, **Q** = Quad, **b** = bathroom, **t** = toilet only, **s** = shower only, **CC** = Credit Card (**V**isa, **M**asterCard, **A**mex), **NSE** = No English.

Book ahead. If necessary, the TI at Plaça de Catalunya has a room-finding service.

Barcelona is Spain's most expensive city. Still, it has reasonable rooms. Cheap places are more crowded in summer; fancier business-class places fill up in winter and offer discounts on weekends and in summer. Prices listed do not include the 7 percent tax or breakfast (ranging from simple 500-ptas spreads to 2,200-ptas buffets) unless otherwise noted. While many recommended places are on pedestrian streets, night noise is a problem almost everywhere (especially in cheap places with single-pane windows). For a quiet night, ask for "*tranquilo*" rather than "*con vista.*"

Sleeping in Eixample

For an elegant and boulevardian neighborhood, sleep in Eixample, a 10-minute walk from the Ramblas action.

Hotel Condes de Barcelona, a four-star business hotel in a grand moderniste building, rents 183 stylish and spacious rooms with all the comforts (Db-31,000 ptas, special Db price—26,000 ptas or less—offered with this book on weekends all year and daily June–mid-Sept, extra bed-5,000 ptas, CC:VMA, air-con, smoke-free floor, elevator, Gaudí-pleasing rooftop sun garden with Jacuzzi, intersection of Mallorca and Passeig de Gracia at Passeig de Gracia 73, 08008 Barcelona, tel. 93-467-4780, fax 93-467-4781, www. condesdebarcelona.com, e-mail: cbhotel@condesdebarcelona.com).

Hotel Regente, another big four-star place, is a notch below Condes de Barcelona but still a fine splurge (80 rooms, Db-23,000 ptas, less June–Aug, CC:VMA, air-con, elevator, roof terrace, Rambla Catalunya 76, 08008 Barcelona, tel. 93-487-5989, fax 93-487-3227, e-mail: regente@hoteles-centro-ciudad.es).

Hotel Gran Vía, filling a palatial mansion built in the 1870s, offers Botticelli and chandeliers in the public rooms; a sprawling, peaceful sun garden; and 54 spacious, comfy, air-conditioned rooms. It's an excellent value (Sb-10,500 ptas, Db-14,500 ptas with this book through 2001, CC:VMA, Internet access, elevator, quiet, Gran Vía de les Corts Catalanes 642, 08007 Barcelona, tel. 93-318-1900, fax 93-318-9997).

Hotel Residencia Neutral, with a classic Eixample address and 35 basic rooms, is popular with backpackers (tiny Sb-3,700 ptas, big Sb-6,000 ptas, Ds-5,500 ptas, Db-6,500 ptas, extra bed-1,500 ptas, includes tax, CC:VM, elevator, thin walls and some street noise, elegantly located 2 blocks north of Gran Vía at Rambla Catalunya 42, 08007 Barcelona, tel. 93-487-6390).

Sleeping near Plaça de Catalunya and at the top of the Ramblas
(zip code: 08002 unless otherwise noted)

The first five of these places are on big but quiet streets within a block or two of Barcelona's exuberant central square. The next are on or near the top of the Ramblas, also just off Plaça de Catalunya. The last is buried in the Gothic Quarter.

Hotel Duques de Bergara boasts four stars with splashy public spaces, slick marble and hardwood floors, 150 comfortable rooms, and a garden courtyard with a pool a world away from the big-city noise (Sb-22,000 ptas, Db-27,000 ptas, extra bed-3,000 ptas, CC:VMA, air-con, elevator, a half block off Plaça de Catalunya at Bergara 11, tel. 93-301-5151, fax 93-317-3442, www.hoteles-catalonia.es, e-mail: cataloni@hoteles-catalonia.es).

Hotel Occidental Reding, a five-minute walk west of the Ramblas and Plaça de Catalunya action on a quiet street, keeps business travelers fat and happy with 44 comfortable rooms (Db-19,000 ptas, extra bed-5,400 ptas, CC:VMA, air-con, elevator, near University metro stop at Gravina 5, 08001 Barcelona, tel. 93-412-1097, fax 93-268-3482, e-mail: reding@occidental-hoteles.com).

Hotel Allegro elegantly fills a renovated old palace with wide halls, hardwood floors, and modern rooms with all the comforts. It overlooks a thriving pedestrian boulevard. Front rooms have views. Balcony rooms on the back are quiet and come with sun terraces (Db-27,000 ptas, extra bed-3,000 ptas, CC:VMA, family rooms, air-con, elevator, a block down from Plaça de Catalunya at Portal de l'Angel 17, tel. 93-318-4141, fax 93-301-2631).

Catalunya Plaza, an impersonal business hotel right on the square, has all the air-conditioning and minibar comforts (Sb-21,000 ptas, Db-26,000 ptas, includes breakfast, CC:VMA, elevator, air-con, free nuts at the desk, Plaça de Catalunya 7, tel. 93-317-7171, fax 93-317-7855, e-mail: catalunya@city-hotels.es).

Hotel Barcelona is another big, American-style hotel with bright, prefab, and comfy rooms (Sb-19,000 ptas, Db-27,000 ptas, Db with terrace-34,000 ptas, CC:VMA, air-con, elevator, a block from Plaça de Catalunya at Caspe 1–13, tel. 93-302-5858, fax 93-301-8674, e-mail: hotelbarcelona@husa.es).

Nouvel Hotel, an elegant Victorian-style building on a fine pedestrian street, has royal lounges and 70 comfy rooms (Sb-13,000 ptas, Db-19,000 ptas, includes breakfast, manager Gabriel promises 10 percent discount with this book, CC:VMA, air-con, Carrer de Santa Ana 18, tel. 93-301-8274, fax 93-301-8370).

Hotel Toledano's, overlooking the Ramblas, is suitable for backpackers and popular with dust-bunnies. Small, folksy, and borderline dumpy, it's warmly run by Juan Sanz, his son Albert, and trusty Daniel on the nightshift (Sb-4,400 ptas, Db-7,600 ptas, Tb-9,500 ptas, Qb-10,600 ptas, cheaper off-season, CC:VMA,

Rambla de Canaletas 138, tel. 93-301-0872, fax 93-412-3142, e-mail: Toledano@ibernet.com). They run **Hostal Residencia Capitol** one floor above—quiet, plain, cheaper, and also appropriate for backpackers (S-3,200 ptas, D-5,200 ptas, Ds-5,800 ptas, cheap 5-bed room).

Hotel Continental has comfortable rooms, double-thick mattresses, and wildly clashing carpets and wallpaper. To celebrate 100 years in the family, José includes a free breakfast and an all-day complimentary coffee bar. Choose a Ramblas-view balcony or quiet back room (Db-10,000–13,000 ptas, extra bed-2,000 ptas, special family room, CC:VMA, fans in rooms, elevator, Internet access, Las Ramblas 138, tel. 93-301-2570, fax 93-302-7360, www.hotelcontinental .com, e-mail: ramblas@hotelcontinental.com).

Hotel Lloret is a big, dark, old-world place on the Ramblas with plain neon-lit rooms (Sb-6,500 ptas, Db-9,500 ptas, Tb-11,000 ptas, extra beds-1,000 ptas each up to qui~ , choose a noisy Ramblas balcony or *tranquilo* in the back, CC:VMA, air-con in summer, elevator dominates stairwell, Rambla de Canaletas 125, tel. 93-317-3366, fax 93-301-9283).

Hosteria Grau is a homey, almost alpine place, family-run with 27 clean and woody rooms just far enough off the Ramblas (S-4,000 ptas, D-6,500 ptas, Ds-7,500 ptas, Db-8,500 ptas, family suites with 2 bedrooms-16,000 ptas, 1,000 ptas extra charged July–Sept, CC:VMA, fans, 200 meters up Calle Tallers from the Ramblas at Ramelleres 27, 08001 Barcelona, tel. 93-301-8135, fax 93-317-6825, www.intercom.es/grau, e-mail: hgrau@lix .intercom.es, Monica SE).

Meson Castilla is clean, comfy and handy, but it's also pricey, a bit sterile, and in all the American guidebooks. It's three blocks off the Ramblas in an appealing university neighborhood (56 rooms, Sb-12,000 ptas, Db-15,000 ptas, Tb-20,000 ptas, Qb apartment-24,000 ptas, includes buffet breakfast, CC:VMA, air-con, elevator, Valldoncella 5, 08001 Barcelona, tel. 93-318-2182, fax 93-412-4020, e-mail: hmesoncastilla@teleline.es).

Citadines Ramblas Aparthotel is a clever concept offering apartments by the day in a bright modern building right on the Ramblas. Prices range with the seasonal demand and rooms come in three categories (studio apartment for 2 with sofa bed and kitchenette-18,000–21,000 ptas, hotel room for 2 with real bed-22,000–24,000 ptas, apartment with real bed and sofa bed for up to 4 people-27,000–31,000 ptas, includes tax, CC:VMA, laundry, Ramblas 122, tel. 93-270-1111, fax 93-412-7421, e-mail: barca @citadines.com).

Hotel Jardi is a hardworking, clean, plain place on the happiest little square in the Gothic Quarter. Balcony rooms overlooking the peaceful leafy square are most expensive (Sb-4,000–7,500 ptas, Db-5,800–7,500 ptas, Tb-6,800–8,500

ptas, extra bed-1,500 ptas, includes tax, 10 percent off with
cash, CC:VMA if bill totals at least 15,000 ptas, air-con, elevator, halfway between Ramblas and cathedral on Plaça Sant
Josep Oriol #1, tel. 93-301-5900, fax 93-318-3664, e-mail:
sgs110sa@retemail.es, Albert SE). Rooms with balconies enjoy
an almost Parisian ambiance and minimal noise.

Humble Places Buried in Gothic Quarter with Youth-Hostel Prices

Pensio Vitoria has loose tile floors and 12 basic rooms, each with
a tiny balcony. It's more dumpy than homey, but consider the
price (D-3,500 ptas, Db-4,500 ptas, CC:VM, a block off day-
dreamy Plaça dei Pi at Carrer la Palla 8, tel. & fax 93-302-0834).

    Hostal Campi—big, quiet, and ramshackle—is a few doors
off the Ramblas (D-5,500 ptas, Db-6,500 ptas, T-7,500 ptas,
Canuda 4, tel. & fax 93-301-3545). **Huéspedes Santa Ana** is
plain and claustrophobic, with head-to-toe twins (S-3,000 ptas,
D-5,000 ptas, Db-7,000 ptas, T-7,500 ptas, Carrer de Santa
Ana 23, tel. 93-301-2246). **Hostal Residencia Lausanne**, filled
with backpackers, has only its location and price going for it
(S-3, 500 ptas, D-5,500 ptas, Ds-6,500 ptas, Db-7,500 ptas,
TV room, Avenida Portal de l'Angel 24, tel. & fax 93-302-1139,
friendly Javier SE). **Hostal Rembrandt** keeps backpackers
happy with 26 simple rooms and a good location (S-3,200 ptas,
Sb-4,300 ptas, D-5,000 ptas, Db-7,000 ptas, Tb-8,500 ptas,
breakfast-400 ptas, Portaferrisa 23, tel. & fax 93-318-1011).
Pension Fina, next to Hostal Rembrandt, offers more cheap
sleeps (S-3,500 ptas, D-5,000 ptas, Db-6,000 ptas, Portaferrissa
11, tel. & fax 93-317-9787).

Eating in Barcelona

Barcelona, the capital of Catalunyan cuisine, offers a tremendous
variety of colorful places to eat. Many restaurants are closed in
August (or sometimes July), when the owners are on vacation.

Eating near the Ramblas and in the Gothic Quarter

Taverna Basca Irati serves 25 kinds of hot and cold Basque
pintxos for 150 ptas each. These are open-faced sandwiches—
like Basque sushi but on bread. Muscle in through the hungry
local crowd. Get an empty plate from the waiter, then help
yourself. It's a Basque honors system: You'll be charged by the
number of toothpicks left on your plate when you're done.
Wash it down with *sidra* (apple wine, 150 ptas) poured from
on high to bring out the flavor (Tue–Sat 12:00–15:00, 19:00–
23:00, Sun 12:00–15:00, closed Mon, a block off the Ramblas,
behind the arcade at Calle Cardenal Casanyes 17, near Metro:
Liceu, tel. 93-302-3084). **Juicy Jones**, next door, is a tutti-frutti

vegetarian place with a hip menu and a stunning array of fresh-squeezed juices (#7, daily 10:00–23:30).

Ria de Vigo III, a nondescript local eatery, is filled with blue-collar workers and cheap, no-nonsense food (open until 21:30, closed Sun, 3 blocks off Ramblas at Carrer Tallers 69, tel. 93-318-4724).

La Taverneta, an artists' bistro, brags it doesn't cater to tourists. It serves good Catalan food seasoned in the evenings with live music (1,200-ptas lunch menus, Mon–Sat 13:00–16:30, 19:00–24:00, closed Sun, 2 blocks off Ramblas near Plaza Villa de Madrid at Pje. Duque de la Victoria 3, tel. 93-302-6152).

Café Granja Viader is a quaint time-trip, family-run since 1870. This feminine place—specializing in baked and dairy delights, toasted sandwiches, and light meals—is ideal for a traditional breakfast (note the "Esmorzars" specials posted). Try a glass of Orxata (Horchata, almond milk, summer only), Llet Mallorquina (Majorca-style milk with cinnamon, lemon, and sugar), or "Suis" (literally Switzerland, hot chocolate with a snowcap of whipped cream). It's a block off the Ramblas behind El Carme church (9:00–13:45, 17:00–20:45, closed Sun and Mon morning, Xucla 4, tel. 93-318-3486).

Egipte offers decent food, indifferent service, and late-19th-century ambience on the Ramblas (daily 13:00–16:00, 20:00–24:00, Rambla 79, downhill from Boqueria, tel. 93-317-7480).

For **groceries,** consider El Corte Ingles on Plaça de Catalunya or the Champion Supermarket at 113 Ramblas (Mon–Sat 9:15–21:15, closed Sun). For a good pizza at the top of the Ramblas, consider La Poma (La Ramblas 117).

Restaurants in the Gothic Quarter

A chain of three bright, modern restaurants with high-quality traditional cuisine in classy bistro settings with great prices has stormed Barcelona. Each can be crowded so arrive early if you can: **La Fonda** (daily 13:00–15:30, 20:30–23:30, a block from Plaça Reial at Escudellers 10, tel. 93-301-7515), **La Dolca Herminia** (2 blocks toward Ramblas from Catalan Concert Hall at Magdalenes 27, tel. 93-317-0676), and **Les Quinze Nits** (on trendy La Plaça Reial at #6—you'll see the line, tel. 93-317-3075).

Els Quatre Gats, Picasso's hangout, still has a bohemian feel in spite of its tourist crowds. Before it was founded in 1897, the idea of a café for artists was mocked as a place where only *quatre gats* ("four cats," meaning only crazies) would go (3,000-ptas meals, Mon–Sat 8:30–02:00, Sun 17:00–01:30, live piano nightly from 21:00, CC:VMA, Montsio 3, tel. 93-302-4140).

Restaurante Agut, buried deep in the Gothic Quarter four blocks off the harbor, is a fine place for local-style food in a local-style setting (Tue–Sat 21:00–24:00, closed Sun, Mon, and July or Aug, Calle Gignas 16, tel. 93-315-1709).

Vegetarian near Plaça de Catalunya

Self Naturista is a quick, no-stress buffet that will make vegetarians and health-food lovers feel right at home. Others may find a few unidentifiable plates and drinks. The food seems tired—pick what you like and microwave it (Mon–Sat 11:30–22:00, closed Sun, near several recommended hotels, just off the top of Ramblas at Carrer de Santa Ana 11–17).

Bio Center, a Catalan soup and salad place popular with local vegetarians, is better but not as handy (Mon–Sat 13:00–17:00, closed Sun, Pintor Fortuny 25, Metro: Catalunya, tel. 93-318-0343). The street has several other good vegetarian places.

Eating in the Eixample

The people-packed boulevards of the Eixample (Passeig de Gràcia and Rambla Catalunya) are lined with appetizing places with breezy outdoor seating. Many trendy and touristic tapas bars offer a cheery welcome and aggressively slam out the appetizers.

La Bodegueta is an unbelievably atmospheric below-street-level bodega serving hearty wines and *flauta* (sandwich on flute-thin baguette, Mon–Sat 8:00–02:00, Sun 19:00–01:00, Rambla Catalunya 100, at intersection with Provenza, Metro: Diagonal, tel. 93-215-4894).

El Hostal de Rita is a fresh and dressy little place serving Catalunyan cuisine just around the corner from Casa Milà. Their three-course-with-wine lunch (1,100 ptas, Mon–Fri at 13:00) and dinner (2,000 ptas, daily from 20:30) specials are a great value (Arago 279, tel. 93-487-2376).

The classy **Quasi Queviures** serves upscale tapas, sandwiches, or the whole nine yards—classic food with modern decor (Passeig de Gràcia 24).

El Café de Internet provides an easy way to munch a sandwich while sending e-mail messages to Mom (600 ptas/30 min, Mon–Sat 9:00–24:00, closed Sun, Gran Vía 656, Metro: Passeig de Gràcia, tel. 93-412-1915, www.cafeinternet.es).

Sandwich Shops

Bright, clean and inexpensive sandwich shops are proudly holding the cultural line against the fast-food invasion hamburgerizing the rest of Europe. You'll find great sandwiches at **Pans & Company** and **Bocatta**, two chains with outlets all over town. Catalunyan sandwiches are made to order with crunchy French bread. Rather than butter, locals prefer *pa amb tomaquet* (pah ahm too-MAH-kaht), a mix of crushed tomato and olive oil. Study the instructive multilingual menu fliers to understand your options.

Eating near the Harbor in Barceloneta

Barceloneta is a charming beach suburb of the big city. A grid plan of long, narrow, laundry-strewn streets surrounds the central Plaça Poeta Boscan. For an entertaining evening, wander around this corner. Drop by the two places listed here or find your own restaurant (15-min walk or Metro: Barceloneta). During the day a lively produce market fills one end of the square. At night kids play soccer and Ping-Pong.

Cova Fumada is the neighborhood eatery. Josep Maria and his family serve famously fresh fish (Mon–Fri 17:30–20:30, closed July, Carrer del Baluarte 56, on the corner at Carrer Sant Carles, tel. 93-221-4061). Their *sardinas a la plancha* (grilled sardines, 350 ptas) are fresh and tasty. *Bombas* (potato croquets with pork, 150 ptas) are the house specialty. It's macho to have it *picante* (spicy with chili sauce); gentler taste buds prefer it with garlic cream (ali-oli). Catalunyan *bruschetta* is *pan tostado* (toast with oil and garlic, 140 ptas). Wash it down with *vino tinto* (house red wine, 80 ptas).

At **Bar Electricidad**, Arturo Jordana Barba is the neighborhood source for cheap wine. Drop in. It's 180 ptas per liter; the empty plastic water bottles are for takeaway. Try a 75-ptas glass of Torroja Tinto, the best local red, or Priorato Dulce, a wonderfully sweet red (Mon–Sat 8:00–13:00, 15:00–19:00, across the square from Cova Fumada, Plaça del Poeta Bosca, #61, NSE).

The Olympic Port, a swanky marina district, is lined with harborside restaurants and eaters enjoying what locals claim is the freshest fish in town (a short taxi ride from the center past Barceloneta).

Tapas on Carrer Merce in the Gothic Quarter

Tapas aren't as popular in Catalunya as they are in the rest of Spain, but Barcelona boasts great *tascas*—colorful local tapas bars. Get small plates (for maximum sampling) by asking for "*tapas*," not "*raciones*."

While trendy uptown places are safer, better lit, and come with English menus and less grease, these places will stain your journal.

From the bottom of the Ramblas (near the Columbus monument), hike east along Carrer Clave. Then follow the small street that runs along the right side of the church (Carrer Merce), stopping at the *tascas* that look fun.

La Jarra is known for its tender *jamón canario con patatas* (baked ham with salty potatoes). Across the street, **La Pulperia** serves up fried fish. A block down the street, **Tasca El Corral** makes one of the neighborhood's best chorizo *al diablo* (hell sausage), which you sauté yourself. It's great with the regional specialty, *pan con tomate*. Across the street, **La Plata** keeps things wonderfully simple, serving extremely cheap plates of sardines and small glasses of keg wine. **Tascael Corral** serves northern Spain mountain favorites such as *queso de cabrales* (very moldy cheese) with *sidra* (apple wine). Have a chat with the parrot at **Bar la Choza del Sopas**. At the end of Carrer Merce, **Bar Vendimia** serves up tasty clams and mussels. Carrer Ample and Carrer Gignas, the streets paralleling Carrer Merce inland, have more refined barhopping possibilities.

Transportation Connections—Barcelona

By train to: Lisbon (1/day, 17 hrs with change in Madrid, $70 with *couchette*), **Madrid** (6/day, 7–9 hrs, $40 with *couchette*), **Paris** (3/day, 11–15 hrs, $100 with *couchette*, night train, reservation required), **Sevilla** (4/day, 11 hrs, $45 with couchette), **Málaga** (3/day, 14 hrs), **Nice** (1/day, 12 hrs, change in Cerbere). Train info: tel. 93-490-0202; international train info: tel. 93-490-1122. RENFE tel. 93-490-0202.

   By bus to: Madrid (12/day, 8 hrs, half the price of a train ticket, departs from station Barcelona Nord at Metro: Marina).

   By plane: To avoid 10-hour train trips, check the reasonable flights from Barcelona to Sevilla or Madrid. Iberia Air (tel. 93-412-5667) and Air Europe (tel. 90-224-0042) offer $80 flights to Madrid. Airport info: tel. 93-298-3838.

NEAR BARCELONA: FIGUERES, CADAQUES, AND MONTSERRAT

Three fine sights are day-trip temptations from Barcelona. For the ultimate in surrealism and a classy but sleepy port-town getaway, consider a day or two in Cadaques with a stop at the Dalí Museum in Figueres. Figueres is an hour from Cadaques and two hours from Barcelona. Pilgrims with hiking boots head 30 miles into the mountains for the most sacred spot in Catalunya—Montserrat.

Figueres

▲▲▲**Dalí Museum**—This is the essential Dalí sight. Inaugurated in 1974, the museum is a work of art in itself. Dalí personally conceptualized, designed, decorated, and painted it, intending to showcase his life's work. Highlights include the epic Palace of the Wind ceiling, the larger-than-life Mae West room (complete with fireplaces for nostrils), fun mechanical interactive art (Dalí was into action; bring lots of 25- and 100-ptas coins), and the famous squint-to-see Abraham Lincoln. Other major and fantastic works include the tiny *Le Spectre Du Sex-Appeal*, *Soft Self Portrait*, and the red-shoe riddle of *Zapato y Vaso de Leche*. The only real historical context provided is on the easy-to-miss and unlabeled earphone info boxes in the Mae West room (100 ptas). A bizarre video (near the exit) shows every half hour. While not in English, it's plenty

Sights Near Barcelona

entertaining (1,000 ptas, daily 9:00–20:00, 22:00–01:00; off-season 10:30–18:00 and closed Mon; last entry 45 min before closing, free bag check has your bag waiting for you at the exit, tel. 97-267-7500). Dalí, who was born in Figueres in 1905, is buried in the museum. From the train station, follow "Museu Dalí" signs to the museum.

Connections: Figueres is an easy day trip from Barcelona or a stopover (trains from France stop in Figueres; lockers at station). Trains from Barcelona depart Sants Station or the RENFE station at Metro: Passeig de Gràcia (hrly, 2 hrs, round-trip-2,300 ptas).

Cadaques

Since the late 1800s, Cadaques has served as a haven for intellectuals and artists alike. Salvador Dalí, raised in nearby Figueres, brought international fame to this sleepy Catalan port in the 1920s. He and his wife, Gala, set up home and studio at the adjacent Port Lligat. Cadaques inspired surrealists such as Eluard, Magritte, Duchamp, Man Ray, Buñuel, and García Lorca. Even Picasso was drawn to this enchanting coastal *cala* (cove), and he painted some of his cubist works here.

In spite of its fame, Cadaques is laid-back and feels off the beaten path. If you want a peaceful beach-town escape near Barcelona, there's no better place. From the moment you descend

into the town, taking in whitewashed buildings and deep blue
waters, you'll be struck by the port's tranquility and beauty. Have a
glass of *vino tinto* or *cremat* (a traditional brandy-and-coffee drink
served flambé style) at one of the seaside cafés and savor the lapping
waves, brilliant sun, and gentle breeze.

The **Casa Museu Salvador Dalí**, once Dalí's home, gives
fans a chance to explore his labyrinthine compound (1,300 ptas,
Tue–Sun 10:30–18:00, closed Mon, closes spring and fall at 17:00,
closed in winter, 15-min walk over the hill from Cadaques to Port
Lligat, limited visits, call to reserve a time, tel. 97-225-1015).

The **TI** is at Carrer Cotxe 2 (Mon–Sat 9:00–14:00, 16:00–
21:00, Sun 10:00–13:00, shorter hours off-season, tel. 97-225-
8315).

Sleeping and Eating: Hotel La Residencia, owned by
Dalí's first manager, Captain Moore, is a pleasant, pricey hotel
strewn with art and sporting a sunny garden patio. One hundred
and twenty original Dalí works—sculptures, prints, paintings, and
photos (in addition to wall coverings and upholstery)—line the
corridors and fill the rooms (Db-11,000 ptas, CC:VM, Avenida
Caritat Serinyana 1, tel. 97-225-8312, fax 97-225-8013, e-mail:
residencia@grn.es). These cheaper options are clean and conveniently located in the main plaza, around the corner from the
TI and across from the beach: **Hostal Marina** (D-4,500 ptas,
Ds-5,500 ptas, Db-8,000 ptas, breakfast-500 ptas, CC:VM,
Riera 3, tel. & fax 97-225-8199) and **Hostal Cristina** (D-4,000
ptas, Ds-6,000 ptas, Db-8,000 ptas, CC:VM, La Riera s/n,
tel. 97-225-8138).

For a fine dinner, try **Casa Anita**, down a narrow street
from La Residencia. Sitting with others around a big table, you'll
enjoy house specialties like *calamars a la plancha* (grilled squid) and
homemade *helado* (ice cream). Muscatel from a glass *porron* finishes
off the tasty meal (Juan and family, tel. 97-225-8471).

Connections: Cadaques is reached by Sarfa buses from
Figueres (3/day, 50 min, 500 ptas) or from Barcelona (5/day,
2.5 hrs, 1,750 ptas, less frequent off-season, tel. 93-265-6508).

Montserrat

Montserrat, set amid spectacular mountains, is a popular day trip
from Barcelona (53 km). This has been Catalunya's most important pilgrimage site for a thousand years. Hymns ascribe this
"serrated mountain" to little angels who carved the rocks with
golden saws. Geologists blame 10 million years of nature at work.

Montserrat's top attraction is **La Moreneta**, a basilica with
the Black Virgin icon (daily 8:00–10:30, 12:00–18:30). The
Moreneta is the patron saint and protector of Catalunya and is
therefore the most revered religious symbol in the province.

Inside the basilica, be sure to see the Virgin close-up (behind the altar). Pilgrims touch her orb; the rest is protected behind glass. Then descend into the prayer room for a view of the Moreneta from behind. Pilgrims dip a memento of their journey into the holy water or even leave a personal belonging here (like a motorcycle helmet for safety) to soak up more blessings.

In the summer watch a 15-minute video in English about the monastery (free, 2/day, ask at TI, tel. 93-877-7701).

The first hermit monks built huts at Montserrat around A.D. 900. By 1025 a monastery was founded. A choir school soon followed. The **Montserrat Escolania**, or choir school, is considered to be the oldest music school in Europe. Fifty young boys, who live and study in the monastery itself, make up the choir, which performs daily at 13:00 and 19:10 (choir on vacation in July).

The **Museu de Montserrat** offers prehistoric tools, religious art, ancient artifacts, and a few paintings by masters such as El Greco, Caravaggio, Monet, Picasso, and Dalí (600 ptas, Mon–Fri 10:00–18:00, Sat–Sun 9:30–18:30, shorter hours in winter).

The Moreneta was originally located in the **Santa Cova** (holy cave), a 40-minute hike down from the monastery and lined with statues depicting scenes from the life of Christ. While the original *Black Virgin* statue is now in the basilica, a replica sits in the cave. (A 3-minute funicular ride cuts 20 minutes off the hike.)

The **Sant Joan funicular** (see below) continues another 250 meters above the monastery (580 ptas one way, 925 ptas round-trip). At the top of the funicular, a 20-minute walk takes you to the Sant Joan chapel and the starting point of numerous hikes, described in the TI's "Six Itineraries from the Monastery" brochure.

Sleeping: You can sleep in the **old monks' cloister** far more comfortably than did its original inhabitants (twin-10,550 ptas, fine restaurant attached, tel. 93-877-7701).

Connections: Ferrocarriles Catalanes trains leave hourly for Montserrat from Barcelona's Plaça Espanya (1,855 ptas round-trip, cash only, Eurailpass not valid, tel. 93-205-1515). From the Metro station, follow signs through several tunnels to the "FF de la Generalitat" underground station, then look for train line R5 (direction Manresa, departures at :36 past each hour, 1 hr; if lost, exit Metro and reenter next to Plaza Hotel). Get off at the Aeri de Montserrat stop at the base of the mountain, where the cable car awaits (the round-trip from Barcelona includes 4/hrly cable-car ride). Returning, you'll find departures at 15 minutes past the hour make the trains leaving at :36 past the hour (last departure 18:45, 17:45 in off-season).

MADRID

Today's Madrid is upbeat and vibrant, still enjoying a post-Franco renaissance. You'll feel it. Even the statue-maker beggars have a twinkle in their eyes.

Madrid is the hub of Spain. This modern capital—Europe's highest, at more than 2,000 feet—has a population of more than 4 million and is young by European standards. Only 400 years ago, King Philip II decided to move the capital of his empire from Toledo to Madrid. One hundred years ago Madrid had only 400,000 people, so 90 percent of the city is modern sprawl surrounding an intact, easy-to-navigate historic core.

Dive headlong into the grandeur and intimate charm of Madrid. The lavish Royal Palace, with its gilded rooms and frescoed ceilings, rivals Versailles. The Prado has Europe's top collection of paintings. The city's huge Retiro Park invites you for a shady siesta and a hopscotch through a mosaic of lovers, families, skateboarders, pets walking their masters, and expert bench-sitters. Make time for Madrid's elegant shops and people-friendly pedestrian zones. Enjoy the shade in an arcade. On Sundays, cheer for the bull at a bullfight or bargain like mad at a mega–flea market. Lively Madrid has enough street singing, barhopping, and people-watching vitality to give any visitor a boost of youth.

Planning Your Time

Madrid's top two sights, the Prado and the palace, are worth a day. On a Sunday (Easter–Oct), consider allotting extra time for a bull-fight. Ideally, give Madrid two days and spend them this way:
Day 1: Breakfast of *churros* (see "Eating," below) before a brisk, good-morning-Madrid walk for 20 minutes from Puerta del Sol to the Prado; 9:00–12:00 at the Prado; afternoon siesta in Retiro

Park or modern art at Centro Reina Sofia (Guernica) and/or Thyssen-Bornemisza Museum; dinner at 8:00, with tapas around Plaza Santa Ana.

Day 2: Follow this book's "Puerta del Sol to Royal Palace Walk" (see below); tour the Royal Palace, lunch near Plaza Mayor; afternoon free for other sights, shopping, or side trip to El Escorial (open until 19:00). Be out at the magic hour—before sunset—when beautifully lit people fill Madrid.

Note that the Prado, Thyssen-Bornemisza Museum, and El Escorial are closed on Monday. For day-trip possibilities from Madrid, see the next two chapters ("Northwest of Madrid" and "Toledo").

Orientation

The historic center is enjoyably covered on foot. No major sight is more than a 20-minute walk or a 600-ptas taxi ride from Puerta del Sol, Madrid's central square. Divide your time between the city's two major sights—the Royal Palace and the Prado—and its barhopping, contemporary scene.

The Puerta del Sol marks the center of Madrid and of Spain itself; notice the "kilometer zero" marker, from which all of Spain is surveyed (southwest corner). The Royal Palace to the west and the Prado Museum and Retiro Park to the east frame Madrid's historic center.

Southwest of Puerta del Sol is a 17th-century district with the slow-down-and-smell-the-cobbles Plaza Mayor and memories of pre-industrial Spain.

North of Puerta del Sol runs Gran Vía, and between the two are lively pedestrian shopping streets. Gran Vía, bubbling with expensive shops and cinemas, leads to the modern Plaza de España. North of Gran Vía is the gritty Malasana quarter, with its colorful small houses, shoemakers' shops, sleazy-looking hombres, milk vendors, bars, and hip night scene.

Tourist Information

Madrid has four Turismos: Plaza Mayor (#3, Mon–Sat 10:00–20:00, Sun 10:00–15:00, tel. 91-588-1636); near the Prado Museum (behind Palace Hotel, Mon–Fri 9:00–19:00, Sat 9:00–13:00, Duque de Medinaceli 2, tel. 91-429-4951); and smaller offices at the Chamartin train station (Mon–Fri 8:00–20:00, Sat 9:00–13:00, tel. 91-315-9976) and at the airport (same hours, tel. 91-305-8656). During the summer small temporary stands with yellow umbrellas and yellow-shirted student guides pop up (at places such as Puerta del Sol), happy to help out lost tourists. Confirm your sightseeing plans and pick up a city map and *Enjoy Madrid*. If interested, ask at the TI about bullfights and Zarzuela (the local light opera).

Madrid

For entertainment listings, the TI's free *En Madrid* is not as good as the easy-to-decipher Spanish weekly entertainment guide *Guía del Ocio* (150 ptas, sold at newsstands), which lists events, restaurants, and movies ("V.O." means a movie is in its original language rather than dubbed).

If you're heading to other destinations in this book, ask any Madrid TI for free maps and brochures. Since many small-town TIs keep erratic hours and run out of these pamphlets, get what you can here. Get bus schedules, too, to avoid unnecessary trips to the various bus stations. The TI's free and amazingly informative *Mapa de Comunicaciones España* lists all the Turismos and highway SOS numbers with a road map of Spain. (If they're out, ask for the Paradores Hotel chain-sponsored route map.)

Arrival in Madrid

By Train: Madrid's two train stations, Atocha and Chamartin, are both on subway lines with easy access to downtown Madrid. Each station has all the services (but there's no TI at Atocha). In Spain, train rides longer than about three hours require reservations, even if you have a Eurailpass. To avoid needless running around, arrange your departure upon arrival.

Chamartin handles most international trains. Atocha runs AVE trains to Sevilla. Both stations offer long-distance trains (*largo recorrido*) as well as local trains to nearby destinations (*cercanías*). Atocha is split into two halves (local and long-distance trains) with separate schedules; this can be confusing if you're in the wrong side of the building. Atocha also has two helpful (necessary) customer-service offices called Atención al Cliente (daily 7:00–23:00)—one office for each half of the building. The Chamartin station is less confusing (customer-service office beside the ticket windows in the middle of the building, TI opposite track #20).

Club AVE in Atocha (upstairs) is a lounge reserved solely for AVE business or first-class ticket-holders or Eurailers with a reservation (free drinks, newspapers, showers, info service, and so on). Club Intercity in Chamartin is less exclusive—you can get in if you have a first-class railpass and first-class seat or sleeper reservations.

Both train stations have Metro stops: Chamartin and Atocha RENFE. (Note that there are 2 Atocha Metro stops in Madrid; the train station's Metro station is "Atocha RENFE"). If you're traveling between Chamartin and Atocha, the Cercanias trains (6/hrly, 12 min, free with railpass—show it at ticket window in the middle of the turnstiles) are far quicker than the subway. These trains depart from Atocha's track #2. At Chamartin, check the Salidas Immediatas board for the next departure.

The downtown RENFE office offers train information, reservations, and tickets (Mon–Fri 9:30–19:00, credit cards accepted, go in person, 2 blocks north of the Prado at Calle Alcala 44, tel. 902-240-202).

By Bus: Madrid's three key bus stations, all connected by Metro, are: Larrea (for Segovia, Metro: Príncipe Pío), Estación Sur Autobuses (for Toledo, Àvila, and Granada, Metro: Méndez Alvaro, tel. 91-468-4200), and Estación Herranz (for El Escorial, in the Metro: Moncloa). For details, see "Transportation Connections" at the end of this chapter.

By Plane: Madrid's Barajas Airport, 10 miles east of downtown, has a 24-hour bank with fair rates, an ATM, a TI, a telephone office (which sells phone cards), a RENFE desk for rail information, a pharmacy, on-the-spot car-rental agencies, and easy public transportation into town. Airport info: tel. 91-393-6000, flight info tel. 90-235-3570. By public transport, take the yellow bus from the airport to Madrid (to Plaza Colón, 385 ptas, 4/hrly, 20 min); then, from Plaza Colón, take a taxi (insist on meter, ride to hotel should be far less than 1,000 ptas) or subway to your hotel (to get to the subway, walk up the stairs and face the blue "URBIS" sign high on a building—the subway stop, M. Serrano, is 50 yards to your right).

The airport's Metro stop, Aeropuerto, provides a cheap (150 ptas) but time-consuming (45 min with changes) way into town (access Metro at check-in level, transfer at Mar de Cristal to brown line #4—direction Arguelles, transfer at Goya to red line #3 to Sol).

For a taxi to or from the airport, allow 3,000 ptas (400-ptas airport supplement is legal). Cabbies routinely try to get 5,000 ptas—a rip off. At the airport, get a rough idea of the price before you hop in. Ask "*¿Cuanto cuesta a Madrid, más o menos?*" ("How much is it to Madrid, more or less?")

Getting around Madrid

By Subway: Madrid's subway is simple, speedy, and cheap (160 ptas/ride). The 735-ptas, 10-ride Metrobus ticket can be shared by several travelers and works on both the Metro and buses (available at kiosks or tobacco shops or in Metro). The city's broad streets can be hot and exhausting. A subway trip of even a stop or two can save time and energy. Pick up a free map (*Plano del Metro*) at most stations. Navigate by subway stops (shown on city maps). To transfer, follow signs to the next subway line (numbered and color-coded). End stops are used to indicate directions. Insert your ticket in the turnstile, then retrieve it as you pass through. Green *Salida* signs point to the exit. Using neighborhood maps and street signs to exit smartly can save lots of walking.

By Bus: City buses, while not as easy as the Metro, can be useful (bus maps at TI or info booth on Puerta del Sol, 160-ptas tickets sold on bus, or 735 ptas for a 10-ride Metrobus—see "By Subway," above).

By Taxi: Taxis are easy to hail and reasonable (180-ptas drop, 100 ptas per km; supplements for airport, train station, and bags). Threesomes travel as cheap by taxi as by subway. A ride from the Royal Palace to the Prado costs only 500 ptas.

Helpful Hints

Theft Alert: Be wary of pickpockets, anywhere, anytime, but particularly on Puerta del Sol (main square), the subway, and crowded streets. Wear your money belt. The small streets north of Gran Vía are particularly dangerous even before nightfall. Fortunately, violent crime against tourists is rare.

Museum Pass: If you plan to visit the Prado, Reina Sofia (*Guernica*), and Thyssen-Bornemisza museums, save 33 percent by buying the Paseo del Arte pass (1,300 ptas, sold at each museum).

Travel Agency and Free Maps: The grand department store, El Corte Inglés, has a travel agency (Mon–Sat 10:00–21:30, just off Puerta del Sol) and gives free Madrid maps (at the information desk, immediately inside the door, just off Puerta del Sol at intersection of Preciados and Tetuan).

Telephones: The telephone office, centrally located at Gran

Vía 30, has metered phones and accepts credit cards for charges over 500 ptas (daily 10:00–23:00).

American Express: The Amex office is at Plaza Cortes 2 (opposite Palace Hotel, 2 blocks from Metro: Banco de España, Mon–Fri 9:00–17:30, Sat 9:00–12:00, tel. 91-322-5455).

Embassies: The U.S. Embassy is at Serrano 75 (tel. 91-587-2200); the Canadian Embassy is at Nuñez de Balboa 35 (tel. 91-431-2350).

Laundromat: The self-service Lavamatique is funky but central (Mon–Fri 9:00–20:00, Sat 9:00–17:00, Cervantes 1).

Internet Access: Zahara is at the corner of Gran Vía and Mesoneros (Mon–Fri 9:00–0:30, Sat–Sun 9:00–01:30).

Tours of Madrid

Hop-on hop-off Bus Tours—Several companies offer virtually identical 15-stop circuits of the city with two or three buses per hour allowing you to hop on and off at the various sights all day. They come with tape-recorded or live commentaries (1,600 ptas, under 15 and over 65 half price, 10:00–18:30).

Private Guided Tour—EuropGuide, a local guide's association, offers excellent private tours (4-hr guided walks for 14,000 ptas, tel. 91-447-0114, www.nauta.es/europguide).

Walking Tours—British expatriate Stephen Drake-Jones gives entertaining, informative walks of historic old Madrid almost nightly (along with more specialized walks, such as "Hemingway," "Civil War," and "Bloody Madrid"). A historian with a passion for the memory of Wellington (the man who stopped Napoleon), Stephen is the founder of the Wellington Society. For 2,500 ptas you become a member of the society and get a free two-hour tour that includes stops at two bars for local drinks and tapas. Eccentric Stephen takes you back in time to sort out Madrid's Habsburg and Bourbon history. Stephen likes his drink. If that's a problem, skip the tour. Tours start at the statue on Puerta del Sol (maximum 10 people, tel. 60-914-3203—a cell phone number that will cost you 100 ptas—to confirm tour and reserve a spot; Stephen also does inexpensive private tours for small groups, e-mail: sdrake _jones@hotmail.com).

Introductory Walk: From Madrid's Puerta del Sol to the Royal Palace

Connect the sights with the following walking tour. Allow an hour for this half-mile walk, not including your palace visit.

▲▲**Puerta del Sol**—Named for a long-gone medieval gate with the sun carved onto it, Puerta del Sol is ground zero for Madrid. It's a hub for the Metro, buses, and pickpockets. The statue of the bear pawing the strawberry bush and the Madrono trees in the big planter boxes are symbols of Madrid.

Heart of Madrid

1. Hotel Europa
2. Hotel Regente
3. Hotel Cliper
4. Hotel Liabeny
5. Rest. Los Galayos
6. Hotels at #44 Gran Via
7. Hostal Tijcal
8. Rest. Puerto Rico
9. Artemisa II
10. Rest. Rodriguez
11. Rest. Botin
12. Torre del Oro Bar
13. Zahara Internet Cafe
14. Artemisa I
15. Casa de las Torrijas

Stand by the statue of King Charles III and survey the square. Because of his enlightened urban policies, Charles III (who ruled until 1788) is affectionately called the "best mayor of Madrid." He decorated the city squares with fine fountains, got those meddlesome Jesuits out of city government, established the public school system, made the Retiro a public park rather than a royal retreat, and generally cleaned up Madrid. The huge palace he faces was the first post office (which Charles established in the 1760s). Today it's remembered for being Franco's police headquarters. An amazing number of those detained and interrogated by the Franco police "tried to escape" by flying out the windows to their deaths. Notice the hats of the civil guardsmen at the entry. It's said the hats have square backsides so they can lean against the wall while enjoying a cigarette.

Crowds fill the square on New Year's Eve. As Spain's "Big Ben" atop the post office chimes 12 times, Madrillinos eat one grape for each ring to bring good luck through the coming year.

A plaque on the post office wall marks the spot where the war against Napoleon started. Napoleon wanted his brother to be king of Spain. Trying to finagle this, Napoleon brought nearly the entire Spanish royal family to France for negotiations. An anxious crowd gathered outside the post office awaiting word of the fate of their royal family. This was just after the French Revolution, and there was a general nervousness between France and Spain. The French guard appeared and the 2nd of May, 1808, massacre took place. Goya, who worked just up the street, observed the event and captured the tragedy in his paintings *2nd of May, 1808*, and *3rd of May, 1808*, which you'll see in the Prado.

Walking from Puerta del Sol to Plaza Mayor: On the corner of Calle Mayor and Puerta del Sol (across from McDonalds), step into the busy *confiteria*, Salon la Mallorquina. It's famous for its sweet Napolitana (creme-filled pastry) or savory, meat-filled *agujas* pastries (200 ptas)—if you can't finish yours, the beggar at the front door would love to; notice the racks with goodies hot out of the oven. Look back toward the entrance and notice the tile above the door with the 18th-century view of the Puerta del Sol. Compare this with the view out the door. This was before the square was widened, when a church stood where the Tío Pepe sign stands today. The French used this church to hold local patriots awaiting execution. (That venerable sign, advertising a famous sherry for over 100 years, is Madrid's first billboard.)

Cross busy Calle Mayor, round McDonald's, and veer left up the pedestrian alley called Calle de Postas. The street sign shows the post coach heading for that famous first post office. Medieval street signs came with pictures so the illiterate could "read" them. After 50 yards, take a left up Calle San Cristobal (passing the local feminist bookshop). At the square notice the big brick 17th-century Ministry of Foreign Affairs building (with the pointed spire)—originally a prison for rich prisoners who could afford the best cells. Turn right and walk down Calle de Zaragoza under the arch into . . .

Plaza Mayor—This square, built in 1619, is a vast, cobbled, traffic-free chunk of 17th-century Spain. Each side of the square is uniform, as if a grand palace were turned inside out. The statue is of Philip III, who ordered the square's construction. Upon this stage, much Spanish history was played out: bullfights, fires, royal pageantry, and events of the gruesome Inquisition. Reliefs serving as seatbacks under the lampposts tell the story. During the Inquisition, many were tried here. The guilty would parade around the square (bleachers were built for bigger audiences, the wealthy rented balconies) with billboards listing their many sins. They were then burned. Some were slowly strangled with a *garrotte*; they'd hold a crucifix and hear the reassuring words of a priest as this life was squeezed out of them. The square is painted a democratic shade of burgundy—the result of a citywide vote. Since Franco's 1975 death, there's been a passion for voting here. Three different colors were painted as samples on the walls of this square, and the city voted for its favorite.

Throughout Spain, lesser *plazas mayores* provide peaceful pools for the river of Spanish life. A stamp-and-coin market bustles here on Sundays from 10:00 to 14:00, and on any day it's a colorful and affordable place to enjoy a cup of coffee. The TI is at #3.

Finish your Plaza Mayor visit with a drink at the Torre del Oro Bar Andalu—a temple to bullfighting. Warning: They push expensive tapas on tourists. A *caña* (small beer) shouldn't cost more than 200 ptas. The bar's ambience is *"Andalu"*...Andalusian. Look under the stuffed head of "Barbero" the bull. At eye level you'll see a *puntilla*, the knife used to put a bull out of its misery at the arena. This was the knife used to kill Barbero.

Notice the incredible action caught in the bar's many photographs. Near Barbero, follow the black and white photo series of a wannabe bullfighter who jumped into the ring and was killed by the bull. Above that is a series of photos showing the scandalous fight in which a banderillero (the guy who puts the arrows into the bull's back) was in trouble and his partners just stood by watching in horror as the man was killed. At the end of the bar in a glass case is the "suit of lights" El Cordobes wore in his ill-fated 1967 fight. With Franco in attendance, El Cordobes went on and on, long after he could have ended the fight, until finally the bull gored him. El Cordobes survived; the bull didn't. Find Franco with El Cordobes at the far end. Under Segador the Bull is a photo of El Cordobes' illegitimate son, El Cordobes, kissing a bull. Disowned by El Cordobes and using his dad's famous name after a court battle, El Cordobes is one of this generation's top fighters.

Walking from Plaza Mayor to the Royal Palace: Leave Plaza Mayor on Calle Cuidad Rodrigo (far right corner from where you entered), passing a series of fine turn-of-the-century storefronts and shops famous for their fried squid-ring sandwiches (*bocadillos calamares*). From the archway you'll see the covered Mercado de San Miguel (green iron posts, on left). Wander

Plaza Mayor to Royal Palace

through this produce market, leaving on the opposite (downhill) side and following the pedestrian lane left. At the first corner, turn right, and cross the small plaza to the modern brick convent. The door on the right says "venta de dulces"; to buy sweets from cloistered nuns, buzz and follow the sign to *torno*, the lazy Susan which lets the sisters sell their baked goods without being seen (smallest quantities: half or *medio* kilo). Follow Calle del Codo (see the street sign—where those in need of bits of armor shopped) around the convent to Plaza de la Villa, the city-hall square. Ahead the flags of city, state, and nation grace the city hall. The statue in the garden is of Don Bazan—mastermind of the Christian victory over the Moslems at the naval battle of Lepanto in 1571. This pivotal battle ended the Moslem threat to Christian Europe. The mayor's office is behind Don.

From here, busy Calle Mayor leads downhill a couple more blocks to the Royal Palace. Halfway down (on the left) there's a tiny square opposite the recommended Casa Ciriaco restaurant (#84). The statue memorializes the 1906 anarchist bombing that killed 23 people as the royal couple paraded by on their wedding day. While the crowd was throwing flowers, an anarchist threw a bouquet lashed to a bomb from a balcony of #84 (which was a hotel at the time). Amazing photos of the event hang just inside the door in the back room of the restaurant.

▲▲**Royal Palace (Palacio Real)**—Europe's third-greatest palace (after Versailles and Vienna's Schönbrunn) is packed with tourists and royal antiques. After a fortress burned down on this site, King Phillip V commissioned this huge 18th-century palace as a replacement. How huge is it? Over 2,000 rooms with miles of lavish tapestries, a king's ransom of chandeliers, priceless porcelain, paintings, and lots of clocks (Charles IV was a huge collector). While the royal family lives in a mansion a few miles away, the place still functions as a royal palace and is used for formal state receptions and tourist daydreams.

A simple one-floor, 24-room, one-way circuit is open to the public. You can wander on your own or join an English tour (get time of next tour and decide as you buy your ticket; tours depart about every 20 minutes). The tour guides, like the museum guidebook, show a passion for meaningless data (900 ptas without a tour, 1,000 ptas with a tour, Mon–Sat 9:00–19:00, Sun 9:30–14:30; Oct–March Mon–Sat 9:30–18:00, Sun 9:00–14:00, last tickets sold an hour before closing; Metro: Opera, tel. 91-559-7404). Your ticket includes the armory and the pharmacy, both on the courtyard.

If you tour on your own, here are a few details you won't find on the little English descriptions posted in each room:

The Grand Stairs: Fancy carpets are rolled down (notice the little metal bar-holding hooks) for formal occasions. At the top of the first landing, the blue and red coat of arms is of the current—and popular—constitutional monarch, Juan Carlos. While Franco chose him to be the next dictator, J.C. knew Spain was ripe for democracy. Rather than become "Juan the Brief" (as some were nicknaming him), he turned real power over to the parliament. At the top of the stairs (before entering first room, right of door) is a bust of J.C.'s great-great-g-g-g-great-grandfather Phillip V. Grandson of France's King Louis XIV, he began the Bourbon dynasty in 1700. The dynasty survives today with Juan Carlos.

Throne Room: Red velvet walls and lions symbolize the monarchy in this rococo riot. The chandeliers are the best in the house. The thrones are only from 1977. This is where ambassadors give their credentials to the king, who receives them relatively informally . . . standing rather than seated in the throne.

Gasparini Anteroom (2 rooms after the throne room): The paintings are of King Charles IV and his wife—all by Goya. Velázquez's masterpiece *Las Meninas* originally hung here.

Gasparini Room: This was the royal dressing room. Dressing, for a divine monarch, was a public affair. The court bigwigs would assemble here as the king, standing on a platform—notice the height of the mirrors—would pull on his leotards. In the next room, the silk wallpaper is new—notice the J.C.S. initials of the king and Sofia (the queen).

Gala Dining Room: Five or six times a year the king entertains up to 150 guests at this bowling lane-sized table. The table in the next room would be lined with an exorbitantly caloric dessert buffet. In the next room you can ogle at glass cases filled with the silver tableware used for these functions.

Stradivarius Room: The queen likes classical music and when you perform for her, you do it with these precious 300-year-old violins. About 300 Antonius Stradivarius-made instruments survive. This is the only matching quartet: two violins, a viola, and a cello.

Royal Chapel: The Royal Chapel is used only for baptisms and funerals. The royal tomb sits here before making the sad trip to El Escorial to join the rest of Spain's past royalty.

Billiards and Smoking Rooms: The billiards room and the smoking room were for men only. The porcelain and silk of the smoking room imitates a Chinese opium den.

Queen's Boudoir: The next room was for the ladies, decorated just after Pompeii was excavated and therefore in fanciful ancient-Roman style. You'll exit down the same grand stairway you climbed 24 rooms ago.

The **Cathedral of Almudena**, Madrid's new cathedral, is ahead of you as you leave the palace. It's worth a look while you're here. Built between 1883 and 1993, its exterior is a contemporary mix and its interior is neo-Gothic with a colorful ceiling.

Sights—Madrid's Museum Neighborhood

These three worthwhile museums are in east Madrid. From Prado to the Thyssen-Bornemisza Museum is a five-minute walk; Prado to Reina Sofia is a 10-minute walk.

▲▲▲**Prado Museum**—The Prado holds my favorite collection of paintings anywhere. With more than 3,000 canvases, including entire rooms of masterpieces by Velázquez, Goya, El Greco, and Bosch, it's overwhelming. Take a tour or buy a guidebook (or bring me along by ripping out and packing the Prado chapter from *Rick Steves' Mona Winks*). Focus on the Flemish and northern (Bosch, Dürer, Rubens), the Italian (Fra Angelico, Raphael, Botticelli, Titian), and the Spanish art (El Greco, Velázquez, Goya).

Follow Goya through his stages, from cheery (*The Parasol*) to political (*2nd of May, 1808* and *3rd of May, 1808*) to dark ("Negras de Goya": e.g., *Saturn Devouring His Children*). In each stage, Goya asserted his independence from artistic conventions. Even the standard court portraits from his "first" stage reflect his politically liberal viewpoint, subtly showing the vanity and stupidity of his royal patrons by the looks in their goony eyes. His political stage, with paintings like the *3rd of May, 1808*, depicting a massacre of Spaniards by Napoleon's troops, makes him one of the first artists with a social conscience. Finally, in his gloomy "dark stage," Goya probed the inner world of fears and nightmares, anticipating our modern-day preoccupation with dreams. Also, seek out Bosch's *The Garden of Earthly Delights*—a three-paneled

altarpiece showing creation, the "transparency of earthly plea-
sures," and the resulting hell. Bosch's self-portrait looks out from
hell (with the birds leading naked people around the brim of his
hat) surrounded by people suffering eternal punishments appropriate for their primary earthly excesses.

The art is constantly rearranged by the Prado's fidgety management, so even the Prado's own maps and guidebooks are out of
date. Regardless of the latest location, most art is grouped by
painter, and better guards can point you in the right direction if
you say "*¿Dónde está . . . ?*" and the painter's name as Españoled as
you can (e.g., Titian is "Ticiano" and Bosch is "El Bosco"). The
Murillo entrance—at the end closest to the Atocha Station—
usually has shorter lines. Lunchtime, from 14:00 to 16:00, is least
crowded (500 ptas, free on Sat afternoon, all day Sun, and to
anyone under 18 and over 65; Tue–Sat 9:00–19:00, Sun 9:00–
14:00, closed Mon; Paseo de Prado, Metro: Banco de España
or Atocha—each a 15-minute walk from the museum, tel.
91-330-2800 or 91-420-2836).

▲▲**Thyssen-Bornemisza Museum**—This stunning museum
displays the impressive collection that Baron Thyssen (a wealthy
German married to a former Miss Spain) sold to Spain for $350
million. It's basically minor works by major artists and major
works by minor artists (the real big guns are over at the Prado).
But art lovers appreciate how the good baron's art complements
the Prado's collection by filling in where the Prado is weak (Impressionism). For a delightful walk through art history, ride the
elevator to the top floor and do the rooms in numerical order.
It's across from the Prado at Paseo del Prado 8 in the Palacio de
Villahermosa (700 ptas, Tue–Sun 10:00–19:00, closed Mon,
Metro: Banco de España or Atocha, tel. 91-369-0151). Tired ones
can hail a cab at the gate and zip straight to Centro Reina Sofia.

▲▲**Centro Reina Sofia**—In this exceptional modern-art
museum, ride the elevator to the second floor and follow the room
numbers for art from 1900 to 1950. The fourth floor continues
the collection from 1950 to 1980. The museum is most famous
for Picasso's *Guernica*, a massive painting showing the horror of
modern war. Guernica, a village in northern Spain, was the target
of the world's first saturation-bombing raid, approved by Franco
and carried out by Hitler. Notice the two rooms of studies for
Guernica filled with iron-nail tears and screaming mouths.
Guernica was exiled in America until Franco's death, and now it
reigns as Spain's national piece of art.

The museum also houses an easy-to-enjoy collection of other
modern artists, including more of Picasso (3 rooms divided among
his pre-civil-war work, *Guernica*, and his post-civil-war art) and a
mind-bending room of Dalís. Enjoy a break in the shady courtyard
before leaving (500 ptas, free Sat afternoon and all day Sun; Mon

and Wed–Sat 10:00–21:00, Sun 10:00–14:30, closed Tue; Santa
Isabel 52, Metro: Atocha, across from Atocha train station, look
for exterior glass elevators, tel. 91-467-5062).

More Sights—Madrid

Chapel San Antonio de la Florida—Goya's tomb stares up at a
splendid cupola filled with his own frescoes (300 ptas, Tue–Fri
10:00–14:00, 16:00–20:00, Sat–Sun 10:00–14:00, closed Mon, July
and Aug only 10:00–14:00, Glorieta de San Antonio de la Florida,
Metro: Príncipe Pío, tel. 91-542-0722).

Royal Tapestry Factory (Real Fabrica de Tapices)—Have a
look at the traditional making of tapestries (250 ptas, some English
tours, Mon–Fri 10:00–14:00, closed Aug, Calle Fuenterrabia 2,
Metro: Menendez Pelayo, take Gutenberg exit, tel. 91-434-0551).

▲Retiro Park—Siesta in this 350-acre green and breezy escape
from the city. At midday on Saturday and Sunday, the area
around the lake becomes a street carnival, with jugglers, puppet-
eers, and lots of local color. These peaceful gardens offer great
picnicking and people watching. From the Retiro Metro stop,
walk to the big lake (El Estanque), where you can rent a rowboat
(450 ptas for 45 min). Past the lake, a grand boulevard of statues
leads to the Prado.

Charles III's Botanical Garden (Real Jardín Botánico)—After
your Prado visit, consider a lush and fragrant break in this sculpted
park wandering among trees from around the world (entry just
opposite Prado's Murillo entry, 250 ptas, daily 9:00–21:00, Plaza
de Murillo 2).

Moncloa Tower—This tower offers the best skyscraper view in
town (200 ptas, elevator takes you 100 meters up).

Teleferico—For a break from the big city, ride this cable car from
downtown over Madrid's sprawling city park to Casa de Campo
(535 ptas round-trip, daily from 12:00, departs from Paseo del
Pintor Rosales, Metro: Arguelles, tel. 91-541-7450).

Shopping

Shoppers can focus on the colorful pedestrian area between Gran
Vía and Puerta del Sol. The giant Spanish department store, El
Corte Inglés, is a block off Puerta del Sol and a handy place to
pick up just about anything you need (Mon–Sat 10:00–21:30,
closed Sun, free maps at info desk, supermarket in basement).

▲El Rastro—Europe's biggest flea market, held on Sundays and
holidays, is a field day for shoppers, people watchers, and thieves
(9:00–15:00, best before 12:00). Thousands of stalls titillate more
than a million browsers with mostly new junk. If you brake for
garage sales, you'll pull a U-turn for El Rastro. Start at the Plaza
Mayor and head south or take the subway to Tirso de Molina.
Hang on to your wallet. Munch on a *relleno* or *pepito* (meat-filled

pastry). Europe's biggest stamp market thrives simultaneously on Plaza Mayor.

Nightlife

▲▲▲**Bullfight**—Madrid's Plaza de Toros hosts Spain's top bullfights on most Sundays and holidays from Easter through October and nearly every day mid-May through early June. Top fights sell out in advance. Fights start punctually at 19:00. Tickets range from 500 to 10,000 ptas. There are no bad seats at Plaza de Toros; paying more gets you in the shade and/or closer to the gore (*filas* 8, 9, and 10 tend to be closest to the action). Booking offices and hotels are convenient but they add 20 percent and don't sell the cheap seats (Calle de Victoria 3, tel. 91-531-2732). If you want to save money, stand in the bullring ticket line. Tickets go on sale the day of the fight at 10:00; 10 percent of the seats are kept available to be sold two hours before the fight (Calle Alcala 237, Metro: Ventas, tel. 91-356-2200, www.las-ventas.com). The bullfighting museum (Museo Taurino) is next to the bullring (free, 9:30–14:30, closed Sat and Mon and early on fight days, Calle Alcala 237, tel. 91-725-1857). See the appendix for more on the "art" of bullfighting.

▲▲**Zarzuela**—For a delightful look at Spanish light opera that even English speakers can enjoy, try Zarzuela. Guitar-strumming Napoleons in red capes; buxom women with masks, fans, and castanets; Spanish-speaking pharaohs; melodramatic spotlights; and aficionados clapping and singing along from the cheap seats where the acoustics are best—this is Zarzuela . . . the people's opera. Madrid's Theater Zarzuela is at Jovellanos 4 (Metro: Banco de España, tel. 91-524-5400). The TI's monthly guide has a special Zarzuela listing.

Flamenco—Save this for Sevilla if you can. In Madrid, Taberna Casa Patas is small, intimate, smoky, and powerful, with one drink included and no hassling after that (tickets around 3,000 ptas, shows at 22:00, Canizares 10, near Plaza Santa Ana, reservations tel. 91-369-0496). The Flamenco House is more touristy (Calle Torija 7, just off Plaza Mayor).

Sleeping in Madrid
(180 ptas = about $1, country code: 34)

Sleep Code: **S** = Single, **D** = Double/Twin, **T** = Triple, **Q** = Quad, **b** = bathroom, **t** = toilet only, **s** = shower only, **CC** = Credit Card (Visa, MasterCard, Amex), **SE** = Speaks English, **NSE** = No English. Breakfast is not included unless noted. In Madrid, the 7 percent IVA tax is generally, but not always, included in the price.

Madrid has plenty of centrally located budget hotels and *pensiónes*. You'll have no trouble finding a sleepable double for $30, a good double for $60, and a modern air-conditioned double with all the comforts for $100. Prices are the same throughout the year, and it's almost always easy to find a place. Anticipate full hotels May 15 to 25 (the festival of Madrid's patron Saint Isidro) and the last week in September (conventions). The accommodations I've listed are within a few minutes' walk of Puerta del Sol.

Sleeping in the Pedestrian Zone between Puerta del Sol and Gran Vía (zip code: 28013)

Predictable and away from the seediness, these are good values for those wanting to spend a little more. Their formal prices may be inflated, and some offer weekend and summer discounts whenever it's slow. Metro: Sol. See map on page 64 for location.

Hotel Europa has red-carpet charm: a royal salon, plush halls with happy Muzak, polished wood floors, attentive staff, and 80 squeaky-clean rooms with balconies overlooking the pedestrian zone or an inner courtyard—which amplifies voices, grunts d'amour, and TV noise. For a better night's sleep, remind the management to enforce the no-TV-after-midnight rule (Sb-6,900 ptas, Db-8,900 ptas, Tb-12,600 ptas, Qb-14,800 ptas, fine lounge on second floor, elevator, fans, easy phone reservations with credit card, CC:VMA, Calle del Carmen 4, tel. 91-521-2900, fax 91-521-4696, www.hoteleuropa.net, e-mail: info@hoteleuropa.net, Antonio Garaban and his very helpful staff SE). The convenient Europa cafeteria/restaurant next door is a great scene and a fine value any time of day.

Hotel Regente is a big, traditional, and impersonal place with 145 plain but comfortable air-conditioned rooms and a great location (Sb-6,500 ptas, Db-11,000 ptas, Tb-12,500 ptas, CC:VMA, midway between Puerta del Sol and Plaza del Callao at Mesonero Romanos 9, tel. 91-521-2941, fax 91-532-3014).

Euromadrid Hotel is like a Motel 6 with 43 nondescript rooms in a modern but well-worn shell (Sb-8,600 ptas, Db-11,500 ptas, Tb-14,000 ptas, includes tax and breakfast, CC:VMA, air-con, Mesonero Romanos 7, tel. 91-521-7200, fax 91-521-4582).

Hotel Cliper is spick-and-span with once-elegant character and basic rooms on a fairly quiet street (Sb-6,300 ptas, Db-8,500 ptas, Tb-9,500 ptas, includes tax and breakfast, fine lounge, air-con, elevator, CC:VMA, Chincilla 6, near Plaza Carmen, tel. 91-531-1700, fax 91-531-1707, e-mail: reservas@hotelclipper.com).

The huge **Hotel Liabeny** feels classy and new, with 222 plush, spacious rooms and all the comforts. It's a business-class hotel that decided to lower its prices to get the tourist trade (Sb-11,900 ptas, Db-16,200 ptas, Tb-19,000 ptas; mid-July and Aug Db-12,000 ptas; CC:VMA, air-con, if one room is smoky ask for another, off Plaza Carmen at Salud 3, tel. 91-531-9000, fax 91-532-7421, e-mail: liabeny@apunte.es).

Hotel Opera, a serious 79-room hotel with all the comforts, is located just off Plaza Isabel II, a ten-minute walk from Puerta del Sol toward the Royal Palace (Sb-12,000 ptas, Db-16,800 ptas, Tb-21,800 ptas, 10 percent off on weekends and in the summer, CC:VMA, air-con, elevator, ask for a higher floor—there are eight—to avoid street noise, consider their "singing dinners," Cuesta de Santo Domingo 2, tel. 91-541-2800, fax 91-541-6923, www.hotelopera.com, e-mail: reservas@hotelopera.com).

Sleeping at Gran Vía #44
(zip code: 28013)
The pulse (and noise) of today's Madrid is best felt along the Gran Vía. This main drag in the heart of the city stays awake all night. Despite the dreary pile of prostitutes just a block north, there's a certain urban decency about it. My choices (all at Gran Vía #44) are across from Plaza del Callao, which is four colorful blocks (of pedestrian malls) from Puerta del Sol. Although many rooms are high above the traffic noise, cooler and quieter rooms are on the back side. The Café & Te next door provides a classy way to breakfast. The Callão Metro stop is at your doorstep, and the handy Gran Vía stop (direct to Atocha) is two blocks away.

Hostal Residencia Miami is clean and quiet, with 11 well-lit rooms, padded doors, and plastic-flower decor throughout. It's like staying at your eccentric aunt's in Miami Beach (S-3,000–4,000 ptas, D-5,000 ptas, Db-7,000 ptas, T-7,000 ptas, Tb-8,000 ptas, includes tax, CC:VM, eighth floor, tel. & fax 91-521-1464).

Across the hall, **Hostal Alibel**, like Miami with less sugar, rents seven big, airy, quiet rooms (D-5,000 ptas, Ds-5,500 ptas, Db-6,000 ptas, tel. 91-521-0051, grandmotherly Terese NSE).

These next two are threadbare and suffer from street noise. **Hostal Residencia Valencia** is a tired old place with 32 big, stark rooms. The friendly manager, Antonio Ramirez, speaks English (Sb-4,400 ptas, Ds-6,000 ptas, Db-6,200 ptas, Tb-8,200 ptas, Qb-9,200 ptas, CC:VMA, fifth floor, tel. 91-522-1115, fax 91-522-1113). A bit smoky and with less character, **Hostal Residencia Continental** is downstairs and closer to the traffic (Sb-4,400 ptas, Db-5,800 ptas, CC:VMA, third floor, tel. 91-521-4640, fax 91-521-4649, e-mail: continental@mundivia.es, SE).

Sleeping on or near Plaza Santa Ana
(zip code: 28012 unless otherwise noted)
The Plaza Santa Ana area has plenty of small, cheap places. While well worn and noisy at night, it has a rough but charming ambience, with colorful bars and a central location (3 min from Puerta del Sol's "Tío Pepe" sign; walk down Calle San Jeronimo and turn right on Príncipe; Metro: Sol). At most of these hotels, fluent Spanish is spoken, bathrooms are down the hall, and there's no heat during winter. To locate hotels, see map on page 79.

Hopeless romantics might enjoy playing corkscrew around the rickety cut-glass elevator to the very simple yet homey **Pensión La Valenciana**'s old and funky rooms with springy beds. All rooms have balconies; three of them overlook the square (S-1,600 ptas, D-3,500 ptas, Príncipe 27, fourth floor, right on Plaza Santa Ana next to the theater with flags, tel. 91-429-6317, Esperanza NSE).

Because of the following two places, I list no Madrid youth hostels. For super-cheap beds in a dingy time warp, consider **Hostal Lucense** (S-1,500 ptas, D-2,800 ptas, Ds-3,000 ptas, Ts-3,500 ptas, 200 ptas per shower, cheaper for 2 nights, Nuñez de Arce 15, tel. 91-522-4888, run by Sr. and Sra. Muñoz, both interesting characters, Sr. SE) and **Casa Huéspedes Poza** (same prices, street noise, and owners—but Sr. does the cleaning, at Nuñez de Arce 9, tel. 91-522-4871).

Hostal R. Veracruz II, between Plaza Santa Ana and Puerta del Sol, rents decent, quiet rooms (Sb-4,800 ptas, Db-6,500 ptas, Tb-8,200 ptas, CC:VM, elevator, air-con, Victoria 1, third floor, tel. 91-522-7635, fax 91-522-6749, NSE).

Splurges: To be on the same square and spend in a day what others spend in a week, luxuriate in **Hotel Reina Victoria** (Sb-24,000 ptas, Db-30,000 ptas, prices generally discounted to "week-end rate" of Db-16,500 on Fri, Sat, Sun in summer and all of July, when this becomes a fine value, CC:VMA, Plaza Santa Ana 14, tel. 91-531-4500, fax 91-522-0307, e-mail: reinavictoria@trypnet .com). For a royal, air-conditioned breather, spit out your gum, step into its lobby, grab a sofa, and watch the bellboys push the beggars back out the revolving doors.

Suite Prado, two blocks toward the Prado from Plaza Santa Ana, is a better value, offering 18 sprawling, air-conditioned suites with a homier feel (Db suite-23,500 ptas, suites are modern and comfortable with refrigerators and sitting rooms, extra adult-4,000 ptas, extra kid free, elevator, CC:VMA, Manuel Fernandez y Gonzalez 10, at intersection with Venture de la Vega, 28014 Madrid, tel. 91-420-2318, fax 91-420-0559, www.suiteprado.com, Monica and Anna SE). Across the street, **Residencia Hostal Lisboa** is also a good value (Sb-6,000 ptas, Db-7,100 ptas, Tb-9,100 ptas, CC:VMA, elevator, Ventura de la Vega 17, tel. 91-429-4676, fax 91-429-9894).

Sleeping Elsewhere in Central Madrid

Halfway between the Prado Museum and Plaza Santa Ana are two good places at #34 Cervantes (28014 Madrid, Metro: Anton Martin). The spotless and comfortable **Hotel Gonzalo**—well-run by friendly and helpful Javier—is in all the guidebooks (Sb-4,900 ptas, Db-5,900 ptas, Tb-7,500 ptas, CC:VMA, elevator, 15 rooms, third floor, tel. 91-429-2714, fax 91-420-2007). The equally polished **Hotel Cervantes** is also good (Sb-5,000 ptas, Db-6,500 ptas, Tb-8,500 ptas, CC:VMA, second floor, tel. & fax 91-429-2745).

(handwritten: We met a couple who said this was good!)

Hostal Tijcal is comfortable, with tons of extras; and just half a block east of the elegant Plaza Mayor on a quiet, traffic-free street (that can attract unsavory characters late at night). Run with pride by Gabriel Caraballo and his parents, the hotel name is an acronym for: work, equality, justice, culture, amigos, and liberty (S-4,500 ptas, Sb-6,000 ptas, D-6,700 ptas, Db-7,500 ptas, includes tax, air-con–1,000 ptas extra per day, elevator, CC:VM, Zaragoza 6, third floor, 28012 Madrid, Metro: Sol, tel. 91-365-5910, fax 91-364-5260, www.hostaltijcal.com).

Eating in Madrid

In Spain, only Barcelona rivals Madrid for taste-bud thrills. You have three dining choices: an atmospheric sit-down meal in a well-chosen restaurant, an unmemorable basic sit-down meal, or a stand-up meal of tapas in a bar or (more likely) in several bars. Many restaurants are closed in August (especially through the last half).

Eating near Puerta del Sol and Plaza Mayor

(handwritten: yes) Many Americans are drawn to Hemingway's favorite, **Sobrino del Botín** (daily 13:00–16:00, 20:00–24:00, Cuchilleros 17, a block downhill from Plaza Mayor, tel. 91-366-4217). It's touristy, pricey, and the last place he'd go now, but still, people love it, and the food is excellent. If phoning to make a reservation, choose between the downstairs (for dark, medieval-cellar ambience) or upstairs (for a still-traditional but airier and lighter elegance).

Restaurante Los Galayos is less touristy and plenty *tipico* with good local cuisine (daily lunch specials, lunch from 13:00, dinner from 20:30, arrive early or make a reservation, 30 meters off Plaza Mayor at Botoneras 5, tel. 91-366-3028). For many, dinner right on the square is worth the premium (consider Restaurante Pulpito, behind the horse).

Plaza Mayor is famous for its *bocadillos calamares*. For a cheap and tasty squid-ring sandwich, line up at **Casa Rua** on Plaza Mayor's southwest corner (behind and to the right of the horse statue).

Restaurante Rodriguez serves basic food which locals return for (closed July, San Cristobal 15, 1 block toward Puertá del Sol from Plaza Mayor, tel. 91-231-1136).

La Casa de las Torrijas, looking much like it did on opening day in 1907, serves cheap home-cooked lunch specials, tapas, and good wine. The sign under the mirror reads: "For hygienic reasons, no spitting on the floor" (Mon–Sat 13:00–16:00, 18:00–24:00, closed Sun, a block off Puerta del Sol at Calle Paz 4, tel. 91-532-1473).

For a fine meal with no tourists and locals who appreciate good local-style cooking, try **Casa Ciriaco** (3,000-ptas meals, Thu–Tue 13:30–16:00, 20:30–24:00, closed Wed and Aug, halfway between Puerta del Sol and Royal Palace at Calle Mayor 84, tel. 91-548-0620). It was from this building in 1906 that an anarchist threw a bomb at the royal couple on their wedding day (for details, see "Introductory Walk," above). Photos of the carnage are on the wall in the dining room.

Restaurante Puerto Rico has good food, great prices, and few tourists (Mon–Sat 13:00–16:30, 20:30–24:00, closed Sun, Chinchilla 2, between Puerta del Sol and Gran Vía, on same street as Hotel Cliper, tel. 91-532-2040).

Hotel Europa Cafeteria is a fun high-energy scene with a mile-long bar, traditionally clad waiters, great people watching, local cuisine, and super prices (next to Hotel Europa, 50 meters off Puerta del Sol at Calle del Carmen 4, tel. 91-521-2900).

Eating near the Prado

Each of the big-three art museums has a decent cafeteria. These two cafés are near the Prado: **La Plateria** is a hardworking little café/wine bar with a good menu for tapas, light meals, and hearty salads. Its tables spill onto the leafy little Plaza de Platarias de Matinez (daily 8:00–24:00, directly across busy highway from Atocha end of Prado, tel. 91-429-1722). Good-looking young tour guides eat cheap and filling salads at **VIPS**, a bright modern place engulfed in a big bookstore (daily 9:00–24:00, in Galeria del Prado at Prado end of San Jeronimo under Palace Hotel).

Vegetarian

Artemisia II is a hit with vegetarians who like good, healthy food in a smoke-free room (great 1,400-ptas 3-course lunch menu, daily 13:30–16:00, 21:00–24:00, closed last half of Aug, CC:VMA, 2 blocks north of Puerta Sol at Tres Cruces 4, just off Plaza Carmen, tel. 91-521-8721). **Artemisia I** is like its sister (4 blocks east of Puerta Sol at Ventura de la Vega 4 off San Jeronimo, tel. 91-429-5092).

Fast Food, Picnics, and Breakfast

Fast Food: For an easy, light, cheap meal, try **Rodilla**—a popular sandwich bar on the northeast corner of Puerta del Sol at #13 (daily 8:30–20:30). **Pans & Company**, with shops throughout Spain, offers healthy, tasty sandwiches and great chef's salads (daily 9:00–24:00, on Puerta del Sol, Plaza Callão, Gran Vía 30, and many more).

Picnics: The department store **El Corte Inglés** has a well-stocked **deli**, but its produce is sold only in large quantities (Mon–Sat 10:00–21:00, closed Sun). A perfect place to assemble a cheap picnic is downtown Madrid's neighborhood market, **Mercado de San Miguel**. How about breakfast surrounded by early-morning shoppers in the market's café? (Mon–Fri 9:00–14:30, 17:15–20:15, Sat 9:00–14:30, closed Sun; from Plaza Mayor, face the colorful building and exit from the upper left-hand corner.)

Churros con chocolate **for breakfast:** If you like hash browns and eggs in American greasy-spoon joints, you must try the Spanish equivalent: greasy *churros* dipped in thick, hot chocolate. **Bar Valladolid** is a good bet for *churros* (open daily from 7:00, 2 blocks off Tío Pepe end of Puerta del Sol, south on Espoz y Mina, turn right on Calle de Cadiz). With luck, the *churros* machine in the back will be cooking. Notice the expressive WC signs.

Tapas: The Madrid Pub-Crawl Dinner

For maximum fun, people, and atmosphere, go mobile and do the "tapa tango," a local tradition of going from one bar to the next, munching, drinking, and socializing. Tapas are the toothpick appetizers, salads, and deep-fried foods served in most bars. Madrid is Spain's tapa capital—tapas just don't get any better. Grab a toothpick and stab something strange—but establish the prices first. Some items are very pricey, and most bars push larger *raciónes* rather than smaller tapas. *Un pincho* is a bite-sized serving (not always available), *una tapa* is a snack, and *una ración* is half a meal. *Un bocadillo* is a tapa on bread. A *caña* (can-yah) is a small glass of draft beer. A *chato* is a small glass of house wine.

Prowl the area between Puerta del Sol and Plaza Santa Ana. There's no ideal route, but the little streets (in this book's map) between Puerta del Sol, San Jeronimo, and Plaza Santa Ana hold tasty surprises. Nearby, Jesus de Medinaceli is also lined with popular tapas bars. Below is a seven-stop tapa crawl. These places are good, but don't be blind to making discoveries on your own. The action is better after 20:00.

1. From Puerta del Sol, walk east a block down Carrera de San Jeronimo to the corner of Victoria Street. Across from Museo del Jamón, you'll find **La Tourina Cervecería**, a bullfighters' Planet Hollywood. Wander among trophies and historic photographs. Each stuffed bull's head is named, along with its farm, awards, and who killed him. Among the photos study the first post: It's Che Guevara, Orson Welles, and Salvador Dalí all enjoying a good fight. Around the corner, the Babe Ruth of bullfighters, El Cordobes, is wounded in bed. The photo below shows him in action. Kick off your pub crawl with a drink here. If inspired, you could go for the *rabo de toro* (bull-tail stew, 1,500 ptas). Across the street at San Jeronimo 5 is...

2. Museo del Jamón (Museum of Ham), tastefully decorated—unless you're a pig. This frenetic, cheap, stand-up bar is an assembly line of fast and deliciously simple *bocadillos* and *raciónes*. Options are shown in photographs with prices. For a small sandwich, ask for a *chiquito* (100 ptas, unadvertised). The pricey Jamon Iberico—from pigs who led stress-free lives in acorn valley—is best. Just point and eat (daily 9:00–24:00, sit-down restaurant upstairs). Next, forage halfway up Calle Victoria to the tiny...

Plaza Santa Ana Area

❶ Tourina Cerveceria	❾ Bar Vallidolid
❷ Museo del Jamon	❿ Artemesia I
❸ Casa del Abuelo	⓫ Pension Valenciana
❹ Casa Toni	⓬ Res. Hostal Lisboa
❺ La Ria	⓭ Hostal Lucense & Poza
❻ Hotel Gonzalo & Cervantes	⓮ Hostal Veracruz II
❼ Torre del Oro Bar	⓯ Hotel Reina Victoria
❽ Chocolateria San Gines	⓰ Suite Prado

3. La Casa del Abuelo, for shrimp lovers who savor sizzling plates of tasty little *gambas*. Try *gambas a la plancha* (grilled shrimp, 600 ptas), *gambas al ajillo* (ahh-hheee-yoh, shrimp version of escargot, cooked in oil and garlic and ideal for bread dipping—750 ptas), and a 150-ptas glass of red wine (daily 11:30–15:30, 18:30–23:30, Calle Victoria 12). Continue uphill and around the corner to...
4. Casa Toni, for refreshing bowls of gazpacho—the popular cold tomato-and-garlic soup (250 ptas, open from 19:30, closed

mid-June–mid-July, Calle Cruz 14). Backtrack halfway down Calle Victoria and turn left, walking through an alley littered with tourist-filled dining tables to...

5. La Ria, a tapas bar that sells plates of 10 mussels—slurp out the meat, scoop the juice with the shells, and toss the shells on the floor as you smack your lips (19:30–23:00, Pasaje Matheu 5). *Mejillones picantes* is spicy (460 ptas). Wash each down with the crude, dry, white Ribeiro wine from Galicia—served in a ceramic bowl to disguise its lack of clarity. The place is draped in mussels. Notice the photo showing the floor filled with litter—a reminder that mussel bars, while lonely these days, have seen better times. In the 1970s they sold 14 tons a month. Now—with other, more trendy evening activities entertaining the cruising youth—it takes a year to sell 14 tons.

6. Head to Plaza Mayor for **La Torre del Oro Bar Andalu** (26 Plaza Mayor, from 11:00, tel. 91-366-5016). Bullfight aficionados hate the gimmicky Bull Bar across from Museo del Jamón (stop #1). This one has soul. The walls are lined with grisly bullfight photos from annual photo competitions. Read the gory description above in the Introductory Walk. Have a drink but be careful not to let the aggressive staff bully you into high-priced tapas you don't want.

7. The classy **Chocolatería San Ginés** is much loved locally for its *churros* (greasy cigar-shaped fritters) and chocolate (Tue–Sun 22:00–7:00, closed Mon). While empty before midnight, it's packed with the disco crowd in the wee hours (the popular Joy disco is next door). Finish off your crawl sweetly, dunking your *churros* into the pudding-like hot chocolate, as locals have done here for over 100 years (from Plaza Mayor, cross Calle Mayor and go down Calle P. de San Ginés to #5, off Calle Arenal, tel. 93-365-6546).

Transportation Connections—Madrid

By train to: Toledo (9/day, 1 hr, from Madrid's Atocha station, if day-tripping there's a direct Madrid–Toledo express at 8:34 or 9:44 and a Toledo–Madrid express at 18:56), **Segovia** (9/day, 2 hrs, both Chamartin and Atocha stations), **Ávila** (6/day, 90 min, from Chamartin and Atocha), **Salamanca** (4/day, 2.5 hrs, from Chamartin), **Barcelona** (6/day, 8 hrs, mostly from Chamartin), **Granada** (6–9 hrs, including an overnight train, from Chamartin), **Sevilla** (15/day, 2.5 hrs by AVE, 3.5 hrs by Talgo, from Atocha), **Córdoba** (16 AVE trains/day, 2 hrs, from Atocha), **Lisbon** (1/day, 10 hrs, overnight from Chamartin), **Paris** (4/day, 12–16 hrs, 1 direct overnight, from Chamartin). Train info: tel. 902-240-202.

Spain's AVE bullet train opens up some good itinerary options. Pick up the brochure at the station. Prices vary with times and class. The basic Madrid–Sevilla fare is 8,400 ptas (1,100-ptas less on the almost-as-fast Talgo). AVE is 85 percent covered by Eurail (so the Madrid–Sevilla–Madrid round-trip costs Eurailers about 2,400 ptas). So far AVE only covers Madrid–Córdoba–Sevilla. Consider this exciting day trip from Madrid: 7:00 depart, 8:45–12:40 in Córdoba, 13:30–21:00 in Sevilla, 23:30 back in Madrid. Reserve each AVE segment (tel. 902-240-202).

By bus to: Segovia (2/hrly, 1.25 hrs, Larrea Lines, Paseo de la Florida 11, just past Hotel Florida Norte, Metro: Príncipe Pío); for **Avila** (7/day, 2 hrs) and **Toledo** (2/hrly, 60 min), buses depart from Estación sur Autobuses (Metro: Méndez Alvaro, tel. 91-468-4200).

By bus, train, and car to El Escorial: Buses leave from the basement of Madrid's Metro stop Moncloa and drop you in the El Escorial center (4/hrly, 45 min, Autocares Herranz, tel. 91-896-9028). One bus a day (except for Mon) is designed to let travelers do the Valley of the Fallen as a side trip from El Escorial; the bus leaves El Escorial at 15:15 (15-min trip) and leaves Valley of the Fallen at 17:30. Trains run to El Escorial but let you off a 20-minute walk (or a shuttle-bus ride, 2/hrly) from the monastery and city center. By car, visiting El Escorial and Valley of the Fallen on the way to Segovia is easy (except on Mon, when both sights are closed).

Drivers' note: Avoid driving in Madrid. Rent your car when you leave. It's cheapest to make car-rental arrangements before you leave home. In Madrid try Europcar (San Leonardo 8, Chamartin station, tel. 91-323-1721, airport tel. 91-393-7235), Hertz (Gran Vía 88, tel. 91-542-5803, Chamartin station tel. 91-733-0400, airport tel. 91-393-7228), or Avis (Gran Vía 60, tel. 91-548-4205, airport tel. 91-393-7222). Ask about free delivery to your hotel. At the airport, most rental cars are returned at Terminal 1.

NORTHWEST OF MADRID:
EL ESCORIAL, VALLEY OF THE FALLEN, SEGOVIA, SALAMANCA

Before slipping out of Madrid by train, consider several fine side trips northwest of Spain's capital city.

Spain has a lavish, brutal, and complicated history. An hour from Madrid, tour the imposing and fascinating palace of Monasterio de San Lorenzo de El Escorial, headquarters of the Spanish Inquisition. Nearby, at the awesome Valley of the Fallen, pay tribute to the countless victims of Spain's bloody civil war.

Segovia, with its remarkable Roman aqueduct and romantic castle, is also an easy side trip from Madrid. Farther out, you can walk the perfectly preserved medieval walls of Ávila. And at Salamanca, enjoy Spain's best town square, caffeinated with a frisky college-town ambience.

Planning Your Time

See El Escorial and the Valley of the Fallen together in less than a day (but not Mon, when sights are closed). By car, do them en route to Segovia; by bus, make it a day trip from Madrid.

Segovia is worth a half day of sightseeing and is a joy at night. Ávila, while not without charm, merits only a quick stop to marvel at its medieval walls, if you're driving in the neighborhood.

Salamanca, with its art, university, and Spain's greatest Plaza Mayor, is worth a day and a night but is stuck out in the boonies. On a three-week Barcelona–Lisbon "open-jaw" itinerary, I'd hook south from Madrid and skip Salamanca. If you're doing a circular trip, Salamanca is a natural stop halfway between Portugal and Madrid.

In total, these sights are worth a maximum of three days if you're in Iberia for less than a month. If you're in Spain for just a week, I'd still squeeze in a look at El Escorial and the Valley of the Fallen.

Sights near Madrid

EL ESCORIAL

The Monasterio de San Lorenzo de El Escorial is a symbol of
power rather than elegance. This 16th-century palace, 30 miles
northwest of Madrid, gives us a better feel for the Counter-
Reformation and the Inquisition than any other building. Built
at a time when Catholic Spain felt threatened by Protestant
"heretics," its construction dominated the Spanish economy for
20 years (1563–1584). Because of this bully in the national budget,
Spain has almost nothing else to show from this most powerful
period of her history.

The giant, gloomy building looks more like a prison than
a palace (grey-black stone, 200 yards long, 150 yards wide, over
100 miles of passages, 2,600 windows, 1,200 doors, 1,600 overwhelmed tourists). Four hundred years ago, the enigmatic, intro-
verted, and extremely Catholic King Philip II ruled his bulky
empire and directed the Inquisition from here. To 16th-century
followers of Luther, this place epitomized the evil of Catholicism.
Today it's a time capsule of Spain's "Golden Age," packed with
history, art, and Inquisition ghosts.

The Monasterio looks confusing at first, but you simply follow the arrows and signs in one continuous walk-through. Guides in each room can answer basic questions. The entrance (off Grimaldi, a minute's walk from TI) is the best place to start. This is the general order you'll follow (though some rooms are sure to be closed for renovation). The small **Museo de Arquitectura** has easy-to-appreciate models of the palace and the machinery used to construct it. The **Museo de Pintura**, packed with big paintings in small rooms, features works by Titian, Veronese, Rubens, Bosch, van Dyck, and van der Weyden. The **king's apartments** are notable for their austerity, with a bed that's barely queen-size. The king made sure his quarters came with a view . . . of the church's high altar. Stairs take you down into the **Pantéon Real**, the gilded resting place of 26 kings and queens, four centuries' worth of Spanish monarchy. The lazy Susan–like **Pantéon de los Infantes** holds the remains of various royal children and relatives. Paintings by Ribera, El Greco, Titian, and Velázquez elegantly decorate the *salas capitulares* (chapter rooms). The **cloister** (which may be partially closed) glows with bright, newly restored paintings by Tibaldi.

Follow the signs to the **church**. The altar is spectacular when illuminated (put 100 ptas in the small box near the church entrance, just before the gated doors), but the highlight is Cellini's marble sculpture *The Crucifixion* (to the left as you enter).

Last comes the *biblioteca*, or the library (have your ticket handy). Savor this room. The ceiling is a burst of color, and the meshed bookcases feature illustrated books. At the far end of the room, the elaborate model of the solar system looks like a giant gyroscope, revolving unmistakably around the earth. Notice the misshapen North America.

Admission to the palace is 900 ptas (Tue–Sun 10:00–19:00, enter before ticket office closes at 18:00, closed Mon; Oct–March closes at 18:00; tel. 91-890-5904). A tour is included if you pay 1,000 ptas for admission, but the tour (available 10:00–18:00) is limited to the apartments and mausoleum only, and English tours occur only if there is an English-speaking guide available and in the mood. You'll find scanty but sufficient captions in English within the palace. For more information, skip the tour and get the *Visitor's Guide: Monastery of San Lorenzo El Real de El Escorial* (1,000 ptas, available at any of several shops in the palace). It follows the general route you'll take and is better than the cheaper but overly comprehensive book-length *Official Guide* (600 ptas).

If you arrive by bus at the town of San Lorenzo de El Escorial, walk from the bus station to the TI (by heading down Juan de Toledo, angling to the right across the plaza onto Avenida Juan de Borbón de Battenberg). The TI (Mon–Thu 11:00–18:00, Fri–Sun 10:00–19:00, tel. 91-890-5313) is on the corner of Grimaldi in front of the entrance of the Monasterio.

Up the hill from the TI on Grimaldi are two pleasant, stair-stepped plazas (Jacinto Benavente and San Lorenzo), dotted with trees and cafés. Nearby is the pedestrian-friendly Calle Juan de Leyra.

The town is worth a browse. To shop for a picnic, stop by the Mercado Publico on Calle del Rey 9, a four-minute walk from the palace (Mon–Fri 9:00–14:00, 17:00–20:00, Sat 10:00–14:00, closed Thu afternoon and Sun). For a change from Spanish fare, consider pizza at Tavolata Reale (Plaza de Las Animas, a block from Monasterio entrance, tel. 91-809-4591) or Restaurante China Hong Kong (Calle San Anton 6, tel. 91-896-1894).

Transportation Connections—El Escorial

From Madrid: Buses leave from the basement level of Madrid's Metro stop Moncloa and drop you in the town center of San Lorenzo de El Escorial, near the Monasterio (4/hrly, 45 min, Autocares Herranz, tel. 91-890-4100).

The **train** is less convenient. Although trains leave twice hourly from Madrid's Atocha station, you're dropped a 20-minute walk (or shuttle-bus ride, 2/hrly) from San Lorenzo de El Escorial town center and Monasterio.

Consider combining a day trip to El Escorial and the Valley of the Fallen. The bus company Autocares Herranz offers one round-trip bus connection every afternoon (except Mon, when sights are closed) from El Escorial to the Valley of the Fallen (see below).

VALLEY OF THE FALLEN (EL VALLE DE LOS CAÍDOS)

Eight kilometers from El Escorial, high in the Guadarrama Mountains, a 150-yard-tall granite cross marks an immense and powerful underground monument to the victims of Spain's 20th-century nightmare—its civil war (1936–1939).

The stairs that lead to the imposing monument are grouped in sets of 10s, meant to symbolize the Ten Commandments (including "Thou shalt not kill"—hmm). The emotional pietà draped over the entrance was sculpted by Juan de Avalos, the same artist who created the dramatic figures of the four evangelists at the base of the cross.

A solemn silence and a stony chill fill the "basilica"—larger (860 feet long) than St. Peter's—as Spaniards pass under the huge, forbidding angels of fascism to visit the grave of General Franco. The term *basilica* normally designates a church built over the remains of a saint, not a fascist dictator. Franco's prisoners, the enemies of the right, dug this memorial out of solid rock.

The sides of the monument are lined with 16th-century Brussels tapestries of the Apocalypse and side chapels containing alabaster copies of Spain's most famous statues of the Virgin Mary.

Interred behind the high altar and side chapels are the remains of the approximately 50,000 people, both Republicanos and Franco's Nacionalistas, who lost their lives in the war. Regrettably the urns are not visible, so it is Franco who takes center stage. His grave, strewn with flowers, lies behind the high altar. In front of the altar is the grave of José Antonio, the founder of Spanish fascism. Between these fascists' graves is the statue of a crucified Christ. The seeping stones seem to weep.

On your way out, stare into the eyes of those angels with swords and two right wings and think about all the "heroes" who keep dying "for God and country," at the request of the latter (700 ptas, Tue–Sun 9:30–19:00, closed Mon).

The expansive view from the monument's terrace includes the peaceful, forested valley and sometimes snow-streaked mountains. A funicular climbs to the base of the cross and a better view (400 ptas round-trip, 10:30–19:00, tel. 91-890-5611). A small snack bar and picnic tables are near the parking lot (and bus stop).

Without a car, the easiest way to get to the Valley of the Fallen is from El Escorial by an Autocares Herranz bus (1/daily except Mon, 15 min, leaves El Escorial at 15:15, leaves Valley of the Fallen at 17:30, 1030-ptas round-trip includes admission to the site). Buy your ticket in El Escorial at the bar on Calle del Rey, just around the corner from the bus stop (the bus driver will point the way).

SEGOVIA

Fifty miles from Madrid, this town of 55,000 boasts a great Roman aqueduct, a cathedral, and a castle. Segovia is a medieval "ship" ready for your inspection. Start at the stern—the aqueduct—and stroll up Calle de Cervantes to the prickly Gothic masts of the cathedral. Explore the tangle of narrow streets around Plaza Mayor and then descend to the Alcázar at the bow.

Orientation

Tourist Information: The two TIs are helpful. One is on Plaza del Azoguejo, under the aqueduct (daily 10:00–20:00, tel. 92-146-2914); the other at Plaza Mayor 10 (daily 10:00–14:00, 17:00–19:00, tel. 92-146-0334).

Arrival in Segovia: The train station is a 30-minute walk from the center. Take a city bus from the station to get to Calle de Colón near Plaza Mayor (2/hrly, 100 ptas, leaving from the same side of the street as the station—confirm by asking, "*¿Para Plaza Mayor?*"). Taxis are a reasonable option (700 ptas). If you arrive by bus, it's a 15-minute walk to the center (turn left out of the bus station and continue straight across the roundabout onto Calle

Ladrera). Day-trippers can store luggage at the train station but not at the bus station. Drivers can park their cars overnight for free in the park facing the Alcázar (gate closes at about 19:00); outside of the old city, parking is plentiful around Via Roma.

Helpful Hints: The Telefónica phone office has handy metered phone booths (Mon–Sat 10:00–14:00, 17:00–20:00, closed Sun, accepts credit cards for charges over 500 ptas, on Plaza de los Huertos). If you buy handicrafts such as tablecloths from street vendors, make sure the item you're buying is the one you actually get; some unscrupulous vendors substitute inferior goods at the last minute. Internet cafés are plentiful but inconveniently located in the new town; ask at the TI for the latest and closest.

Sights—Segovia

▲**Roman Aqueduct**—Built by the Romans, who ruled Spain for more than 500 years, this 2,000-year-old *acueducto Romano* is 2,500 feet long and 100 feet high, has 118 arches, was made without any mortar, and still works. It's considered Segovia's backup plumbing. From underneath the aqueduct, climb the steps off Plaza Azoguejo for an overhead view.

▲**Cathedral**—Segovia's cathedral was Spain's last major Gothic building. Embellished to the hilt with pinnacles and flying buttresses, the exterior is a great example of the final overripe stage of Gothic, called Flamboyant. The dark, spacious, and elegantly simple interior provides a delightful contrast. In the chapel to the immediate left of the entry, notice the dramatic gilded "Carroza de la Custadia." (If it's not here, look in the cathedral museum.) The Holy Communion is placed in the top of this templelike cart and paraded through town each year during the Corpus Christi festival. The *Tree of Life*, by Ignacio Ries, is also worth finding (in the rear left as you face the front). It shows hedonistic mortals dancing atop the tree of life. Look closely to see a skeletal Grim Reaper preparing to receive them into hell and Jesus ringing a bell imploring them to wake up before it's too late. The cathedral is free—just walk by the ticket counter unless you want to see the small but interesting museum and cloister (museum admission 300 ptas, tour of church and museum included—ask if an English-speaking guide is available, daily 9:00–19:00, off-season 9:30–18:00).

▲**Alcázar**—This Disneyesque rebuild, an exaggeration of an old castle that burned down here in 1862, is fun to explore and worthwhile for the view of Segovia. While it's said that Isabel first met Ferdinand here and that Columbus came here to get his fantasy financed, the tower is of little importance historically. Only a portion of the keep, which you'll pass through as you enter, is from the original castle (400 ptas, daily 10:00–19:00, off-season until 18:00, get the 25-ptas English brochure).

Strolling—Roman and Romanesque Segovia was made for

Segovia

HOTELS:
1. PLAZA
2. LOS LINAJES
3. INFANTA ISABEL
4. SIRENAS
5. DON JAIME
6. CUBO
7. SOL CRISTINA + HOSTEL

roamin'. Rub shoulders with Segovian yuppies parading up and down Calle Juan Bravo. For subtler charm, wander the back streets, away from the trinket shops and ladies selling lace. Segovia has a wealth of 12th- and 13th-century Romanesque churches (usually open during Mass, often around 8:00 and 19:30, ask at TI). Look Catholic and drop in. The San Justo church has well-preserved 13th-century frescoes (free, daily 12:00–14:00, 17:00–19:00, off-season until 18:00; near base of aqueduct, a couple of blocks from Plaza Azoguejo, in the newer side of town). The caretaker, Rafael, might invite you to climb the bell tower for "the best view of Segovia."

▲**Vera Cruz Church**—This 12-sided 13th-century Romanesque church was built by the Knights Templar and used to house a piece of the "true cross" (200 ptas, Tue–Sun 10:30–13:30, 15:30–19:00, closed Mon, Oct–May until 18:00, closed Nov, outside of town beyond the castle, a 20-min walk from main square). There's a postcard view of the city from here, and more views follow as you continue around Segovia on the small road below the castle labeled *ruta turistica panoramica*.

▲**La Granja Palace**—This "Little Versailles," 10 kilometers south of Segovia, is much smaller and happier than El Escorial. The palace and gardens were built by the homesick French King Philip V, grandson of Louis XIV. It's a must for tapestry lovers. Fountain displays send local crowds into a frenzy at 17:30 on most summer Wednesdays, Saturdays, Sundays, and holidays; July 25th and August 25th have the best shows of the year (confirm schedule at Segovia TI). Entry to the palace includes a required 45-minute guided tour, usually in Spanish (700 ptas, Tue–Sun 10:00–18:00, closed Mon; off-season Tue–Sat 10:00–13:30, 15:00–17:00, Sun 10:00–14:00; tel. 92-147-0019). Eight buses a day make the 30-minute trip from Segovia.

Sleeping in Segovia
(180 ptas = about $1, country code: 34, zip code 40001)
Sleep Code: **S** = Single, **D** = Double/Twin, **T** = Triple, **Q** = Quad, **b** = bathroom, **t** = toilet only, **s** = shower only, **CC** = Credit Card (**V**isa, **M**asterCard, **A**mex), **SE** = Speaks English, **NSE** = No English.

The best places are on or near the central Plaza Mayor. This is where the city action is: the cheapest and best bars, most touristic and *típico* eateries, and the TI. Segovia is crowded on weekends and in July and August, so arrive early or call ahead. The 7 percent IVA tax and breakfast are rarely included.

Hostal Plaza is just off Plaza Mayor toward the aqueduct. You'll find *serioso* management and long, snaky corridors, but the 26 rooms are clean and cozy (S-3,300 ptas, 1 Sb-5,300 ptas, D-4,800 ptas, Db-6,000 ptas, Tb-8,100 ptas, CC:VM, Cronista Lecea 11, tel. 92-146-0303, fax 92-146-0305, SE).

Hotel Los Linajes is ultra-classy, with rusticity mixed into its newly poured concrete. This poor-man's parador is a few blocks beyond the Plaza Mayor, with commanding views and modern, air-conditioned niceties (Sb-8,000–9,400 ptas, Db-12,500–16,000 ptas, depending on room size, Tb-15,200 ptas, cheaper off-season, breakfast-950 ptas, parking-1,200 ptas, CC:VMA, air-con, elevator, Dr. Velasco 9, tel. 92-146-0475, fax 92-146-0479). From Plaza Mayor, take Escuderos downhill; at the five-way intersection, angle right on Dr. Velasco. Drivers, follow brown signs from aqueduct.

Hotel Infanta Isabel, right on Plaza Mayor, is the ritziest hotel in the old town. It's friendly, elegant, and pricey, but 20 percent cheaper off-season (Sb-8,400 ptas, Db-12,000–14,000 ptas depending on room size, some rooms with plaza views, CC:VMA, elevator, tel. 92-146-1300, fax 92-146-2217, e-mail: hinfanta @teleline.es, SE).

A place I don't like that fills a void in Segovia is the big, stuffy, hotelesque **Hotel Sirenas** (Sb-5,500–6,500 ptas, Db-7,500–9,000 ptas, air-con, elevator, CC:VMA, 3 blocks down from the Plaza Mayor at Calle Juan Bravo 30, tel. 92-146-2663 fax 92-146-2657, NSE).

Hostal Don Jaime, near the base of the aqueduct, is shiny-new, well maintained, and friendly (S-3,400 ptas, Db-5,800 ptas, Tb-7,300 ptas, Qb-8,000 ptas, CC:VM, Ochoa Ondategui 8; from TI at aqueduct, cross under the aqueduct, go right, angle left, then snake uphill for 2 blocks; tel. 92-144-4787, SE).

Right on Plaza Mayor at #4 is a tiny and dark but clean-enough place (look hard for "Hospedaje Habitaciones" sign). The **Hospedaje Cubo** has five simple, sinkless but tidy rooms; request a room *con ventana* to avoid the windowless room (S-1,800 ptas, D-3,400 ptas, T-5,000 ptas, ask at the ground-level La Oja Blanca Bar if rooms are available before climbing up, Plaza Mayor 4, tel. 92-146-0318, Maria Jesus Cubo NSE). **Pensión Ferri**, around the corner, is a last resort (S-1,600 ptas, D-2,500 ptas, shower-350 ptas, Escuderos 10, half block off Plaza Mayor, tel. 92-146-0957, NSE).

Across from the train station is **Hostal Sol Cristina** (S-2, 500 ptas, D-4,800 ptas, Db-5,800 ptas, T-6,500 ptas, Tb-6,800 ptas, Calle Obispo Quesada 40, tel. 92-142-7513, NSE) and its nearby twin, **Hostal Residencia Sol Cristina-Dos** (same prices, same phone number).

The **Segovia Youth Hostel** is a great hostel—easygoing, comfortable, clean, friendly, and very cheap (2,100-ptas beds, open July–Aug only, Paseo Conde de Sepulveda 4, between the train and bus stations, tel. 92-144-1111).

Eating in Segovia

Look for Segovia's culinary claim to fame, roast suckling pig (*cochinillo asado*: 21 days of mother's milk, into the oven, and onto your plate—oh, Babe). It's worth a splurge here or in Toledo or Salamanca. While you're at it, try *sopa Castellana*—soup mixed with eggs, ham, and garlic bread.

Mesón de Candido, one of the top restaurants in Castile, is the place to spend 4,000 ptas on a memorable dinner (daily 12:30–16:30, 20:00–23:00, Plaza Azoguejo 5, under aqueduct, tel. 92-142-8103 for reservations, gracious Alberto SE).

Narizotas, a more modern place, attracts locals and tourists with 2,000-pta *platos combinados* (daily 13:00–16:00, 21:00–24:00, CC:VM, Plaza de Medina del Campo 1, tel. 92-146-2679).

The cheapest bars and eateries line Calle de Infanta Isabel, just off Plaza Mayor. For nightlife, the bars on Plaza Mayor, Calle de Infanta Isabel, and Calle Isabel la Católica are packed. And there are a number of discos along the aqueduct.

Have breakfast at the cafeteria bar **Korppus** (Plaza del Corpus 1, a block down Calle Isabel la Católica from the Plaza Mayor, look for blue awnings). A **supermarket** is in the old town (at Traviesa Dr. Laguna, near Telefónica office). An **outdoor produce market** thrives on Plaza de los Huertos (Thu 8:00–14:00).

Transportation Connections—Segovia

By train to: Madrid (9/day, 2 hrs, both Chamartin and Atocha stations). If day-tripping from Madrid, look for the Cercanías (commuter train) ticket window and departure board in either of Madrid's train stations and get a return schedule. Train info: tel. 92-142-0774.

By bus to: La Granja Palace (8/day, 30 min), **Ávila** (3/day, 45 min), **Salamanca** (3/day, 3–4 hrs, transfer in Labajos; consider busing from Segovia to Ávila for a visit then continuing to Salamanca by bus or train), **Madrid** (hrly, 1.25 hr, quicker than train, Madrid's Larrea bus station, Metro: Príncipe Pío, just past Hotel Florida Norte at Paseo de la Florida 11, tel. 92-142-7707).

ÁVILA

A popular side trip from Madrid, the birthplace of St. Teresa is famous only for its perfectly preserved medieval walls. You can climb onto them through the gardens of the parador. Ávila's old town is charming, with several fine churches and monasteries. Pick up a box of the famous local sweets called *yemas*—like a soft-boiled egg yolk cooled and sugared.

Ávila is well connected to **Segovia** (3 buses/day, 45 min), **Madrid** (1 train/hrly, 2 hrs, both Chamartin and Atocha stations), and **Salamanca** (4 trains/day, 2 hrs; 4 buses/day, 2 hrs). While there are no lockers at the bus station, you can leave bags at the train station—a 10-minute walk away. By car, it's easy and worth a look if you're driving from Segovia or Madrid to Salamanca. Train info: tel. 92-125-0202.

SALAMANCA

This sunny sandstone city boasts Spain's grandest plaza, its oldest university, and a fascinating history, all swaddled in a strolling, college-town ambience.

Salamanca is a youthful and untouristy Toledo. The city is a series of monuments and clusters of cloisters. The many students help keep prices down. Take a paseo with the local crowd down Rua Mayor and through Plaza Mayor. The young people congregate until late in the night, chanting and cheering, talking and singing. When I asked a local woman why young men all alone on the Plaza Mayor suddenly break into song, she said, "Doesn't it happen where you live?"

Orientation

Tourist Information: The more convenient Turismo is on Plaza Mayor (under the arch, on your right as you face the clock; Mon–Sat 9:00–14:00, 16:30–18:30, Sun from 10:00, tel. 92-321-8342). Pick up their free map, city brochure, and current listing of museum hours. The other TI, covering Salamanca and the Castile region, is in Casa de las Conchas on Rua Mayor (daily 10:00–14:00, 17:00–19:00, tel. 92-326-8571). Ask for brochures on the Castile and Leon regions. Summertime-only TIs also spring up at the train and bus stations.

Arrival in Salamanca: From Salamanca's train and bus stations it's a 20-minute walk or an easy bus ride (100 ptas) to Plaza Mayor. From the train station, turn left out of the station and walk down to the ring road, cross it at Plaza España, then angle slightly left up Calle Azafranal. Or you can take bus #1 from the train station, which lets you off at Plaza Mercado (the market), next to Plaza Mayor. Day-trippers can store bags in a train-station locker (300–600 ptas).

From the bus station, turn right and walk down Avenue Filiberto Villalobos; take a left on the ring road and the first right on Ramon y Cajal. Or take bus #4 from the station to the city center; the closest stop is on Gran Vía, about four blocks from Plaza Mayor (ask a fellow passenger, "*¿Para Plaza Mayor?*"). Taxis to the center cost around 500 ptas.

Helpful Hints

Bus Tickets: Some travel agencies, such as Viajes Salamanca next to the Turismo on Plaza Mayor, sell city-to-city bus tickets.

Local Guide: Maria Cruz is good (2-hr tour/8,000 ptas for small group, tel. 92-319-3166, cellular 60-922-0757).

Internet Access: Campus Cibermatico charges 400 ptas per half hour (Mon–Fri 10:00–14:00, 17:00–21:00, Sat 10:00–14:00, Plaza Mayor 10, first floor, tel. 92-327-1131).

Parking: A handy underground parking lot is at Plaza Santa Eulalia; some hotels give you a discount stamp on your parking receipt.

Sights—Salamanca

▲**Plaza Mayor**—Built in 1755, this ultimate Spanish plaza is a fine place to nurse a cup of coffee and watch the world go by. The town hall, with the clock, grandly overlooks the square. The Arch of the Toro (built into the eastern wall) leads to the covered market. Imagine the excitement of the days, just 100 years ago, when bullfights were held in the square. How about coffee at the town's oldest café, Café Novelty?

▲▲**Cathedrals, Old and New**—These cool-on-a-hot-day cathedrals share buttresses and are both richly ornamented. You get to the old through the new. Before entering the new church, check out the ornate Plateresque facade (Spain's version of Flamboyant Gothic). At the side door of the facade, look for the astronaut added by a capricious restorer in 1993. This caused an outrage in town, but now locals shrug their shoulders and say, "He's the person closest to God."

Salamanca

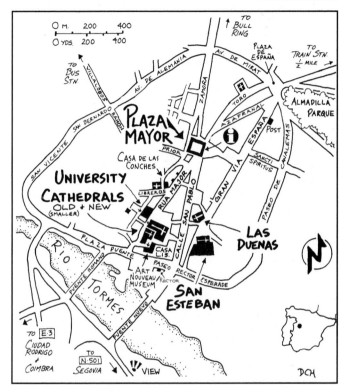

The "new" cathedral, built from 1513 to 1733, is a mix of Gothic, Renaissance, and baroque (free and lackluster). The recorded music helps. The *coro*, or choir, blocks up half of the church, but its wood carving is sumptuous; look up to see the elaborate organ.

The entrance to the old cathedral (12th-century Romanesque) is near the rear of the new one (300 ptas, daily 9:00–14:00, 16:00–20:00; Oct–March 9:00–13:00, 16:00–18:00). Sit in a front pew to study the 53 altarpiece scenes from Mary's life (by the Italian Florentino, 1445) and the dramatic Last Judgment fresco above it—notice Jesus sending condemned souls into the literal jaws of hell.

Then head into the cloister and explore the chapels, notable for their unusual tombs, ornate altarpieces, and ceilings with leering faces. Capilla San Bartolome de Los Anajas has a gorgeously carved 16th-century alabaster tomb and wooden Moorish organ.

▲▲**University**—Salamanca University, the oldest in Spain (est. 1230), was one of Europe's leading centers of learning for 400 years. Columbus came here for travel tips. Today many Americans enjoy its excellent summer program. The old lecture halls around the cloister, where many of Spain's Golden Age heroes studied, are open to the public (300 ptas, Mon–Sat 9:30–13:30, 16:00–18:30, Sun 10:00–13:00, free English info sheet is full of details; enter from Patio de Escuela, off Calle Libreros, tel. 92-329-4400, ext. 1150). Some of the rooms are still used by the university for prestigious academic ceremonies.

In the Hall of Fray Luis de León, the tables and benches are made of narrow wooden beams, whittled down by centuries of studious doodling. Professors spoke from the church-threatening *catedra*, or pulpit. It was here that free-thinking Fray Luis de León, after the Inquisition jailed and tortured him for four years, returned to his place and started his first post-imprisonment lecture with, "As we were saying … "

The altarpiece in the chapel depicts professors swearing to Mary's virginity (how did they know?), and the library upstairs is definitely worth the climb. Check out the cloister's ceiling outside the library for home-decorating ideas.

The entrance portal of the university is a great example of Spain's Plateresque style—masonry so intricate it looks like silver work. The people studying the facade aren't art fans. They're trying to find a tiny frog on a skull that students looked to for good luck.

As you leave the university, you'll see the statue of Fray Luis de León. Behind him, to your left (his right), is the entrance to a peaceful courtyard containing the Museum of the University, notable for Gallego's fanciful 16th-century *Sky of Salamanca* (included in university admission).

▲**Museo Art Nouveau y Art Deco**—Located in the Casa Lis, this museum, with its beautifully displayed collection of stained glass, jewelry, and statues (300 ptas, Tue–Fri 11:00–14:00, 17:00–21:00, Sat–Sun 11:00–21:00, closed Mon, Calle Gibraltar 14, between the cathedrals and the river, tel. 92-312-1425), is a refreshing change of pace.

Casa de las Conchas—The aptly named "House of Shells," dating from 1503, is a landmark on Rua Mayor (free, patio open Mon–Fri 9:00–21:00, Sat 9:00–14:00, 16:00–19:00, Sun 10:00–14:00, 16:00–19:00, tel. 92-326-9317). If you see shells broken off or missing, it's because long ago people believed there were pearls beneath each shell. Go upstairs for a close-up view of the powerful towers of the 17th-century Clerecia church. The church, worth a look, is open sporadic afternoons.

Church of San Esteban—Dedicated to St. Stephen (Esteban) the martyr, this complex contains a cloister, a pantheon of tombs, a museum, a sacristy, and a church. Before you enter, notice the Plateresque facade and its bas-relief of the stoning of St. Stephen. The crucifixion above is by Cellini. Once inside, follow the free English pamphlet and arrows. Upstairs you'll find the museum (with illustrated 16th-century choir books at the far end) and the entrance to the choir. The church is overwhelmed by a Churriguera altarpiece, a textbook example of the style named after him. Quietly ponder the gold-plated cottage cheese, as tourists retch and say "too much" in their mother tongue (200 ptas, Mon–Fri 9:00–13:30, 16:00–20:00, Sat–Sun 9:30–13:30, 16:00–20:00).

Convento de las Dueñas—Next door, the much simpler *convento* is a joy. It consists of a double-decker cloister with a small museum of religious art. Check out the stone meanies exuberantly decorating the capitals on the cloister's upper deck (200 ptas, daily 10:30–13:00, 16:30–19:00). The nuns sell sweets daily except Sunday (400 ptas for a box).

Honorable Mention—Romantics will enjoy the low-slung Roman bridge, much of it original, spanning the Rio Tormes. The ancient (pre-Roman) headless bull, blindly guarding the entrance to the bridge, is a symbol of the city. Nearby, at Parque Fluvial, you can rent rowboats.

Sleeping in Salamanca
(180 ptas = about $1, country code: 34)

Sleep Code: **S** = Single, **D** = Double/Twin, **T** = Triple, **Q** = Quad, **b** = bathroom, **t** = toilet only, **s** = shower only, **CC** = Credit Card (**V**isa, **M**asterCard, **A**mex), **SE** = Speaks English, **NSE** = No English.

Salamanca, being a student town, has plenty of good eating and sleeping values. Most of my listings are on or within a three-minute walk of the Plaza Mayor. Directions are given from the Plaza Mayor, assuming you are facing the building with the clock (e.g., 3 o'clock is 90 degrees to your right as you face the clock). The 7 percent IVA tax is included only in the prices charged by the cheaper hotels.

Hostal Los Angeles, at about three o'clock, has simple but cared-for rooms, with a few overlooking the square. Stand on the balcony and inhale the essence of Spain (S-2,200 ptas, D-3,300 ptas, Db-4,500 ptas, T-5,000 ptas, Tb-6,500 ptas, all rooms with plaza views have full bathrooms, Plaza Mayor 10, 37002 Salamanca, tel. & fax 92-321-8166, Luis and Sabina NSE). To try for a view, request, "*Con vista, por favor.*" If that fails, avoid the windowless room by requesting, "*Con ventana*" (window).

Hotel Las Torres, another on-the-square option, has 44 modern, spacious rooms with all the amenities (Sb-9,500 ptas, Db-12,500 ptas, CC:VMA, avoid their restaurant, entrance just off square at Consejo #4, Plaza Mayor 47, under the clock, 37002

Plaza Mayor

Salamanca, tel. 92-321-2100, fax 92-321-2101, www.mmteam
.interbook.net/lastorres, SE). Rooms with views cost the same as
viewless rooms.

Hotel Don Juan, just off Plaza Mayor, has 16 classy, comfy
rooms and an attached restaurant (Sb-6,500 ptas, Db-9,000 ptas,
Tb-12,000 ptas, CC:VM, breakfast is cheaper off-season, elevator,
air-con, double-paned windows; exit Plaza Mayor at about 5 o'clock
and turn right to Quintana 6, 37001 Salamanca; tel. 92-326-1473,
fax 92-326-2475, e-mail: hoteldonjuan@wanadoo.es, SE).

Consider **Hotel Residencia Rector** for a four-star splurge,
complete with 14 stately but stiff rooms and a pleasant staff (Sb-
11,500 ptas, Db-17,000–20,000 ptas, Tb-22,000 ptas, CC:VMA,
includes breakfast, located south of university, exit Plaza Mayor at
about 5 o'clock, continue for several blocks on San Pablo, turn right
to Rector Esperabe 10, tel. 92-321-8482, fax 92-321-4008, www
.teleline.es/personal/hrector, e-mail: hotelrector@teleline.es, SE).

The handy **Hostal Tormes** is a student-type residence with
13 clean but spartan rooms on the pedestrian street connecting
Plaza Mayor and the university (S-2,700 ptas, D-4,500 ptas,
Db-5,100 ptas, Rua Mayor 20, 37008 Salamanca, tel. & fax
92-321-9683, NSE).

Hostal Plaza Mayor has 19 small but welcoming rooms
and a good location just southwest of Plaza Mayor (Sb-5,000 ptas,
Db-8,500 ptas, Tb-10,000 ptas, CC:VM, exit Plaza Mayor at

7 o'clock, Plaza del Corrillo 20, attached restaurant, tel. 92-326-2020, fax 92-321-7548).

Hotel Milan, formerly a budget hotel, is closed for renovation and may reopen in 2001 with higher rates (Db-5,900 ptas, CC:VM, elevator, leave Plaza Mayor at 5 o'clock and go left around fancy hotel to Plaza del Angel 5, 37001 Salamanca, tel. 92-321-7518, fax 92-321-9697, NSE).

Eating in Salamanca

There are plenty of good, inexpensive restaurants between Plaza Mayor and Gran Vía and as you leave the Plaza Mayor toward Rua Mayor. Just wander and eat at your own discovery or try **Café Novelty** (Plaza Mayor's oldest coffee shop) or any of several places on Calle Bermejeros, such as **Taberna de Pilatos** (at #5, Mon–Sat 13:00–15:00, 21:00–03:00, closed Sun).

Restaurante Isidro has a super assortment of seafood and meat dishes (menu of the day 1,500 ptas, Mon–Sat 13:00–16:00, 20:00–23:00, Sun 13:00–16:00, Pozo Amarillo 19, about a block north of covered market, close to Plaza Mayor, tel. 92-326-2848). **Restaurante Dulcinea** is a classier, pricier version of the Isidro (menu of the day 1,400–1,950 ptas, Pozo Amarillo 5, tel. 92-321-7843).

Mandala is popular with the younger crowd for its tasty tapas, attractive setting, and good prices (daily 8:00–24:00, Calle Serranos 9–11; from Casa de las Conchas follow Rua Antigua alongside Clerecia church for 2 blocks, tel. 92-312-3342). Wash down your tapas or *plato combinado* with a *batido* (milkshake).

Tops for tapas in Salamanca is **Café Chinitas**, one of several tapas bars lining Calle Van Dyck. It's a 15-minute walk from Plaza Mayor, but its prices and selection are great. On a hot day the iced gazpacho hits the spot. It's offered daily in summer; otherwise, hope for the "Hay Gazpacho" sign (daily 8:00–01:00, Van Dyck 14–16; from Plaza Mayor, follow Toro north as it changes its name to Maria Auxiliadora; after you cross Avenida de Portugal, take the third left; tel. 92-325-0293). Runner-up, and far more central, is **Bar Bambu**, offering cheap, good tapas just off the southwest corner of Plaza Mayor (daily 9:00–01:30, Calle Prior 4, pass the Burger King and immediately head downstairs). Overlooking Plaza Mayor, **Cervantes Bar** (next to TI) serves great tapas, salads, and meals to a mainly local crowd of all ages.

Salamanca's high student population supports a vast array of trendy hangouts. The best way to locate current hot spots is to find the touts handing out fliers and coupons at the clock tower around 23:00. Popular places include **Country**, with great music, a student vibe, and dice-for-free-drinks games (Juan de Almeida 5); **Cum Laude** (across from Bar Bambu); and the tacky **De Laval**

Genoves Submarino, with its submarine-like interior (Calle San Justo 27–31, 5-min walk east of Plaza Mayor). Other good, centrally located tapas bars are **El Candil** (on Ventura Ruiz Aguilera) and **La Covachuela**, where the waiter will amaze you with coin tricks (in Portales de San Antonio; establish prices before ordering).

The covered *mercado* (market) on Plaza Mercado (Mon–Sat 8:00–14:00, closed Sun) is ideal for picnic gatherers. And if you always wanted seconds at Communion, buy a bag of giant Communion wafers, a local specialty called *obleas*.

Transportation Connections—Salamanca

By train to: Madrid (4/day, 2.5 hrs, new and fast Finnish-made TRD trains require 300-ptas reservation, Chamartin station), **Ávila** (3/day, 1 hr; also 3 buses/day), **Barcelona** (1/day, 10 hrs), **Coimbra** (1/day, 5 hrs, departs Salamanca station at about 04:40; buses leave a bit later, see below); taxis to the station are available at any hour at Plaza Mercado for about 500 ptas. Train info: tel. 92-312-0202.

By bus to: Segovia (3/day, 4 hrs, transfer in Labajos or Ávila; consider a brief visit to Ávila en route), **Ciudad Rodrigo** (7/day, 1 hr), **Barcelona** (1/day, 12 hrs), **Coimbra** (5/weekly, all early-morning departures, 6:30 Mon–Tue and Sat–Sun, 02:15 Fri, 5 hrs; get tickets 1–2 days in advance from bus station or at Viajes Salamanca Travel Agency on Plaza Major, or take your chances and just show up). Bus info for Coimbra, Barcelona, and more: tel. 92-323-6717, bus info for Segovia and Ciudad Rodrigo: tel. 92-323-2266.

CIUDAD RODRIGO

(Worth a visit only if you're traveling from Salamanca to Coimbra.) This rough-and-tumble old town of 16,000 people caps a hill overlooking the Río Agueda. Spend an hour wandering among the Renaissance mansions that line its streets and exploring its cathedral and Plaza Mayor. Have lunch or a snack at El Sanatorio (Plaza Mayor 14). The tapas are cheap, the crowd is local, and the walls are a Ciudad Rodrigo scrapbook, including some bullfighting that makes the Three Stooges look demure.

Ciudad Rodrigo's cathedral—pockmarked with scars from Napoleonic cannon balls—has some entertaining carvings in the choir and some pretty racy work in its cloisters. Who said, "When you've seen one Gothic church, you've seen 'em all"?

The TI (tel. 92-346-0561) is just inside the old wall near the cathedral and can recommend a good hotel such as Hotel Conde Rodrigo. The Plaza Mayor is a two-block walk from the TI.

Ciudad Rodrigo is a convenient stop on the Salamanca-to-Coimbra drive. Buses connect Salamanca and Ciudad Rodrigo with surprising efficiency in about an hour. From there you can connect (with less ease) to Coimbra.

Route Tips for Drivers

Madrid to El Escorial to the Valley of the Fallen to Segovia (50 miles): Taxi to your car-rental office (or ask if they'll deliver the car to your hotel). Pick up the car by 8:30 and ask directions to highway A6. Follow "A6-Valladolid" signs to the clearly marked exit on M505 to El Escorial. Get to El Escorial by 9:30 to beat the crowds. The nearby **Silla de Felipe** (Philip's Seat) is a rocky viewpoint where the king would come to admire his palace being built.

From El Escorial, follow "C600-Valle de los Caídos" signs to the Valley of the Fallen. You'll see the huge cross marking it in the distance. After the tollbooth, follow "Basilica" signs to the parking place (toilets, tacky souvenirs, and cafeteria). As you leave, turn left to Guadarrama on C600, go under the highway, and follow signs to Puerto de Navacerrada. From there, you climb past flocks of sheep, over a 6,000-foot-high mountain pass (Pto. de Navacerrada) into old Castile, and through La Granja to Segovia. (Segovia is much more important than La Granja, but garden lovers enjoy a quick La Granja stop.)

At the Segovia aqueduct, turn into the old town (the side where the aqueduct adjoins the crenellated fortress walls) and park on or as close to the Plaza Mayor as possible. To be legal— and they do issue expensive tickets—buy a ticket from the nearby machine to park in areas marked by blue stripes; place the ticket on your dashboard (45 ptas/30 min, 90-min maximum 9:00–20:00; free parking 20:00–9:00, Sat afternoon, and all day Sun). You should be safe on the square. Plenty of parking is also available outside the old town near Via Roma.

Segovia to Salamanca (100 miles): Leave Segovia by driving around the town's circular road, which offers good views from below the Alcázar. Then follow signs for Ávila (road N110). Notice the fine Segovia view from the three crosses at the crest of the first hill. Just after the abandoned ghost church at Villacastin, turn onto N501 at the huge Puerta de San Vicente (cathedral and TI are just inside). The Salamanca road leads around the famous Ávila walls to the right. The best wall view is from the signposted Cuatro Postes, a mile northwest of town. Salamanca (N501) is clearly marked, about an hour's drive away.

A few miles before Salamanca, you might want to stop at the huge bull on the left of the road. There's a little dirt path leading right up to it. The closer you get, the more you realize it isn't real. Bad boys climb it for a goofy photo, but I wouldn't. For a great photo op of Salamanca, complete with river reflection, stop at the edge of the city (at the light before the first bridge).

Parking in Salamanca is terrible. Gamblers park at their own risk over the river or in the city between Rua Palomino and Avenida de Portugal wherever there are blue parking lines (100 ptas for 90 min, 9:00–14:00, 16:00–20:00, free Sat afternoon and Sun). Leave nothing of value in your car. The only safe parking is in a garage (try the underground lot at Plaza Santa Eulalia).

TOLEDO

An hour south of Madrid, Toledo teems with tourists, souvenirs, and great art by day, delicious roast suckling pig, echoes of El Greco, and medieval magic by night. Incredibly well preserved and full of cultural wonder, the entire city has been declared a national monument.

Spain's historic capital is 2,000 years of tangled history—Roman, Visigothic, Moorish, and Christian—crowded onto a high, rocky perch protected on three sides by the Tejo River. It's so well preserved that the Spanish government has forbidden any modern exteriors. The rich mix of Jewish, Moorish, and Christian heritages makes it one of Europe's art capitals.

Toledo was a Visigothic capital back in 554 and—after a period of Moorish rule—Spain's political capital until 1561, when it reached its natural limits of growth as defined by the Tejo River Gorge. Though the king moved to more spacious Madrid, Toledo remains the historic, artistic, and spiritual center of Spain. In spite of tremendous tourist crowds, Toledo just sits on its history and remains much as it was when Europe's most powerful king and El Greco each called it home.

Planning Your Time

To properly see Toledo's museums (great El Greco), cathedral (best in Spain), and medieval atmosphere (best after dark), you'll need two nights and a day.

Toledo is just 60 minutes away from Madrid by bus (2/hrly), train (6/day), or taxi (10,000 ptas max from Puerto del Sol—negotiate the ride without a meter). A car is useless in Toledo. See the town outside of car-rental time (pick up or drop your car here).

Toledo

1 Hotel Residencia Imperio
2 Hotel Santa Isabel
3 Hotel Alfonso VI
4 Hotel Pintor El Greco
5 Hotel Maria Christina
    Hostal Gavilanes II &
    Hostal Madrid
6 Restaurante-Meson Palacios

7 Casa Aurelio
8 Zamorano Knives
9 Tickets & Cathedral Entry
10 Sinagoga Street &
    Aurelio 2 & 3 Restaurants
11 Hostal Centro
12 Hotel Sol

Orientation

Lassoed into a tight tangle of streets by the sharp bend of the Tejo River (called the Tagus where it hits the Atlantic, in Lisbon), Toledo has Spain's most confusing medieval street plan. But it's a small town of 65,000, major sights are well signposted, and most locals will politely point you in the right direction.

Look at the map and take a mental orientation walk past Toledo's main sights. Starting in the central Plaza Zocódover, go

Toledo's Plaza Zocódover

southwest along the Calle de Comércio. After passing the cathedral on your left, follow the signs to Santo Tomé and the cluster of other sights. The visitor's city lies basically along one small but central street—and most tourists never stray from this axis. Make a point to get lost. It's a small town, bounded on three sides by the river. When it's time to get somewhere, I pull out the map or ask, "*¿Dónde está Plaza Zocódover?*"

Tourist Information
The TI is just outside the Bisagra Gate where those arriving by train or bus enter the old town (Mon–Sat 9:00–19:00, Sun 9:00–15:00; Oct–June Mon–Fri 9:00–18:00, Sat 9:00–19:00,

El Greco's Art

Born on Crete and trained in Venice, Domenikos Theoto-
copoulos (tongue-tied friends just called him "The Greek")
came to Spain to get a job decorating El Escorial. He failed
there but succeeded in Toledo, where he spent the last 37
years of his life. He mixed all three regional influences into
his palette. From his Greek homeland, he absorbed the
solemn, abstract style of icons. In Venice he learned the bold
use of color and dramatic style of the later Renaissance.
These styles were then fused in the fires of fanatic Spanish-
Catholic devotion.

Not bound by the realism so important to his 16th-
century contemporaries, El Greco painted dramatic visions
of striking colors and figures—bodies unnatural and elon-
gated as though stretched between heaven and earth. He
painted souls, not faces. His work is on display at nearly
every sight in Toledo. Thoroughly modern in its disregard
of realism, it seems as fresh as contemporary art.

Sun 9:00–15:00; can recommend local guides, tel. 92-522-0843).
There's a second TI in front of the cathedral. Consider the readable local guidebook, *Toledo, Its Art and Its History* (small version—
900 ptas, sold all over town). It explains all the sights (which
generally provide no on-site information) and gives you a photo
to point at and say, "*¿Dónde está…?*"

Arrival in Toledo

"Arriving" in Toledo means getting to Plaza Zocódover. From the
train station, that's a 20-minute hike, taxi ride (400 ptas), or easy
bus ride (#5 or #6, 120 ptas, pay on bus, confirm by asking, "*Para
Plaza Zocódover?*"). If you're walking, turn right as you leave the
station, cross the bridge, pass the bus station, go straight through the
roundabout, and continue uphill to the TI and north gate (Puerta
Bisagra is the last surviving gate of the 10th-century fortifications).
From the bus station, Plaza Zocódover is a 15-minute walk or short
bus ride (#5, see directions from train station, above).

Getting around Toledo

This small city is walkable. But for great city views, consider
hopping on the cheesy Tren Imperial Tourist Tram. Crass as
it feels, you get a no-effort 50-minute putt-putt through Toledo
and around the Tagus River Gorge (600 ptas, daily from 11:00,
tape-recorded English/Spanish commentary, hop on at Plaza
Zocódover, tel. 925-142-274).

Sights—Toledo

▲▲▲**Cathedral**—Holy Toledo! Spain's leading Catholic city has a magnificent cathedral. Shoehorned into the old center, its exterior is hard to appreciate. But the interior is so lofty, rich, and vast that it grabs you by the vocal cords, and all you can do is whisper, "Wow."

While the basic cathedral is free, seeing the great art—in four separate places within the cathedral—requires a 700-ptas ticket (well worthwhile, sold in shop opposite church entrance, Mon–Sat 10:30–18:30, Sun 14:00–18:00).

Holy redwood forest, Batman! Wander among the pillars. Sit under one and imagine when the light bulbs were candles and the tourists were pilgrims—before the "No Photo" signs, when every window provided spiritual as well as physical light. The cathedral is primarily Gothic, but since it took more than 200 years to build (1226–1493), you'll see a mix of styles—Gothic, Renaissance, and Baroque. Enjoy the elaborate wrought-iron work, lavish wood carvings, window after colorful window of 500-year-old stained glass, and a sacristy with a collection of paintings that would put any museum on the map.

This confusing collage of great Spanish art deserves a guided tour. Hire a private guide, freeload on a tour (they come by every few minutes), or follow this quick tour. Here's a framework for your visit:

First, walk to the center to marvel through the iron grill at one of the most stunning high altars in Spain. Real gold on pine wood, by Flemish, French, and local artists, it's one of the country's best pieces of Gothic art. About-face...

The **choir**, facing the high altar, is famous for its fine carving and requires a piece of your four-part ticket. The lower wooden stalls are decorated with scenes from the Christian victory over the Moslems at Granada. The upper stalls feature Old Testament figures carved out of alabaster. The iron grill of the choir is notable for the dedication of the man who built it. Domingo de Cespedes, a Toledo ironworker, accepted the commission to build the grill for 6,000 ducats. The project, which took from 1541 to 1548, was far more costly than he anticipated. The medieval Church didn't accept cost overruns, so, to finish it, he sold everything he owned and went into debt. He died a poor—but honorable—man.

The *transparente*, behind the high altar, is a unique feature of the cathedral. In the 1700s a hole was cut into the ceiling to let a sunbeam brighten the Mass. Melding this big hole into the Gothic church presented a challenge that resulted in a Baroque masterpiece. Gape up at this riot of angels doing flip-flops, babies breathing thin air, bottoms of feet, and gilded sunbursts. I like it, as did, I guess, the long-dead cardinal whose red hat hangs from the edge of the hole. (A perk that only cardinals enjoy is choosing the place in the cathedral in which their hat will hang until it rots.)

Toledo Cathedral

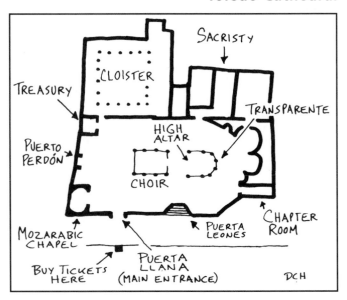

The cathedral's **sacristy** has 20 El Grecos and masterpieces by Goya, Titian, Rubens, Velázquez, and Bellini. First, look at the fine perspective work on the ceiling. Then walk to the most important painting in the collection (end of room). El Greco's first masterpiece, from 1579, *The Spoiliation* (a.k.a. *The Denuding of Christ*) hangs above the marble altar. This was one of El Greco's first Toledo commissions after arriving from Venice. Notice the parallel contrasts: Jesus' delicate hand before a flaming red tunic and Jesus' noble face among the sinister mob. On the right is a rare religious painting by Goya, the *Betrayal of Christ*, which shows Judas preparing to kiss Jesus, identifying him to the Roman soldiers. Enjoy the many other El Grecos. Find the lifelike 17th-century carving of St. Francis by Pedro de Mena.

The *sala capitular*, or chapter house (there goes another part of your ticket), has a rich gilded ceiling, interesting Bible-story-telling frescoes, and a pictorial review of 1,900 years of Toledo archbishops (the upper row of portraits were not painted from life; the lower portraits were, and therefore hold more historic and artistic interest). Imagine sitting down to church business surrounded by all this tradition and theology. As you leave, notice the iron-pumping cupids carved into the panels lining the walls.

The **treasury** (*tesoro*) has plenty to see. The highlight is the 10-foot-high, 430-pound monstrance—the tower designed to hold

the Holy Communion bread (the Host) during the festival of
Corpus Christi (body of Christ) as it parades through the city.
Built in 1517 by a man named Arfe, it's made of 5,000 individual
pieces held together by 12,500 screws. There are diamonds, emer-
alds, rubies, and 400 pounds of gold-plated silver. The inner part
is 35 pounds of solid gold. Yeow. The base is a later addition,
from the Baroque period. Traditionally, it's thought that much of
this gold and silver arrived on Columbus' first load home. To the
right of the monstrance find the fancy sword of Franco. To the
right of that is a gift from St. Louis, the king of France—a 700-
year-old Bible printed and beautifully illustrated by French monks.
Imagine the exquisite experience of reading this with its lavish
illustrations through medieval eyes. The finely painted crucifix
on the opposite side—by the great Gothic Florentine painter Fra
Angelico—depicts Jesus alive on the back and dead on the front.
This was a gift from Mussolini to Franco. Hmmm. There's even
a gift in this room from Toledo's sister city, Toledo, Ohio.

If you're at the cathedral between 9:30 and 9:45, you can peek
into the otherwise-locked **Mozarabic Chapel** (Capilla Mozarabe).
The Visigothic Mass, the oldest surviving Christian ritual in
Western Europe, starts at 9:45. You're welcome to partake in this
stirring example of peaceful coexistence of faiths—but once the
door closes, you're a Visigoth for 30 minutes.

▲▲**Santa Cruz Museum**—This great Renaissance building was
an orphanage, built from money left by Cardinal Mendoza when
he died in 1495. It's in the form of a Greek cross under a Moorish
dome. The arms of the building—formerly wards—are filled with
16th-century art, tapestries, furniture, armor, and documents. It's
a stately, classical, music-filled setting with a cruel lack of English
information.

Eighteen El Grecos gather in one wing upstairs, including the
impressive *Assumption of Mary*—a spiritual poem on canvas (notice
old Toledo on the bottom). Painted one year before his death in
1614, this is considered the culmination of El Greco's artistic
development.

An enormous blue banner hangs like a long, skinny tooth
opposite the entry. This flew from the flagship of Don Juan of
Austria and recalls the pivotal naval victory over the Moslems at the
Battle of Lepanto in 1571. Lepanto was a key victory in the centuries-long Moslem threat to Christian Europe (400 ptas, Mon
10:00–18:30, Tue–Sat 10:00–18:30, Sun 10:00–14:00, Cervantes 3).

▲**Alcázar**—This huge former imperial residence—built on the
site of Roman, Visagothic, and Moorish fortresses—dominates the
Toledo skyline. The Alcázar became a kind of right-wing Alamo
during Spain's civil war when a force of Franco's Nationalists (and
hundreds of hostages) were besieged for two months. Finally, after
many fierce but futile Republican attacks, Franco sent in an army

that took Toledo and freed the Alcázar. The place was rebuilt and glorified under Franco. Today you can see its civil-war exhibits, giving you an interesting—and right-wing—look at the horrors of Spain's recent past (200 ptas, Tue–Sun 9:30–14:30, closed Mon).

▲**Santo Tomé**—A simple chapel holds El Greco's most loved painting. *The Burial of the Count of Orgaz* couples heaven and earth in a way only The Greek could. It feels so right to see a painting left where the artist put it 400 years ago. Take this slow. Stay a while—let it perform. It's 1323. You're at the burial of the good count. After a pious and generous life, he left his estate to the Church. Saints Augustine and Steven have even come down for the burial—to usher him directly to heaven. "Such is the reward for those who serve God and his saints."

More than 250 years later, in 1586, a priest hired El Greco to make a painting of the burial to hang over the count's tomb. The painting has two halves divided by a serene—but not sad—line of noble faces. The physical world ends with the line of nobles. Above them a spiritual wind blows as colors change and shapes stretch. Notice the angel, robe caught up in that wind, "birthing" the soul of the count through the neck of a celestial womb into Heaven—the soul abandoning the physical body to join Christ the Judge. Mary and John the Baptist both intervene on behalf of the arriving soul. Each face is a detailed portrait. El Greco himself (eyeballing you, seventh figure in from the left) is the only one not involved in the burial. The boy in the foreground is El Greco's son (200 ptas, daily 10:00–18:45, until 17:45 in off-season, tel. 92-525-6098).

▲**Museo El Greco**—This old house, often wrongly called El Greco's, gives you a good look at the interior of a traditionally furnished Renaissance home. You'll see El Greco's masterful View of Toledo and portraits of the Apostles (400 ptas, free Sat after-noon and all day Sun; Tue–Sat 10:00–14:00, 16:00–18:00, Sun 10:00–14:00, closed Mon; Samuel Levi 3).

Sinagoga del Transito (Museo Sefardi)—Built in 1366, this is the best surviving slice of Toledo's Jewish past (near Museo El Greco, with same price and hours, on Calle de los Reyes Católicos).

Sinagoga del Santa Maria Blanca—This synagogue-turned-church with Moorish arches is an eclectic but harmonious gem (200 ptas, daily 10:00–14:00, 15:30–19:00, closes off-season at 18:00, Reyes Católicos 2-4).

Shopping

Toledo probably sells as many souvenirs as any city in Spain. This is the place to buy medieval-looking swords, armor, maces, three-legged stools, and other nouveau antiques. It's also Spain's damascene center, where, for centuries, craftspeople have inlaid black steel with gold, silver, and copper wire.

At the workshop of English-speaking Mariano Zamorano (Calle Ciudad 19, near the cathedral and Plaza Ayuntamiento), you can see swords and knives being made (and the damascene process in action). Judging by what's left of Mariano's hand, his knives are among the best.

El Martes, Toledo's colorful outdoor flea market, bustles on Paseo del Carmen (below the Alcazar) Tuesday from 9:00 to 14:00.

Sleeping in Toledo
(180 ptas = about $1, country code: 34)
Sleep Code: **S** = Single, **D** = Double/Twin, **T** = Triple, **Q** = Quad, **b** = bathroom, **t** = toilet only, **s** = shower only, **CC** = Credit Card (**V**isa, **M**asterCard, **A**mex), **SE** = Speaks English, **NSE** = No English. Breakfast and the 7 percent IVA tax aren't included unless noted.

Madrid day-trippers darken the sunlit cobbles, but few stay to see Toledo's medieval moonrise. Spend the night. Spring and fall are high season; November through March and July and August are low. There are no private rooms for rent.

Sleeping near Plaza Zocódover
Hotel Residencia Imperio is well-run, offering 21 rooms with solid air-conditioned comfort in a handy old-town location (Sb-4,400 ptas, Db-6,500 ptas, Tb-8,700 ptas, includes tax, 5 percent discount with this book, CC:VMA, elevator, cheery café, from Calle Comercio at #38 go a block uphill to Calle Cadenas 5, tel. 92-522-7650, fax 92-525-3183, e-mail: himperio@teleline.es, Pablo SE).

Hostal Centro rents 23 modern, clean, and comfy rooms just around the corner (Sb-4,500 ptas, Db-6,500 ptas, Tb-9,000 ptas, 50 meters off Plaza Zocódover, first right off Calle Comercio at Calle Nueva 13, roof garden, tel. 92-525-7091, fax 925-257-848).

Hotel Maravilla is wonderfully central and convenient with claustrophobic halls and simple rooms (Sb-4,000 ptas, Db-6,500 ptas, Tb-8,800 ptas, Qb-10,700 ptas, includes tax, CC:VMA, back rooms are quieter, air-con, a block behind Plaza Zocódover at Plaza de Barrio Rey 7, 45001 Toledo, tel. 92-522-8317, fax 92-522-8155, Ana and Felisa Maria SE).

Hotel Carlos V overlooks the cathedral midway between the Alcázar and Plaza Zocódover. While suffering from the obligatory stuffiness of a correct hotel, it has bright, pleasant rooms and bathrooms you could make love in (Sb-9,500 ptas, Db-14,000 ptas, Tb-18,000 ptas, breakfast-1,100 ptas, less off-season, CC:VMA, air-con, elevator, Plaza Horno Magdalena 3, 45001 Toledo, tel. 92-522-2100, fax 92-522-2105, SE). Ask for a room with a view of the cathedral.

Around the corner, the quiet, modern **Hostal Nuevo Labrador** is just as nice, with clean, shiny, and spacious rooms for about half the price (Sb-3,800 ptas, Db-6,400 ptas, Tb-8,500 ptas, Qb-10,000 ptas, includes tax, CC:VMA, Juan Labrador 10, 45001 Toledo, tel. 92-522-2620, fax 92-522-9399, NSE).

Across from the Alcázar is **Hotel Alfonso VI**, a big, touristy establishment with large, airy rooms, tour groups, and souvenirs for sale all over the lobby (Sb-10,500 ptas, Db-14,500 ptas, Tb-18,500 ptas, breakfast-1,200 ptas, includes tax, CC:VMA, some air-con, General Moscardo 2, 45001 Toledo, tel. 92-522-2600, fax 92-521-4458, e-mail: alfonsovi@macom.es, SE). Ask for a room with a view.

Hotel Sol, which is plain, modern, clean, and actually on a quiet street, isn't exactly glamorous but is a great value halfway between the Bisagra Gate and Plaza Zocódover (Sb-4,500 ptas, Db-6,500 ptas, Tb-8,300 ptas, CC:VM, air-con, easy parking, 50 meters down lane off busy main drag at Hotel Real, Azacares 8, 45003 Toledo, tel. 925-213-650, fax 925-216-159, e-mail: hotel.sol@to.adade.es). Their "Hostal Sol" annex across the street is just as comfortable and a bit cheaper.

Sleeping beyond the Cathedral, Deep in Toledo

Hotel Santa Isabel, in a 15th-century building two blocks from the cathedral, has 23 clean, modern, and comfortable rooms and squeaky tile hallways. Avoid the few *atico* rooms that have only a skylight (Sb-4,200 ptas, Db-6,500 ptas, Tb-8,000 ptas, includes tax, breakfast-600 ptas, parking-900 ptas, CC:VMA, air-con, elevator; buried deep in old town so take a taxi, not the bus; drivers enter from Calle Pozo Amargo, Calle Santa Isabel 24, 45002 Toledo, tel. 92-525-3120, fax 92-525-3136, www.santa-isabel.com).

Hotel Pintor El Greco, at the far end of the old town, is plush and modern-feeling, with all the comforts, yet it's in a historic 17th-century building. A block from Santo Tomé in a Jewish Quarter garden, it's very quiet (Sb-12,600 ptas, Db-16,400 ptas, plus tax, includes breakfast, CC:VMA, 33 rooms, air-con, elevator, Alamillos del Transito 13, tel. 92-528-5191, fax 92-521-5819, e-mail: elgreco@estancias.es).

Sleeping Cheap near Plaza Zocódover

The very central **Pensión Segovia** is old, rickety, and dingy, with questionable beds, head-banger doorways, and memorable balconies (D-3,000 ptas, T-4,500 ptas; from Plaza Zocódover go down Calle de la Sillería, take second right and another right to Calle de Recoletos 2, 45001 Toledo, tel. 92-521-1124).

Another family-run cheapie, but modern and more comfortable, is **Pension Castilla**. It's just around the corner (S-2,200 ptas, Db-4,000 ptas, fans, 6 rooms, Calle Recoletos 6, tel. 925-256-318, José SE).

The family-run **Pensión Lumbreras** has a tranquil courtyard and 12 rooms, some with views—such as room #6 (D-3,200 ptas, T-4,500 ptas; their huge, view Q for 6,000 ptas can sleep up to 6; includes tax, breakfast-225 ptas, Juan Labrador 9, 45001 Toledo, tel. 92-522-1571, Gonzalez family NSE).

Sleeping Outside of Town
On the road to Madrid (near bullring): There's a conspiracy of clean, modern, and hard-working little hotels with comfy rooms a five-minute walk beyond Puerta Bisagra near the bullring (Plaza de Toros), bus station, and TI. Drivers will enjoy easy parking here. The downside: It's a 15-minute uphill hike to the old-town action. Two good bets are **Hostal Gavilánes II** (Sb-5,000 ptas, Db-6,000 ptas, Db suite-8,600 ptas, Tb-7,500 ptas, Qb-9,000 ptas, sporadic air-con, CC:VM, Marqués de Mendigorría 14, 45003 Toledo, tel. & fax 92-521-1628, NSE) and **Hostal Madrid** (Sb-3,500 ptas, Db-5,200 ptas, Tb-7,020 ptas, CC:VM, air-con, Calle Marqués de Mendigorría 7, 45003 Toledo, tel. 92-522-1114, fax 925-228-113, NSE). This *hostal* rents lesser rooms from an annex across the street (Db-5,000 ptas without air-con). **Hotel Maria Cristina** is a sprawling modern hotel with all the comforts under a thin layer of prefab tradition (Sb-8,500 ptas, Db-12,800 ptas, extra bed-4,400 ptas, plus tax, CC:VMA, air-con, elevator, Marques de Mendigorria 1, next to bullring, tel. 92-521-3202, fax 92-521-2650, SE).

Near train station: The **Albergue Juvenil San Servando** youth hostel is lavish but cheap, with small rooms, a swimming pool, views, and good management (1,400 ptas per bed, youth hostel membership required, in San Servando castle 10-min walk from train station, over Puente Viejo outside town, tel. 92-522-4554, NSE).

Hostal de Cardenal, a 17th-century cardinal's palace built into Toledo's wall, is quiet and elegant with a cool garden and a stuffy restaurant. This poor-man's parador is at the dusty old gate of Toledo, closest to the station but a hike below the old-town action (Sb-8,500 ptas, Db-13,700 ptas, Tb-17,800 ptas, 5 percent discount with this book, cheaper in winter, CC:VMA, air con, no fun staff likely because of the management, enter through town wall 100 meters below Puerta Bisagra, Paseo de Recaredo 24, 45004 Toledo, tel. 92-522-4900, fax 92-522-2991, e-mail: cardenal@macom.es).

Sleeping Outside of Town with the Grand Toledo View
Toledo's **Parador Nacional Conde de Orgaz** is one of Spain's most famous, enjoying the same Toledo view El Greco made famous from across the Tejo Canyon (Db-20,000 ptas, CC:VMA, 2 windy miles from town at Cerro del Emperador, 45002 Toledo,

tel. 92-522-1850, fax 92-522-5166, www.parador.es, SE). Take a
cab here just to see the sunset from the terrace (700 ptas one way).
   Hotel Residencia La Almazara was the summer residence of
a 16th-century archbishop of Toledo. With its classic Toledo
view, El Greco hung out here for inspiration. A lumbering old
place with cushy public rooms, simple bedrooms, and a sprawling
garden, it's truly in the country but just two miles out of Toledo
(Sb-6,000 ptas, Db-7,000 ptas, Tb-9,000 ptas, 10 of 24 rooms
with view, 1,000 ptas less without view, CC:VMA, fans, Ctra. de
Piedrabuena 47, kilometer 3,400 on the Toledo-Arges road, P.O.
Box 6, Toledo 45080, tel. 92-522-3866, fax 92-525-0562, e-mail:
hotelalmazara@ribernet.es).

Eating in Toledo

A day full of El Greco and the romance of Toledo after dark
puts me in the mood for partridge (*perdiz*), roasted suckling pigs
(*cochinillo asado*), or baby lamb (*cordero*), similarly roasted after a
few weeks of mother's milk.
   Toledo's three **Casa Aurelio** restaurants each offer traditional cooking, reasonable prices, and classy atmosphere (2,500-
ptas *menu*, 13:00–16:30, 20:00–23:00, all closed Sun, each closed
either Mon, Tue, or Wed, CC:VA). All are within three blocks of
the cathedral: Plaza Ayuntamiento 4 (tel. 92-522-7716), Sinagoga
1 (tel. 92-522-1392), and Sinagoga 6 (tel. 92-522-2097).
   Restaurante-Meson Palacios serves good food at cheap
prices (lunch from 13:00, dinner from 19:30, on Alfonso X, near
Plaza de San Vicente). **Rincón de Eloy** is more elegant (1,500-
ptas *menu*, Juan Labrador 16, near the Alcazar).
   Restaurants La Parrilla and **Plaza** share a tiny square
behind Plaza Zocódover (9:00–24:00, take the alley from Plaza
Zocódover 30 meters past Café Casa Telesforo to Plaza de Barrio
Rey). The bars and cafés on Plaza Zocódover are reasonable,
seasoned with some fine people watching.
   Picnics are best assembled at the **Mercado Municipal** on
Plaza Mayor (on the Alcázar side of cathedral, open until 14:00,
closed Sun). This is a fun market to prowl, even if you don't need
food. If you feel like munching a paper plate–size Communion
wafer, one of the stalls sells crispy bags of *obleas* (a great gift for
your favorite pastor).
   Toledo's famous almond-fruity-sweet *mazapan* is sold all over
town. On Plaza Zocodover try the modern **Santo Tomé** or **Casa
Telesforo**. Each has a great window display, is open long hours
daily, and sells single *mazapan* goodies (125 ptas each) or small
mixed boxes.
   For a sweet and romantic evening moment, get a pastry and
head down to the cathedral. Sit on the Plaza del Ayuntamiento
(there's a comfortable perch atop the stone fence 10 meters down

the lane from the huge granite bowling ball). The fountain is on your right, Spain's best-looking city hall is behind you, and her top cathedral, built back when Toledo was Spain's capital, shines brightly against the black night sky before you.

Transportation Connections—Toledo

Far more buses than trains connect Toledo with Madrid.

To Madrid by bus (2/hrly, 60 min, Madrid's Estación sur Autobuses, Metro: Méndez Alvaro, 92-522-3641), **by train** (9/day, 50 or 75 min, Madrid's Atocha station), **by car** (40 miles, 1 hr). Toledo bus info: tel. 92-521-5850; train info: tel. 92-522-3099.

Car Rental: Avis is within Toledo's city walls at Galeria Comercial 107, Paseo del Miradero (tel. 92-521-4535), and Hertz is in the train station (tel. 92-525-3890).

LA MANCHA

(Visit only if you're driving between Toledo and Granada.) Nowhere else is Spain so vast, flat, and radically monotonous. La Mancha, Arabic for "parched earth," makes you feel small—lost in rough seas of olive-green polka dots. Random buildings look like houses and hotels hurled off some heavenly Monopoly board. It's a rough land where roadkill is left to rot, where bugs ricochet off the windshield and keep on flying, and where hitchhikers wear red dresses and aim to take you for the ride.

This is the setting of Cervantes' *Don Quixote*, published in the 17th century, after England sank the Armada and the Spanish Empire began its decline. Cervantes' star character fought doggedly for good, for justice, and against the fall of Spain and its traditional old-regime empire. Ignoring reality, Don Quixote was a hero fighting a hopeless battle. Stark La Mancha was the perfect stage.

The epitome of Don Quixote country, the town of **Consuegra** must be the La Mancha Cervantes had in mind. Drive up to the ruined 12th-century castle and joust with a windmill. It's hot and buggy here, but the powerful view overlooking the village, with its sun-bleached, light-red roofs; modern concrete reality; and harsh, windy silence makes for a profound picnic (a 1-hour drive south of Toledo). The castle belonged to the Knights of St. John (12th and 13th centuries) and is associated with their trip to Jerusalem during the Crusades. Originally built from the ruins of a nearby Roman circus, it has been newly restored (200 ptas). Sorry, the windmills are post-Cervantes, only 200 to 300 years old.

If you've seen windmills, the next castle north (above Almonacid, 12 kilometers from Toledo) is more interesting than the Consuegra castle and free. Follow the ruined lane past the ruined church up to the ruined castle. The jovial locals hike up with kids and kites.

Route Tips for Drivers

Granada to Toledo (250 miles, 5 hrs): The Granada–Toledo drive is long, hot, and boring (see "La Mancha," above). Start early to minimize the heat and make the best time you can. Follow signs for Madrid/Jaen/N323 into what some call the Spanish Nebraska—La Mancha. After Puerto Lapice, you'll see the Toledo exit.

View the city from many angles along the Circumvalación road across the Tejo Gorge. Drive to Parador Conde de Orgaz just south of town for the view (from the balcony) El Greco made famous in his portrait of Toledo.

Enter Toledo by the north gate and park in the open-air guarded lot (cheap but not safe overnight) or in one of two garages. The garage just past the Alcázar is easy and as central as you need (1,900 ptas/24 hrs). You can usually park free in the lot just down the street from the garage or in the huge dirt lot below and behind the Santa Cruz Museum.

Toledo to Madrid (40 miles, 1 hr): It's a speedy *autovía* north, past one last bullboard, to Madrid. The highways converge into M30, which circles Madrid. Follow it to the left ("Nor y Oeste") and take the Plaza de España exit to get back to Gran Vía. If you're airport bound, keep heading into Madrid until you see the airplane symbol (N-II). Turn in your rental car at terminal T-1.

GRANADA

For a time, Granada was the grandest city in Spain; but in the end, it was left in the historic dust. Today it's a provincial town with more than its share of history and bumper stickers reading, "Life is short. Don't run." We'll keep things fun and simple, settling down in the old center and exploring monuments of the Moorish civilization and monuments of its conquest. And we'll taste the treats of an African-flavored culture that survives today.

Granada's magnificent Alhambra fortress was the last stronghold of the Moorish kingdom in Spain. The city's exotically tangled Moorish quarter bustles under the grand Alhambra, which glows red in the evening while locals stroll, enjoying the city's cool late-night charms.

There is an old saying: "Give him a coin, woman, for there is nothing worse in this life than to be blind in Granada." This city has much to see, yet it reveals itself in unpredictable ways. It takes a poet to sort through the jigsaw-puzzle pieces of Granada. Peer through the intricate lattice of a Moorish window. Hear water burbling, sight unseen, among the labyrinthine hedges of the Generalife garden. Listen to a flute trilling deep in the swirl of alleys around the cathedral. Don't be blind in Granada—open your senses.

Planning Your Time

Granada is worth one day and two nights. Consider the night train connection with Madrid (or Barcelona), giving the city a night and a day. The Costa del Sol's best beach town, Nerja, is just two quick hours away (by bus), postcard-perfect white hill towns such as Ronda are three hours away (bus or train), and Sevilla is an easy three-hour train ride.

In the morning, tour the cathedral and Royal Chapel (both closed roughly 13:00–16:00) and stroll the pedestrian-zone shopping scene. Do the Alhambra in the early evening (reserve ahead; see "Sights—Granada's Alhambra," below). Be at the Albaicín viewpoint for sunset and then wander the Moorish Quarter (Albaicín) until you find the right place for a suitably late dinner.

Orientation

While modern Granada sprawls (300,000 people), its sights are all within a 20-minute walk of Plaza Nueva, where dogs wag their tails to the rhythm of the street musicians. Nearly all my recommended hotels are within a few blocks of Plaza Nueva. Make this the hub of your Granada visit.

Plaza Nueva was a main square back when kings called Granada home. This historic center is in the Darro River Valley, which separates two hills (and now flows under the square): one with the great Moorish palace, the Alhambra; and the other with the best-preserved Moorish quarter in Spain, the Albaicín. To the southeast are the cathedral, Royal Chapel, and Alcaicería (Moorish market), where the city's two main drags, Gran Vía de Colón and Calle Reyes Católicos, lead away into the modern city.

Tourist Information

There are three TIs. The handiest—in the courtyard of what was a Moorish hotel 500 years ago—is at Corral del Carbon (Mon–Sat 9:00–19:00, Sun 10:00–14:00; from Plaza Isabel la Católica, take Reyes Católicos in the opposite direction from Alhambra, take first left, walk through keyhole arch, tel. 95-822-5990). Another TI is on Plaza de Mariana Pineda (Mon–Fri 9:30–19:00, Sat 10:00–14:00, closed Sun, tel. 95-822-6688). Get the free Granada map and verify your Alhambra plans. Check the posted bus and train schedules. The other TI is at the Alhambra (Mon–Fri 10:00–14:00 only).

Arrival in Granada

By Train: Granada's train station is connected to the center by frequent buses, a 600-ptas taxi ride, or a 20-minute walk down Avenida Constitución and Gran Vía de Colón. The train station has lockers. Reserve your train out upon arrival.

Exiting the train station, walk straight ahead down the tree-lined road. At the first major intersection (Avenida de la Constitución), you'll see the bus stop on your right. Take buses #9 or #11 and confirm by asking the driver, "*¿Catedral?*" (kat-ay-dral; the nearest stop to Plaza Nueva, ticket-130 ptas, pay driver). Get off when you see the fountain of Plaza Isabel la Católica in front of the bus at the stop near the cathedral; cross the busy Gran Vía and walk two blocks to Plaza Nueva.

Granada

1	HOTEL RESIDENCIA MACIA	**7**	HOTEL LOS TILOS	**13**	HOTEL ANACAPRI
2	HOSTAL RESIDENCIA BRITZ	**8**	ROYAL CHAPEL ENTRY	**14**	HOSTAL RESIDENCIA LISBOA
3	HOSTAL GOMEREZ	**9**	CATHEDRAL ENTRY	**15**	CALLE NAVAS: HOTEL NAVAS
4	HOSTAL NAVARRO RAMOS	**10**	NATURI ALBAICIN REST.	**16**	BODEGA CASTANEDA
5	HOSTAL LANDAZURI	**11**	PLAZA DE LOS TRISTES	**17**	HOTEL INGLATERRA
6	HOSTAL VIENA	**12**	ALCAICERIA		

By Bus: Granada's main bus station, where all long-distance buses stop, is a bus or taxi ride from the center (bus info: tel. 95-818-5480). To get to the city center, take bus #3 (130 ptas) and get off just after turning right through the Plaza Isabel la Católica (with the fountain) at the stop opposite the cathedral. Plaza Nueva is two blocks east.

By Car: Driving in Granada's historic center is restricted to buses, taxis, and tourists with hotel reservations (tell the police officer). The *autovía* (freeway) circles the city with a *circumvalación* road. To reach Plaza Nueva, take exit #132, direction *"Centro, Recogidas."* Calle Recogidas leads directly into the heart of town. There will probably be a police block at Puerta Real (Victoria Hotel). Ask here for Plaza Nueva. Double-park at Plaza Nueva long enough to get directions to a parking garage near your hotel (but, considering the risk of both police and thieves, don't leave your car unattended). A handy garage, Parking San Agustín, is just off Gran Vía (1,800 ptas/24 hrs).

Getting around Granada

With such cheap taxis, efficient Alhambra minibuses, and nearly all points of interest an easy walk from Plaza Nueva, you may not even need the regular city buses. Two handy little red minibuses depart from Plaza Nueva to the Alhambra and for the circuit around Albaicín. You buy bus tickets (130 ptas) from the driver. Sharable *bonobus* strips of 15 tickets cost 1,000 ptas (buy at tobacco shop or on bus; valid on minibuses and city buses).

Helpful Hints

When you see women wanting to give you leaves or flowers, avoid them like the plague.

Long-Distance Bus and Train Tickets: To save yourself a trip to the train or bus stations, get schedule information from the TI or a travel agency. Most travel agencies sell long-distance bus or train tickets (generally open Mon–Fri 9:30–13:30, 17:00–20:00, Sat 9:30–13:30, closed Sun; Viajes Bonanza is convenient at Reyes Católicos 30, tel. 95-822-3578).

Post Office: The P.O. is on Puerta Real (Mon–Fri 8:30–20:30, Sat 9:00–13:00, tel. 95-822-1138).

American Express: Amex is across from the main TI (Reyes Católicos 31, tel. 95-822-4512).

Internet Access: Madar Internet is at Calderia Nueva 12, amid *teterias* (tea shops), and two blocks off Plaza Nueva (400 ptas/hr, Mon–Sat 10:00–24:00, Sun 12:00–24:00).

Festivals: From late June to mid-July the International Festival of Music and Dance offers some of the world's best classical music in the Alhambra at reasonable prices.

Local Guide: Margarita Landazuri, a local English-speaking guide, knows how to teach and has reasonable rates (tel. 95-822-1406). If she's busy, her partner, Miguel Angel, is also good.

Sights—Granada's Alhambra

A ▲▲▲ sight, this last and greatest Moorish palace is one of Europe's top attractions. Attracting up to 8,000 visitors a day, it's the reason most tourists come to Granada. Nowhere else does the splendor of Moorish civilization shine so brightly.

The last Moorish stronghold in Europe is, with all due respect, really a symbol of retreat. Granada was only a regional capital for centuries. Gradually the Christian Reconquista moved south, taking Córdoba (1236) and Sevilla (1248). The Moors held Granada until 1492. As you tour their grand palace, remember that while Europe slumbered through the Dark Ages, Moorish magnificence blossomed—busy stucco, plaster "stalactites," colors galore, scalloped windows framing Granada views, exuberant gardens, and water, water everywhere. Water—so rare and precious in most of the Islamic world—was the purest symbol of life to the Moors. The Alhambra is decorated with water: standing still, cascading, masking secret conversations, and drip-dropping playfully.

Getting there: There are three ways to get to the Alhambra.

1. From Plaza Nueva, hike 20 minutes up the street Cuesta de Gomerez. Keep going straight, with the Alhambra high on your left, and follow the street to the ticket pavilion at the far side of the Alhambra, near the Generalife garden.

2. Catch the red minibus #30 marked "Alhambra-Plaza Nueva" from Plaza Nueva (130 ptas, every 10 min).

3. Take a taxi (450 ptas, taxi stand on Plaza Nueva).

Don't drive. If you do, you'll park on the far, far side of the Alhambra, and when you leave, one-way streets will send you into the traffic-clogged center of New Granada.

Cost: While Charles V's Palace is free, the Alcazaba fort, Moorish palace (Palacios Nazaries), and Generalife gardens require a 1,000-ptas combo ticket.

Getting Tickets: Tickets are limited to 8,000 per day (6,000 available in advance through the BBV Bank reservation system and 2,000 given out at the door). You can reserve one of the 6,000 tickets in advance or be one of the first 2,000 people to get one at the main Alhambra ticket office (daily 8:00 until sold out—as late as 19:00 but generally before noon, Generalife entrance near parking lot). Ideally, arrive by 8:15 and get an entry time. On a slow day you'll get in right away. During busy times you'll have an appointment for later that day.

You can reserve in advance (at least a day) from the BBV Bank in town (Banco Bilbao Vizcaya, Mon–Fri 9:00–14:00, Plaza Isabel la Católica, 125-ptas surcharge) or from any BBV bank in Spain. Or you can reserve by phone (between 2 days and a year in advance, CC:VM, 125-ptas surcharge, tel. 90-222-4460), pay by credit card, and get a reference number that will allow you to pick up your ticket at any BBV Bank (a minimum of a day before your visit) or at the main Alhambra entrance. Bigger hotels can make a reservation for you (request this with your reservation).

Only 400 visitors per half hour are allowed in the Moorish palace (Palacios Nazaries). Your 30-minute time span is printed on your ticket; you can request a particular half hour when you pay. While you must enter the Palacios Nazaries within this time, once inside you may linger as long as you like.

Hours: The Alhambra is open daily from 8:30 to 20:00 (closes in winter at 18:00). If you're looking for something to do while you await your appointment for Palacios Nazaries, you can see the fort, Generalife garden, or museums in Charles V's

Alhambra

Palace—requiring a ticket but no entry time. Or, for those on vacation, kill time luxuriously in and around the parador bar (actually within the Alhambra walls). While drinks, WCs, and guidebooks ring the Palacios Nazaries, you'll find none inside.

Guidebook: Consider the guidebook *The Alhambra and the Generalife*, available at souvenir shops across from Charles V's Palace (600 ptas, great layout plan included), or buy it in town and read it the night before to understand the layout and history of this remarkable sight before entering.

Alhambra by moonlight: Late-night visits (Tue–Sat, usually 22:00–23:30; Tue and Sat only 20:00–21:30 in winter) include only the Moorish palace and not the fort or garden—but hey, the palace is 80 percent of the Alhambra thrills, and by moonlight there's no waiting or obnoxious crowds.

The Alhambra in Four Parts

The Alhambra—not nearly as confusing as it is—consists of four sights: Charles V's Palace (free, Christian Renaissance palace plopped on top of the Alhambra after the reconquest), Alcazaba (empty old fort), Palacios Nazaries (exquisite Moorish palace), and Generalife (fancy garden).

1. Charles V's Palace—It's only natural for a conquering king to build his own palace over his foe's palace—and that's exactly what the Christian King Charles V did. The Alhambra palace wasn't good enough for Charles, so he built this one—destroying the dramatic Alhambra facade and financing his new palace with a salt-on-the-wound tax on Granada's defeated Moorish population.

This palace—a unique circle within a square—is Spain's most impressive Renaissance building. It was designed by Pedro Machuca, a devotee of Michelangelo and Raphael. Stand in the circular courtyard, then climb the stairs. Imagine being here for one of Charles' bullfights. Charles' palace was never finished because his son Philip II moved the royal building focus to El Escorial. Inside the palace are two free, but boring, museums: Museo de Bellas Artes (9:00–20:00, closed Sun afternoon, all day Mon, Tue morning) and Museo de Alhambra, showing off some of the Alhambra's best Moorish art (Tue–Sat 9:00–14:30).

2. Alcazaba—The fort—the oldest and most ruined part of the Alhambra—offers exercise and fine city views. What you see is mid-13th century, but there was probably a fort here in Roman times. Once upon a time this tower defended a town (or medina) of 2,000 Arabs living within the Alhambra walls. From the top find Plaza Nueva, the Albaicín viewpoint, and the mountains. Is anybody skiing today? Look to the south and think of that day in 1492 when the cross and flags of Aragon and Castille were raised on this tower and the fleeing Moorish King Boabdil looked back and wept. His mom chewed him out, saying, "Don't weep like a woman for what you couldn't defend like a man." Much later, Napoleon stationed his troops here, contributing substantially to its ruin when he left. Follow the arrows down and around to the . . .

3. Palacios Nazaries—During the 30-minute window of time stamped on your ticket, enter the jewel of the Alhambra: the Moorish royal palace. You'll walk through three basic sections: royal offices, ceremonial rooms, and private quarters. Built mostly in the 14th century, this palace offers your best possible look at the refined, elegant Moorish civilization of Al-Andalus. If you can imagine a few tapestries, carpets, pillows, ivory-studded wooden furniture, and painted stucco, the place is much as it was for the Moorish kings. Rather then hire an interior decorator, the Moors just read the Koran: recommended color scheme—red (blood), blue (heaven), green (oasis), and gold (wealth). As you tour the palace, keep the palace themes in mind: water, no images, "stalactite" ceilings throughout—and no signs telling you where you are. Even today, the route constantly changes. Use the map to locate these essential stops:

Court of Myrtles: Walk through a few administrative rooms (the *mexuar*) until you hit a big rectangular courtyard with a pond lined by a myrtle bush hedge—the Court of Myrtles (Patio de los Arrayanes). Moors loved their patios—with a garden, water, and under the sky. Women, who rarely went out, stayed in touch with nature here. The living quarters for the wives (the Koran allowed a man "all the women you can maintain with dignity") were upstairs. Notice the wooden "jealousies"—screens (erected by

Palacios Nazaries

jealous husbands) allowing the cloistered women to look out but not be seen.

Boat Room: Head left (north) from the entry into the long, narrow antechamber to the throne room, called the "Boat Room." While it's understandable that many think this is named for the upside-down hull shape of its fine cedar ceiling, the name is actually a corruption of the Arab word *baraka*, meaning "divine blessing and luck." This was the waiting room for meetings with the sultan, and blessings and luck are exactly what you'd need if you had business in the next room. Oh, it's your turn now...

The Hall of the Ambassadors (Grand Salon de Embajadores) functioned like a throne room. It was here that the sultan received foreign emissaries. The king's throne stood opposite the entrance. The ceiling, made of cedar of Lebanon—8,000 inlaid pieces—is original. The walls, even without their original paint and gilding, are still glorious. Note the finely carved Arabic script. Muslims couldn't make images of living things—that was God's work. But they could carve decorative religious messages. One phrase—"only Allah is victorious"—is repeated 9,000 times throughout the palace. Find the character for Allah—it looks like a cursive W with a nose on its left side. The swoopy toboggan blades underneath are a kind of artistic punctuation marking off one phrase.

In 1492 two historic events took place in this room. Culminating a 700-year-long battle, the Reconquista was completed here as the last Moorish king, Boabdil, signed the terms of his surrender before packing light and fleeing to Africa. For four years Isabel had put off Columbus as she focused on the Reconquista. That accomplished, Isabel and Ferdinand finally received Columbus in this room. Imagine the scene: The king, queen, and the greatest minds from the University of Salamanca gathered here to hear Columbus make his case that the world was round—then a still-loony notion that got people burned a few years earlier. Ferdinand and the professors laughed, calling Columbus mad. But Isabel said *"Sí, señor."* Columbus fell to his knees (promising to wear a moneybelt and use the most current guidebooks available) and she gave him a wad of traveler's checks.

Continue deeper into the palace to a court where, 600 years ago, only the royal family and their servants could enter. It's the much-photographed...

Court of the Lions: The Patio de los Leones features a fountain with 12 lions. Why 12? Since the fountain was a gift from a Jewish leader celebrating good relations with the sultan (Granada had a big Jewish community), the lions probably represent the 12 tribes of Israel. During Moorish times, the fountain functioned as a clock, with a different lion spouting water each hour. (Conquering Christians disassembled the fountain to see how it worked and it's never worked since.) From the center, four streams went out—figuratively to the corners of the earth and literally to various apartments of the royal family. Notice how the court resembles, with its 124 columns, the cloister of a Catholic monastery. Six hundred years ago the Muslim Moors could read the Koranic poetry that ornaments this court, and they could understand the symbolism of this lush, enclosed garden (considered the embodiment of paradise or truth). Imagine—they enjoyed this part of the palace even more than we do today.

On the right, off the courtyard, is a square room called the **Hall of the Abencerrajes (Sala de los Abencerrajes)**. According to legend, the father of Boabdil took a new wife and wanted to disinherit the children of his first marriage—one of whom was Boabdil. In order to deny power to Boabdil and his siblings, he killed nearly the entire pro-Boabdil Abencerrage family. The sultan thought this would pave the way for the son of his new wife to be the next sultan. Happily, he stacked 36 Abencerrage heads in the pool under this sumptuous honeycombed stucco ceiling. But his scheme failed, and Boabdil ultimately assumed the throne. Bloody power struggles like this were the norm here in the Alhambra.

The Hall of the Kings (Sala de los Reyes) is at the end of the court opposite where you entered. Notice the ceilings of the three chambers branching off this gallery. Breaking from the tradition of imageless art, paintings on goat leather depict scenes of the sultan and his family. The center room shows a portrait of the first

10 of the Alhambra's 22 sultans. The scene is a fantasy, since these people lived over a span of many generations. The two end rooms show scenes of princely pastimes, such as hunting and shooting skeet. In a palace otherwise devoid of figures, these offer a rare look at royal life in the palace.

The next room, the **Hall of the Two Sisters**, named for the two great stone slabs that flank the fountain, has another oh-wow stucco ceiling but no figures—only geometric patterns and stylized Arabic script quoting verses from the Koran.

Washington Irving Room: That's about it for the palace. From here you wander through a few more rooms including one (marked with a large plaque) where Washington Irving wrote *Tales of the Alhambra*. While serving as the U.S. ambassador to Spain in 1829, Irving lived in the Alhambra. It was a romantic time when the place was home to Gypsies and donkeys. His "tales" kindled interest in the place, causing it to become recognized as a national treasure.

Hallway with a view: Stop at the open-air hallway for the best-in-the-palace view of the labyrinthine Albaicín—the old Moorish town on the opposite hillside. Find the famous viewpoint at the base of the white St. Nicolás church tower breaking the horizon. Creeping into the mountains on the right are the Gypsy neighborhoods of Sacromonte. Still circling old Granada is the Moorish wall (built by the Moors in the 1200s to protect the city's population, swollen by Moslem refugees driven south by the Reconquista.

Leaving the Palacios Nazaries you walk through a garden and follow signs directing you left to Generalife or right to the exit.
4. Generalife—On the hillside to the east, the garden with carefully pruned hedges is Generalife (henneraw-LEEF-ay). This most perfect Arabian garden in Andalucía was the summer home of the Moorish kings, the closest thing on earth to the Koran's description of heaven. If you have a long wait before your entry to the Palacios, tour these gardens first.

Sights—Central Granada
▲▲**Royal Chapel (Capilla Real)**—Without a doubt Granada's top Christian sight, this lavish chapel holds the dreams—and bodies—of Queen Isabel and King Ferdinand (350 ptas, Mon–Sat 10:30–13:00, 16:00–19:00, Sun 11:00–13:00, 16:00–19:00; Oct–March, Mon–Sat 10:30–13:00, 15:30–18:30, closed Sun; entrance on Calle Oficios).

In the lobby notice the painting of Boabdil (on the black horse) giving the key of Granada to the conquering King Ferdinand. Boabdil wanted to fall to his knees, but the Spanish king, who had great respect for his Moorish foe, embraced him instead. They fought a long and noble war (for instance, respectfully returning the bodies of dead soldiers). Ferdinand is in red, and Isabel is behind him in white and blue. Behind her (under a black hood) is their daughter Juana. And behind her, wearing a crown, is Juana's husband, Philip the Fair. Philip died young, and for two years Juana kept his casket at her bedside, kissing his embalmed body good night. These four people are buried in this chapel. The painting is flanked by two large portraits of Ferdinand and Isabel.

Isabel decided to make Granada the capital of Spain (and burial place for Spanish royalty) for three reasons: 1) With the conquest of Granada, Christianity had overcome Islam in Europe; 2) her marriage with Ferdinand, followed by the conquest of Granada, had marked the beginning of a united Spain; and 3) Granada had been the departure point for Columbus.

Step into the **chapel**. It's Plateresque Gothic—light and lacy, named for and inspired by the fine silverwork of the Moors. This was the most lavish interior money could buy 500 years ago. Because of its speedy completion, the chapel is an unusually harmonious piece of architecture.

The four **royal tombs** are Renaissance style. Carved in Italy in 1521 out of Carrara marble, they were sent by ship to Spain. The faces—based on death masks—are considered accurate. If you're facing the altar, Ferdinand and Isabel are on the right. (Isabel fans attribute the bigger dent she puts in the pillow to brains.) Philip the Fair and Juana are on the left. Philip was a Hapsburg. Their son, Charles V (known as Charles I in Spain), was a key character in European history, as his coronation merged the Holy Roman Empire (Hapsburg domain) with the Spanish empire. Europe's top king, he ruled a vast empire stretching from Budapest to Bolivia (1519–1556).

When the son of Charles V decided to build El Escorial and establish Madrid as the single capital of a single Spain, Granada lost power and importance.

More important, Spain declined. After Charles V, Spain squandered her awesome wealth trying to maintain this impossible empire—not for material riches but to defend the romantic Quixote-esque dream of a Catholic empire ruled by one divinely ordained Catholic monarch against an irrepressible tide of nationalism and Protestantism. Spain's relatively poor modern history can be blamed, in part, by her stubborn unwillingness to accept the end of this "old regime" notion.

Look at the fine carving on the tombs (unfortunately vandalized by Napoleon's troops). It's a humanistic statement with healthy, organic, realistic figures rising above the strict and heavy Gothic past.

From the feet of the marble tombs, step downstairs to see the actual coffins. They are plain. Isabel was originally buried as a simple monk at the Franciscan monastery (in what is today the parador at the Alhambra). The fifth coffin (with PM on it) is that of a young Prince Michael, who would have been king of a united Spain and Portugal. A sad—but too-long—story...

The **high altar** is one of the finest Renaissance works in Spain. It's dedicated to John the Baptist and John the Evangelist. In the center, you can see the Baptist and the Evangelist chatting as if over tapas (an appropriately humanist scene). Scenes from the Baptist's life are on the left: John beheaded after Salome's fine dancing and (below) John baptizing Jesus. Scenes from the Evangelist's life are on the right: John's martyrdom (a failed attempt to boil him alive in oil) and John on Patmos (where he wrote the last book of the Bible, Revelation). John is talking to the eagle that, according to legend, flew him to Heaven.

Anyone who paid for church art got their mug in it. Find Ferdinand and Isabel kneeling in prayer in opposite corners. The eagle banners around the room are not the aggressive, two-headed, claws-exposed Hapsburg eagles but eagles with halos (and crowns for bras). These are symbolic of the eagle that inspired John on Patmos.

The Plateresque (silver-filigree-style) arch leads to a small glass pyramid in the **treasury**. This holds the silver crown of Queen Isabel, ringed by pomegranates (symbolizing Granada), and the sword of Ferdinand. Beside the entry arch you'll see the devout Isabel's prayer book, in which she followed the Mass. The book and its sturdy box date from 1496. The fancy box on the other side of the door is the one that Isabel (cash-poor because of her military expenses) filled with jewels and gave Columbus. Columbus sold these to finance his journey. Next, in the corner (and also behind glass), is the cross Cardinal Mendoza carried into the Alhambra on that historic day in 1492. Next, the big silk, silver, and gold tapestry is the altar banner for the mobile campaign chapel of Ferdinand and Isabel, who always traveled with their army. In the next case you'll see the original Christian army flags raised over the Alhambra in 1492.

The room holds the first great art collection ever established by a woman. Queen Isabel amassed more than 200 great paintings. After Napoleon's visit, only 30 remain. Even so, this is a fine collection, all on wood, featuring works by Botticelli, Perugino, the Flemish master Memling, and less-famous Spanish masters.

Finally, at the end of the room, the two carved portraits of Ferdinand and Isabel were the originals from the high altar. Charles V considered them primitive and replaced these with the ones you saw earlier.

Cathedral—The only Renaissance church in Spain, Granada's cathedral is the second-largest in Spain after Sevilla's. Its spacious and bright interior is a refreshing break from the dark Gothic and gilded-lily Baroque of so many Spanish churches. In a modern move back in the 18th century, the choir walls were taken out so that people could be involved in the worship. To make matters even better, an 18th-century bishop ordered the interior painted with lime (for hygienic reason, during a time of disease). The people liked it, and it stayed white. Most of the side chapels are decorated in Baroque style. On the far wall (right of the high altar) is St. James the Moor-slayer, with his sword raised high and an armored Moor under his horse's hooves. The Renaissance facade and paintings of the Virgin in the rotunda are by Granada's own Alonso Cano (1601–1661) and can be lit by dropping a coin in the box (entry: 300 ptas, Mon–Sat 10:30–13:30, 16:00–19:00, Sun 16:00–19:00; Oct–March, Mon–Sat 10:30–13:30, closed Sun; entrance off Gran Vía de Colón).

Alcaicería—Originally an Arab silk market, this neighborhood (around the cathedral) still functions as a silk and jewelry market. Ignore the obnoxious Gypsy women giving tourists sprigs of rosemary for good luck. (The flowers they used to give became too expensive. After somehow rerouting the magic power, they now use rosemary, which comes from the parks—for free.) By accepting the sprig you start a relationship. This, while free, leads to palm reading, which isn't.

Explore the mesh of tiny shopping lanes between the cathedral and Calle Reyes Católicos. Go on a photo and sound safari: popcorn machines popping, men selling balloons, leather goods spread out on streets, kids playing soccer, the whirring grind of knife sharpeners, barking dogs, dogged shoeshine boys.

The exuberant square behind the cathedral is **Bib-Rambla**. While today it's fine for a coffee or meal amidst the color and fragrance of flower stalls, in Moorish times this was a place of public execution. The small Mercado Municipal is liveliest on Saturday, spilling out into the nearby streets (off Plaza Romanilla, best in mornings until 14:00, closed Sun).

Plaza Isabel la Católica—Granada's two grand boulevards, Gran Vía and Reyes Católicos, meet a block off Plaza Nueva at Plaza Isabel la Católica. Here you'll see a fine statue of Columbus unfurling a long contract with Isabel. It lists the terms of Columbus' MCDXCII voyage.

Isabel was driven by her desire to spread Catholicism. Columbus was driven by his desire for money. For adding territory to Spain's Catholic empire, she promised Columbus the ranks of Admiral of the Oceans and Governor of the New World. To sweeten the pie, she tossed in 10 percent of all the riches he brought home. Isabel died thinking Columbus had found India or China. Columbus died poor and disillusioned.

From here, Reyes Católicos leads to Puerta Real. There Acera de Darro takes you through modern Granada to the river via the huge El Corte Inglés department store and lots of modern commerce.

Paseo de los Tristes—In the cool of the evening (with dinner as a popular destination), consider strolling the Paseo de los Tristes ("walk of the sad ones"—the route of funeral processions to the cemetery at the edge of town). Start at Plaza Nueva. The Church of Santa Anna, which stands at the far end of the square, was originally a mosque, its tower a minaret. Notice the ceramic brickwork. This is Mudejar art, the technique of the Moors used by Christians. Inside you'll see a fine Alhambra-style cedar ceiling. Follow Carrera del Darro along the River Darro under the Alhambra. (Nine kilometers upstream, part of the Darro is diverted to provide water for the Alhambra's many fountains.) On the left you'll pass the Arab Baths (below) and the Convent de Santa Catalina de Zafra, a home of cloistered nuns (they worship behind a screen that divides the church's rich interior in half). On the right, across from the Archeological Museum, is the Church of San Pedro, the parish church of Sacromonte's Gypsy community. Within its rich interior is an ornate oxcart used to carry the Holy Host on the annual pilgrimage to Rocio near Portugal. Finally, you reach the Plaza de los Tristes. Covered with happy diners, this is a great spot at night, under the floodlit Alhambra. From here the road arches up (past a rank of "burro taxis" for those into adventure sports) into Sacromonte. And from here a lane (called Cuesta de los Chinos or Carretera del Rey Chico) leads up to the Alhambra "through the back door."

Arab Baths—Consider a visit to the Arab baths at Hammam Baños Arabes Al Andaluz. The soak and a 15-minute massage cost 2,700 ptas (open until 24:00, co-ed with swimsuits, just off Plaza Nueva at Santa Ana 16, reservation necessary, tel. 95-822-9978).

Sights—Albaicín

Explore Spain's best old Moorish quarter, with countless colorful corners, flowery patios, and shady lanes to soothe the 21st-century-mangled visitor. Climb high to the San Nicolás church for the best view of the Alhambra. Then wander through the mysterious backstreets.

A handy city minibus threads its way around the Albaicín from Plaza Nueva (see below). It gets you scenically and sweatlessly to the St. Nicolás viewpoint. You can also taxi to the St. Nicolás church and explore from there. Consider having your cabby take you on a Sacromonte detour en route.

If walking up, leave the west end of Plaza Nueva on Calle Elvira. After about 200 meters, turn right on Calderería Nueva. Follow this stepped street past tapas bars and *teterias* (see "Eating," below) as it goes left around the church, slants, winds, and zigzags up the hill, heading basically straight. Pass the pink building on your left (resisting the temptation to turn left on Muladar Sancha). Near the crest, turn right on Camino Nuevo de San Nicolás, then

Albaicín Neighborhood

NOTE:
NOT TO SCALE
PLAZA NUEVA TO
SAN NICOLAS IS
A 20 MIN WALK
UPHILL

① BUS STOP FOR ALBAICIN LOOP

② CALDERERIA NUEVA
(TAPAS BARS, TETERIAS)

③ PLAZA DE CARVAJALES

④ RESTAURANT LADRILLO I

⑤ RESTAURANT LADRILLO II

⑥ CASA TORCUATO

⑦ EL AGUA CASA DE VINOS

⑧ MIRADOR DE MORAYMA

⑨ NATURI ALBAICIN

⑩ BODEGA CASTANEDA

⑪ BUS TO ALHAMBRA

⑫ ARAB BATHS

walk several blocks to the street that curves up left, leading to the steps up to the church's viewpoint.

▲▲**San Nicolás Viewpoint**—For one of Europe's most romantic viewpoints, be here at sunset when the Alhambra turns red and the Albaicín widows share the benches with local lovers and tourists. In 1997 President Clinton made a point to bring his family here— a favorite spot from a trip he made as a student. Many now know this as "The Clinton Mirador."

Exploring the Albaicín: From the San Nicolás viewpoint you're at the edge of a neighborhood even people of Granada rec- ognize as a world apart. From the viewpoint turn your back to the Alhambra and walk north (passing the church on your right and the Biblioteca Municipal on your left). A lane leads past a white arch—now a chapel built into the old Moorish wall. At the end of the lane, step down to the right through the 11th-century "New Gate" (Puerta Nueva—older than the Alhambra) and into **Plaza Larga.** In medieval times this tiny square (called "large" because back then it was) was the local marketplace. It still is a busy market each morning, with locals blaring their cheap, pirated cassettes as if to prove there is actually music on them. Casa Pasteles, at the end of the square, serves good coffee and cakes. From Plaza Larga, Calle del Agua (named for the public baths that used to line it) shows evidence of the Moorish plumbing system. Back when Europe's streets were filled with muck, Granada actually had Roman Empire–style gutters with drains leading to clay and lead pipes.

This is the heart of the Albaicín. Poke into an old church. They're plain by design—to go easy on the Moslem converts who weren't used to being surrounded by images as they worshiped. You'll see lots of real Moslem culture living in the streets, including many recent Spanish converts. Those aren't the Spice Girls, just Gypsy teenagers—as influenced as any teenagers these days by TV. **Albaicín Circular Bus Tour**—The handy Albaicín bus (#32) makes the 15-minute loop, departing from Plaza Nueva about every 10 minutes (pay driver 130 ptas, best views on the right). While good for a lift to the top of the Albaicín, I'd stay on for an entire circle (and return to the Albaicín later for dinner). While a few buses detour up Sacromonte, all pass its entrance (you'll see the humble brown statue of the Gypsy king on the right). Two stops later the driver announces the San Nicolas mirador (view-point). The next stop is San Miguel el Bajo (a fun, untouristy square with several fine little restaurants). Just after that you get a commanding view of modern Granada on the left. Hitting the city's main drag, Gran Via, you make a U-turn at the Garden of the Triumph, celebrating the Immaculate Conception of the Virgin Mary (notice her statue atop a column). Behind Mary stands the old Royal Hospital—built in the 16th century for Granada's poor by the Catholic Kings after the Reconquista in hopes of winning the favor of Granada's conquered residents. From here you zip past the cathedral and home to Plaza Nueva.

Sights—Sacromonte and Granada's Gypsies

Spain's Gypsies came from India via Egypt. The Spanish word for Gypsy, *Gitano*, means "Egyptian." They settled mostly in the south, where they found people less racist and more tolerant. Ages ago a Spanish king, exasperated by Gypsy problems, actually declared that these nomads must stay in one place and get a religion—any religion. In most of Spain, Gypsies are more assimilated into the general community, but Granada's Sacromonte district is a large and distinct Gypsy community. Granada's Gypsies arrived in the 16th century and have stuck together ever since. Today 50,000 Gypsies call Granada home.

Local Spaniards, who consider themselves accepting and not racist, claim that in maintaining such a tight community, the

Gypsies segregate themselves. The Gypsies call Spaniards *Payo* ("whites").

Sacromonte has one main street. Camino del Sacromonte is lined with caves primed for tourists and restaurants ready to fight over the bill. Intriguing lanes run above and below this main drag. Notice the statue of a Gypsy "king"—actually a wise community elder—in traditional attire marking the start of Sacromonte.

Formerly Europe's most disgusting tourist trap, famous for its cave-dwelling, foot-stomping, flamenco-dancing Gypsies, Sacromonte is not quite as bad as it used to be. Still, don't go here expecting to get a good value for anything. Flamenco is better in Sevilla.

Sights—Near Granada

Carthusian Monastery (La Cartuja)—A church with an interior that looks as if it squirted out of a can of whipped cream, La Cartuja is nicknamed the "Christian Alhambra" for its elaborate white baroque stucco work. In the rooms just off the cloister, notice the gruesome paintings of martyrs placidly meeting their grisly fate. It's located a mile out of town on the way to Madrid. Go north on Gran Vía and follow the signs or take bus #8 from Gran Vía (entry: 350 ptas, daily 10:00–13:00, 16:00–20:00, shorter hours Sun mornings, Oct–March, Mon–Sat 10:00–13:00 and 15:30–18:00).

Sleeping in Granada
(180 ptas = about $1, country code: 34)

Sleep Code: **S** = Single, **D** = Double/Twin, **T** = Triple, **Q** = Quad, **b** = bathroom, **t** = toilet only, **s** = shower only, **CC** = Credit Card (**V**isa, **M**asterCard, **A**mex), **SE** = Speaks English, **NSE** = No English. Breakfast and the 7 percent IVA tax are not included.

In July and August, when the streets are littered with sunstroke victims, rooms are plentiful. Crowded months are April, May, June, September, and October. Except for the Alhambra listings, all recommended hotels are within a five-minute walk of Plaza Nueva. While almost none of the hotels have their own parking facilities, all can direct you to a garage (such as Parking San Agustin, just off Gran Vía, 1,800 ptas/24 hrs.)

Hotels on or near Plaza Nueva
(zip code: 18009 unless otherwise noted)

Each of these is big, professional, plenty comfortable, and perfectly located. Prices vary with the demand. You'll generally get the low price on weekends (Fri, Sat, and Sun) and throughout July and August.

Hotel Residencia Macia, right on the colorful Plaza Nueva, is a clean, modern, classy, and hotelesque place. Choose between an on-the-square view or a quieter interior room (Sb-6,600 ptas,

Db-9,900 ptas, Tb-13,900 ptas, show this book upon arrival to get a 10 percent discount, good buffet breakfast-725 ptas, CC:VMA, 44 rooms, elevator, air-con, Plaza Nueva 4, tel. 95-822-7536, fax 95-822-7533, e-mail: maciaplaza@maciahoteles.com, SE).

Hotel Anacapri is a bright, cool, marble oasis with 49 modern rooms and a quiet lounge (Sb-9,000–10,000 ptas, Db-12,000–14,000 ptas, extra bed-3,000 ptas, CC:VMA, elevator, air-con, 2 blocks toward Gran Vía from Plaza Nueva at Calle Joaquin Costa 7, tel. 95-822-7477, fax 95-822-8909, e-mail: acapri@batch-pc.es, helpful Kathy speaks Iowan).

Hotel Inglaterra—modern, peaceful, and pastel with 39 rooms offering all the comforts—feels like a chain hotel (Sb-11,100–13,500 ptas, Db-11,100–15,000 ptas, extra bed-5,000 ptas, CC:VMA, elevator, air-con, Cettie Meriem 4, 18010 Granada, tel. 95-822-1559, fax 95-822-7100, e-mail: nhinglaterra@nh-hoteles.es).

Hotel Gran Vía, right on Granada's main drag, has a stately lobby with Euro-modern business-class rooms (Sb-7,000–8,000 ptas, Db-10,900–12,400 ptas, Tb-14,700–16,800 ptas, show this book for a 10 percent discount, CC:VMA, elevator, air-con, 5-min walk from Plaza Nueva, Gran Vía de Colón 25, tel. 95-828-5464, fax 95-828-5591, e-mail: granvia@maciahoteles.com, SE).

Cheaper Places on Cuesta de Gomerez
(zip code: 18009)
These are cheap and ramshackle on the street leading from Plaza Nueva up to the Alhambra.

Hostal Landazuri is run by friendly, English-speaking Matilda Landazuri and her son Manolo. While well-worn, it's lovingly decorated and homey. It has a great roof garden with an Alhambra view and a hardworking, helpful management (18 rooms, Sb-4,000 ptas, D-3,400 ptas, Db-5,000 ptas, Tb-7,000 ptas, simple 250-ptas breakfast or their hearty 650-ptas English breakfast, Cuesta de Gomerez 24, tel. & fax 95-822-1406). The Landazuris also run a good, cheap café.

Hostal Residencia Britz is a simple, no-nonsense 24-room place with questionable beds overlooking Plaza Nueva (S-2,400 ptas, D-3,900 ptas, Db-5,400 ptas, CC:VM, coin-op washing machine, elevator, Plaza Nueva y Gomerez 1, tel. & fax 95-822-3652).

Hostal Navarro Ramos is shiny and well-assembled but has almost no warmth or character (15 rooms, S-1,650 ptas, D-2,600 ptas, Db-4,000 ptas, Tb-5,400 ptas, Cuesta de Gomerez 21, tel. 95-825-0555, NSE).

Hostal Viena, run by English-speaking Austrian Irene ("ee-RAY-nay"), is on a quieter side street with basic backpacker-type rooms (S-2,500 ptas, Sb-4,000 ptas, D-4,000 ptas, Db-5,500–6,000 ptas, T-5,000 ptas, Tb-7,000 ptas, family rooms, CC:VM, air-con, Hospital de Santa Ana 2, 10 meters off Cuesta de Gomerez, tel. &

fax 95-822-1859, e-mail: austria@arrakis.es). Irene also manages the similar **Hotel Austria** nearby.

Hostal Gomerez is run by English-speaking Sigfrido Sanchez de León de Torres (who will explain to you how Spanish surnames work if you've got the time). Clean and basic and listed in nearly every country's student-travel guidebook, this is another fine cheapie (S-1,700 ptas, D-2,800 ptas, T-3,800 ptas, Q-4,400 ptas, laundry service, Cuesta de Gomerez 10, 1 floor up, tel. 95-822-4437).

Hostal Venecia is a perfect student pension run by kind Mary Carmen and Sergio. Rooms are basic, clean, and tastefully decorated (S-2,000 ptas, D-3,600 ptas, T-5,100 ptas, Cuesta de Gomerez 2, second floor, CC:VM, tel. 95-822-3987, NSE).

Sleeping near Plaza Carmen
Two blocks from the TI is the pleasant Plaza Carmen and the beginning of Calle Navas, a pedestrian street offering a couple of good values.

Hotel Residencia Lisboa, which overlooks Plaza Carmen opposite Granada's city hall, offers 28 basic but well-maintained rooms with modern bathrooms and friendly, helpful owners (S-2,600 ptas, Sb-3,900 ptas, D-3,900 ptas, Db-5,600 ptas, T-5,200 ptas, Tb-7,500 ptas, includes tax, no public rooms, CC:VM, elevator, Plaza de Carmen 27, tel. 95-822-1413, fax 95-822-1487).

Hotel Navas, a block down Calle Navas, is a modern, well-run, tour-friendly and business-class hotel with 49 spacious rooms (Sb-7,800 ptas, Db-11,600 ptas, Tb-15,000 ptas, breakfast buffet-800 ptas, CC:VMA, air-con, Calle Navas 24, tel. 95-822-5959, fax 95-822-7523, e-mail: alixares@jet.es, SE).

Sleeping near the Cathedral
Hotel Los Tilos offers comfortable rooms on the charming, traffic-free Bib-Rambla square behind the cathedral. Some rooms have balconies, and everyone's welcome to the fourth-floor view terrace overlooking a great café, shopping, and people-watching neighborhood (Sb-5,145 ptas, Db-7,875 ptas, Tb-10,630 ptas, includes tax, 20 percent discount with this book and cash, breakfast buffet-650 ptas or free in winter, CC:VM, air-con, elevator, Plaza Bib-Rambla 4, tel. 95-826-6712, fax 95-826-6801, e-mail: hoteltilos@jazzfree.com, friendly Jose-Maria SE).

Sleeping in or near the Alhambra
(zip code: 18009)
If you want to stay on or bordering the Alhambra grounds, three popular options are a kilometer up the hill from Plaza Nueva. The first two—famous, overpriced, and often booked up—are actually within the Alhambra grounds.

Parador Nacional San Francisco, offering 36 air-conditioned rooms in a converted 15th-century convent, is called Spain's premier parador (Sb-23,600–26,400 ptas, Db-29,500–33,000 ptas, breakfast-1,600 ptas, free parking, CC:VMA, Real de la Alhambra, tel. 95-822-1440, fax 95-822-2264, SE). You must book ahead several months to spend the night in this lavishly located, stodgy, classy, and historic place. Any peasant, however, can drop in for coffee or a drink.

Next to the parador, the elegant and cozy **Hotel America** rents 13 rooms (Sb-10,700 ptas, Db-17,400 ptas, Tb-24,000 ptas, includes breakfast and tax, CC:VMA, closed Nov–Feb, tel. 95-822-7471, fax 95-822-7470, e-mail: hamerica@moebius.es, SE). Book months in advance.

The ramshackle old **Hotel Washington Irving** is pleasant, spacious, and charmingly rundown. Not quite as romantically located, it offers the best reasonable beds in this prestigious neighborhood (Sb-10,000 ptas, Db-16,000 ptas, Tb-19,000 ptas, Qb-22,000 ptas, buffet breakfast-1,350 ptas, CC:VMA, elevator, Paseo del Generalife 2, tel. 95-822-7550, fax 95-822-7559, SE).

Eating in Granada

Traditionally, Granada bars serve a tapa plate free with any beer or wine ordered. Two well-chosen beers can actually end up being a light meal. In search of an edible memory? A local tradition, *tortilla Sacromonte*, is a spicy omelet with pig's brain and other organs.

In the Albaicín: The most interesting meals hide out deep in the Albaicín quarter. Two good squares are near the San Nicolás viewpoint. Plaza San Miguel el Bajo has no tourists…just a few charming restaurants and kids playing soccer (don't miss the view over the modern city a block away). Plaza Larga (ask any local or follow directions above, in Sights—Albaicín), within two blocks of the first three listings below, also has good eateries.

For fish, consider **El Ladrillo**, with outdoor tables on a peaceful square (Placeta de Fatima, just off Calle Pages), or **Ladrillo II**, with indoor dining and a more extensive menu (Calle Panaderos 35, tel. 95-829-2651). They each serve a popular *barca* (1,200-ptas "boatload" of mixed fried fish), a fishy feast that stuffs two to the gills. The smaller *canoa*, for 800 ptas, fills one adequately. (A *canoa* and a salad feed two.) Each restaurant is open daily (lunch from 12:00, dinner from 20:00). For fewer tourists, fewer fish, more village atmosphere, and great inexpensive food, eat at **Casa Torcuato** (closed Sun, 2 blocks beyond Plaza Larga on Placeta de Carniceros).

For a more romantic, candlelit setting with Alhambra views, splurge at **El Agua Casa de Vinos** (2,500-ptas 3-course meals—most with cheese fondue, daily from 20:00, also Wed–Sun 13:30–16:00, Placeta Aljibe de Trillo 7, halfway up Albaicín hill, below San Nicolás viewpoint, reservations necessary, tel. 95-822-4356).

Mirador de Morayma, with a similarly intimate, garden-view-mansion ambience, also requires reservations (3,000-ptas meals, Calle Pianista Garcia Carrillo 2, tel. 95-822-8290).

The Albaicín is peppered with lively tapas bars (as is Calle Elvira near Plaza Nueva).

Hippie Options on Calle Calderería Nueva: From Plaza Nueva walk two long blocks down Calle Elvira and turn right onto the wonderfully hip and Arabic-feeling Calderería Nueva, which leads uphill into the Albaicín. The street is lined with trendy *teterias*. These small tea shops, open all day, are good places to linger, chat, and imagine an America where marijuana was legal. Some are conservative and unmemorable, and others are painfully romantic, filled with incense, beaded cushions, live African music, and effervescent young hippies. They sell light meals and a world-wide range of teas. The plush **Kasbah** has good (canned) music.

Naturi Albaicín is a great vegetarian place with 1,000-ptas three-course meals featuring classy couscous (daily 13:00–16:00, 19:00–23:00, Calle Calderería Nueva 10, tel. 95-822-0627). Wafting up to the end of the teahouse street you'll find **Bar Restaurant Las Cuevas**—its rickety tables spilling onto the street—serving salads, pizzas, tapas, and wine to a fun family/bohemian crowd.

A block off Plaza Nueva, the cheap and easy **Bodega Castaneda** serves a fine *ensalada de casa* and baked potatoes with a fun variety of toppings (on Calle Elvira). For people-watching ambience, consider the many restaurants on Plaza Nueva, Bib-Rambla, or Plaza de los Tristes.

Transportation Connections—Granada

By train to: Barcelona (3/day, 12 hrs, handy night train), **Madrid** (3/day, 6–9 hrs, 1 night-train; or go via Córdoba and catch the AVE train), **Toledo** (3/day, 1/night, 9 hrs, transfer in Aranjuez), **Algeciras** (5/day, 5 hrs, possible transfer in Antequera), **Ronda** (4/day, 3 hrs), **Sevilla** (4/day, 3 hrs, transfer in Bobadilla; also 10 buses/day, 3 hrs), **Córdoba** (1/day, 4 hrs, transfer in Bobadilla; also 6 buses/day, 3 hrs), **Málaga** (2/day, 3.5 hrs, transfer in Bobadilla; also hrly buses, 2 hrs). Granada train info: tel. 90-224-0202.

By bus to: Nerja (2/day, 2 hrs, more frequent with transfer in Motril), **Sevilla** (10 buses/day, 3 hrs; plus trains, above), **Córdoba** (6 buses/day, 3 hrs; plus trains above), **Málaga** (hrly, 2 hrs; plus trains, above), **Algeciras** (6/day, 4.5 hrs), **La Línea/Gibraltar** (2/day, 5 hrs). Bus info: tel. 95-818-5480.

SEVILLA

This is the flamboyant city of Carmen and Don Juan, where bullfighting is still politically correct and where little girls still dream of growing up to become flamenco dancers. While Granada has the great Alhambra, and Córdoba the remarkable Mezquita, Sevilla has a soul. It's a great-to-be-alive-in kind of place.

Sevilla, the gateway to the New World in the 16th century, boomed when Spain did. Explorers such as Amerigo Vespucci and Ferdinand Magellan sailed from its great river harbor. In the 17th century, local artists such as Velázquez, Murillo, and Zurbarán made it a cultural center. Sevilla's Golden Age, with its New World riches, ended when the harbor silted up and the Spanish empire crumbled.

In the 19th century, Sevilla—the city of Carmen, Don Juan, flamenco, and bullfighting—was a big stop on the Romantic grand tour of Europe. To build on this tourism, Sevilla planned the World Exposition of 1929. Bad year. The Expo crashed with the stock market. In 1992 Sevilla got a second chance at a World's Fair. This Expo was a success, leaving the city with an impressive new infrastructure: new airport, train station, seven bridges, and the super AVE bullet train to Madrid. Next, Sevilla hopes to host the 2008 Olympics.

Today Spain's fourth-largest city (pop. 700,000) is Andalucía's leading city, buzzing with festivals, life, color, and castanets. James Michener wrote, "Sevilla doesn't *have* ambience, it *is* ambience." Sevilla has its share of impressive sights, but the real magic is the city itself, with its tangled Jewish Quarter, riveting flamenco shows, thriving bars, and teeming evening paseo.

Planning Your Time

If ever there was a big Spanish city to linger in, it's Sevilla. With three weeks in Iberia, spend two nights and a day in Sevilla. On a shorter trip, at least zip down here via the slick AVE train for a day trip from Madrid.

The sights—the cathedral and the Alcázar (about 3 hours) and a wander through the Santa Cruz district (1 hour)—are few and simple for a city of this size. You could spend half a day touring its other sights (described below). An evening is essential for the paseo and a flamenco show. Sevilla's Alcázar is closed on Monday. Bullfights are on most Sundays, April through October.

Córdoba (described at the end of this chapter) is worth a stopover if you're taking the AVE.

Orientation

For the tourist, this big city is small. Sevilla's major sights, including the lively Santa Cruz district and the Alcázar, surround the cathedral. The central boulevard, Avenida de la Constitución (with TI, banks, and a post office), zips right past the cathedral to Plaza Nueva (the shopping district). Nearly everything is within in easy walking distance. Taxis are reasonable (400 ptas minimum), friendly, and easy. The horse-and-buggy rides are popular (around 5,000 ptas for a 60-minute clip-clop).

Tourist Information

Handy TIs are in the center and at the train station. The central TI is a block toward the river from the cathedral (Mon–Fri 9:00–19:00, Sat 10:00–14:00, 15:00–19:00, Sun and festivals 10:00–14:00, Avenida de la Constitución 21, tel. 95-422-1404). The train station TI (Mon–Fri 9:00–20:00, Sat–Sun 10:00–14:00, tel. 95-453-7626) offers the same services. Ask for the city map (far better than the one in the promo city magazine); a current listing of sights, hours, and prices; and a schedule of bullfights. The free monthly events guide, *El Giraldillo*, in nearly readable Spanish, covers cultural events in all of Andalucía with a focus on Sevilla. If heading south, ask for the "Route of the White Towns" brochure and a Jerez map (100 ptas each). If arriving by bus or train, you'll find helpful TIs in or near your station (see "Arrival," below).

Arrival in Sevilla

By Train: Trains arrive at the sublime Santa Justa station (banks, ATMs, TI, luggage storage). The town center, marked by the ornate Giralda Cathedral bell tower (visible from the front of the station), is a 30-minute walk, 500-ptas taxi ride, or short bus ride away (bus #32 takes you to Plaza de la Encarnación in the center; pay the driver 125 ptas as you board).

By Bus: Sevilla's two major bus stations have information

Sevilla

1	HOSTALE MONREAL	**13**	HOTEL LA RABIDA
2	HOTEL DONA MARIA	**14**	HOP ON - HOP OFF TOUR BUS STOP
3	HOSTAL ARIAS & PENSION ALCAZAR	**15**	HOSTAL PICASSO
4	HOSTAL CORDOBA / GOOD SLEEP	**16**	HOTEL SEISES
5	HOSTAL SIERPES	**17**	HOTEL CASAS MERCADERES
6	HOSTAL SANCHEZ SABARIEGO	**18**	HOTEL INGLATERRA
7	HOTEL ALCAZAR	**19**	PLAZUELA SANTA ANA TABERNA PLAZUELA
8	HOTEL SIMON	**20**	RESTAURANTS RIO GRANDE, PRIMERA DEL & PUERTO
9	HOTEL FERNANDO III	**21**	REST. MARIA ANGELES & PUENTE ISABEL II
10	HOTEL LAS CASAS DE LA JUDERIA	**22**	REST. MESON DON RAIMUNDO
11	FLAMENCO LOS GALLOS		
12	FLAMENCO EL ARENAL		

offices, cafés, and luggage storage. The Prado de San Sebastian station covers Andalucía, Barcelona, and points east. To get downtown from the station, turn right on the major street Carlos V, then right again on Avenida de la Constitución (10-minute walk).

The Plaza de Armas station (near the river, opposite EXPO '92 site) serves southwest Spain, Madrid, Salamanca, and Portugal.

To get downtown from this station, head toward the angled brick apartment building and cross the busy Boulevard Expiración. Go a half-block up Calle Arjona to the stop for bus #C4, which goes into town (125 ptas, pay driver; get off at Puerta de Jerez, near main TI) or continue walking a couple more blocks to a TI at Calle Arjona #28 (near Isabel II Bridge, daily 8:00–20:30, tel. 95-450-5600). From here you can catch bus #C4 or walk 15 minutes into the center (following map from TI).

By Car: Driving in Sevilla is difficult and many cars are broken into. I'd pay to park in a garage. To enter Sevilla, follow signs to Centro Ciudad (city center) and drive along the river. If you need a brief place to park (to get set up), find a place near the cathedral and tower (leave your partner in the car). Paseo de Cristobal Colón has free street parking but is particularly theft-prone in the summer.

Helpful Hints

Sevilla Festivals: Sevilla's peak season is April and May. And it has two festival periods when the city is packed. All over Spain, Semana Santa (Holy Week—the week between Palm Sunday and Easter Sunday) is big, but it's biggest in Sevilla.Then, after taking enough time off to catch its communal breath, the city holds its April Fair, beginning a week or two after Easter. This is a celebration of all that's Andalusian, with plenty of eating, drinking, singing, and having fun. Book rooms in advance during festival times.

Telephone: A telephone office, Locutorio Público, has metered phone booths. Calls are slightly more expensive than calls made with Spanish phone cards, but you get a quiet setting with a seat (Mon–Fri 10:00–14:00, 17:00–21:00, Sat 10:00–14:00, in the passage at Sierpes 11, near intersection with Calle de Rafael Padura, tel. 95-422-6800).

Post Office: The post office is on Avenida de la Constitución 32, across from the cathedral (Mon–Fri 8:30–20:30, Sat 9:30–14:00).

Train Tickets: The downtown RENFE office gives out train schedules and sells train tickets (Mon–Fri 9:00–13:15, 16:00–19:00, CC:VMA, Calle Zaragoza 29, tel. 95-421-7998, you can't work here if you speak English). Many travel agencies sell train tickets for the same price as the train station (look for train sticker in agency window). Usit Student Travel is at Mateos Gago 2, just off the cathedral square.

Internet Access: Cibercenter is central (9:00–22:00, closed Sun, just off Reyes Católicos at Julio Cesar 8, tel. 95-422-8899).

Laundromat: Lavanderia Roma offers quick and economical drop-off service (Mon–Sat 9:30–13:30, 17:00–20:30, Sun 9:00–14:00, near Hotel La Rabida at Castela 2, tel. 95-421-0535). -

Sights—Sevilla

▲▲**Cathedral and Giralda Tower**—This is the third-largest church in Europe (after the Vatican's St. Peter's and London's St. Paul's) and the largest Gothic church anywhere. When they ripped down a mosque on the site in 1401, the Reconquista Christians bragged, "We'll build a cathedral so huge that anyone who sees it will take us for madmen." They built for 120 years. Even today, the descendants of those madmen proudly display an enlarged photocopy of their *Guinness Book of Records* letter certifying, "The cathedral with the largest area is: Santa Maria de la Sede in Sevilla, 126 meters long, 82 meters wide, and 30 meters high" (700 ptas, Mon–Sat 11:00–18:00, free on Sun 14:00–19:00, last entry 1 hour before closing). There's only one way in for tourists, on the west end. Here's a six-stop tour:

1. Giralda Tower exterior: Before going in, step across the street from the entry and look at the bell tower. Formerly a Moorish minaret from which Muslims were called to prayer, it became the cathedral's bell tower after the Reconquista. It's named for the 4,500-pound bronze statue symbolizing the Triumph of Faith that caps it and serves as a weathervane. In fact, the name of the tower comes from the Spanish word for turning (*girando*). In 1356 the original top of the tower fell. You're looking at a 16th-century Christian-built top with a ribbon of letters proclaiming, "This is stronger now, made in the name of God." Needing more strength than their bricks could provide for the lowest section of the tower, the Moors used Roman-cut stones. (At the end of your visit, when you leave the cathedral, look at the corner of the tower at ground level; you can actually read the Latin on one of the stones.)

Notice also the fine Moorish-style arch (it's actually 16th-century Christian—the banners are a give-away). Like so much other Moorish-looking art in town, it's done by Moorish artists under Christian rule. The relief above the door shows the Bible story of Jesus ridding the temple of the merchants…just a reminder to contemporary merchants that there will be no retail activity in the church. The plaque on the right is one of many scattered throughout town showing a place Cervantes—the great 16th-century Spanish writer—mentioned in his books. (In this case, the topic was pickpockets.) Crossing the chains that ring the church you have entered the protective sanctuary of this house of God (handy if you were a medieval criminal). The huge green doors are a bit of the surviving pre-1248 mosque—wood covered with bronze. As you go in, knock on wood.

2. Cloister: The cloister used to be the mosque's Court of the Naranjos (Oranges). 12th-century Muslims stopped at the fountain in the middle to wash their hands, face, and feet before praying. The lanes between the bricks were once irrigation streams—

a reminder that the Moors introduced irrigation to Iberia. The mosque was made of bricks; the church was made of stone.

3. Giralda Tower climb: From inside the church you can enter and climb the bell tower. Notice the beautiful Moorish simplicity as you climb to its top, 100 yards up, for a grand city view. The spiraling ramp is designed to accommodate riders on horseback, so find the entrance (just inside the church on the left, same hours and ticket as cathedral) and gallop up the 34 ramps for a Pegasus'-eye view of Sevilla.

4. Sanctuary: Hike through the sanctuary. Then sit down in front of the main chapel (*capilla mayor*) in the center. The incredible main altarpiece (*retablo mayor*) has 4,000 pounds of gold (imported in Spain's post-1492 "free trade" era). Sixty feet tall, with 36 scenes from the life of Jesus, it's composed of 1,500 figures.

5. Tomb of Columbus: Opposite the entry you'll see four kings carrying the tomb of Christopher Columbus. His pallbearers are the kings of Castile, Aragon, Leon, and Navarra (identify them by their team shirts). Columbus even traveled a lot posthumously. He was buried in Santo Domingo, then Cuba, and—when Cuba gained independence from Spain, around 1900—he sailed home to Sevilla. Are the remains actually his? Sevilla likes to think so.

6. Treasury: The treasury (*tesoro*) is scattered in several rooms at the exit. Find the Corona de la Virgen de los Reyes, Spain's most valuable crown, with 11,000 precious stones and the world's largest pearl, made into the torso of an angel. Also on display: relics (thorns, chunks of the cross, splinters from the Last Supper table) and some of the lavish Corpus Christi festival parade regalia.

The cathedral is wonderfully floodlit at night. A good place to view it is from the rooftop bar of the huge Hotel Dona Maria across the square (open in the summer, just step in and ride the elevator).

▲**Alcázar**—Originally a 10th-century palace built for the governors of the local Moorish state, this still functions as a royal palace ... the oldest still in use in Europe. What you see today is an extensive 14th-century remodel job, done by Moorish workmen (Mudejar) for the Christian King Pedro I. Pedro was nicknamed either "the Cruel" or "the Just," depending on which end of his sword you were on.

The Alcázar is a thought-provoking glimpse of a graceful Al-Andalus (Moorish) world that might have survived its Castilian conquerors—but didn't. But I have a tough time hanging any specific history on it. The throne room (#7, Salon de Embajadores) is most impressive. Sit here for a while and freeload off passing tours. The floor plan is intentionally confusing, part of the style designed to make experiencing the place more exciting and surprising.

With a grand collection of royal courts, halls, patios, and apartments, it's been a Spanish royal residence for 600 years (and maintains that function today). The upper floors are more European-style palatial. Seek out the Grand Hall, with its fine tapestries celebrating Emperor Charles V's 1535 victory in Tunis over the Turks. Trace your itinerary on the south-up tapestry map of Iberia and Northern Africa.

The garden is full of tropical flowers, wild cats, cool fountains, and hot tourists (700 ptas, Tue–Sat 9:30–19:00, Sun 9:00–17:00, off-season Tue–Sat 9:30–17:00, Sun 10:30–13:00, closed Mon, tel. 95-450-2323). The 400-ptas audio guide is tempting and tries hard. But sorry, there's no way to make this palace worth a flowery hour of hard-to-follow commentary.

Archivo de Indias, the archive of the documents of the discovery and conquest of the New World, could be fascinating, but little of importance is on display (old maps of Havana) and there's not a word of English (free, Mon–Fri 10:00–13:00, closed Sat–Sun, in Lonja Palace, across street from Alcázar).

▲▲**Barrio de Santa Cruz**—Only the tangled street plan survives from the days this was Sevilla's Jewish Quarter. The narrow streets—some with buildings so close they're called "kissing lanes"—were actually designed to maximize shade. Even today, locals claim the Barrio de Santa Cruz is three degrees cooler than the rest of the city. While its charm is trampled by tour groups in the mornings, this classy maze of lanes too narrow for cars, whitewashed houses with wrought-iron latticework, and *azulejo* tile-covered patios is a great refuge from the summer heat and bustle of Sevilla. The TI map has a helpful Barrio de Santa Cruz inset, but it's best to just get lost.

Forget about eating any of the oranges. They're bitter and used only to export to Britain where they're made into that awful marmalade you can't avoid in England's B&Bs.

Hospital de la Caridad—Between the river and the cathedral is the charity hospital founded by the original Don Juan. One of history's great hedonists, his party was crashed by a vision that tuned him on to his own mortality. He paid for the construction of this hospital for the poor and joined the Brotherhood of Charity. Peek into the fine courtyard. On the left, the chapel has some gruesome art (above both doors) illustrating that death is the great equalizer, and an altar sweet as only a Spaniard could enjoy (400 ptas, Mon–Sat, 9:00–13:30, 15:30–18:30, Sun 9:00–13:00, tel. 95-422-3232).

Torre del Oro/Naval Museum—Sevilla's historic riverside "golden tower" was the starting point and ending point for all shipping to the New World. It's named for the golden tiles that once covered it—not for all the New World booty that landed here. Since the 13th century it has been part of the city's fortifications, with a heavy chain draped across the river to protect the harbor. Today it houses a dreadful little naval museum with charts showing various knots, models of ships, dried fish, and an interesting mural of Sevilla in 1740 (100 ptas, free Tue, Tue–Fri 10:00–14:00, Sat–Sun 11:00–14:00, closed Mon).

Plaza Nueva/Calle Sierpes—While many tourists never get beyond the cathedral and Santa Cruz, it's important to wander west into the lively shopping center of town, which also happens to be the oldest part of town. Plaza Nueva—a 19th-century square facing the ornate city hall and serving as the starting point of half of Sevilla's city buses—features a statue of Ferdinand III, a local favorite because he freed Sevilla from the Moors in 1248. Wander down Calle Tetuan into Sevilla's pedestrian-zone shopping center—a delightful alternative to the suburban mall.

Take a right on Jovellanos street and notice the tiles. The Moors gave this region its characteristic glazed tiles...but without any figures. In later centuries, Christians decorated their tiles with social scenes. Either way, the tiles made sense because they kept buildings cooler in the summer heat.

Calle Sierpes has been a commercial center for 500 years. It's also the main street of the Holy Week processions when the street is packed and the balconies bulge with spectators.

Find Sagasta street and notice it has two names—the modern version and a medieval one: "Antiqua Calle de Gallegos" ("Ancient Street of the Gallacians"). With the Christian victory in 1248, the Muslims were given one month to evacuate. To consolidate Christian control here, settlers from the north were planted. This street was home to people from Gallacia.

Continue down Sagasta street to Plaza del Salvador and Sevilla's number-two church. This is the high ground where Phoenicians established the town. The Romans built their Forum here. But the shops are open, so scram (wedding dresses fill the lane behind the church).

Hop-on Hop-off Bus Tours—Two competing city bus tours leave from the curb near the golden tower, Torre del Oro (on the river). You'll see the buses parked with a salesperson handing out fliers. Each does about an hour-long swing through the city with a tape-recorded narration. The routes are heavy on Expo '29 and Expo '92 neighborhoods of little interest in '01. While the narration does its best, Sevilla is most interesting where buses can't go (1,500 ptas, departures daily 10:00–20:00).

Guided City Walks—Concepción Delgado, an enthusiastic teacher and a joy to listen to, takes small groups on English-language-only walks. Concepción has designed a fine two-hour introduction to the city sharing important insights the average visitor misses. This is two hours well-spent, even on a one-day visit (1,500 ptas, daily except Sun at 9:30 and 11:30, starting from Plaza Nueva, tel. 90-215-8226, www.seviruta.com). For other guides, contact the Guides Association of Sevilla (tel. 95-421-0037, e-mail: apitsevilla@alehop.com).

O 90-215-8226

University—Today's university was yesterday's *fabrica de tabacos* (tobacco factory), which employed 10,000 young female *cigareras*—including Bizet's Carmen. In the 18th century, it was the second-largest building in Spain, after El Escorial. Wander through its halls as you walk to the Plaza de España. The university's bustling café is a good place for cheap tapas, beer, wine, and conversation (Mon–Fri 8:00–21:00, Sat 9:00–13:00, closed Sun).

▲**Plaza de España**—The square, the surrounding buildings, and the nearby María Luisa Park are the remains of a 1929 fair that crashed with the U.S. stock market. This delightful area, the epitome of World's Fair–style building, is great for people-watching (especially at early-evening paseo time). Stroll through the park and along the canal. The highlight is what was the Spanish Pavilion. Its *azulejo* tiles (a trademark of Sevilla) show historic scenes and maps from every province of Spain (arranged in alphabetical order from Alava to Zaragoza). Climb to one of the balconies for a fine view.

▲**Museo de Bellas Artes**—Spain's second-best collection of paintings (after Madrid's Prado) has 50 Murillos and works by Zurbarán, El Greco, and Velázquez. Rather than exhausting, the museum—which fills a former convent—is pleasantly enjoyable (250 ptas, Wed–Sat 9:00–20:00, Sun 9:00–14:00, Tue 15:00–20:00, closed Mon, Plaza Museo 9, tel. 95-422-0790).

▲▲**Basilica Macarena**—Sevilla's Holy Week celebrations are Spain's grandest. During the week leading up to Easter, the city's packed with pilgrims witnessing 50 processions carrying about 100 religious floats. Get a feel for this event by visiting Basilica Macarena (built 1947) to see the two most impressive floats and the darling of Semana Santa, the Weeping Virgin (Virgen de la Macarena or La Esperanza, church free, museum-400 ptas, daily 9:30–13:00, 17:00–20:00, taxi to Puerta Macarena or bus #C4 from Puerta Jerez).

Grab a pew and study Mary, complete with crystal teardrops. She's like a 17th-century doll—with human hair and articulated arms, and even dressed with underclothes. Her beautiful expression—halfway between smiling and crying—is moving, in a Baroque way. Her weeping can be contagious—look around you. La Macarena is considered the protector of bullfighters (she's big in bullring chapels). In 1912 the bullfighter José Ortega—hoping for protection—gave her the five emerald brooches she wears. It worked for eight years…until he was gored to death in the ring. Filling a side chapel (on left) is "Christ of the Sentence" showing Jesus the day he was condemned (from 1654).

To see the floats that Mary and Jesus ride every Good Friday, head for the museum (through door, left of altar).

The three-ton float, slathered in gold leaf, shows a commotion of figures acting out the sentencing of Christ (who's placed in the front of this crowd). Pontius Pilate is about to wash his hands. Pilate's mother cries as a man reads the death sentence. Relays of 50 men carry this—only their feet showing under the drapes—as they shuffle through the streets from midnight to 14:00 each Good Friday. Shuffle upstairs for another perspective.

The weeping Mary—called La Esperanza—follows the Sentencing of Christ in the procession. Her smaller (1.5 ton) float, in the next room, seems all silver and candles—"strong enough to support the roof but slender enough to quiver in the soft night breeze." Mary has a wardrobe of three huge mantels (each displayed here) worn in successive years. The big green one is from 1900. Her six-pound gold crown/halo is from 1913. This float has a mesmerizing effect on the local crowds. They line up for hours, clapping, weeping, and throwing roses as it slowly works its way through Sevilla.

Before leaving, find the case of matador outfits (also upstairs) given to the church over the years by bullfighters in thanks for the protection they feel they received from La Macarena.

Outside, notice the best surviving bit of Sevilla's old walls. Originally Roman, what remains today is 12th-century Moorish, a reminder that for centuries, Sevilla was the capital of the Moorish kingdom in Iberia.

▲**Bullfights**—Spain's most artistic and traditional bullfighting is done in Sevilla's Plaza de Toros, with fights on most Sundays, Easter through October. Serious fights with adult matadors—called *corrida de toros*—are in April and October. Summer fights are usually *novillada*, with teenage novices doing the killing. (*Corrida de toros* seats range from 3,000–13,000 ptas; *novillada* seats are half that; get information at TI, your hotel, or tel. 95-422-8229.)

▲▲**Bullfight Museum**—Follow a two-language, 20-minute guided tour through the Plaza de Toros' strangely quiet and empty arena, its museum, and the chapel where the matador prays before the fight (500 ptas, daily 9:30–14:00, 15:00–19:00; or 10:00–15:00 on fight days). See the appendix for more on the dubious "art" of bullfighting.

Across Paseo de Cristobal Colón from the bullring, note the statue of **Carmen**. This beautiful girl from the cigar factory was the inspiration for Bizet's famous opera.

Nightlife
▲▲**Evening Paseo**—Sevilla is meant for strolling. The areas along either side of the river between the San Telmo and Isabel II bridges (Paseo de Cristobal Colón and Triana district; see "Eating," below), around Plaza Nueva, at Plaza de España, and throughout Barrio de Santa Cruz thrive every non-winter evening. Spend some time rafting through this sea of humanity. Savor the view of floodlit Sevilla by night from the far side of the river—perhaps over dinner.

▲▲▲**Flamenco**—This music-and-dance art form has its roots in the Gypsy and Moorish cultures. Even at a packaged "Flamenco Evening," sparks fly. The men do most of the flamboyant machine-gun footwork. The women concentrate on graceful turns and a smooth, shuffling step. Watch the musicians. Flamenco guitarists, with their lightning finger-roll strums, are among the best in the world. The intricate rhythms are set by castanets or the hand-clapping (called *palmas*) of those who aren't dancing at the moment. In the raspy-voiced wails of the singers you'll hear echoes of the Moslem call to prayer.

Like jazz, flamenco thrives on improvisation. Also like jazz, good flamenco is more than just technical proficiency. A singer or dancer with "soul" is said to have *duende*. Flamenco is a happening, with bystanders clapping along and egging on the dancers with whoops and shouts. Get into it.

For a tourist-oriented flamenco show, your hotel can get you nightclub show tickets. **Los Gallos** gives nightly two-hour shows at 21:00 and 23:30 (3,000-ptas ticket plus a 500-ptas drink, manager Nuria promises goose bumps and a 10 percent discount to those with this book—maximum 2 per book, Plaza de Santa Cruz 11, tel. 95-421-6981, reservations by fax: 95-421-3436). **El Arenal** also does a good show (4,300 ptas, shows at 21:30 and 23:30, near bullring at Calle Rodo 7, tel. 95-421-6492). **El Patio Sevillano** is more of a variety show (shows at 19:30 and 22:00, next to bullring at Paseo de Cristobal Colón, tel. 95-421-4120). These prepackaged shows can be a bit sterile, and an audience of tourists doesn't help. But I find both Los Gallos and El Arenal professional and riveting. El Arenal may have a slight edge on talent, but Los Gallos has a more intimate setting, with cushy rather than hard chairs—and it's cheaper.

The best flamenco erupts spontaneously in bars throughout the old town after midnight. Just follow your ears as you wander down Calle Betis, leading off Plaza de Cuba across the bridge. The **Lo Nuestro** and **Rejoneo** bars are local favorites for impromptu flamenco (at Calle Betis 30 and 32).

In the Barrio Santa Cruz, a mix of students and tourists gathers in **La Carboneria** to hear free flamenco—usually Thursdays after 23:00 (Levies 10, unsigned door, music only, no dancing).

Shopping

The popular pedestrian streets Sierpes, Tetuan, and Valázquez and the surrounding lanes near Plaza Nueva are packed with people and shops. Nearby is Sevilla's top department store, El Corte Inglés. While small shops close between 13:30 and 16:00 or 17:00, big ones like El Corte Inglés stay open (and air-conditioned) right through the siesta. It has a supermarket downstairs and a good but expensive restaurant (Mon–Sat 10:00–21:30, closed Sun). **Flea**

markets hop on Thursday on Calle La Feria and Sunday along Alameda de Hércules.

Sleeping in Sevilla
(180 ptas = about $1, country code: 34, zip code: 41004)
Sleep Code: **S** = Single, **D** = Double/Twin, **T** = Triple, **Q** = Quad, **b** = bathroom, **t** = toilet only, **s** = shower only, **CC** = Credit Card (Visa, MasterCard, Amex), **SE** = Speaks English, **NSE** = No English.

All of my listings are centrally located and within a five-minute walk of the cathedral. The first ones are near the charming but touristy Santa Cruz neighborhood. The last group is just as central but closer to the river, across the boulevard in a more workaday, less touristy zone. See map on page 138.

Room rates as much as double during the two Sevilla fiestas (roughly the week before Easter and a week or so after Easter). In general, the busiest and most expensive months are April, May, September, and October. Hotels put rooms on the discounted push list in July and August. Prices rarely include the 7 percent IVA tax. A price range indicates low- to high-season prices (but I have not listed festival prices). Hoteliers speak enough English. Skip ground-floor rooms (because of noise) and ask for upper floors (*piso alto*). Many of these hotels are reportedly unreliable for reservations, particularly the small, family *pensiónes* (as opposed to normal big hotels). Always telephone to reconfirm what you think is a reservation.

Sleeping near the Santa Cruz Neighborhood
Off Calle Santa Maria la Blanca: The **Hostal Córdoba** has 12 tidy, quiet, air-conditioned rooms, solid modern furniture, and a showpiece plant-filled courtyard (S-4,000 ptas, Sb-5,000 ptas, D-6,500 ptas, Db-7,500 ptas, a tiny lane off Calle Santa Maria la Blanca, Farnesio 12, tel. 95-422-7498).

Hostal Good Sleep is a homey, backpacker-type place filled with cheery tiles, caged birds, family ambience, and 20 neon-lit and cheaply furnished rooms (S-2,000 ptas, D-4,000 ptas, Db-5,000 ptas, T-5,000 ptas, Tb-6,000 ptas, CC:VM, laundry service, fans in rooms, birds wake at 8:00, welcoming rooftop terrace for picnicking and socializing, next to Hostal Córdoba at Farnesio 8, tel. 95-421-7492, friendly Rene and Myriam speak English). *our hotel*

Off Plaza Santa Maria: The **Hotel Las Casas de la Juderia** has quiet, elegant rooms and suites tastefully decorated with hardwood floors and a Spanish flair. The rooms surround a series of peaceful courtyards. This is a romantic splurge and a fine value (Sb-11,000–13,000 ptas, Qb-16,000–19,500 ptas, Db suite-17,500–21,000 ptas, Qb suite-25,000–29,000 ptas, extra bed-5,000 ptas; low-season prices—July, Aug, late-Nov–Feb—are discounted a further 10 percent to those with this book who ask; CC:VMA, great breakfast, air-con, elevator, on small traffic-free lane off Plaza Santa Maria, Callejon de Dos Hermanas 7, tel. 95-441-5150, fax 95-442-2170, e-mail: juderia@zoom.es, SE).

Hotel Fernando III is cavernous, comfortable, modern, and popular with groups (Db-17,000 ptas, CC:VMA, mostly twin beds—all with plastic sheets, air-con, rooftop pool, garage, elevator, San Jose 21, just off Plaza Santa Maria, tel. 95-421-7307, fax 95-422-0246, e-mail: fernando3@altur.com).

On Corral del Rey: Walking from the cathedral square straight up Argote de Molina (200 meters) you come to **Hostal Sierpes**, a sprawling, 40-room place with fine lounges and a big, cool, airy courtyard. Rooms are small and basic but air-conditioned, with shiny new bathrooms. When you arrive, show this book to the hardworking and ever-serious Melquiades for a 15 percent discount (Sb-4,200–5,400 ptas, Db-8,000 ptas, Tb-10,500 ptas, CC:VMA, some air-con, quieter rooms upstairs, Corral del Rey 22, tel. 95-422-4948, fax 95-421-2107).

Across the street, **Hostal Sanchez Sabariego** is a homier, 10-room place with a folksy garden courtyard. The higher floors are most peaceful and air-conditioned (S-3,000 ptas, Db-8,000 ptas, Corral del Rey 23, tel. 95-421-4470, friendly Macu speaks English and does everything).

Near Old Bus Station: The **Hotel Alcázar**, on the big and busy Menendez y Pelayo boulevard, is air-conditioned, with lavish, shiny public areas and everything you'd find in a modern, big-city American hotel (Sb-11,350 ptas, Db-15,700 ptas, includes breakfast, CC:VMA, elevator, Menendez y Pelayo 10, tel. 95-441-2011, fax 95-442-1659, SE). Ask for a quiet room off the street.

Sleeping near the Alcázar

In a quiet eddy of lanes on the side of the Alcázar nearest the river, **Hostal Arias** is cool, clean, and no-nonsense. Its 14 rooms are air-conditioned, comfortable, and come equipped with medieval disco-balls (Sb-5,500 ptas, Db-7,200 ptas, Tb-11,000 ptas, CC:VMA, Calle Mariana de Pineda 9, tel. 95-422-6840, fax 95-421-8389, e-mail: riena@arrakis.es, helpful manager Manuel Reina SE). Around the corner, **Pensión Alcázar** rents eight pleasant rooms. The lower rooms have ceiling fans, the three top rooms are air-conditioned with terraces (Db-7,500 ptas, extra bed-2,000 ptas, Qb-11,000 ptas, Dean Miranda 12, tel. 95-422-8457, SE). **Hostal Picasso** is a fresh new place painted happily throughout with 17 fine rooms (D-6,800 ptas, Db-7,500 ptas, extra bed-3,200 ptas, 10 percent off with this book, CC:VMA, air-con, Calle San Gregorio 1, tel. & fax 95-421-0864, e-mail: hpicasso@arrakis.es, Rocio SE).

Hotel Residencia Doña María tries to be elegant but is just big and stuffy. Facing the cathedral on Plaza Vírgen de los Reyes, it brags that it's "very modern but furnished in an ancient style," with four-poster beds, armoires, and a rooftop swimming pool with a view of Giralda Tower (Sb-8,000–11,000 ptas, Db-14,000–19,000 ptas, CC:VMA, elevator, Don Remondo 19, tel. 95-422-4990, fax 95-421-9546, e-mail: reservas@hdmaria.com).

Hotel Seises—a modern business-class place spliced into the tangled old town—offers a fresh and spacious reprieve for anyone ready for good old contemporary luxury. Its rooftop garden comes with a pool and a great cathedral view (Sb-14,000–20,000 ptas, Db-18,000–27,000 ptas, extra bed-4,000 ptas, lower prices in July, Aug, and winter, CC:VMA, elevator, air-con, 2 blocks northwest of the cathedral at Segovias 6, tel. 95-422-9495, fax 95-422-4334, e-mail: seises@jet.es).

Hotel Las Casas de los Mercaderes feels like the Hotel Casas de la Juderia because it's run by the same people. Traditionally Andalusian in a modern way with all the comforts, it's beautifully located between the cathedral and the best shopping streets (Db-14,500–17,500 ptas, extra bed-3,500 ptas, CC:VMA, air-con, elevator, 47 rooms, Calle Alvarez Quintero 9, tel. 95-422-5858, fax 95-422-9884, e-mail: mercaderes@zoon.es).

Hotel Inglaterra, a big four-star place on the no-nonsense Plaza Nueva, is big and modern, with all the professional comforts (high season: April–May, low season: rest of year, Sb-12,600–17,600 ptas, Db-19,000–23,000 ptas, extra bed-5,000 ptas, CC:VMA, air-con, elevator, Plaza Nueva 7, tel. 95-422-4970, fax 95-456-1336, e-mail: hotelinglaterra@svq.servicom.es).

Sleeping West of Avenida de la Constitución

Hotel Simón is a classic 18th-century mansion with a faded-elegant courtyard. Room quality varies; many are decorated with period furniture under high ceilings. On weekends, avoid rooms on the noisy street (Sb-6,500–8,000 ptas, Db-9,500–12,500 ptas, extra person-3,000 ptas, high prices are only for April–May, CC:VMA, air-con, a block west of the cathedral at Calle García de Vinuesa 19, tel. 95-422-6660, fax 95-456-2241, e-mail: hotel-simon@jet.es).

Hotel La Rabida has 100 business-class rooms surrounding a spacious lobby, a delightful garden courtyard, and a classy breakfast room (Sb-6,300 ptas, Db-9,600 ptas, Tb-12,000 ptas, CC:VMA, 10 percent discount with this book, air-con, elevators, Castelar 24, tel. 95-422-0960, fax 95-422-4375, hotel-rabida @sol.com, SE). From the cathedral, go down Calle García de Vinuesa and turn right on Calle Castelar.

Eating in Sevilla

Do the tapa tango, using the "Tapa Tips" from this book's introduction. For an Anadalusian twist, try *salmorejo*, Córdoba-style super-thick gazpacho. Wash down your tapas with *fino* (dry sherry) or, more refreshing, *tinto de Verano* (literally "summer" red), an Andalusian red wine with soda, like a light sangria.

Eating in Triana across the River

South of the river between the San Telmo and Isabel II bridges is the colorful Triana District—filled with fine and fun eateries. The riverside street, Calle Betis (the Roman name for the Guadalquivir River), is classier than Calle Pureza, a block inland, and best for tapas bars. Before sitting down, walk to the Santa Ana church (midway between the bridges) to check out two great tapas bars. Each has tables spilling into the street and square in the shadow of the floodlit church spire. It feels like the whole neighborhood is out celebrating. **Taberna la Plazuela**, on the square, is bigger with more of a menu (Plazuela de Santa Ana, tel. 95-427-0471, daily) and **Bar Santa Ana** is draped in bullfighting memorabilia with a fun list of tapas (Pureza 82, tel. 95-427-2102). The Pena Sevillista de Triana (at Pureza 61) is Triana's soccer fans' club-house (satellite TV for all the best matches and bullfights—wild on weekend soccer nights).

For a riverside restaurant dinner (with properly attired waiters and full menus as opposed to tapas), consider these three (each are neighbors on Calle Betis, next to the San Telmo bridge): **Río Grande** is the place for a candlelight-fancy meal (daily 13:00–16:00, 20:00–24:00, tel. 95-427-8371). Its terrace is less expensive and more casual. Next door, **Restaurante La Primera Del** (Thu–Tue 11:30–17:00, 19:30–24:00, closed Wed, tel. 95-427-6918) and **Restaurante El Puerto** (closed Mon) serve about the same thing with about the same view for half the price.

At the Isabel II bridge, in the yellow bridge tower, **Restaurante Maria Angeles** offers romantic dining atop the tower (daily 3-course *menus* from around 2,000 ptas) and cheaper, more casual tables filling the sidewalk along the riverside (fried fish *raciónes*, daily 13:00–17:00, 19:30–24:00, Puente de Isabel II, tel. 95-433-7498).

Eating in the Santa Cruz Area

Plenty of atmospheric-but-touristy restaurants fill the old quarter near the cathedral and along Calle Santa Maria la Blanca.

For tapas, the Barrio de Santa Cruz is trendy, touristic, and *romántico*. From the cathedral, walk up Mateos Gago where several classic old bars now keep tourists and locals well-fed and watered. **Cerveceria Giralda** (Mateos Gago 1), a standard meeting place for locals, is famous for its fine tapas (see the award it won at the Spanish tapas convention posted on the wall). Turn right off Mateos Gago at Meson del Moro which leads to **La Teresas**, a fine and characteristic little bar draped in fun photos (including one of Ted Kennedy sandwiched between matadors and local intellectuals) and serving good tapas from a user-friendly menu (Santa Teresa 2, tel. 95-421-3069). Just past La Teresas is the artist Murillo's house (free when open and a good example of a local courtyard). The lane continues past a convent of cloistered nuns (notice the spiked window) to the most romantic little square in Santa Cruz (where you'll find the Las Gallos flamenco club).

Restaurante Meson Don Raimundo, proudly serving traditional Andalusian cuisine drenched in Andalusian ambience in a museum-like building, is a good choice for a full meal in a fancy indoor restaurant (2,800-ptas 3-course *menu*, CC:VMA, daily 12:30–17:00, 19:30–24:00, air-con, 2 blocks northwest of cathedral at Argote de Molina 26, tel. 95-422-3355).

Eating along Calle García de Vinuesa

This street (across from the cathedral) has several colorful and cheap tapas places. On the corner, the slick and chrome **Horno San Buenaventura** is handy for coffee and dessert (tapas are posted on the pillar). Farther down the street you'll find **Bodega Morales** (#11, closed Sun, tel. 95-422-1242). Go in the back section to munch tiny sandwiches (*montaditos*) and tapas and sip wine among huge kegs. Farther along is a **fried-fish joint** (*pescado frito*) that also sells homemade potato chips, and the lonely but potent **Bodegas Diaz Salazar**. More restaurants, tapas bars, and a recommended flamenco bar (**El Arenal** at Calle Rodo 7) are in the streets just beyond.

Picnickers forage at the covered fish-and-produce **Mercado del Arenal** (with a small café/bar for breakfast inside, Mon–Sat 9:00–13:00, closed Sun, on Calle Pastor y Landero at Calle Arenal, just beyond bullring).

Transportation Connections—Sevilla

To: Madrid (2.5 hrs by AVE express train, from 7:00–23:00 departures are on the hour—except 13:00, 1,500-ptas reservation fee with railpass; 10 buses/day for 2,700 ptas), **Córdoba** (15 trains/day, 1.5 hrs; 50 min by speedy AVE; 10 buses/day, 2 hrs), **Málaga** (5 trains/day, 3 hrs; 10 buses/day, 3 hrs), **Ronda** (3 trains/day, 3 hrs, change at Bobadilla; 5 buses/day, 3 hrs), **Tarifa** (4 buses/day, 3 hrs), **La Línea/Gibraltar** (4 buses/day, 4 hrs), **Granada** (4 trains/day, 3 hrs; 8 buses/day, 4 hrs), **Arcos** (2 buses/day, 2 hrs), **Jerez** (7 buses/day, 2 hrs), **Barcelona** (4 trains/day, 10–12 hrs), **Algeciras** (3 trains/day, 5 hrs, change at Bobadilla; 10 buses/day, 4 hrs), **Lisbon** (2 buses most days, 10 hrs, 4,500 ptas; or AVE to Madrid and night train). Train info: tel. 90-224-0202. Bus info: tel. 95-490-8040.

For driving ideas south into Andalucía and west into Portugal's Algarve, see those chapters.

From Sevilla to Portugal's Algarve

By bus to: Tavira (2 buses/day, 3.5 hrs, departs Sevilla's Plaza de Armas station, easy transfer in Huelva; 1 direct bus runs 4 mornings/week, 3 hrs, no transfer, see below).

By bus/train to Lagos/Salema: The direct bus between Lagos and Sevilla is a godsend (Thu, Fri, Sat, Sun, 5 hrs, 2,600 ptas). The bus departs from Sevilla's Plaza de Armas bus station and arrives at the Lagos bus station, with stops at Algarve towns such as Tavira. From Lagos catch a one-hour bus to Salema. On days there's no bus to Lagos, catch the daily bus to Faro (3 hrs). Tel. 95-490-8040 or 95-490-1160.

Other than the direct bus, it's a long day of bus, ferry, and train rides: Sevilla–Ayamonte bus (4/day from Plaza de Armas station, 2.5 hrs) to Ayamonte at the border, ferry to Vila Real in Portugal (17/day, 15 min), train to Lagos (3/day, more with transfer in Tunes, 4 hrs). Get an early start.

Taking the train from Sevilla to the Algarve is slower and requires a transfer to a bus at Huelva (Sevilla–Huelva: 4 trains/day, 90 min; Huelva–Ayamonte: 6 buses/day, 1 hr, Huelva bus station tel. 95-125-6900). The Sevilla–Ayamonte bus (almost hrly, none on Sun) is preferable, cheap, direct, and less hassle. In Vila Real the train station, the buses, and the ferry dock are clustered together. Saturdays and Sundays are dead in Vila Real. Ayamonte is much livelier and tourist-friendly by comparison.

Small groups with more money than time can ride a taxi from Sevilla to Tavira.

CÓRDOBA

Córdoba is one of Spain's three big Moorish cities. Even though it was the center of Moorish civilization in Spain for 300 years (and an important Roman city), Sevilla and Granada are far more interesting. Córdoba has a famous mosque surrounded by the colorful Jewish quarter, and that's it.

The **Mezquita** (meh-SKEET-ah) was the largest Islamic mosque in its day. Today you can wander past its ramshackle "patio of oranges" and into the cavernous 1,200-year-old building. Grab the English pamphlet at the door (which predictably describes the church history much better than the mosque's). The interior is a moody world of 800 rose- and blue-marble columns and as many Moorish arches. If a guide told me I was in the basement of something important, I'd believe him. The center was gutted to make room for an also-huge Renaissance cathedral (900 ptas, Mon–Sat 10:00–19:00, Sun 14:00–19:00, tel. 95-747-0512). The mosque is near the TI (Mon–Fri 9:30–20:00, Sat 10:00–20:00, Sun 10:00–14:00, closes early in winter, tel. 95-747-1235). The TI also has a handy kiosk at the train station (with a room-finding service).

From the station to the mosque it's a 400-ptas taxi ride or a pleasant 30-minute walk (left on Avenida de America, right on Avenida del Gran Capitan, which becomes a pedestrian zone; when it ends ask someone "*¿Dónde está Mezquita?*" and you'll be directed downhill through the whitewashed old Jewish Quarter).

Sleeping and Eating in Córdoba: Two comfortable, air-conditioned, and expensive hotels are located within a five-minute walk of the station. **Hotel Gran Capitan** is closer (Db-20,000 ptas, Avenida de America 5, tel. 95-747-0250, fax 95-747-4643). **Hotel Sol los Gallos** is cheaper and has a pool (Db-12,250 ptas, Avenida de Medina Azahara 7, tel. 95-723-5500, fax 95-723-1636). For food, try **Taverna Salinas** (Tendidores 3, near mosque).

Transportation Connections—Córdoba

Now that Córdoba is on the slick AVE train line, it's an easy stopover between **Madrid** and **Sevilla** (15 trains/day, about 1 hour from each city, reservations required on all AVE trains).

By bus to: Granada (9/day, 3 hrs), **Málaga** (5/day, 3 hrs), **Algeciras** (2/day, 6 hrs).

ANDALUCÍA'S WHITE HILL TOWNS

Just as the American image of Germany is Bavaria, the Yankee dream of Spain is Andalucía. This is the home of bullfights, flamenco, gazpacho, pristine-if-dusty whitewashed hill towns, and glamorous Mediterranean resorts. The big cities of Andalucía (Granada, Sevilla, and Córdoba) and the Costa del Sol are covered in separate chapters. This chapter explores its hill-town highlights.

The Route of the White Towns, Andalucía's charm bracelet of cute towns, gives you wonderfully untouched Spanish culture. Spend a night in the romantic queen of the white towns, Arcos de la Frontera. Towns with "de la Frontera" in their names were established on the front line of the centuries-long fight to recapture Spain from the Muslims, who were slowly pushed back into Africa. The hill towns, no longer strategic, no longer on any frontier, are now just passing time peacefully. Join them. Nearby, the city of Jerez is worth a peek to see its famous horses in action and for a sherry bodega tour.

Planning Your Time

While the towns can be (and often are) accessed from the Costa del Sol resorts via Ronda, Arcos makes the best home base. Arcos, near Jerez and close to interesting smaller towns, is conveniently situated halfway between Sevilla and Tarifa.

On a three-week Iberian vacation, the region is worth two nights and two days sandwiched between Sevilla and Tarifa. Spend both those nights in Arcos. See Jerez (horses and sherry) on your way in or out, spend a day hopping from town to town (Grazalema and Zahara, at a minimum) in the more remote interior, and enjoy Arcos early and late in the day.

Without a car you might keep things simple and focus only on Arcos and Jerez (both well served by public buses). Spring and

Andalucía

O KM 50
O MI 20

TO CORDOBA

TO AYAMONTE & PORTUGAL

SEVILLA

AGUILAR

PUENTE GENIL

ESTEPA

← FREEWAY A·4

334

ESPAÑA • MADRID
FR.
PORT.

GRAZALEMA

ZAHARA

382

TEBA

CHORRO GORGE

382

ARCOS D.L.F.

344

SETENIL

CARRA-TRACA

JEREZ D.L.F.

UBRIQUE

PILETA CAVES

RONDA

TO MALAGA

CÁDIZ

S. PEDRO

MARBELLA

GAUCIN

ESTE-PONA

340

VEJER D.L.F.

JIMENA D.L.F.

COSTA DEL SOL

LA LINEA

340

M E D.

ALGE-CIRAS

GIBRALTAR (U.K.)

S E A

TARIFA

ATLANTIC

TANGIER

CEUTA (SPAIN)

OCEAN

MOROCCO

DCH.

fall are high season throughout this area. In summer you'll find empty hotels and no crowds.

ARCOS DE LA FRONTERA

Arcos, smothering its hilltop and tumbling down all sides like an oversized blanket, is larger than the other Andalusian hill towns but equally atmospheric. The old center is a labyrinthine wonderland, a photographer's feast. Viewpoint-hop through town. Feel the wind funnel through the narrow streets as cars inch around tight corners. Join the kids' soccer game on the churchyard patio.

There are two towns: the fairy-tale old town and the fun-loving lower or new town. Check out the pleasant evening paseo and café scene, best at Plaza España and the adjacent Paseo Andalucía, the base of the hill where the new and old towns meet. Enjoy the moonlit view from the main square in the old town.

Though it tries, Arcos doesn't have much to offer other than its basic whitewashed self. The locally produced English guide-book on Arcos waxes poetic and at length about very little. Since the church is open until early evening and the town market is open in the morning, you can arrive late and leave early.

Orientation

Tourist Information: The TI, on the main square across from the parador, is helpful and loaded with information, including bus schedules (Mon–Fri 10:00–14:00, 17:30–19:30, Sat 10:00–14:00, 17:00–18:30, Sun 10:30–13:30, no change Oct–Feb except Mon–Fri 17:00–19:00, Plaza del Cabildo, tel. 95-670-2264, fax 95-670-0900).

Walking Tours: Year-round the TI organizes two different one-hour walking tours: "Old Town" and "Patios of Arcos." They leave from the main square, are given in Spanish and/or English, and cost 400 ptas. Old-town walks include the church and general history (Mon–Fri 10:30 and 17:00, Sat 10:30 only, 1.5 hrs). Patio walks get you into private courtyards and cover lifestyles and Moorish influences (Mon–Sat 12:00 and 18:30, 2 hrs). On Sunday they do only one tour (at 12:30, a combo of both). Groups can hire a private guide for any walk any time (7,000 ptas).

Arrival in Arcos: The bus station is on Calle Corregidores. To get to the old town, catch a bus marked "*Centro*" (2/hrly, 105 ptas), hop a taxi (400 ptas), or take a 15-minute uphill walk. As you leave the station, turn left on Corregidores, angle left uphill, cross the four-way intersection, angle right uphill, and take Muñoz Vazquez up into town. Go up the stairs by the church to the main square and TI.

Helpful Hints: Before you go, visit www.andalucia.com for information on hotels, festivals, museums, nightlife, and sports in the region. Arcos' little post office is a few doors away from Hotel Los Olivos (Mon–Fri 8:30–14:30, Sat 9:30–13:00, Paseo Boliches 26). Parking is available in Arcos' main square (ticket from machine 110 ptas/hr, only necessary 9:30–14:00 and 18:00–21:00, can get half-price ticket from old-town hotels, free Sat afternoon and all day Sun).

Self-Guided Tour of the Old Town

Avoid this walk during the midday siesta.

1. Plaza del Cabildo: Stand at the viewpoint opposite the church on the town's main square. Survey the square, which in the old days doubled as a bullring: On your right is the parador, a former palace of the governor. On your left is the **city hall** (with the TI), below the 11th-century Moorish **castle** where Ferdinand and Isabel met to plan the Reconquista (closed to the public). Directly in front is the Church of Santa Maria. Notice the fine but unfin-ished **church bell tower**. The old one fell in the earthquake of

Arcos de la Frontera

1755 (famous for destroying Lisbon). The new baroque replacement was intended to be the tallest in Andalucía after Sevilla's—but money ran out. It looks like someone lives on an upper floor. They do. You can go through the brown door on the right and climb up to a living room hung with bell-ringing ropes and ask the church guardian if you can go to the top of the tower. He may give you the key (tip 100 ptas per person), or he may say "scram."

Enjoy the square's viewpoint. The people of Arcos boast that only they see the backs of the birds as they fly. Ponder the parador's erosion concerns, orderly orange groves, flower-filled greenhouses, and fine views toward Morocco. Belly up to the railing and look down—the town's suicide departure point.

2. Inside the Church of Santa Maria: After Arcos was retaken from the Moors in the 13th century, this church was built—atop a mosque. The fine Renaissance **high altar** covers up a Muslim prayer niche surviving from the older mosque. The altar shows God with a globe in his hand on top and scenes from the life of Jesus on the right and from Mary's on the left. While most of the architecture is Gothic, the elaborate **chapels** are decorated Baroque and rococo. The ornate statues are used in the Holy Week processions. In the choir notice the historic **organ** (1,500 pipes, from 1789). Sniff out the "incorruptible body" of St. Felix (a third-century martyr). Rome sent it in 1764 after recognizing this church as the most important in Arcos. Study the finely carved stalls and, if you're tired, flip up a seat to see how priests used to rest and "stand" at the same time. In the back of the church, under a huge fresco of St. Christopher (carrying his staff and baby Jesus), is a giant votive candle from 1767 (150 ptas, Mon–Fri 10:00–13:00, 15:30–18:30, Sat 10:00–13:00, closed Sun).

3. Church Exterior: Circle clockwise around the church. Down four steps find the third-century **Roman votive altar** with a carving of the palm tree of life. While the Romans didn't build this high, they did have a town and temple below Arcos. This was found in the foundation of the old Moorish mosque that stood here before the first church was built.

Down a few more steps you come to the **main entrance** (west portal) of the church—open for worship every evening at 19:00 and Sundays. This is a fine example of Plateresque Gothic (Spain's last and most ornate kind of Gothic), not counting the minaret incorporated into the wall. In the pavement notice the 15th-century **magic circle**: 12 red and 12 white stones—the white ones with various constellations marked. When a child came to the church to be baptized, the parents would stop here first for a good Christian exorcism. The exorcist would stand inside the protective circle and cleanse the baby of any evil spirits. While locals no longer use this (and a modern rain drain now marks the center), Sufis from a sect of Islam still come here in a kind of magical pilgrimage.

Continue around the church to the intersection below the **flying buttresses**. These buttresses were built to shore up the church when it was wounded by an earthquake in 1699. Thanks to this, the church survived the bigger earthquake of 1755. Look at the arches supporting the houses downhill on the left. All over town, arches support earthquake-damaged structures. The spiky security grill over the window above protected cloistered nuns when this building was a convent. Sr. Gonzalez Oca's tiny barbershop at the corner has some exciting posters of bulls running Pamplona-style through the streets of Arcos during Holy Week—an American from the nearby Navy base at Rota was killed here by a bull in 1994. (Sr. Gonzalez Oca is happy to show off his posters; drop in and say, "*Hola*." Need a haircut? 800 ptas.) Continuing along under the buttresses, notice the scratches of innumerable car mirrors on each wall (and be glad you're walking).

4. From the Church to the Market: Completing your circle around the church, turn left under more earthquake-damaged arches and walk down the bright white Calle Escribanos. From now until the end of this walk you're going basically straight until you come to the town's second big church (St. Peter's). After a block you hit Plaza Boticas. At the end of the street on your left is the finest restaurant in town (El Convento—see "Eating," below). On your right is the last remaining **convent** in Arcos. Notice the no-nunsense window grills above, with tiny peepholes for the cloistered nuns. Step into the lobby under the fine portico to find a one-way mirror and a blind spinning cupboard. Push the buzzer and one of the eight sisters inside will spin some boxes of freshly baked cookies for you to consider buying (700 ptas). If you ask for *magdalenas*, bags of cupcakes will swing around (250 ptas). These are traditional goodies made from completely natural ingredients (daily 8:30–14:30, 17:00–19:00). Buy some cupcakes to support their church work and give them to kids as you complete your walk.

The covered **market** (*mercado*) at the bottom of the plaza resides in an unfinished church. Notice the half-a-church wall at the entry. This was being built for the Jesuits, but construction stopped in 1767 when King Charles III, tired of the Jesuit appetite for politics, expelled the order from Spain. (Jesuits encountered no such tough treatment in South America.) The market is closed on Sunday and on Monday—when you rest on Sunday there's no produce, fish, or meat ready for Monday. Poke inside (public WC).

5. From the Market to the Church of St. Peter: Continue straight (passing the market on your right) down Calle Boticas. Peek into private **patios**. These wonderful, cool-tiled courtyards filled with plants, pools, furniture, and happy family activities are typical of Arcos (and featured on the TI's "Patios" walks).

Look for Las Doce Campanas bakery, which sells traditional *sultana* cookies. These big, dry macaroons (named for sultans) go back to Moorish times. At the next corner, squint back above the bakery to the corner of the tiled rooftop. The tiny mask was placed here to scare evil spirits from the house. This is Arcos' last surviving mask from a tradition that lasted until the mid-19th century.

At the next intersection notice the **ancient columns** on each corner. All over town these columns, many actually Roman (appropriated from their ancient settlement at the foot of the hill), were put up to protect buildings from reckless donkey carts.

As you walk down the next block, notice that the walls are scooped out on either side of the windows—a reminder of the days when women stayed inside but wanted the best possible view of any people action in the streets.

At the old facade of San Miguel, duck right into the first of two **courtyards**. Retired men hang out here and play poker and dominoes. See the historic photos on the walls of the second courtyard.

Just beyond is Arcos' second church, **St. Peter's**. It really is the second church, having had an extended battle with Santa Maria for papal recognition as the leading church in Arcos. When the pope finally recognized Santa Maria, parishioners from St. Peter's even changed their prayers. Rather than say "Maria," they prayed "Saint Peter, mother of God."

In the cool of the evening, the tiny **square** in front of the church—about the only flat piece of pavement around—serves as the old-town soccer field for neighborhood kids. Until a few years ago this church also had a resident bellman—notice the cozy balcony halfway up. He was a basket maker and a colorful character—famous for bringing a donkey into his quarters that grew too big to get back out. Finally, he had no choice but to kill and eat the donkey.

Twenty meters beyond the church is a fine **gallery**, Galería de Arte San Pedro, featuring painting, pottery, and artisans in action.

From St. Peter's church, circle down and around back to the main square, wandering the tiny neighborhood lanes, peeking into patios, kicking a few soccer balls, and enjoying the views.

Nightlife

New-Town Evening Action—The newer part of Arcos has a modern charm, as all the generations are out enjoying life in the cool of the evening around Plaza Espana (a 10-minute walk from the old town). Several fine tapas bars border the square along with a good Egyptian restaurant (see "Eating," below). The big park below the square (Recinto Ferial) is the late-night fun zone in the summer (June–Sept)—the *carpas* (tents) fill with merrymakers, especially on weekends, when the scene includes open-air tapas bars, disco music, and dancing. There are free live concerts on Friday evenings throughout the summer.

Flamenco—On Plaza Cananeo in the old town, amateur flamenco sizzles on Thursday evening (free, from 22:00 July–August).

Sleeping in Arcos
(180 ptas = about $1, country code: 34, zip code: 11630)
Sleep Code: **S** = Single, **D** = Double/Twin, **T** = Triple, **Q** = Quad, **b** = bathroom, **t** = toilet only, **s** = shower only, **CC** = Credit Card (**V**isa, **M**asterCard, **A**mex), **SE** = Speaks English, **NSE** = No English. A price range reflects off-season to peak-season prices. Breakfast is not included; nor is the 7 percent IVA tax (unless noted below).

Hotel El Convento, deep in the old town just beyond the parador, is the best value in town. Run by a hardworking family, this cozy, newly renovated hotel offers 11 fine rooms—all with great views, half with view balconies. In 1998 I enjoyed a big party with most of Arcos' big shots present as they dedicated a fine room with a grand-view balcony to "Rick Steves Periodista Turistico" (all rooms Db-10,000 ptas plus tax, third person or balcony-2,000 ptas extra, CC:VMA, Maldonado 2, tel. 95-670-2333, fax 95-670-4128, Estefania SE). Enjoy a bird-watching breakfast on their view terrace with all of Andalucía spreading beyond your *café con leche*. The family also runs a good restaurant (see "Eating," below).

Parador de Arcos de la Frontera is royally located, recently refurbished, and, for all its elegance, reasonably priced. If you're going to experience a parador (and you can't get into El Convento), this might be the one (Sb-14,000 ptas, Db-18,500 ptas, 1,000 ptas more with a terrace—well worthwhile if you're into relaxing, CC:VMA, elevator, air-con, minibars, free parking, Plaza del Cabildo, tel. 95-670-0500, fax 95-670-1116, www.parador.es, e-mail: arcos@parador.es, SE).

Hotel Los Olivos is a bright, cool, and airy new place with a fine courtyard, roof garden, bar, view, friendly English-speaking folks, and easy 700-ptas/day parking. This is a poor-man's parador (Sb-5,000–6,000 ptas, Db-8,000–10,000 ptas, third person-3,000 ptas, includes tax, 10 percent discount for readers of this book, CC:VMA, San Miguel 2, tel. 95-670-0811, fax 95-670-2018, e-mail: mmoreno0237@viautil.com, Raquel SE).

Hotel La Fonda is a great traditional Spanish inn with all 19 rooms off one grand hall (Sb-4,500 ptas, Db-7,500 ptas, third person-2,000 ptas, no breakfast, CC:VM, across from Egyptian restaurant at Calle Corredera 83, tel. 95-670-0057, fax 95-670-3661, e-mail: lafonda@rrakis.es, SE).

Hotel Marques de Torresoto is a restored 17th-century palace with 15 classy rooms (few views), a peaceful courtyard, and a view terrace (Sb-6,800 ptas, Db-9,100 ptas, Db with salon-11,200 ptas, air-con, CC:VMA, across from Restaurante El Convento, Marques de Torresoto 4, tel. 95-670-0717, fax 95-670-4205, SE).

Hostal San Marcos offers four air-conditioned rooms above a neat little bar in the heart of the old town and a great sun terrace (Db-4,000 ptas, Tb-5,000 ptas, includes tax, Marques de Torresoto 6, tel. 95-670-0721, Loli NSE).

La Casa Grande has four shipshape rooms with porthole windows and Moroccan-tiled bathrooms, plus a terrace with fine views (Db-9,000–11,000 ptas, Db suite-13,000 ptas, Qb suite with kitchen-14,000 ptas, Maldonado 10, tel. & fax 95-670-3930, www.lacasagrande.net).

Hostal Callejon de las Monjas offers the closest thing to budget beds in the old town but is on a noisy street behind the Church of Santa Maria. Its nine simple, decent, clean rooms have fans (Sb-3,000 ptas, D-3,500 ptas, Db-5,000 ptas, CC:VM, Dean Espinosa 4, tel. 95-670-2302, NSE). Friendly Sr. Gonzalez Oca runs a tiny barbershop in the foyer and a restaurant in the cellar.

If for some reason you want to sleep on the big, noisy road

at the Jerez edge of town, two fine hotels nestle between truck stops on A-382: **Hostal Málaga** is surprisingly nice, with 15 clean, attractive rooms and a breezy two-level roof garden (Sb-3,000–3,500 ptas, Db-5,000–5,500 ptas, CC:VMA, air-con, TV, parking-500 ptas/day, Ponce de Leon 5, tel. & fax 95-670-2010, e-mail: hostalmalaga@teleline.es, NSE). **Hostal Voy-Voy** is next door (Sb-2,500–3,000 ptas, Db-5,000–6,000 ptas, attached restaurant, CC:VMA, Ponce de Leon 9, tel. 95-670-1412, NSE).

Eating in Arcos

The parador is very expensive, though a costly drink on its million-dollar-view terrace can be a good value. **Restaurante El Convento** has a wonderful atmosphere and is graciously run by Señora María Moreno-Moreno and her husband, Señor Roldan (daily 13:00–16:00, 19:00–22:30, near parador at Marques Torresoto 7, reservations necessary, tel. 95-670-3222). The food is the best of traditional local cuisine and well worth the splurge. The hearty 3,000-ptas *menu* of the day includes a fine red house wine and circular bread sticks (*picos de Arcos*), a local specialty. Many readers report this to be the best meal of their trip.

The *típico* **Alcaravan** is two blocks off Plaza Cabildo under the castle. You can enjoy your tapas on its classy patio or inside what was actually the dungeon of the castle (closed Mon, Calle Nueva 1).

Los Faraones serves good Egyptian cuisine in the new town near the paseo zone of Plaza España (1,500 ptas, Tue–Sun from 20:00, closed Mon, Debajo del Corral 8, tel. 95-670-0612, Hussein SE).

Transportation Connections—Arcos

By bus to: Jerez (hrly, 30 min), **Ronda** (4/day, 2 hrs), **Cadiz** (9/day, 1 hr), **Sevilla** (2/day, 2 hrs). From Jerez there are hourly connections to Sevilla. Two bus companies share the Arcos bus station. Their Jerez offices keep longer hours and know the Arcos schedules (Jerez tel. 95-634-2174 or 95-634-1063—make it clear you're in Arcos).

RONDA

With 40,000 people, Ronda is one of the largest white towns; and with its gorge-straddling setting, it's also one of the most spectacular. While it can be crowded with day-trippers, nights are peaceful. And since it's served by train and bus, Ronda makes a relaxing break for nondrivers traveling between Granada, Sevilla, and Córdoba.

Ronda's main attractions are its gorge-spanning bridges, the oldest bullring in Spain, and an interesting old town. Spaniards know it as the cradle of modern bullfighting and the romantic home of old-time banditos. Its cliffside setting is as dramatic today as it was practical yesterday. For the Moors it provided a tough bastion, taken by the Spaniards only in 1485, seven years before Granada fell. To 19th-century bandits it was a Bolivia without the boat ride.

Ronda's breathtaking ravine divides the town's labyrinthine old Moorish quarter and its new, noisier, and more sprawling Mercadillo quarter. A massive-yet-graceful 18th-century bridge connects these two neighborhoods. Most things of touristic importance (TI, post office, hotels, and bullring) are clustered within a few blocks of the bridge. While day-trippers from the touristy Costa del Sol clog the streets during the day, locals retake the town in the early evening. The paseo scene happens in the new town, on Ronda's major pedestrian street, Carrera Espinel.

Orientation

Tourist Information: The TI is on the main square, Plaza España, opposite the bridge (Mon–Fri 9:00–19:00, Sat–Sun 10:00–14:00, tel. 95-287-1272). Get their free Ronda map, their excellent Andalusian road map, and a listing of the latest museum hours; consider buying maps of Granada, Sevilla, or the "Route of the White Towns" (100 ptas each). While the town has precious little organized for tourism, you may see the tiny Tajotur bus parked in front of the TI gathering tourists for a drive outside of town to the most scenic places from which to view the gorge and bridge (1,500 ptas, 45 min, English narration, runs erratically, up to 8/day).

Arrival in Ronda: The train station is a 15-minute walk from the center. Turn right out of the station on Avenida Andalucía, turn left at the roundabout (the bus station is on your right), and then walk four blocks and you'll cross Calle Almendra (where several recommended hotels are located). At the pedestrian street (Carrera Espinel, a few blocks farther), turn right to reach the TI. From the bus station, cross the roundabout and follow directions above.

Drivers coming up from the coast catch A376 at San Pedro de Alcantara and wind 30 miles into the mountains. The handiest place to park is the underground lot at Plaza del Socorro (1 block from bullring, 150 ptas/hr, 1,800 ptas/24 hrs).

Excursions: Helena Wirtanen, a personable Finnish guide, will take you to nearby Roman ruins and hill towns (starting at 5,000 ptas for 2 people, 4 hrs, tel. 95-287-5556, cellular 65-693-2820).

Sights—Ronda

▲▲▲**The Gorge and New Bridge**—Ronda's main bridge, called Puente Nuevo (New Bridge), mightily spans the gorge. A bridge was built here in 1735 but fell after six years. This one was built from 1751 to 1793. The ravine, called El Tajo—360 feet down and 200 feet wide—divides Ronda into the whitewashed old Moorish town (called La Cuidad) and the new town (El Mercadillo), which was built after the Christian reconquest in 1485.

Ronda

200 YARDS

SOUTH

TO COSTA DEL SOL, MALAGA

SANTA MARIA LA MAYOR

MONDRAGON PALACE

CITY WALL

ARMIÑAN

MOORISH QUARTER

ARAB BRIDGE

PUENTE NUEVO

GUADALEVIN RIVER

PARA-DOR

PEÑAS

CANTOS

LOS REMEDIOS

PLAZA C. ABELA

VILLA

PLAZA ESPAÑA

MERCA-DILLO

CORTES

NARANJA

ESPINEL

NUEVA

VIRGEN

POST

PLAZA DE TOROS

ALAMEDA

QUARTER

RAMON

ALMENDRA

SOUVIRON

POZO

CRUZ

BOLO

MADRID

SAN JOSE

PLAZA MERCED

DR. FLEMING

MONTEREJAS

ANDALUCIA

TO TRAIN STATION & HOSTAL ANDALUCIA

BUS STATION

TO SEVILLA, ARCOS & PILETA CAVES

1 ROYAL	**7** VIRGIN DEL ROCIO	**12** CASA DEL MARQUES DE SALVATIERRA
2 RONDA SOL	**8** DON MIGUEL	**13** PUENTE VIEJO
3 BIARRITZ	**9** REINA VICTORIA	**14** HOSTAL SAN FRANCISCO
5 EL TAJO	**10** MUSEO DEL BANDOLERO	**15** LOS BANOS
6 LA ESPANOLA	**11** CASA DEL REY MORO	**16** HOTEL SAN GABRIEL

Look down...carefully. The architect fell to his death while inspecting it, and hundreds from both sides were thrown off this bridge during Spain's brutal civil war.

You can see the foundations of the original bridge (and a great view of the New Bridge) from the park named Vista Panoramica Jardines Ciudad de Cuenca. From Plaza España walk down Calle Villanueva and turn right on Calle Los Remedios at the sign for the park.

▲▲**Bullfighting Ring**—Ronda is the birthplace of modern bullfighting, and this ring is the first great Spanish bullring. In the early 1700s Francisco Romero established the rules of modern bullfighting and introduced the scarlet cape, held unfurled with a stick. His son Juan further developed the ritual or sport, and his grandson Pedro was one of the first great matadors (killing nearly 6,000 bulls in his career).

To see the **museum**, buy tickets from the shop to the right of the bullring's central door. You get to walk across the actual arena, with plenty of time to play "*toro*" surrounded by 5,000 empty seats. The arena was built in 1784. Notice the 176 classy Tuscan columns. With your back to the entry, look right and you can see the ornamental columns and painted doorway where the dignitaries sit (near the gate where the bull enters). On the left is the place for the band—in the case of a small town like Ronda, a high-school band. *Sol* means "sun" (cheap seats) and *sombra* means "shade." Straight ahead, where the horses drag out the dead bull after each fight, is the gate leading to the museum. The tiny museum—with not a word of English information available—is a shrine to bullfighting and the historic Romero family. You'll see stuffed heads (of bulls), photos, artwork, posters, and costumes (400 ptas, daily 10:00–20:00, Oct–April 10:00–19:00, on the main drag in the new town, 2 blocks up from the bridge and TI, tel. 95-287-4132).

Bullfights are scheduled for the first weekend of September and occur only rarely in the spring. For September bullfights, tickets go on sale the preceding July (tel. 95-287-6967). The Alameda del Tajo park, a block away, is a fine place for people-watching or a snooze in the shade.

Santa Maria la Mayor Cathedral—This 15th-century church shares a fine parklike square with orange trees and the city hall. Its Renaissance bell tower still has parts of the old minaret. It was built on and around the remains of Moorish Ronda's main mosque (which was itself built on the site of a temple to Julius Caesar). Partially destroyed by an earthquake, the reconstruction of the church resulted in the Moorish/Gothic/Renaissance/Baroque fusion (or confusion) you see today. Enjoy the bright frescoes and elaborately carved choir and altar. The treasury displays vestments that look curiously like matadors' brocaded outfits (250 ptas, daily 10:00–19:30, Oct–April 10:00–18:00, in the old town).

Mondragon Palace (Palacio de Mondragon)—This beautiful Moorish building was built in the 14th century, possibly as the residence of Moorish kings, and lovingly restored in the 16th century. It houses an enjoyable prehistory museum, with exhibits on Neolithic toolmaking and early metallurgy (many captions in English). Even if you have no interest in your ancestors, this is worth it for the architecture alone (250 ptas, Mon–Fri 10:00–19:00, Sat–Sun 10:00–15:00, Oct–April 10:00–18:00, on Plaza Mondragon in the old town, tel. 95-287-8450). Linger in the two small gardens, especially the shady one. Wander out to the nearby Plaza de Maria Auxiliadora for more views.

Museo del Bandolero—This tiny museum, while not as intriguing as it sounds, is an interesting assembly of *bandito* photos, guns, clothing, and knickknacks. The Jesse Jameses of Andalucía called this remote area home, and brief but helpful English descriptions make this a fun detour. One brand of romantic bandits were those who fought Napoleon's army—often more effectively than the regular Spanish troops (350 ptas, daily 10:00–20:00, Oct–April 10:00–18:00, across the main street below the Church of Santa Maria at Calle Arminan 65, tel. 95-287-7785).

Parador National de Ronda—Walk around and through this newest of Spain's fabled paradors. The views from the walkway just below the outdoor terrace are magnificent. Anyone is welcome at the cafés, but you have to be a guest to use the pool.

Hot-Air Balloon Ride—For a bird's eye view of Ronda, consider a balloon ride with Graham Elson (starting at 20,000 ptas, half-day, Aviacon Del Sol, tel. 95-287-7249, www.andalucia.com/balloons).

Walk through Old Town—From the New Bridge you can descend into a world of whitewashed houses, tiny grilled balconies, and winding lanes—the old town. The romantic-sounding but not very interesting **Casa del Rey Moro** (600 ptas, daily 10:00–20:00, Oct–April 10:00–19:00) offers no *casa*, just a fine old garden combining Muslim, Hispanic, and French traditions and "the Mine," an exhausting series of 365 stairs (like climbing down and then up a 20-story building) leading to the floor of the gorge. The Moors cut this zigzag staircase into the wall of the gorge in the 14th century. They used Spanish slaves to haul water to the thirsty town.

Fifty meters downhill from Casa del Rey Moro is **Casa del Marques de Salvatierra** (closed to public, but may reopen). With the "distribution" following the Reconquista here in 1485, the Spanish king gave this fine house to the Salvatierra family. The façade is rich in colonial symbolism from Spanish America. Note the pre-Columbian-looking characters flanking the balcony above the door and below the family coat of arms.

Continuing downhill you come to **Puente Viejo** (Old Bridge), built in 1616 upon the ruins of a Roman bridge. From here look down to see the old Puente Arabe, originally built by the Moors. Far to the right you can glimpse some of the surviving highly fortified old Moorish city walls. Crossing the bridge you see stairs on the right leading scenically along the gorge back to the New Bridge via a fine viewpoint. Straight ahead bubbles the welcoming "Eight Springs" fountain.

Pileta Caves—These caves with prehistoric paintings (22 km from Ronda) will be closed the next two years for study.

Sleeping in Ronda
(180 ptas = about $1, country code: 34, zip code: 29400)

Ronda has plenty of reasonably priced, decent-value accommodations. It's crowded only during Holy Week (the week before Easter) and through September. My recommendations are in the new town, a short walk from the New Bridge and a 10-minute walk from the train station. (The exceptions are Hostal Andalucía, across from the station, and Reina Victoria, at the edge of town—and the gorge.) In the cheaper places, ask for a room with a *ventana* (window) to avoid the few interior rooms. Breakfast and the 7 percent IVA tax are usually not included.

Hotel La Española is perfectly located on a pedestrian street just off Plaza España around the corner from the TI. Each of its 18 rooms is newly remodeled and comfy, with air-conditioning and modern bathrooms (Sb-6,000–6,500 ptas, Db-11,000–13,000 ptas, big Db suite-13,000–15,000 ptas, includes breakfast but not tax, José Aparicio 3, tel. 95-287-1052, fax 95-287-8001, e-mail: laespanola@ronda.net, NSE).

Hotel Royal has 29 clean, boring rooms—many on a busy street. Ask for a *tranquilo* room in the back (Sb-3,800 ptas, Db-6,000 ptas, Tb-7,500 ptas, CC:VMA, air-con, 42 Virgen de la Paz, 3 blocks off Plaza España, tel. 95-287-1141, fax 95-287-8132, www.ronda.net/usuar/hotelroyal/, e-mail: hroyal@ronda.net, some English spoken).

The friendly **Hostal Ronda Sol** has a homey atmosphere with 15 cheap but monkish rooms (S-1,700 ptas, D-2,800 ptas, Almendra 11, tel. 95-287-4497, NSE). Next door, and run by the same man, **Hostal Biarritz** offers 21 similar rooms, some with private baths (Sb-1,700 ptas, D-2,800 ptas, Db-3,500 ptas, T-4,000 ptas, Tb-5,200 ptas, includes tax, Almendra 7, tel. 95-287-2910, NSE).

The 65-room **Hotel El Tajo** has pleasant, quiet rooms once you get past the tacky Moorish decoration in the foyer (Sb-4,000 ptas, Db-7,000 ptas, includes tax, parking-1,000 ptas/day, CC:VMA, air-con, Calle Cruz Verde 7, a half-block off the pedestrian street, tel. 95-287-4040, fax 95-287-5099, helpful Puri and Beli SE).

Hostal Virgin del Rocio, spotless and central, won't overwhelm you with friendliness (Db-5,500–7,000 ptas, Calle Nueva 18, near Plaza España, tel. & fax 95-287-7425).

Hostal San Francisco offers 15 small, humble rooms a block off the main pedestrian street in the town center (Sb-2,000 ptas, Db-4,000 ptas, Tb-6,000 ptas, includes tax, CC:VM, Maria Cabrera 18, tel. & fax 95-287-3299).

Hostal Andalucía, a plain but clean place with 11 comfortable rooms and a low metabolism, is immediately across the street from the train station (Sb-3,000 ptas, Db-5,000 ptas, includes tax, air-con, Martinez Astein 19, tel. & fax 95-287-5450, Sra. Campos Garcia NSE).

Hotel San Gabriel has 16 pleasant rooms, a friendly staff, and a fine garden terrace (Sb-9,000 ptas, Db-11,000 ptas, Db suite-13,000 ptas, CC:VMA, air-con, Calle Jose M. Holgado 19, just off Plaza Poeta Abul-Beca, tel. 95-219-0392, fax 95-219-0117, www .ronda.net/usuar/hotelsgabriel, e-mail: sangabriel@ronda.net, SE).

Alavera de Los Banos, located next to ancient Moorish baths, has 10 clean and colorful rooms (Sb-7,000 ptas, Db-9,000–11,000 ptas, includes tax and breakfast, CC:VMA, Calle San Miguel, tel. & fax 95-287-9143, www.andalucia.com/alavera, e-mail: alavera @ctv.es, Christian SE).

Splurges: Ronda offers three tempting splurges. The gorge-facing **Don Miguel** is just left of the bridge. Many of its 19 red-tiled, comfortable rooms have balconies and gorgeous views at no extra cost, but street rooms come with a little noise (Sb-6,500 ptas, Db-9,500 ptas, cheaper off-season, breakfast-475 ptas, CC:VMA, parking garage a block away-750 ptas/day, air-con, elevator, Calle Villanueva 8, tel. 95-287-7722, fax 95-287-8377, SE).

You can't miss the striking **Parador de Ronda** on Plaza España. It's an impressive integration of stone, glass, and marble. All rooms have hardwood floors and fantastic view balconies (ask about family-friendly duplexes) and are surprisingly reasonable. There's also a pool overlooking the bridge (Sb-12,600–15,600 ptas, Db-15,800–19,500 ptas, breakfast-1,300 ptas, garage-1,200 ptas, CC:VMA, Plaza España, tel. 95-287-7500, fax 95-287-8188, e-mail: ronda@parador.es, SE). Consider at least a drink on the terrace.

The royal **Reina Victoria**, hanging over the gorge at the edge of town, has a great view—Hemingway loved it—but you'll pay for it (Sb-11,000–12,200 ptas, Db-15,000–18,500 ptas, CC:VMA, air-con, elevator, 10-min walk from city center and easy to miss, look for intersection of Avenida Victoria and Calle Jerez, Jerez 25, tel. 95-287-1240, fax 95-287-1075, SE).

Eating in Ronda

Dodge the tourist traps. They say the best meal in Ronda is at the **parador** (*muy* elegant, figure 3,500 ptas). **Plaza del Socorro**, a block in front of the bullring, is a wonderful local scene, where families enjoy the square and its restaurants. Take a paseo with the locals down pedestrian-only Carrera Espinel and choose a place with tables spilling out into the action. The best drinks and views in town are sipped on the terraces of the **Don Miguel Hotel** or the parador.

Restaurant Pedro Romero, assuming a shrine to bullfighting draped in *el toro* memorabilia doesn't ruin your appetite, gets good reviews (2,500 ptas meals, lunch from 12:30, dinner from 20:00, air-con, across the street from bullring at Calle Virgen de la Paz 18, tel. 95-287-1110).

Restaurant "Casa Santa Pola" serves unmemorable but cheap *típico* food with friendly service, gorge views, and a great Moorish cliffside ambience (3-course dinners 1,800 ptas, lunch from 12:30, dinner 19:00–23:30; crossing New Bridge, take the first left downhill and you'll see the sign, Calle Santo Domingo, tel. 95-287-9208).

The no-frills **Café & Bar Faustina** offers the cheapest tapas in town mixed with a lively crowd of locals and internationals (Tue–Sun 12:00–01:00, closed Mon, just off Plaza Carmen Abela, Santa Cecilia 4, tel. 95-287-6746).

Transportation Connections—Ronda

By bus to: Arcos (4/day, 2 hrs), **Benoajan** (2/day, 30 min), **Jerez** (5/day, 3 hrs), **Grazalema** (2/day, 1 hr), **Zahara** (2/day, Mon-Fri only, 1 hr), **La Línea** (1/day, Mon-Fri only, 3 hrs), **Sevilla** (5/day, 2.5 hrs; also see trains below), **Málaga** (10/day, 3 hrs; access other Costa del Sol points from Málaga), **Marbella** (6/day, 75 min), **Fuengirola** (5/day, 2 hrs), **Nerja** (4 hrs, transfer in Málaga; can take train or bus from Ronda to Málaga). There's no efficient way to call "the bus company" because there are four sharing the same station; it's best to just drop by and compare schedules (on Plaza Concepción García Redondo, several blocks from train station).

By train to: Algeciras (4/day, 2 hrs) **Bobadilla** (4/day, 1 hr), **Málaga** (3/day, 2.5 hrs, transfer in Bobadilla), **Sevilla** (3/day, 3.5 hrs, transfer in Bobadilla), **Granada** (3/day, 3.5 hrs, transfer in Bobadilla), **Córdoba** (4/day, 3.5 hrs, transfer in Bobadilla), **Madrid** (5/day, 5 hrs, 1 direct night train—23:20–8:40). It's a sleepy station serving only 11 trains a day. Transfers are a snap and time-coordinated in Bobadilla; with four trains arriving and departing simultaneously, double-check that you've jumped on the right one. Ronda train info: tel. 95-287-1673.

MORE ANDALUSIAN HILL TOWNS: THE ROUTE OF THE PUEBLOS BLANCOS

There are plenty of undiscovered and interesting hill towns to explore. About half the towns I visited were memorable. Unfortunately, public transportation is frustrating; I'd do these towns only by car. Good information on the area is rare. Fortunately, a good map, the tourist brochure (pick it up in Sevilla or Ronda), and a

The White Hill Towns

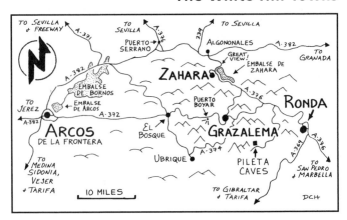

spirit of adventure work fine. Along with Arcos, here are my favorite white villages.

▲▲**Zahara**—This tiny town with a tingly setting under a Moorish castle (worth the climb) has a spectacular view. While the big church, facing the town square, is considered one of the richest in the area, the smaller church has the most-loved statue. The Virgin of Dolores is Zahara's answer to Sevilla's Virgin of Marcarena (and is similarly paraded through town during Holy Week). Zahara is a fine overnight stop for those who want to hear only the sounds of wind, birds, and elderly footsteps on ancient cobbles. (TI open daily 9:00–14:00, plus Fri–Sat 17:00–20:00, tel. 95-612-3114.)

▲**Zahara Castle**—During Moorish times Zahara lay within the fortified castle walls above today's town. It was considered the gateway to Granada and a strategic stronghold for the Moors by the Christian forces of the Reconquista. Locals tell of the Spanish conquest of the Moors' castle as if it happened yesterday: After the Spanish failed several times to seize the castle, a clever Spanish soldier noticed that the Moorish sentinel would check to see if any attackers were hiding behind a particular section of the wall by tossing a rock to set the pigeons to flight. If they flew, the sentinel figured there was no danger. One night a Spaniard hid there with a bag of pigeons and let them fly when the sentinel tossed his rock. Seeing the birds fly, the guard assumed he was clear to enjoy a snooze. The clever Spaniard then scaled the wall and opened the door to let his troops in, and the castle was conquered. That was in 1482. Ten years later Granada fell, the Muslims were back in Africa, and the Reconquista was completed. Today the castle is little more than an evocative ruin (always open, free) offering a commanding view. The lake is actually a reservoir. Before 1991 the valley had only a tiny stream.

Sleeping and Eating in Zahara: The **Hostal Marques de Zahara** is the best central hotel and a good value, with 10 comfortable rooms gathered around a cool, quiet courtyard and mother cooking traditional specialties in the restaurant (Sb-4,000–4,500 ptas, Db-5,700–6,500 ptas, breakfast-500 ptas, CC:VM, San Juan 3, 11688 Zahara, tel. & fax 95-612-3061, Santiago SE). **Pensión Los Tadeos** is a simple, blocky place just outside of town by the municipal swimming pool (*piscina*) offering basic rooms with great views (S-1,500 ptas, D-3,000 ptas, Paseo de la Fuente, tel. 95-612-3086, family Ruix NSE). Sr. Manolo Tardio runs **Meson Los Estribos**, a fine little restaurant across from the church, and rents an apartment (Db-4,000 ptas, CC:VMA, tel. 95-612-3145).

▲**Grazalema**—Another postcard-pretty hill town, Grazalema offers a royal balcony for a memorable picnic, a square where you can watch old-timers playing cards, and plenty of quiet, whitewashed streets to explore. Plaza de Andalucía, a block off the view terrace, has several decent little bars and restaurants and a popular candy store. Grazalema, situated on a west-facing slope of the mountains, catches clouds and is famous as the rainiest place in Spain—but I've had only blue skies on every visit (TI open Tue–Sun 10:00–14:00, 18:00–20:00, closed Mon, tel. 95-613-2225).

Sleeping in Grazalema: The **Casa de las Piedras** has 30 comfortable rooms just a block up from the town center—ask for a room in their new wing (S-1,500 ptas, Sb-3,800 ptas, D-3,000 ptas, Db-5,500 ptas, T-4,000 ptas, Tb-6,500 ptas, breakfast-250 ptas, Calle Las Piedras 32, 11610 Grazalema, tel. 95-613-2014, NSE). **Villa Turistica Grazalema** is a big, popular, happy place for locals enjoying their national park. It has apartments and regular hotel rooms, with balconies on the first floor or opening onto the swimming-pool garden on the ground floor (Db-7,500 plus tax, extra person-1,600 ptas, apartments-10,000 ptas, CC:VM, game rooms, restaurant, half mile outside town, tel. 95-613-2136, fax 95-613-2213).

JEREZ

Jerez, with nearly 200,000 people, is your typical big-city mix of industry, garbage, car bandits, and dusty concrete suburbs, but it has two claims to touristic fame: horses and sherry.

Jerez is ideal for a noontime (or midday) visit on a weekday. See the famous horses, sip some sherry, wander through the old quarter, and swagger out.

Orientation

Tourist Information: The helpful TI gives out free maps and info on the sights (Mon–Fri 9:00–19:00, Sat–Sun 10:00–14:00, 17:00–19:00, Oct–March 9:00–14:00, 17:00–20:00, closed Sun, Calle Larga 39, tel. 95-633-1150).

Arrival in Jerez: The bus station (at Calle Cartuja and Madre de Dios) has a simple baggage checkroom (120 ptas, if it looks closed, knock on the window; it's open until 22:00). *Consigna* is the Spanish word for "baggage check." The train station, a block away, has 30 lockers. Buy a 400-ptas locker token (*ficha*) at the ticket window.

Exit the bus station farthest from the WCs and turn left. The center of town and the TI are a 20-minute walk away. At the five-way intersection angle right on Honda; then, at the fountain, make a sharp left on the pedestrian street, Calle Larga, to reach the TI.

If you're arriving by train, angle right as you leave the station. Cross the intersection. The bus station is on your left. Continue straight, following directions from the bus station (above). Taxis from the station to the horses cost about 500 ptas.

Sights—Jerez

▲▲**Royal Andalusian School of Equestrian Art**—If you're into horses, this is a must. Even if you're not, this is horse art like you've never seen. The school does its Horse Symphony show at noon every Thursday, and from March through October on Tuesday as well (2,000–3,000 ptas, CC:VM, reservations tel. 95-631-9635 or 95-631-8008, fax 95-631-8015, call for current schedule). This is an equestrian ballet with choreography, purely Spanish music, and costumes from the 19th century. The stern horsemen and their talented and obedient steeds prance, jump, and do-si-do in time to the music, to the delight of an arena filled with mostly local horse aficionados. Training sessions, open to the public on Monday, Wednesday, and Friday from 11:00 to 13:00, offer a 1,000-ptas sneak preview. Practice sessions can be exciting or dull, depending on what the trainers are working on. Amble along (Mon and Wed only) during a one-hour guided tour of the stables, horses, tack room, and horse health center. Sip sherry in the arena's bar to complete this Jerez experience. If you're driving, follow signs from the center of Jerez to Real Escuela Andaluza de Arte Ecuestre (street parking). Otherwise it's a 30-minute walk from the train station, a 10-minute walk from the TI, or a short taxi ride.

▲▲**Sherry Bodega Tours**—Spain produces more than 10 million gallons per year of this fortified wine, ranging in taste from fino (dry) to amontillado (medium) to oloroso (sweet). The name *sherry* comes from English attempts to pronounce Jerez. While traditionally the drink of England's aristocracy, today it's more popular with Germans. Your tourist map of Jerez is speckled with wine barrels. Each of these barrels is a sherry bodega that offers tours and tasting.

Sandeman Sherry Tour: Just over a fence from the horse school is the venerable Sandeman Bodega (which has been pro-ducing sherry since 1790 and is the longtime choice of English royalty). This tour is the aficionado's choice for its knowledgeable

Jerez

guides and their quality explanations of the process (500 ptas, tours Mon–Fri 10:00–16:00 on the hour, Sat 11:00–14:00, bottling finishes at 14:00, finale is a chance to taste 3 varieties, tel. 95-630-1100 for English tour times and to reserve a place, fax 95-630-2626). During the high season, flamenco dancers perform just after the Horse Symphony concludes next door (March–Oct, some Tue and every Thu at 14:00, 300 ptas).

Harvey's Bristol Creme: Their English/German tours (Mon–Fri at 10:30 and 12:00 or by arrangement) aren't substantial but include a 10-minute video and all the sherry you like in the tasting room (450–750 ptas, Calle Pintor Munoz Cebrian, reservations recommended, tel. 95-634-6004, fax 95-634-9427).

Gonzalez Byas: The makers of the famous Tío Pepe offer a tourist-friendly tour with more pretense and less actual sherry-making on display (it's done in a new, enormous plant outside of town), but it's the only bodega that offers daily tours (1,000 ptas, open year-round, Manuel Maria Gonzalez 12, tel. 95-635-7000, fax 95-635-7046). Gonzales Byas is Disneyfying their tours, and schedules change frequently—call for the latest.

Alcazar—This gutted castle looks tempting, but don't bother. The 200-ptas entry fee doesn't even include the ramparts. Its underground parking is convenient for those touring Gonzalez Byas Bodega (150 ptas/hr).

Transportation Connections—Jerez

Jerez's bus station is shared by three bus companies, each with its own schedules, some specializing in certain destinations, others sharing popular destinations such as Sevilla and Algeciras. Shop around for the best departure time (Comes tel. 95-634-2174, Linesur tel. 95-634-1063, Los Amarillos tel. 95-632-9347). By car it's a zippy 30 minutes from Jerez to Arcos.

By bus to: Tarifa (3/day, 3 hrs), **Algeciras** (8/day, 2.5 hrs), **Cadiz** (10/day, 50 min), **Arcos** (hrly, 30 min), **Ronda** (5/day, 2.5 hrs), **Sevilla** (10/day, 90 min), **Málaga** (2/day, 5 hrs), **Córdoba** (1/day, 3.5 hrs), **Madrid** (6/day, 7 hrs).

By train to: Cadiz (2/hr, 50 min), **Sevilla** (12/day, 1 hr), **Madrid** (2/day, 4 hrs), **Barcelona** (2/day, 12 hrs). Train info: tel. 95-633-7975.

Drivers' note: In Jerez, blue-line zones require prepaid parking tickets on your dashboard on weekdays from 9:00 to 13:30 and 17:00 to 20:00 and on Saturday from 9:00 to 14:00; Sundays and July and August afternoons are free. Otherwise there's the handy underground parking lot near the Alcazar.

Easy Stops for Drivers

If you're driving between Arcos and Tarifa, here are two towns to explore:

Medina Sidonia—This place has no TI (read "no tourists"). It is whitewashed as can be surrounding its church and castle ruins–topped hill. Give it a quick look. Signs to Vejer and then Centro Urbano route you through the middle to Plaza de España—great for a coffee stop. Or, if it's lunchtime, consider buying a picnic, as all the necessary shops are nearby and the plaza benches afford a fine workaday view of a perfectly untouristy Andalusian town at play. You can drive from here up to the church (Plazuela de la Yglesia Mayor), where, for a tip, the man will show you around. Even without a tip you can climb yet another belfry for yet another vast Andalusian view. The castle ruins just aren't worth the trouble.

Vejer de la Frontera—Vejer, south of Jerez and just 20 miles north of Tarifa, will lure all but the very jaded off the highway. Vejer's strong Moorish roots give it a distinct Moroccan (or Greek island) flavor—you know, black-clad women whitewashing their homes and lanes that can't decide if they're roads or stairways. Only a few years ago women wore veils. The town has no real sights (other than its women's faces) and very little tourism, but it makes for a pleasant stop. (TI open Mon–Sat 10:00–14:00, 17:00–20:00, closed Sun, tel. 95-645-0191.)

The coast near Vejer is lonely, with fine but windswept beaches. It's popular with windsurfers and sand flies. The Battle of Trafalgar was fought just off Cabo de Trafalgar (a nondescript lighthouse today). I drove the circle so that you need not.

Sleeping in Vejer: A newcomer on Andalucía's tourist map, the old town of Vejer has only two hotels. **Convento de San Francisco** is a poor-man's parador in a classy refurbished convent (Sb-6,800 ptas, Db-9,100 ptas, breakfast-525 ptas, prices negotiable in off-season, CC:VMA, La Plazuela, 11150 Vejer, tel. 95-645-1001, fax 95-645-1004, e-mail: convento-san-francisco.tugasa@cadiz.org, Ines SE). They have the rare but unnecessary Vejer town map. A much better value is the clean and charming **Hostal La Posada** (S-3,000 ptas, Db-5,000 ptas, cheaper off-season, Los Remedios 21, tel. 95-645-0258, NSE). Both are at the entrance to the old town, at the top of the switchbacks past the town's lone traffic cop.

Route Tips for Drivers—Andalucía

Arcos to Tarifa (80 miles): Drive from Arcos to Jerez in 30 minutes. If you're going to Tarifa, take the tiny C343 road at the Jerez edge of Arcos toward Paterna and Vejer. Later you'll pick up signs to Medina Sidonia and then to Vejer and Tarifa.

Sevilla to Arcos: The remote hill towns of Andalucía are a joy to tour by car with Michelin map #446 or any other good map. Drivers can zip south on N-IV from Sevilla along the river, following signs to Cádiz. Take the fast toll freeway (blue signs, E5, A4). The toll-free N-IV is curvy and dangerous. About halfway to Jerez, at Las Cabezas, take CA403 to Villamartin. From there, circle scenically (and clockwise) through the thick of the Pueblos Blancos—Zahara and Grazalema—to Arcos.

It's about two hours from Sevilla to Zahara. You'll find decent but winding roads and sparse traffic. It gets worse if you take the tortuous series of switchbacks over the 4,500-foot summit of Puerto de Las Palomas on the direct but difficult road from Zahara to Grazalema. Remember to refer to your "Ruta de Pueblos Blancos" pamphlet.

Traffic flows through old Arcos only from west to east (coming from the east, circle south under town). The TI, my recommended hotels, and parking (Paseo Andalucía) are all in the west. Driving in Arcos is like threading needles. But if your car is small and the town seems quiet enough, follow signs to the parador, where you'll find the only old-town car park.

COSTA DEL SOL: SPAIN'S SOUTH COAST

It's so bad, it's interesting. To northern Europeans the sun is a drug, and this is their needle. Anything resembling a quaint fishing village has been bikini-strangled and Nivea-creamed. Oblivious to the concrete, pollution, ridiculous prices, and traffic jams, tourists lie on the beach like game hens on skewers—cooking, rolling, and sweating under the sun.

Where Europe's most popular beach isn't crowded by high-rise hotels, most of it's in a freeway choke hold. Wonderfully undeveloped beaches between Tarifa and Cádiz and east of Alveria are ignored, while lemmings make the scene where the coastal waters are so polluted that hotels are required to provide swimming pools. It's a fascinating study in human nature.

Laugh with Ronald McDonald at the car-jammed resorts. But if you want a place to stay and play in the sun, unroll your beach towel at Nerja.

You're surprisingly close to jolly olde England. The land of tea and scones, fish and chips, pubs and bobbies awaits you—in Gibraltar. And beyond "The Rock," the whitewashed port of Tarifa, the least-developed piece of Spain's generally overdeveloped south coast, provides an enjoyable springboard for a quick trip into Morocco (next chapter).

Planning Your Time

My opinions on the "Costa del Turismo" are valid for peak season. If you're there during a quieter time and you like the ambience of a beach resort, it can be a pleasant stop. Off-season it can be neutron-bomb quiet.

The whole 150-mile-long coastline takes four hours to drive or six hours by bus. You can resort-hop by bus across the entire

Costa del Sol

Costa del Sol and reach Nerja for dinner. If you want to party on the beach, it can take as much time as Mazatlán.

NERJA

Somehow Nerja, while cashing in on the fun-in-the-sun culture, has actually kept much of its quiet, old-world charm. It has good beaches, a fun evening paseo that culminates in the proud Balcony of Europe terrace, enough pastry shops and nightlife, and locals who get more excited about their many festivals than the tourists do. For a taste of the British expatriate scene, pick up the monthly *Street Wise* magazine or tune in to Coastline Radio at 97.7 FM. The weekly market is colorful, lively, and fun (Tue 9:30–14:00, open Sun 9:30–14:00 with older, antique items, along Calle Antonio Fernandiz at the edge of town).

Orientation

Tourist Information: The helpful, English-speaking TI has town maps, bus schedules, and tips on beaches and side trips (Mon–Fri 10:00–14:00, 17:30–20:30, Sat 10:00–13:00, closed Sun, Puerta del Mar 2, just off Balcony of Europe, tel. 95-252-1531). Ask for the TI's free "Cultural Center Guide" with the latest theater and musical events, and the "Leisure Guide" with a comprehensive listing of activities. Another TI is located at the Caves of Nerja (Mon–Fri 10:30–14:00, 16:00–18:30, Sat 10:00–13:00, closed Thu afternoon and Sun).

Getting Around: A goofy little tourist train does its 30-minute loop twice an hour (400 ptas, daily 10:30–24:00). Nerja taxis charge a set 700-ptas fee (e.g., to Burriana beach).

Nerja

* NOT TO SCALE -
BUS INFO KIOSK TO
BALCON DE EUROPA
IS A 10 MIN WALK

BUS INFO KIOSK

TO CAVES, SALOBREÑA & GRANADA

N-340

N-340   AV. DE PESCIA

← TO MALAGA

PLAZA CANTARERO

SAN MIGUEL

ALEJ.

NUÑEZ

USA

MENDEZ

BUENO

HERR. ORIA

CRISTO

SAN PAB.

TAPAS

S. JUAN

RUPERTO

PLAZA ERMITA

PINTADA

COLON

FERRANDIZ

CARRETAS

LA PARRA

LOS   HUERTOS

TO N-340

ANGUSTIAS

BRONCE

CRUZ

ANIMAS

CRUZ

PASEO NUEVO

ALMIRANTE

CRISTO

LOTS OF CASAS PARTICULARES

PEREZ

GRANADA

TO PARADOR

CASTILLA

DIPUTACIÓN

EL BARRIO

PROV.

TEL.

PASEO DEL MAR

Post/Correos

CARABEO

PLAZA CAVANA

PLAYA CARABED

PLAYA BURRIANA

PLAYA CALAHONDA

BALCON DE EUROPA

PLAYA DEL SALON (BEST BEACH)

← TO PLAYA LA TORRECILLA & HOTEL PERLA MARINA

MEDITERRANEAN SEA

❶ DON PEQUE	❺ BALCON DE EUROPA	❾ BAR EL PULGUILLA
❷ ATEMBENI	❻ HOSTAL LORCA	❿ BAR EL CHISPA
❸ MENA	❼ PENSION EL PATIO	
❹ PLAZA CAVANA	❽ LOS CUNAOS BAR	

Sights—Nerja
▲▲**Balcony of Europe (Balcón de Europa)**—This promenade on a bluff over the beach is the center of the town's paseo. It overlooks miles of coastline as well as a few little coves and caves below.
Beaches—Nerja has several good beaches. The sandiest (and most crowded) is down the walkway to the right of the Restaurante Marissal, just off the Balcony of Europe. The pebblier beach, full of fun pathways, crags, and crannies (head down through the arch to the right of the TI office), has a trail leading east to a bigger beach, Playa de Burriana. This is Nerja's leading beach, with all the jet-ski, paddleboat, and entertainment options. Playa de la Torrecilla, a 10-minute walk west of the Balcony of Europe, is the cleanest. All have showers, bars, restaurants, and beach chairs (400–500 ptas/day). Beware of red flags on the beach, which indicate when seas are too rough for safe swimming.
▲**Caves of Nerja (Cuevas de Nerja)**—These caves, four kilometers east of Nerja, have the most impressive array of stalactites and stalagmites I've seen anywhere in Europe, with huge caverns filled with expertly backlit formations and appropriate music. The visit is a 30-minute unguided ramble deep into the mountain, up and down lots of dark stairs congested with Spanish families. At the end you reach the Hall of the Cataclysm, where you'll circle what, according to Guinness, is the world's largest stalactite-made column. Then you hike out. Someone figured that it took 1 trillion drops to make the column (750 ptas, daily 10:00–14:00, 16:00–20:00, closes off-season at 18:30, tel. 95-252-9520). To get to the caves, catch a bus from the Nerja bus stop on Avenida de Pescia (105 ptas, 16/day, 15 min).
Frigiliana—This picture-perfect whitewashed village, only six kilometers from Nerja, is easy by bus or car. It's a worthwhile detour from the beach, particularly if you don't have time for the Pueblos Blancos hill towns.

Sleeping in Nerja
(180 ptas = about $1, country code: 34, zip code: 29780)
Sleep Code: **S** = Single, **D** = Double/Twin, **T** = Triple, **Q** = Quad, **b** = bathroom, **t** = toilet only, **s** = shower only, **CC** = Credit Card (**V**isa, **M**asterCard, **A**mex), **SE** = Speaks English, **NSE** = No English spoken.
The entire Costa del Sol is crowded during August and Holy Week (when prices are at their highest). Reserve in advance for peak season, basically mid-July through mid-September, prime time for Spanish workers to hit the beaches. Any other time of year you'll find Nerja has plenty of comfy, low-rise, easy-going, resort-type hotels and rooms. Room rates are three-tiered, with the highest being only for August or, at most, July through September.

Sleeping in Hotels

Hotel Plaza Cavana overlooks a plaza lily-padded with cafés. If you like a central location, marble floors, modern furnishings, an elevator, and a small rooftop swimming pool, dive in (Sb-8,500–11,500 ptas, Db-11,000–16,000 ptas, extra bed-3,500 ptas, some view rooms, includes breakfast, tax extra, air-con, your car can ride an elevator into the basement for 1,000 ptas/day, CC:VM, 2 blocks from Balcony of Europe at Plaza Cavana 10, tel. 95-252-4000, fax 95-252-4008, e-mail: hotelplazacavana@infonegocio.com, SE).

The best place in town is **Balcón de Europa**, right on the water and on the square, with the prestigious address Balcón de Europa 1. With all the modern comforts and an elevator down to your own private beach, you'll feel like you own the town. Suites all have a sea-view balcony. Most regular rooms come with a sea view (Sb-9,000–13,750 ptas, Db-13,750–19,000 ptas, add about 4,000 ptas for a suite, third person pays 3,500 ptas, air-con, elevator, parking-1,000 ptas/day, CC:VMA, tel. 95-252-0800, fax 95-252-4490, e-mail: balconeuropa@spa.es, SE).

Hotel Perla Marina is a big, modern, splashy place with sprawling public rooms, no soul, and plenty of fun-in-the-sun package groups. It's right on a fine beach a 15-minute walk from the center. Most of its 100 rooms overlook the sea. If you're here for the beach, not the town, this place is ideal (Sb-6,000, 7,000, or 8,500 ptas, Db-9,500, 12,000, or 14,000 ptas, suites for 3,000 ptas extra, breakfast and tax extra, CC:VMA, air-con, elevator, grassy backyard faces the surf, free on-street parking, Calle Merida 7, tel. 95-252-3350, fax 95-252-4083, SE). **Hotel Riu Monica**, next door, is much bigger, classier, and twice as expensive (tel. 95-252-1100).

Nerja's **parador**, housed in a new office-type building rather than a castle, lacks character but has spacious, suite-like rooms. The parador will be closed part of the year for renovations— call first rather than show up (Sb-12,000–15,200 ptas, Db-15,000–19,500 ptas, CC:VMA, air-con, free parking, swimming pool, 15-min walk from town center, Almuñecar 8, tel. 95-252-0050, fax 95-252-1997, e-mail: nerja@parador.es, SE).

Sleeping in Cheaper Hostals

The new **Hostal Marissal**, just next door to the fancy Balcón de Europa hotel, has 14 modern, spacious rooms, four with small view balconies directly above the Balcony of Europe (Db-6,500–8,000 ptas, CC:VM, air con, Balcón de Europa 3, reception at café, tel. & fax 95-252-0199, SE).

Hostal Residencia Don Peque, also in the center, has 10 tastefully decorated rooms, all with balconies. Front rooms over the noisy street have air-conditioning (Db-4,000–5,800 ptas,

Tb-start at 5,500 ptas, includes tax, CC:VM, Diputación 13, tel. 95-252-1318, some English spoken).

Hostal Atembeni, across the street from Don Peque, is more basic (Sb-2,700–4,400 ptas, Db-3,800–5,600 ptas, includes tax, ceiling fans, no air-con, CC:VMA, Diputación 12, tel. 95-252-1341, some English spoken).

Hostal Residencia Mena is erratically run but has homey rooms and a breezy garden (Sb-2,500–3,500 ptas, Db-3,500–5,500 ptas, includes tax, street noise, El Barrio 15, tel. & fax 95-252-0541, Maria speaks some English).

A quiet residential section five minutes from the center (and 3 blocks from the bus stop) offers two good options:

The new **Hostal Lorca**, run by a friendly Dutch couple, has nine modern, comfortable rooms and a pool (Sb-3,000–5,000 ptas, Db-4,000–6,000 ptas, extra bed-1,500 ptas, includes tax, Mendez Nunez 20, look for yellow house, tel. & fax 95-252-3426, www.hostallorca.com).

Pensión El Patio is clean, homey, and really local—worth the communication struggles (Db-4,000–5,000 ptas, Tb-4,500–7,000 ptas, Mendez Nuñez 12, tel. 95-252-2930, NSE). The kids of the family always seem to be dressed up and heading off to some festival, dance, or concert. If no one answers, ask at the nearby fruit shop.

Your cheapest and often most interesting bet may be a room in a private home (*casa particular*). Walk around the residential streets within about six blocks of Calle La Parra or on Calle Nueva with your rucksack. Ask around.

Eating in Nerja

There are three Nerjas: the private domain of the giant beachside hotels; the central zone packed with fun-loving expatriates and tourists enjoying great food with trilingual menus; and the back-streets, where local life goes on as if there were no tomorrow (or tourists). The whole old town around the Balcony of Europe sizzles with decent restaurants. It makes no sense for me to recommend one over the others. Wander around and see who's eating best.

Farther inland, prices go down and locals fill the bars and tables. A 10-minute hike uphill takes you into the residential thick of things, where the sea views come thumbtacked to the walls. These three great places cluster within two blocks of each other around Herrera Oria (see map). Each specializes in seafood and is fine for a sit-down meal or a stop on a tapas crawl. Remember that tapas are snack-size portions. To turn tapas into more of a meal, ask for a *ración* or two.

Los Cunaos is most fun late in the evening, when families munch tapas, men watch soccer on TV, women chat, and stray kids wander around like it's home (good seafood and prices,

Herrera Oria 19, tel. 95-252-1107). **El Pulguilla** specializes in seafood, with clams so fresh they squirt (Bolivia 1, tel. 95-252-1384). **El Chispa** is similarly big on seafood, with an informal restaurant terrace in the back (San Pedro 12, tel. 95-252-3697).

If you're out late, consider **Bar El Molino** for folk singing after 23:00. It's a bit touristy but worth the effort (Calle San Jose 4).

Transportation Connections—Nerja

The Nerja bus station is actually just a bus stop on Avenida de Pescia with an info booth (daily 8:00–20:00, helpful schedules posted on booth, tel. 95-252-1504).

By bus to: Nerja Caves (16/day, 15 min), **Málaga** (14/day, 90 min), **Granada** (2/day, more frequent with Motril transfer, 2–3 hrs), **Córdoba** (2/day, 4 hrs; only 1/day in the off-season), **Sevilla** (3/day, 4 hrs).

Transportation Connections—Málaga

The nearest train station to Nerja is an hourly 90-minute bus ride away in Málaga.

From Málaga by train to: Ronda (3/day, 2.5 hrs, transfer in Bobadilla), **Madrid** (6/day, 4.5 hrs on Talgo train), **Córdoba** (6/day, 2 hrs on Talgo), **Granada** (2/day, 3–4 hrs, transfer in Bobadilla), **Sevilla** (2/day, 3 hrs), **Barcelona** (3/day, 14 hrs). Malaga train info: tel. 95-236-0202.

Buses: Málaga's bus station, a block from the train station, has a helpful information office with an invaluable listing combining all the schedules offered by the different bus companies (on Paseo de los Tilos, tel. 95-235-0061).

By bus to: Algeciras (12/day, 3 hrs), **Nerja** (14/day, 90 min), **Ronda** (4/day, 2.5 hrs), **La Línea** (5/day, 3 hrs), **Sevilla** (10/day, 3 hrs), **Granada** (14/day, 2 hrs), **Córdoba** (4/day, 3 hrs), **Madrid** (12/day, 7 hrs).

Sights—From Nerja to Gibraltar

Buses take five hours to make the Nerja-to-Gibraltar trip. They leave nearly hourly and stop at each town mentioned.

Fuengirola/Torremolinos—The most built-up part of the region, where those most determined to be envied settle down, is a bizarre world of Scandinavian package tours, flashing lights, pink flamenco, multilingual menus, and all-night happiness. Fuengirola is like a Spanish Mazatlán with a few less-pretentious, older, budget hotels between the main drag and the beach. The water here is clean and the nightlife fun and easy. James Michener's idyllic Torremolinos has been strip-mauled and parking-metered.

Marbella—This is the most polished and posh of the Costa del Sol's resorts. Look for the *"Turismo"* sign to the right as you enter the center of town. Cross the main street at the signal closest to the *turismo* and walk up to the old city's pedestrian section, veering right. While the high-priced boutiques, immaculate streets, and beautifully landscaped squares are testimony to Marbella's arrival on the world-class-resort scene, cheap accommodations can still be found in old Marbella. Have a *café con leche* on the beautiful Plaza de Naranjas before wandering back down to new Marbella and the high-rise beachfront apartment buildings. Check out the beautiful beach scene before leaving. Marbella is an easy stop on the Algeciras–Málaga bus route (as you exit the bus station, take a left to reach the center of town).

San Pedro de Alcantara—This town's relatively undeveloped sandy beach is popular with young travelers. San Pedro's neighbor, Puerto Banus, is "where the world casts anchor." This luxurious jet-set port, complete with casino, is a strange mix of Rolls-Royces, yuppies, boutiques, rich Arabs, and budget browsers.

GIBRALTAR

One of the last bits of the empire upon which the sun never sat, Gibraltar is a fun mix of Anglican propriety, "God Save the Queen" tattoos, military memories, and tourist shops. The British soldiers you'll see are enjoying this cushy assignment in the Mediterranean sun as a reward for enduring and surviving an assignment in another remnant of the British Empire: Northern Ireland. While things are cheaper in pounds, your Spanish money works as well as your English words here.

The 30,000 Gibraltarians have a mixed and interesting heritage. The Llanitos (yah-nee-tohs), as the Spanish call them, speak a Creole-like Spanglish. They are a fun-loving and tolerant mix of British, Spanish, Genoese, Maltese, Portuguese, and Moroccan.

You'll need your passport to cross the border (and you may still be able to charm an official into stamping it—ask or you'll get just a wave-through). Make Gibraltar a day trip; rooms are expensive.

Planning Your Time

For the best day in Gibraltar, consider this plan: Walk across the border, catch bus #3, and ride it to the end, following a self-guided tour (see below). Catch bus #3 back to the cable-car station, ride to the top, and then walk down via O'Hara's Battery, St. Michael's Cave, and the monkeys. From there catch the cable car back into town. Spend your remaining free time in town before returning to Spain.

Orientation

(tel. code: 9567 from Spain, or 350 from other countries)
Tourist Information: The main TI is at the Duke of Kent House

Gibraltar

on Cathedral Square, a few blocks from the town center (Mon–Fri 9:00–17:30, bus #3 stops here, tel. 9567/74950). Other TIs are on Main Street (also open Sat–Sun 10:00–16:00, inside the House of Assembly, tel. 9567/74982), at Customs where you cross the border, and at Coach Park (the bus terminal). The TIs can arrange extensive WWII tunnel and cave tours.

Helpful Hints: A Checkout supermarket is on Main Street, off Cathedral Square, next to Marks & Spencer (Mon–Sat 8:30–20:00). Fruit stands bustle at the Market Place (Mon–Sat 9:00–15:00, north end of Main Street). Café Cyberworld has Internet access for a pricey £4.50/hr (daily 12:00–24:00, 14 Queensway, in Ocean Heights Gallery, tel. 9567/51416). To telephone Gibraltar from Spain, dial 9567 followed by the five-digit local number.

Arrival in Gibraltar

By Bus: Spain's La Línea bus station is a five-minute walk from the Gibraltar border. If you're day-tripping to Gibraltar it's easy to store luggage in the lockers at the La Línea bus station (15 lockers, 400 ptas each) or the Algeciras train station.

From the La Línea bus station it's a five-minute walk to the border (flash your passport) and then a 30-minute walk into downtown Gibraltar (straight across the runway and up Winston Churchill Avenue, angling right at the Shell station on Smith Dorrien Avenue). Otherwise you can take the #3 minibus from the border to the TI at Cathedral Square (or continue on the self-guided tour, below) or the double-decker bus #9 to the beginning of Main Street (100 ptas or 40 pence, every 15 min).

By Car: After taking the La Línea-Gibraltar exit off the main Costa del Sol road, continue as the road curves left with the Rock to your right. The traffic light with the Aduana (customs) sign is just at the border; a right turn will take you into Gibraltar, or a left turn will take you immediately to La Línea (the Gibraltarians call this street Winston Churchill Avenue, the Spanish call it the 20th of April). Avoid long lines of cars going into Gibraltar by turning left and parking in La Línea. From here you make the five-minute walk across the border on foot. The handiest place to park is at Fo Cona parking lot (150 ptas/hour, left on 20th of April, 100 meters on your left). You will also find blue-lined parking spots in this area (130 ptas/hr from meter, bring 100-ptas coins, leave ticket on dashboard, Sun free). The days of con artists dressed as cops taking bogus entrance fees from hapless tourists are nearly gone. Today you will only find blue-uniformed Spanish police making sure all goes smoothly.

If you insist on driving into Gibraltar, there are plenty of parking lots (like the huge one near the cable car), but be prepared for a 90-minute wait both ways at the border.

Tours of Gibraltar

By Minibus: Organized tours such as Blands (tel. 9567/76226), Thomas Cook's Travel Exchange (tel. 9567/76151), and Parody-tour (tel. 9567/76070) have predictable set fees (around £10–12) regardless of the number of people on the tour. Standard tours last about 90 minutes and include the Upper Rock Nature Reserve. Travel Exchange has a 2.5-hour tour of the entire Rock.

By Taxi: You'll find lots of aggressive cabbies at the border who would love to give you a tour. For those with more money than time, this can be a good value (as low as £8 per person if the taxi is packed) for a ride up the Rock to the Apes' Den and St. Michael's Cave (90 min)—but not all taxis go to the very top of the Rock, so ask. More people in a taxi means a lower cost per person; try to buddy up with other travelers.

The Quick, Cheap, Bus #3 Self-Guided Orientation Tour

At the border, pick up a map at the customs TI. Then walk straight ahead for 200 meters to the bus stop on the right. Catch minibus #3 (4/hrly, pay driver 100 ptas or 40 pence) and enjoy the ride.

You enter Gibraltar by crossing an **airstrip**. Forty times a week, the entry road into Gibraltar is closed to allow airplanes to land or take off. (You can fly to London for as low as $170.) The airstrip, originally a sports stadium, was filled in with stones excavated from the 34 miles of military tunnels in the Rock. This airstrip was a vital lifeline in the days when Spain and Britain were quarreling over Gibraltar and the border was closed.

Just after the airstrip, the bus passes a road leading left (which heads clockwise around the Rock to the town of Catalan Bay, peaceful beaches, and the huge mountainside rainwater "catch-ment" wall). As you pass apartments on the left, find the **Moorish castle** above (now a prison; only the tower is open to the public).

Over the bridge and on the right after the next stop you'll see **World War I memorials**. The first is the American War Memorial, built in 1932 to commemorate American sailors based here in World War I. Farther along you'll see 18th-century cannons and a memorial to Gibraltarians who died in that same war.

Passing the Natwest House office tower on the left, you'll see the **synagogue**. In the 19th century half of Gibraltar was Jewish. The Jewish community now numbers 600.

Zigzagging past cute **Cathedral Square** (TI) and the Moorish-looking Anglican church, you reach Main Street. On the left, polished cannons protect the sentry house. Across the street the stately brick residence has housed the British governor since 1728.

The bus stops before the old **Charles V wall**. The wall was built in response to a 1552 raid in which the pirate Barbarossa stole 70 Gibraltarians into slavery.

Passing under the wall, on the left, you'll see the **Trafalgar cemetery**. Buried here are the British sailors who died defeating the French off the coast of Portugal's Cape Trafalgar in 1805.

The next stop is at the big parking lot for the **gondola** to the top of the Rock. You can get off now or later, on the ride back into town.

Heading uphill out of town you pass the big ugly casino and the path leading up the Rock (a 2.5-hour hike). Reaching the end of the Rock you pass modern apartments and the new mosque. The lighthouse marks the windy Europa Point—end of the line. Buses retrace the route you just traveled, departing about every 15 minutes (check schedule before exploring farther).

The **Europa Point**, up the mound from the bus stop and tourist shop (on right), is an observation post. A plaque here identifies the mountains of Morocco 15 miles across the straits. The light of the lighthouse (from 1841, closed to visitors) can be seen from Morocco.

The **King Fahad Mosque**, a gift from the Saudi Sultan, was completed in 1997. Gibraltar's 300 Muslims worship here each Friday. Here—as across the straits in Morocco—five times a day the imam sings the call to prayer. Visitors (without shoes) are welcome (daily 17:00–18:00).

Sights—Gibraltar's Upper Rock Nature Reserve

▲▲▲**The Rock**—The real highlight is the spectacular Rock itself. From the south end of Main Street, catch the cable car to the top (1,000 ptas/£3.65 one way, 1,300 ptas/£4.90 round-trip, Mon–Sat 9:30–17:15, 6/hrly, closed Sun and when it's windy). The cable car drops you at a slick **restaurant/view terrace** at the very top of the Rock, from which you can explore old ramparts and drool at the 360-degree view of Morocco, the Straits of Gibraltar, Algeciras and its bay, and the twinkling Costa del Sol arcing eastward. Below you stretches the giant water catchment system that the British built to catch rainwater in the not-so-distant past, when Spain allowed neither water nor tourists to cross its disputed border. The views are especially crisp on brisk off-season days.

Buying a one-way ticket up saves a little money and gives you a chance to hike down to all of the sites. Allow 90 minutes to hike down—or up to 2.5 hours if you stop at the following six sights in the Upper Rock Nature Reserve, which you'll see in order as you descend from the top of the Rock.

With a round-trip ticket, your best strategy is to take the cable car up, hike downhill to St. Michael's Cave and the Apes' Den, and then take the cable car down into town from the Apes' Den, skipping the other sights. Why hike at all, you ask? Because you'd miss St. Michael's Cave if you relied solely on the cable car.

The entire Upper Rock Nature Reserve is open daily from
9:30 to 19:00. O'Hara's Battery, St. Michael's Cave, and the Apes'
Den are free with your cable-car ticket. A pass for admission to
the other sites is 1,400 ptas/£5 (or 1,000 ptas/£4 with your cable-
car ticket).

▲▲**O'Hara's Battery**—At 426 meters, this is the highest point
on the Rock. While some taxi tours don't come here, you can hike
here in 20 minutes from the top of the cable-car lift. (The Battery
may still be closed for restoration; check at the TI, cable-car lift,
or restaurant before you make the hike.) A 28-ton, 9-inch gun sits
on the summit where a Moorish lookout post once stood. It was
built after World War I, and the last test was fired in 1974. Locals
are glad it's been mothballed. During test firings, if locals didn't
open their windows to allow air to move freely after the concus-
sion, their windows would shatter. Thirty-four miles of tunnels,
like the tiny bit you see here, honeycomb this strategic rock.
During World War II it was thought that an entire garrison could
survive six months with the provisions stored in this underground
base (Mon–Sat 10:00–17:30, closed Sun; from the cable-car stop
walk 10 min down and then 10 min up). As you explore the mountain, you may see iron rings. These anchored pulleys used to haul
up guns such as the huge one at O'Hara's Battery.

▲**St. Michael's Cave**—Studded with stalagmites and stalactites,
eerily lit and echoing with classical music, this cave is dramatic,
corny, and slippery when wet. Considered a one-star sight since
Neolithic times, these were alluded to in ancient Greek legends—
when the Rock was one of the Pillars of Hercules, marking the
end of the world, and the caves were believed to be the Gates of
Hades. In our century they were prepared (but never used) as a
World War II hospital and are now just another tourist site with
an auditorium for musical events. Notice the polished cross section of a stalagmite showing weirdly beautiful rings similar to a
tree's. Spelunkers who'd enjoy a three-hour subterranean hike
through the lower cave can make arrangements in advance at the
TI (£5 per person).

Apes' Den—This small zoo without bars gives you a chance for a
close encounter with some of the famous (and very jaded) apes of
Gibraltar. Keep your distance from the apes and beware of their
kleptomaniac tendencies. The man at the little booth posts a
record of the names of all the apes. If there's no ape action, wait
for a banana-toting taxi tour to stop by and stir some up. (The
cable car stops here.)

▲**Siege Tunnels**—Also called the Upper Galleries, these chilly
tunnels were blasted out of the rock by the Brits during the
Spanish and French siege of 1779 to 1783. Hokey but fun diora-
mas help recapture a time when Brits were known more for con-
quests than for crumpets. The tunnels are at the northern end of

the Rock, about a mile from the Apes' Den (at the fork in the road, follow the sign for "All Directions").

Gibraltar, A City Under Siege **Exhibition**—A spin-off of the siege tunnels, this excuse for a museum gives you a look at life during the siege. It's worth a stop only if you already bought a combo ticket (just downhill from Siege Tunnels).

Moorish Castle—Actually more tower than castle, this building offers a tiny museum of Moorish remnants and carpets. The original castle was built by the Moorish Tarik-ibn-Zeyad in 711, but his name lasted longer than the castle; Gibel-Tarik (or Tarik's Hill) became Gibraltar. The tower marks the end of the Upper Rock Nature Reserve. Head downhill to reach the lower town and Main Street.

Sights—Lower Gibraltar

Gibraltar Museum—Built atop a Moorish bath, this museum in Gibraltar's lower town tells the story of a rock that has been fought over for centuries. Highlights are a 15-minute history film and the cavelike room that features prehistoric remains and artifacts (oddly hidden away in a room off the art gallery). The first Neanderthal skull was actually found in Gibraltar in 1848, though no one realized its significance until a similar skull found years later in Germany's Neanderthal Valley was correctly identified, stealing the name, claim, and fame from Gibraltar (530 ptas/£2, Mon–Fri 10:00–18:00, Sat 10:00–14:00, closed Sun, on Bomb House Lane off Main Street, ignore misleading "closed" entrance).

▲**Catalan Bay**—Gibraltar's tiny second town originated as a settlement of Italian shipwrights whose responsibility was keeping the royal ships in good shape. Today it's just a huddle of apartments around a cute little Catholic church and the best beach on the Rock (fully equipped). Catch bus #4A from opposite the Governor's Residence or the roundabout near the airport.

Sleeping in Gibraltar

(£1 = about $1.60, tel. code: 9567 from Spain, or 350 international, zip code: 29780)

Sleep Code: **S** = Single, **D** = Double/Twin, **T** = Triple, **Q** = Quad, **b** = bathroom, **t** = toilet only, **s** = shower only, **CC** = Credit Card (Visa, MasterCard, Amex), **SE** = Speaks English, **NSE** = No English spoken.

Cannon Hotel is a friendly B&B run by gregarious Swedish sailors who settled in Gibraltar. Centrally located on a quiet street a block off Cathedral Square, the Cannon offers the best-value accommodations (S-£22.50, D-£34.50, Db-£42, includes English breakfast, 9 Cannon Lane, tel. 9567/51711, fax 9567/51789, www.cannonhotel.gi).

Bristol Hotel offers dark, dumpy rooms in a central location at a premium price (Sb-£47–51, Db-£61–66, Tb-£71–78, break-fast-£5, 10 Cathedral Square, tel. 9567/76800, fax 9567/77613 e-mail: bristhtl@gibnet.gi).

Queen's Hotel has reasonable rates and free parking nearby plus special rates for young travelers, but it's noisy and lacks character (student S-£17, student D-£25, Db-£43, across from cable-car station and a few blocks from city center, 1 Boyd Street, tel. 9567/74000, fax 9567/40030).

Transportation Connections—Gibraltar

If you're leaving Gibraltar without a car, you must walk five minutes from Gibraltar's border into Spain to reach La Línea, the nearest bus station. The region's main transportation hub is Algeciras, with lots of train, bus, and ferry connections. (For Algeciras connections, see "Tarifa," below.)

La Línea by bus to: Algeciras (2/hrly, 45 min), **Tarifa** (8/day, 1 hr), **Málaga** (4/day, 3 hrs), **Granada** (2/day, 5 hrs).

TARIFA

Europe's most southerly town is a pleasant alternative to gritty, noisy Algeciras. It's an Arabic-looking town with a lovely beach, an old castle, restaurants swimming in fresh seafood, inexpensive places to sleep, and enough windsurfers to sink a ship.

As I stood on the town promenade under the castle, looking out at almost-touchable Morocco across the Straits of Gibraltar, I regretted only that I didn't have this book to steer me clear of wretched Algeciras on earlier trips. Tarifa, with usually daily one-hour trips to Tangier, is the best jumping-off point for a Moroccan side trip—if the boats are accepting non-Europeans. Call ahead to travel agencies listed below. (Non-Europeans *are* always allowed on the boats departing from Algeciras.)

Tarifa has no blockbuster sights (and is pretty dead off-season), but it's a town where you just feel good to be on vacation.

Orientation

Tourist Information: The TI is on Paseo Alameda (Mon–Fri 11:00–14:00, 18:00–19:00, tel. 95-668-0993).

Arrival in Tarifa: The bus station (just a ticket office) is at Batalla de Salado 19 (Mon–Fri 7:15–11:00, 15:00–19:00, Sat–Sun 15:00–20:00, tel. 95-668-4038). When you get off the bus, orient yourself by facing the old-town gate. The recommended hotels in the old town are through the gate; the hotels in the newer part of town are a couple of blocks behind you.

Ferry to Morocco: If you're going to Morocco, call to make sure the boat is running (Tarifa travel agencies: Marruecotur, tel. 95-668-4751 and FRS Maroc at the boat dock, tel. 95-668-1830). Get your boat ticket as soon as possible—there are only a few

Tarifa

ferries a day, and they do sell out. Prices are the same in the many travel agencies and hotels, so you might book ahead or stop by the first agency you see when you get to town. The going rate is 7,000 ptas for a round-trip all-day tour or 6,000 ptas for a round-trip without a tour. See the Morocco chapter for more information.

Sights—Tarifa

Castle of Guzman El Bueno—This castle was named after a 13th-century Christian general who gained fame in a sad show of courage while fighting the Moors. Holding Guzman's son hostage, the Moors demanded he surrender the castle or they'd kill the boy. Guzman refused, even throwing his own knife down from the ramparts. It was used on his son's throat. Ultimately, the Moors withdrew to Africa, and Guzman was a hero. *Bueno*. The castle itself is a concrete hulk in a vacant lot, interesting only for the harbor views from the ramparts (200 ptas, Tue–Sun 10:00–14:00, 18:00–20:00, Dec–April 10:00–14:00, 16:00–18:00, closed Mon).

Church of St. Matthew—Tarifa's main church faces its main drag. Most nights it seems life squirts from the church out the front door and into the fun-loving Calle El Bravo. Wander inside (English leaflets inside on the right).

    1. Find the tiny (one-foot-square) piece of **ancient tombstone** in the wall just before the transept on the right side. Probably the most important historic item in town, it proves there was a functioning church here during Visigothic times, before the Moorish conquest. The tombstone reads, in a kind of Latin Spanish, "Flaviano lived as a Christian for 50 years, a little more or less. In death he received forgiveness as a servant of God on March 30, 674. May he rest in peace." If that gets you in the mood to light a candle, switch on an electronic "candle" for 25 ptas on your left.

    2. Step into the transept beyond the candles. The centerpiece of the **altar** is a boy Jesus. By Andalusian tradition he used to be naked, but these days he's clothed with outfits that vary with the Church calendar. On the right is a fine 17th-century statue of the "Virgin [protector] of the Fishermen."

    3. A statue of **St. James the Moorslayer** (missing his sword) is on the right wall of the main central altar. Since the days of the Reconquista, James has been Spain's patron saint.

    4. The altar on the left harbors several **statues** that go on parade through town during Holy Week. The **Captive Christ** (with hands bound) goes back to the days when Christians were held captive by Moors.

    5. Circling around to the left side you'll find a side door, the **"door of pardons."** For a long time, Tarifa was a dangerous place—on the edge of the Reconquista. To encourage people to live here, the Church offered a huge amount of forgiveness to anyone who lived in Tarifa for a year. One year and one day after moving to Tarifa, they would have the privilege of passing through this special "door of pardons," and a Mass of thanksgiving would be held in that person's honor.

Bullfighting—Tarifa has a third-rate bullring where novices botch fights most Saturdays through the summer. Professional bullfights takes place the first two weeks of September. The ring is a short walk from the town. You'll see posters everywhere.

Whale Watching—Daily whale- and dolphin-watching excursions are offered by two eco-tourism organizations, FIRMM (4,500 ptas per person, Pedro Cortés 3, next to Café Central, tel. 95-662-7008, fax 95-668-1424) and Whale Watch España (4,000 ptas per person, Avenida de la Constitución, tel. 63-947-6544). Trips last 2.5 hours and advance reservations are advised.

▲**Windsurfing**—**Playa Punta Paloma** is a vast, sandy beach about eight kilometers northwest of town. On windy summer days the sea is littered with sprinting windsurfers while the beach holds a couple hundred vans and fun-mobiles from northern Europe. Under mountain ridges lined with modern energy-generating windmills, it's a fascinating scene. Drive down the sandy road and stroll along the beach. You'll find a cabana-type hamlet with rental gear, beachwear shops, a bar, and a hip, healthy restaurant with great lunch salads.

Sleeping in Tarifa
(180 ptas = about $1, country code: 34, zip code: 11380)
The first four listings (listed in the order you'll see them if you drive in from Sevilla) are right off the main drag—Batalla del Salado—with easy parking, in the modern, plain part of town. To reach these hotels if arriving by bus, turn left out of the station ticket office and head away from the old-city center. The rest are inside or border the old town. Room rates vary with the season (3 tiers vary but are, roughly: high—always August, as much as July–September; mid—spring and fall; and low—winter). Breakfast and a 7 percent tax are extra. There's a handy laundry service (drop off and pick up later) at the big Consum supermarket on Calle San José near the recommended hotels in the newer part of town.

   Hotel La Mirada is shiny new, with 25 modern rooms, some of which come with sea views (Sb-4,000, 5,000, or 6,000 ptas, Db-6,000, 6,500, or 8,000 ptas, extra bed-1,000 ptas, breakfast-550 ptas, elevator, great views from large terrace, attached restaurant, CC:VMA, Calle San Sebastián 41, tel. 95-668-4427, fax 95-668-1162, www.hotel-lamirada.com, some English spoken). It's two blocks to the right of the main drag and about five blocks away from the old town.

   The 10-room motel-style **Hostal Tarik** is clean and pleasant but short on windows (Db-4,500–8,000 ptas, Tb-5,500–9,000 ptas,

CC:VMA, Calle San Sebastián 32, tel. 95-668-0648, SE).
Surrounded by warehouses, it's one block toward the town
center from Hotel La Mirada.

Hostal Alborada is a squeaky-clean place with an attractive
courtyard. It's a couple of blocks closer to the old town on a plain
street (Sb-3,000, 4,000, or 5,000 ptas, Db-4,500, 5,500, or 7,000
ptas, Tb-6,000–9,000 ptas, high season is July–Sept, get your price
and then show this book for a 10 percent discount, laundry and
Internet services, CC:VM, Calle San José 52, tel. 95-668-1140,
fax 95-668-1935, www.hotelalborada.com, fun-loving Rafael
Mesa Rodriguez and Juaquina speak only a little English).

The family-run **Hostal Avenida** has 11 tidy, comfy rooms
and a pretty courtyard, but it's on a busy street leading into town.
Ask for one of the four *tranquilo* rooms off the street (Sb-
3,000–5,000 ptas, Db-4,000–6,500 ptas, Tb-5,000–8,000 ptas,
Calle Pío XII, just off main drag, tel. 95-668-4818, Maria NSE).

Hostal Villanueva is your best budget bet. It's friendly,
though no English is spoken, and includes a great terrace overlooking the old town. It's on a busy street, and the quiet rooms in
the back come with the best views (Sb-2,000–2,500 ptas, Db-
5,000–8,000 ptas, extra bed-2,500 ptas, some more expensive new
rooms, breakfast-300 ptas, attached restaurant, Avenida de
Andalucía 11, just west of the old-town gate, tel. 95-668-4149).

The following are inside the old city: **Hostal La Calzada** has
eight well-appointed, quiet, and airy rooms right in the noisy-
at-night, old-town thick of things (Db-6,000–8,000 ptas, Tb-
7,000–9,000 ptas, closed Oct–March, CC:VMA, Calle Justino
Pertinez 3, veer left and down from the old-town gate, tel. 95-
668-0366 or 95-668-1492, NSE).

Hostal Alameda glistens with pristine marble floors and
pastels. It overlooks a square where the local children play (Db-
5,000–6,000 ptas, Tb-8,000–9,500 ptas, breakfast–450 ptas,
CC:VM, Paseo Alameda 4, tel. 95-668-1181, some English spoken). Its 11 bright rooms are above its restaurant (great gazpacho).

La Casa Amarilla (the Yellow House) offers posh apartments
with modern décor and mini-kitchens (Db-7,000–8,000 ptas,
Tb-8,000–10,000 ptas, across the street from Café Central, Calle
Sancho IV El Bravo #9, tel. 95-668-1993, fax 95-668-0590,
e-mail: lacasaamarilla@via.goya.es).

Eating in Tarifa

You'll find good tapas throughout the old town. **Café Central** is
the happening place nearly any time of day (all tapas are priced at
150 ptas—go to the bar and point; great and ingenious 600-ptas
salads—study the menu; healthy fruit drinks are impressively thera-
peutic; off Plaza San Mateo, tel. 95-668-0560). Across the street
is a *panadería* offering tasty, cheap sandwiches. Next door, in

front of the church, **Restaurant Morilla** serves good local-style food and paella on the town's prime piece of people-watching real estate (long hours, every day, Calle Sancho IV El Bravo, tel. 95-668-1757).

From Café Central follow the cars 100 meters to the first corner on the left to reach **Bar El Frances** for its fine tapas (generally 125 ptas), especially snails (*caracoles*, June–mid-July only). The nearby **Cafe Bar los Melli** is family friendly and serves a good chorizo sandwich. **Bar El Pasillo**, next to Melli, has tapas.

From Melli you can circle around toward the church past some very gritty and colorful tapas bars. Just to the seaside of the church you'll see the mysterious **Casino Tarifeno**. This is an old-boys' social club "for members only," but it offers a big, musty Andalusian welcome to visiting tourists—even women. Wander through. There's a bar with tapas, a TV room, a card room, and a lounge.

From the town center, walk the narrow Calle San Francisco to survey a number of good restaurants, such as the classy, quiet **Guzman El Bueno** and the cheap and easy **Pizzeria La Capricciosa**.

While tricky to find, the street Buerta del Rey is punctuated with snack bars, and a family scene at night (outside the old city walls, 2 blocks west). Stop by the *heladeria* for ice cream or **La Dulce Campesina** for tasty pastries and coffee.

Confiteria la Tarifeña serves super pastries and flan (at the top of Calle Nuestra Sra. de la Luz, near the arch).

Picnics: Try a grocery, the *mercado* municipal (Mon–Sat 8:00–14:00, closed Sun, in old town), or **Consum supermarket** (Mon–Sat 9:00–14:00, 17:00–21:00, closed Sun, simple cafeteria, at Callao and San José, near the hotels in the new town).

Transportation Connections—Tarifa

By bus to: La Línea and Gibraltar (7/day, 1 hr, 455 ptas; first departure at 9:40, last return at 20:00), **Jerez** (3/day, 2 hrs, 1,220 ptas), **Sevilla** (4/day, 3 hrs, 2,075 ptas), **Málaga** (3/day, 3.5 hrs, 1,575 ptas), **Algeciras** (10/day, 30 min, 235 ptas), **Huelva** (1/day, 5 hrs, 3,025 ptas), **Cadiz** (9/day, 2 hrs, 1,030 ptas). Bus info: tel. 95-668-4038.

Transportation Connections—Algeciras

Algeciras is only worth leaving. Use it as a transfer point—and then only if necessary. The train station is four blocks inland on the far side of Hotel Octavio (up Juan de la Cierva, tel. 95-663-0202). Head toward the sea for the TI and bus stations. The TI (Mon–Fri 9:00–14:00, Juan de la Cierva, tel. 95-657-2636) is midway between the train station and the port.

Algeciras has three bus stations: The Comes bus station

(half-block away from train station, next to Hotel Octavio, tel. 95-665-3456) offers frequent service to La Línea and Tarifa, less-frequent service to other Andalusian destinations and Madrid. The Portillo bus station (on waterfront, kitty-corner from the port, Calle Virgen Carmen, tel. 95-665-1055) offers frequent, direct buses to Málaga and Granada. The Linesur bus station (also on waterfront, 1 block north of Portillo station, Calle Virgen Carmen, tel. 95-660-3400) offers the most direct buses to Sevilla and Jerez. The many travel agencies along the waterfront all sell ferry tickets and accept credit cards (for ferries to Morocco, see Morocco chapter).

By bus to: **La Línea/Gibraltar** (2/hrly, 45 min), **Tarifa** (10/day, 30 min), **Jerez** (8/day, 1.5 hrs), **Sevilla** (8/day, 3 hrs), **Granada** (4/day, 3.5 hrs), **Málaga** (11/day, 3 hrs), **Madrid** (2/day, 12 hrs).

By train to: **Ronda** (4/day, 2 hrs), **Málaga** (3/day, 4 hrs, transfer in Bobadilla), **Granada** (3/day, 5 hrs, transfer in Bobadilla), **Sevilla** (3/day, 5 hrs, transfer in Bobadilla). All four rides offer great scenery; the mountainous trip to Málaga via Bobadilla is one of Spain's most scenic train rides. There are also five trains to Madrid (2 direct, 1 overnight, 6–9 hrs).

Route Tips for Drivers

Tarifa to Gibraltar (45 min): It's a short drive, passing a silvery-white forest of windmills, from peaceful Tarifa past Algeciras to La Línea (the Spanish town bordering Gibraltar). Passing Algeciras, continue in the direction of Estepona. At San Roque take the La Línea-Gibraltar exit.

Gibraltar to Nerja (130 miles): Barring traffic problems, the trip along the Costa del Sol is smooth and easy by car—much of it on new highways. Just follow the coastal highway east. After Málaga follow signs to Almería and Motril.

Nerja to Granada (80 miles, 90 min, 100 views): Drive along the coast to Salobrena, catching N323 north for about 40 miles to Granada. While scenic side trips may beckon, don't arrive late in Granada without a firm reservation.

MOROCCO

Go to Africa. As you step off the boat you realize that the hour-long crossing has taken you farther culturally than did the trip from the United States to Iberia. Morocco needs no museums; its sights are living in the streets. The one-day excursions (usually daily, year-round) from Tarifa are well organized and reliable, and given the steep price of the boat passage alone, the tour package is a good value for those who can spare only a day for Morocco. Call ahead to travel agencies (see page 206) to make sure boats departing from Tarifa are accepting non-Europeans. If they aren't, catch a boat from Algeciras.

Morocco in a Day?

There are many ways to experience Morocco, and a day in Tangier is probably the worst. But all you need is a passport (no visa or shots required), and if all you have is a day, this is a real and worthwhile adventure. Tangier is the Tijuana of Morocco, and everyone there seems to be expecting you.

The tours organized in Tarifa charge 7,000 ptas and give you a round-trip crossing, a good guide to meet you at the harbor in Tangier and hustle you through the hustlers and onto your bus, and a bus tour. The latter includes a city tour, a trip to the desolate Atlantic Coast for some rugged African scenery, the famous ride-a-camel stop, a walk through the medina (old town) with a too-thorough look at a sales-starved carpet shop, and a big lunch in a palatial Moroccan setting with live music.

Sound cheesy? It is. But no amount of packaging can gloss over how exotic and different this culture really is. This kind of cultural voyeurism is almost embarrassing, but it's nonstop action and more memorable than another day in Spain. The shopping is—Moroccan. Bargain hard!

Morocco

The day trip is so tightly organized you'll have hardly any time alone in Tangier. For many people, that's just fine. Some, however, spend a night there and return the next day. Ask the Tarifa TI about the two-day tour for 12,500 to 13,500 ptas. (See "Ferry Connections," on page 205, for travel agencies.) You can buy and sell dirhams at the Bank of Morocco branch in the Algeciras terminal. But for a short one-day trip, there's no need to change money. Everyone you meet will be happy to take your pesetas or dollars.

Extended Tour of Morocco

Morocco gets much better as you go deeper into the interior. The country is incredibly rich in cultural thrills—but you'll pay a price in hassles and headaches. It's a package deal, and if danger's your business, it's a great option.

To get a fair look at Morocco, you must get past the hustlers and con artists of the north coast (Tangier, Tétouan). It takes a minimum of four or five days to make a worthwhile visit—ideally seven or eight. Plan at least two nights in either Fès or Marrakech. A trip over the Atlas Mountains gives you an exciting look at Saharan Morocco. If you need a vacation from your vacation, check into one of the idyllic Atlantic beach resorts on the south coast. Above all, get past the northern day-trip-from-Spain, take-a-snapshot-on-a-camel fringe. Oops, that's us. Oh, well.

If you're relying on public transportation for your extended tour, sail to Tangier, blast your way through customs, listen to no hustler who tells you there's no way out until tomorrow, and hop into a Petit Taxi for the Morora train station four kilometers away (15 dirhams, or $1.50). From there, set your sights on Rabat, a dignified, European-type town with fewer hustlers, and make it your get-acquainted stop in Morocco. Trains go farther south from Rabat.

If you're driving a car, sail from Algeciras to Ceuta, a Spanish possession. Crossing the border is a bit unnerving, since you'll be jumped through several bureaucratic hoops. You'll go through customs, buy Moroccan insurance for your car (cheap and easy), and feel at the mercy of a bristly bunch of shady-looking people you'd rather not be at the mercy of. Most cars are shepherded through by a guy who will expect a tip. Relax and let him grease those customs wheels. He's worth it. As soon as possible, hit the road and drive to Chefchaouen, the best first stop for those with their own wheels.

Orientation (Mental)

Thrills: Morocco is culture shock—both bad and good. It makes Spain and Portugal look meek and mild. You'll encounter oppressive friendliness, the Arabic language, squiggly writing, the Islamic faith, and ancient cities. It is a photographer's delight, very cheap, and comes with plenty of hotels, surprisingly easy transportation, and a variety of terrain, from Swiss-like mountain resorts to fairytale mud-brick oasis towns to luxuriously natural beaches to bustling desert markets.

Spills: Many travelers are overwhelmed by its intensity, poverty, aggressive beggars, brutal heat, and slick con men. Most of the English-speaking Moroccans that the tourist meets are hustlers. Most visitors have some intestinal problems. Most women are harassed on the streets by horny but generally harmless men. Things don't work smoothly. In fact, compared to Morocco, Spain resembles Sweden for efficiency. People don't see the world through the same filters we do, and some very good parents proudly name their sons Saddam. This is Islam.

Leave busy itineraries and split-second timing in Europe. Morocco must be taken on its own terms. In Morocco things go smoothly only *"Inshallah"*—if God so wills.

Helpful Hints

Friday: Friday is the Muslim day of rest, when most of the country (except Tangier) closes down.

Money: Change money only at banks, or even easier, at ATMs (available at most major banks), all of which have uniform rates. The black market is dangerous. Change only what you need and keep the bank receipt to reconvert if necessary. Don't leave the country with Moroccan money. (If you do, the Bank of Morocco branch in Algeciras may buy it back from you.)

Arabic Numerals

0	•	SIFR
1	١	WAAHID
2	٢	ITNEEN
3	٣	TALAATA
4	٤	ARBA'A
5	٥	KHAMSA
6	٦	SITTA
7	٧	SAB'A
8	٨	TAMANYA
9	٩	TIS'A
10	١٠	'ASHRA

Health: Morocco is much more hazardous to your health than Spain or Portugal. Eat in clean— not cheap—places. Peel fruit, eat only cooked vegetables, and drink reliably bottled water (Sidi Harazem or Sidi Ali). When you do get diarrhea, and you should plan on it, adjust your diet (small and bland meals, no milk or grease) or fast for a day but make sure you replenish lost fluids. Relax; most diarrhea is not serious, just an adjustment that will run its course.

Information: For an extended trip, bring travel information from home or Spain. The guides published by Lonely Planet, Rough Guide, and Let's Go (*Let's Go: Spain and Portugal* includes Morocco) are good. The green *Michelin Morocco* guidebook is worthwhile (if you read French). Buy the best map you can find locally—names are always changing, and it's helpful to have towns, roads, and place-names written in Arabic.

Language: The Arabic squiggle-script, its many difficult sounds, and the fact that French is Morocco's second language make communication tricky for English-speaking travelers. A little French goes a long way, but learn a few words in Arabic. Have your first local friend help you pronounce *min fadlik* ("please"; meen FAD-leek), *shókran* ("thank you"; SHOW-kron), *ismahli* ("excuse me"; ees-MAY-lee), *yeh* ("yes"; EE-yuh), *lah* ("no"; lah), and *maa salama* ("good-bye"; mah sah-LEM-ah). In markets, I sing "la la la la la" to my opponents. *Lah shókran* means, "No, thank you." Listen carefully and write new words phonetically. Bring an Arabic phrase book. Make a point of learning the local number symbols; they are not like ours (which we call "Arabic").

Keeping your bearings: Navigate the labyrinthine *medinas* (old towns) by altitude, gates, and famous mosques or buildings. Write down what gate you came in so you can enjoy being lost— temporarily. *Souk* is Arabic for a particular market (such as leather, yarn, or metalwork).

Hustlers: While Moroccans are some of Africa's wealthiest people, you are still incredibly rich to them. This imbalance causes predictable problems. Wear your money belt. Assume con artists are more clever than you. Haggle when appropriate (prices skyrocket for tourists). You'll attract hustlers like flies at every famous tourist sight. They'll lie to you, get you lost, and pester you. Never leave your car or baggage where you can't get back to it without your "guide." Anything you buy in their company gets them a 20 percent commission. Normally locals, shopkeepers, and police will come to your rescue when the hustlers' heat becomes unbearable. I usually hire a guide, since it's helpful to have a translator, and once you're "taken," the rest seem to leave you alone.

Marijuana: In Morocco marijuana (*kif*) is as illegal as it is popular, as many Westerners in local jails would love to remind you. Some dealers who sell it cheap make their profit after you get arrested. Cars and buses are stopped and checked by police routinely throughout Morocco—especially in the north and in the Chefchaouen region, which is Morocco's *kif* capital.

Getting around Morocco: Moroccan trains are quite good. Second class is cheap and comfortable. Buses connect all smaller towns quite well. By car, Morocco is easy, but drive defensively and never rely on the oncoming driver's skill. Night driving is dangerous. Pay a guard to watch your car overnight.

TANGIER
Tangier is split into two. The new town has the TI and fancy hotels. The medina (old town) has the markets, the Kasbah (with its palace), cheap hotels, decrepit homes, and 2,000 wannabe guides. The twisty, hilly streets of the old town are caged within a wall accessible by keyhole gates. The big square, Grand Socco, is the link between the old and new parts of town.

Orientation (area code: 039)
Many assume they'll be lost in Tangier—because it's in Africa. This makes no sense. The town is laid out very simply. From the boat dock you'll see the old town—circled by its medieval wall—on the right (behind Hotel Continental). The new town sprawls past the industrial port zone to the left. Everything is within a 15-minute walk from the port. Petit Taxis are a godsend. Use them generously and go ahead and just pay double the meter for any ride (10 dirhams = about $1). See "Sleeping" below for tips on making calls to and within Morocco.

Planning Your Time
Consider hiring a guide at the port (see "Guides," below). If you're a shopper, head straight for the market. Otherwise, head to the TI for a map and advice (Mon–Sat 8:30–12:00, 14:30–18:30, Boulevard Pasteur 29, tel. 94-80-50, fax 94-86-61). From there

you can walk to the Grand Socco and market. Or, for the more complete tour, catch a taxi to the Place de la Kasbah at the top of the old town and work your way downhill to the port. Start at the Museum of the Kasbah, then wander through the fortress (Dar el-Makhzem) and the Old American Legation Museum, and shop through the Petit Socco. Walk out of the old town into the noisy Grand Socco. From there, catch a taxi to the beach (Place el Cano) and sightsee along the beach and then along Avenue d'Espagne back to the port.

From Tarifa to Tangier

Departing Tarifa: At the Tarifa port, bring or buy your boat ticket (if you're doing Tangier on your own). If you're taking a tour, bring the tour voucher you bought at the travel agency to the boat office and get your ticket. If you have confirmed your boat's departure time carefully the night before, there's no reason to show up more than 15 minutes before departure.

On the boat: If you're on your own and plan to stay only one day, do what you can to get your ticket stamped twice (*"Entree"* and *"Sortie"*) by the Moroccan customs man. (Those taking the tour get this done automatically.) If you manage this, show your ticket—not your passport—upon arrival and departure in Morocco and you'll save 30 minutes of messing around as you leave Tangier. If, on the other hand, you plan to stay longer than a day in Morocco (or you want the option to stay longer than a day), make sure your passport is stamped only once (*"Entree"*). The boat has a gruesome cafeteria bar, plenty of WCs, stuffy indoor chairs, and grand top-deck views. Carefully confirm the time your return boat departs from Tangier. The time difference between the countries can be up to two hours.

Arriving in Tangier: If you're on a tour, look for your leader. Note that your leader meets you in Tangier after you get off the boat from Spain (not in Spain when you board). In Tangier you'll be corralled at the gangplank onto your waiting tour bus.

Independent travelers will take a five-minute walk from the boat, through customs, and out of the port. Taxis at the port are more expensive. Ask the cost before taking one. The big yellow Port de Tanger gateway defines the end of the port area and the start of the city. Leave mental bread crumbs so you can find your way back to your boat. It will just stay put all day. Just outside the port gate on the busy traffic circle you'll find plenty of fair, metered Petit Taxis along with a line of decent fish restaurants, the boulevard arcing along the beach into the new town, and stairs leading up into the old town (on the right). Catch a taxi to the TI.

Guides

If you're on your own, you'll be fighting off "guides" all day. In order to have your own translator and a shield from less scrupulous

Tangier

❶ HOTEL CONTINENTAL	❸ HOTEL TANJAH - FLANDRIA	❺ OLD AMERICAN LEGATION MUSEUM
❷ HOTEL REMBRANDT	❹ HOTEL PARIS	

touts that hit up tourists constantly throughout the old town, I recommend hiring a guide. Stress your interest in the people and culture rather than shopping. Guides, hoping to get a huge commission from your purchases, can cleverly turn your Tangier day into a Marco Polo equivalent of the Shopping Channel.

I've had good luck with the private guides who meet the boat. These hardworking, English-speaking, and licensed guides offer their services for the day for 2,000 ptas. Aziz Begdouri is good ($12 for 5 hrs, easier to reach him on his Spanish cellular, tel. 60-789-7967, than his Moroccan cellular, tel. 00-212-61-63-9332, e-mail: aziztour@hotmail.com). The TI also has official guides (half-day for $12, 2,000 ptas or 120 dirhams).

If you don't want a guide, ask directions of people who can't leave what they're doing (such as the only clerk in a shop) or of women who aren't near men. Ask "Kasbah?" or wherever you want to go, and you'll get pointed in the right direction. Fewer hustlers are in the new (but less interesting) part of town.

Sights—Tangier

Kasbah—This is the fortress atop old Tangier. You'll find a history museum in a former palace on Place de la Kasbah (10 dirhams, Wed–Mon 9:00–12:30, 15:00–17:00, closed Tue) and a colorful gauntlet of Kodak moments waiting to ambush tour groups as they wander through: snake charmers, squawky dance troupes, and colorful water vendors. Before descending out of the Kasbah, don't miss the ocean viewpoint, the Mosque de la Kasbah, and Dar el-Makhzen, the fortress of the pasha of Tangier.

The *Medina* and Petit Socco—From the Kasbah, a maze of winding lanes and tiny alleys weave through the old-town market area. Petit Socco, a little square in the old town, is lined with tea shops. A casual first-time visitor cannot stay oriented. I just wander, knowing that if I keep going downhill, I'll eventually pop out at the port; if I veer to the right while going downhill, I'll come to a gate leading into the modern town probably via the Grand Socco, the big and noisy market square. The market is filthy and reportedly dangerous after dark. Plain-clothed tourist police are stationed throughout, making sure you are safe as you wander.

Tangier American Legation Museum—Morocco was the first country to recognize the United States as an independent country. This building, given to the United States by the sultan of Morocco, became the American government's first foreign possession. It served as our embassy or consulate from 1821 to 1956, is still owned by the United States, and is the only U.S. national historic landmark overseas. Today this 19th-century mansion is a strangely peaceful oasis within Tangier's intense old town. It offers a warm welcome, lots of interesting paintings, and a reminder of how long the United States and Morocco have had good relations (free, donations accepted, Mon–Fri 10:00–13:00, 15:00–17:00, Rue America 8, tel. 93-53-17).

Grand Socco—This big square is a transportation hub. From here, a gate leads into the old-town market; Rue de la Kasbah leads uphill along the old wall to Port de la Kasbah (a gate leading into the Kasbah); Rue de la Liberte leads to Place de France and Boulevard Pasteur (TI and recommended hotels); and Rue de la Plage leads to the train station, the port, and the beach.

Tangier Beach—This fine, white-sand crescent beach, stretching eastward from the port, is lined by fun eateries and packed with locals doing what people around the world do at the beach—with a few variations: You'll see lazy camels and people, young and old, covered in hot sand to combat rheumatism.

Sleeping in Tangier

(10 dirhams = about $1, country code: 212, area code: 039)
Sleep Code: **S** = Single, **D** = Double/Twin, **T** = Triple, **Q** = Quad, **b** = bathroom, **t** = toilet only, **s** = shower only, **CC** = Credit Card (**V**isa, **M**asterCard, Amex), **SE** = Speaks English, **NSE** = No English.

These hotels are centrally located, near the TI and American Express (Boulevard Pasteur 54), and within walking distance of the market. The first two are four-star hotels. To reserve from Spain, dial 00 (Spain's international access code), 212 (Morocco's country code), 039 (Tangier's area code without the initial zero), then the local number. When calling from anywhere within Morocco, dial Tangier's area code with the zero, then the six-digit number. July through mid-September is high season, when rooms may be a bit more expensive and a reservation is wise.

Hotel Rembrandt, with a restaurant, bar, and swimming pool surrounded by a great grassy garden, has 75 clean, comfortable rooms, some with views (Sb-371 dirhams, Db-453 dirhams, elevator, CC:VMA, tel. 93-78-70 or 33-33-14, fax 93-04-43, SE). Across the street, **Hotel Tanjah-Flandria** is more formal, stuffy, and comfortable but soulless, and a lesser value (Sb-639 dirhams, Db-792 dirhams, discounts for 3-night stays, breakfast-65 dirhams, CC:VMA restaurant, elevator, air-con, rooftop terrace, pool, tel. 93-32-79, fax 93-43-47, e-mail: Rembrand@Iam.net.ma, SE).

Hotel Continental, the Humphrey Bogart option, is a grand old place in the old town. It overlooks the port, with lavish, public spaces, a chandeliered breakfast room, and 70 spacious bedrooms with hardwood floors. Jimmy, who runs the place with a Moroccan flair, says he offers everything but Viagra. When I said, "I'm from Seattle," he said, "206." Test him. He knows your area code (Db-307 dirhams, includes tax and breakfast, Dar Baroud 36, tel. 93-10-24, fax 93-11-43, SE).

Hotel Paris, across from the TI, is noisy, dingy, and friendly. Ask for a room in the back—and a mop. (Sb-249 dirhams, Db-296 dirhams, Boulevard Pasteur 42, tel. 93-18-77; the helpful and informative manager, Abdullatif, SE.)

Ferry Connections from Spain

Boats run daily year-round (but call to make sure the boat is running). Some Spanish hotels also sell the tours (same price as travel agencies). In summer Tangier is two hours earlier than Tarifa (1 hour in winter). Confirm the time of departure. I'd keep my watch on Spanish time and get my departure times clear in Spanish time. For each departure you'll go through two different passport-stamping lines (unless you managed to get your ticket prestamped; see "From Tarifa to Tangier," above). Plan on spending one hour of your day in lines. Departing from Spain, passports are checked on the boat.

Tarifa to Tangier: There are two to three crossings every morning (2 boats depart daily at 9:00; 1 boat departs Sun–Thu at 11:00). The fast ferry (FRS Maroc) gets you to Tangier in 40 minutes (but you can't go out on the deck); the regular ferry (Southern Ferries) takes 60 minutes. If you travel without a tour, you'll pay 6,000 ptas round-trip (free parking at Tarifa boat dock). Tour options cost 7,000 ptas for one day, 12,500 to 13,500 ptas for two days (includes crossing). Two-day tours are the same as the one-day tour, but you just go to a fancy hotel (with dinner) rather than the afternoon boat (15:00, 16:00, 18:00) and catch the same boat 24 unstructured hours later.

If you'll leave Tarifa at 9:00, you'll return by 18:00. Note that returns on Friday tours are delayed four hours, which for some means being bored and killing time at the port and for others means getting lots more time for exploring Tangier. If considering Friday, also remember that it is the Muslim Sabbath, which means there will be less business action in the streets.

You rarely need to book more than a day in advance, even during peak season. Boats are most crowded on Tuesday, Wednesday, and Thursday, when the Costa del Sol groups come en masse. They can book up the boat entirely in August. Only about seven crossings a year are canceled because of storms (mostly in winter), but if you're going to Tarifa for the sole purpose of catching the boat to Morocco, call one of the travel agencies below to make sure the boats are running.

Get your ticket any way you like. Many hotels and travel agencies sell the same boat tickets and tours for the same price. The major travel agencies in Tarifa are Marruecotur and FRS Maroc.

Marruecotur has a handy office across from the Tarifa TI on Avenida di Constitutión (daily 8:30-21:00, Nov–April 8:30–20:00, CC:VMA, tel. 95-668-4751, fax 95-668-0256, e-mail: mctotravel@hotmail.com). If you choose Marruecotur, you'll sail with Southern Ferries (the office at the dock sells tickets, daily 8:00–13:00, 16:00–19:00, tel. 95-662-7044). If you want to take your car, Southern Ferries will transport it for 9,300 to 13,000 ptas, depending on its size. There is plenty of parking at the dock if you go on foot.

FRS Maroc is at the far end of the dock (daily 8:00–13:00, 16:00–20:00, shorter hours at whim, CC:VMA, tel. 95-668-1830, fax 95-668-4835).

Algeciras to: Tangier (5 ferries/day, 1/hrly in summer, 2.5 hrs, 3,500 ptas each way, 10,000 ptas for a car; plus an occasional hydrofoil, 1 hr, 3,800 ptas), **Ceuta** (7 ferries/day, 1/hrly in summer, 90 min, 2,000 ptas each way, 9,000 ptas for a car; plus 12 hydrofoils/day, 35 min, 3,100 ptas each way). **Ceuta**, an uninteresting Spanish possession in North Africa, is the best car-entry point but is not for those relying on public transport. From Ceuta, drive into Morocco. For more info on ferry schedules, call the Algeciras TI (Mon–Fri 9:00–14:00, tel. 95-657-2636). Moroccans clog the Algeciras port, especially in July and August, making Tarifa a relatively relaxing and easygoing option.

Sights—Moroccan Towns

▲▲**Chefchaouen**—Just two hours by bus or car from Tétouan, this is the first pleasant town beyond the Tijuana-type north coast. Monday and Thursday are colorful market days. Stay in the classy old Hotel Chaouen on Plaza el-Makhzen. This former Spanish parador faces the old town and offers fine meals and a refuge from hustlers. Wander deep into the whitewashed old town from here.

▲▲**Rabat**—Morocco's capital and most European city, Rabat is the most comfortable and least stressful place to start your North African trip. You'll find a colorful market (in the old neighboring town of Salé), bits of Islamic architecture (Mausoleum of Mohammed V), the king's palace, mellow hustlers, and fine hotels.

▲▲▲**Fès**—More than just a funny hat that tipsy Shriners wear, Fès is Morocco's religious and artistic center, bustling with craftsmen, pilgrims, shoppers, and shops. Like most large Moroccan cities, it has a distinct new town from the French colonial period and an exotic—and stressful—old Arabic town, where you'll find the market. The Fès marketplace is Morocco's best.

▲▲▲**Marrakech**—Morocco's gateway to the south, this market city is a constant folk festival bustling with djellaba-clad Berber tribespeople and a colorful center where the desert, mountain, and coastal regions merge. The new city has the train station, and the main boulevard (Mohammed V) is lined with banks, airline offices, a post office, a tourist office, and comfortable hotels. The old city features the mazelike market and the huge Djemaa el-Fna, a square seething with people—a 43-ring Moroccan circus.

▲▲▲**Over the Atlas Mountains**—Extend your Moroccan trip several days by heading south over the Atlas Mountains. Take a bus from Marrakech to Ouarzazate (short stop) and then to Tinerhir (great oasis town, comfy hotel, overnight stop). The next day go to Er Rachidia and take the overnight bus to Fès.

By car, drive from Fès south, staying in the small mountain town of Ifrane, and then continue deep into the desert country past Er Rachidia and on to Rissani (market days: Sun, Tue, and Thu). Explore nearby mud-brick towns still living in the Middle Ages. Hire a guide to drive you past where the road stops and head cross-country to an oasis village (Merzouga) where you can climb a sand dune and watch the sun rise over the vastness of Africa. Only a sea of sand separates you from Timbuktu.

Transportation Connections—Morocco

In Tangier, all train traffic comes and goes from the suburban Morora train station, four kilometers from the city center and a short Petit Taxi ride away (15 dirhams, $1.50). Upon your return, catch the bus, which meets every train arrival and takes passengers all the way to the port for 2.5 dirhams. The bus also goes from downtown one hour before each departure but is not worth the trouble.

From Tangier by train to: Rabat (4/day, 6 hrs), **Casablanca** (5/day, 6 hrs), **Marrakech** (5/day, 10 hrs), **Fès** (2/day, 6 hrs), **Ceuta** and **Tétouan** (hrly buses, 1 hr).

From Fès to: Casablanca (8/day, 5 hrs), **Marrakech** (4/day, 9 hrs), **Rabat** (7/day, 4 hrs), **Meknes** (10/day, 1 hr), **Tangier** (5/day, 5 hrs).

From Rabat to: Casablanca (12/day, 90 min), **Fès** (6 buses/day, 5.5 hrs), **Tétouan** (2 buses/day, 4 hrs).

From Casablanca to: Marrakech (6/day, 5 hrs).

From Marrakech to: Meknes (4/day, 10 hrs), **Ouarzazate** (4 buses/day, 4 hrs).

By Plane: Flights within Morocco are convenient and cheap (around $60).

LISBON

Lisbon is a ramshackle but charming mix of now and then. Old wooden trolleys shiver up and down its hills, bird-stained statues mark grand squares, taxis rattle and screech through cobbled lanes, and well-worn people sip coffee in Art Nouveau cafés.

Lisbon, like Portugal in general, is underrated. The country seems somewhere just beyond Europe. The pace of life is noticeably slower than in Spain. Roads are rutted. Prices are cheaper. While the unification of Europe is bringing sweeping changes, the traditional economy is based on fishing, cork, wine, and textiles. Be sure to balance your look at Iberia with enough Portugal.

While Lisbon's history goes back to the Romans and Moors, its glory days were the 15th and 16th centuries, when explorers such as Vasco da Gama opened new trade routes around Africa to India, making Lisbon one of Europe's richest cities. (These days, in the wake of the 500th anniversary of his 1498 voyage, da Gama has a higher profile.) Portugal's "Age of Discovery" fueled an economic boom, which fueled the flamboyant art boom called the Manueline period—named after King Manuel I (ruled 1495–1521). In the early 18th century, the gold and diamonds of Brazil, one of Portugal's colonies, made Lisbon even wealthier.

Then, on All Saints' Day in 1755, while most of the population was in church, the city was hit by a tremendous earthquake. Candles quivered as far away as Ireland. Lisbon was dead center. Two-thirds of the city was leveled. Fires started by the many church candles raged through the city, and a huge tidal wave blasted the waterfront. Of Lisbon's 270,000 people, 30,000 were killed.

Under the energetic and eventually dictatorial leadership of Prime Minister Marques de Pombal—who had the new city planned within a month of the quake—Lisbon was rebuilt in a

Lisbon

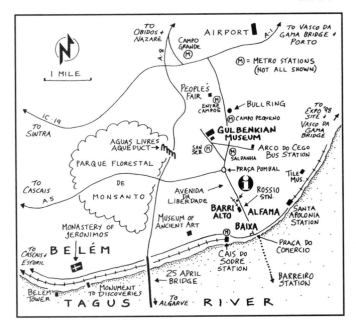

progressive grid plan, with broad boulevards and square squares. Remnants of pre-earthquake Lisbon charm survive in Belém, the Alfama, and the Baírro Alto district.

The heritage of Portugal's Age of Discovery was a vast colonial empire. Except for Macao and the few islands off the Atlantic coast, the last bits of the empire disappeared with the 1974 revolution, which delivered Portugal from the right-wing Salazar dictatorship. Emigrants from former colonies such as Mozambique and Angola have added diversity and flavor to the city, making it more likely that you'll hear African music than Portuguese fado these days.

But Lisbon's heritage survives. The city seems better organized, cleaner, and more prosperous and people-friendly than ever. With its elegant outdoor cafés, exciting art, entertaining museums, a hill-capping castle, a salty sailors' quarter, and the boost given the city after hosting the 1998 World's Fair, Lisbon is a world-class city. And with some of Europe's lowest prices, enjoying Lisbon is easy on the budget.

Planning Your Time

With three weeks in Iberia, Lisbon is worth two days.

Day 1: Start by touring Castle São Jorge, at the top of the Alfama, and surveying the city from its viewpoint. Hike down to another fine viewpoint, Miradouro de Santa Luzia, and descend into the Alfama. Explore. Back in the Baixa (bai-shah; "lower city"), have lunch on or near Rua Augusta and walk to the funicular near Praça dos Restauradores. Kick off the described walk through the Baírro Alto with a ride up the funicular. Take a joyride on trolley #28. If it's not later than 14:00, art lovers can Metro or taxi to the Gulbenkian Museum. Consider dinner at a fado show in the Baírro Alto. If one of your nights is a summer Thursday, consider a bullfight.

Day 2: Trolley to Belém and tour the Tower, Monastery, and Coach Museum (note: Belém's sights are closed Mon). Have lunch in Belém. You could continue westward, catching the train to Sintra to tour the Pena Palace and explore the ruined Moorish castle.

A third day could easily be spent at the Museum of Ancient Art and browsing through the Rossio, Baírro Alto, and Alfama neighborhoods.

The side trip to Sintra is time-consuming and rushes Lisbon. If you'd appreciate more time to absorb the ambience of the city, spend a full two days in Lisbon and do the Sintra side trip on a third day (but not on Monday, when Sintra's Pena Palace is closed).

Orientation

Greater Lisbon has around 3 million people and some frightening sprawl, but for the visitor, the city can be a delightful small-town series of parks, boulevards, and squares bunny-hopping between two hills down to the waterfront. The main boulevard, Avenida da Liberdade, goes from the high-rent district downhill, ending at the grand square called Praça dos Restauradores. From here the Baixa—the post-earthquake, grid-planned lower town, with three fine squares—leads to the riverfront. Rua Augusta is the grand pedestrian promenade running through the Baixa to the river.

Most travelers focus on the three characteristic neighborhoods that line the downtown harborfront: Baixa (flat, in the middle), the Baírro Alto (literally "high town," Lisbon's "Latin Quarter" on a hill to the west), and the tangled, medieval Alfama (topped by the castle on the hill to the east).

From ye olde Lisbon, Avenida da Liberdade storms into the no-nonsense real world, where you find the airport, bullring, Edward VII Park, and breezy botanical gardens.

Tourist Information

Lisbon's city TI is in the peach-colored Palacio Foz at the bottom of Praça dos Restauradores (daily 9:00–20:00, tel. 21-346-3314; national TI for Portugal is in the same office, tel. 21-346-3658). The airport has another TI (daily 6:00–02:00). The free city map lists all museums and has a helpful inset of the town center. The free biweekly *Follow Me Lisboa* is better than the TI's *Cultural*

Agenda. Each summer cheery little "Ask Me about Lisbon" info booths, staffed by tourism students, pop up all over town (less busy and jaded, actually eager to help you enjoy their town). The city has no regular walking tours, but for a private guide you can call the Guides' Union (14,000$/4 hrs, 23,000$/full day, tel. 21-346-7170). Angela da Silva is a good local guide (tel. 21-479-3597, cellular 96-605-9518, e-mail: jsfonseca@mail.pt).

Arrival in Lisbon

By Train: Lisbon has four train stations—Santa Apolonia (to Spain and most points north), Rossio (for Sintra, Óbidos, and Nazaré), Barreiro (for Algarve), and Cais do Sodre (Cascais and Estoril). If leaving Lisbon by train, see if your train requires a reservation (boxed "R" in timetable).

Santa Apolonia Station covers international trains and nearly all of Portugal (except the south). It's just past the Alfama and includes foreign-currency change machines and good bus connections to the town center (buses #9, #39, #46, and #90 go from station through center, up Avenida da Liberdade). A taxi from Santa Apolonia to any hotel I recommend should cost around 700$. If there's a long taxi-stand lineup, walk a block away and hail one off the street.

Rossio Station is in the town center (within walking distance of most of my hotel listings) and handles trains from Sintra (and Óbidos and Nazaré, with transfers at Cacém). Its all-Portugal ticket office on the ground floor is handy (Mon–Fri 7:00–20:00).

Barreiro Station, a 30-minute ferry ride across the Tagus River (Rio Tejo) from Praça do Comércio, is for trains to the Algarve and points south (the 180$ ferry ticket is generally sold to you with a train ticket).

Caís do Sodre Station handles the 40-minute rides to Cascais and Estoril.

By Bus: Lisbon's bus station is at Arco do Cego (200 meters from Metro: Saldanha, tel. 21-354-5439).

By Plane: Lisbon's easy-to-manage airport is eight kilometers northeast of downtown, with a 24-hour bank, ATMs, a TI (daily 6:00–02:00), reasonable taxi service (1,800$ to center), good bus connections into town (#44, #45, 165$), and an airport bus.

The Aero-Bus #91 runs from the airport to Restauradores, Rossio, and Praça do Comércio (460$, 3/hrly, 30 min, 7:00–21:00, buy ticket on bus). Your ticket is actually a one-day Lisbon transit pass that covers bus, tram, and elevator rides. If you fly in on TAP airline, show your boarding pass to get a free lift into town on Aero-Bus #91 (TAP tel. 21-841-6990). A Lisbon transit pass (sold in 1-day and 3-day versions) covers the Aero-Bus trip to the airport if you're flying out of Lisbon. (Airport info: tel. 21-841-3500; flight info: tel. 21-841-3700.)

Central Lisbon

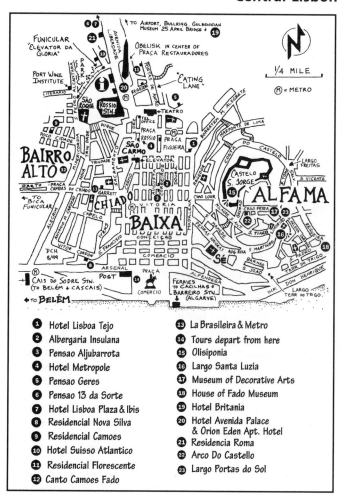

- ❶ Hotel Lisboa Tejo
- ❷ Albergaria Insulana
- ❸ Pensao Aljubarrota
- ❹ Hotel Metropole
- ❺ Pensao Geres
- ❻ Pensao 13 da Sorte
- ❼ Hotel Lisboa Plaza & Ibis
- ❽ Residencial Nova Silva
- ❾ Residencial Camoes
- ❿ Hotel Suisso Atlantico
- ⓫ Residencial Florescente
- ⓬ Canto Camoes Fado
- ⓭ La Brasileira & Metro
- ⓮ Tours depart from here
- ⓯ Olisiponia
- ⓰ Largo Santa Luzia
- ⓱ Museum of Decorative Arts
- ⓲ House of Fado Museum
- ⓳ Hotel Britania
- ⓴ Hotel Avenida Palace & Orion Eden Apt. Hotel
- ㉑ Residencia Roma
- ㉒ Arco Do Castello
- ㉓ Largo Portas do Sol

Getting around Lisbon

By Metro: Lisbon's simple, fast subway is handy for trips to the Gulbenkian Museum, bullfights, the Colombo mall, the Expo '98 site, and the long-distance bus station. Bring change for the machines, as many stations are not staffed (100$ per ride or 250$ all day). Remember to stamp your ticket in the machine. Metro stops are marked with a red "M." *Saida* means exit.

By Trolley: For fun and practical public transport, use the trolley and the funicular. One ride costs 165$ (no transfers). Transit passes cover all public transportation—including the extensive city bus system—except for the Metro (1-day/460$, 3-day/1,080$). Like San Francisco, Lisbon sees its trolleys as part of its heritage and is keeping a few. Trams #12 and #28 are here to stay.

By Taxi: Lisbon cabbies are good-humored, abundant, and use their meters. Rides start at 320$, and you can go anywhere in the center for under 500$. Decals on the window clearly spell out all charges in English. Especially if you're traveling with a companion, Lisbon cabs are a cheap time-saver. For an average trip, couples save less than a dollar by taking public transport and spend an extra 15 minutes to get there—bad economics. If time is limited, taxi everywhere. If you're having a hard time flagging one down, ask for a taxi stand (prah-sah dee taxi).

Helpful Hints

Calendar Concerns: Bullfights take place most summer Thursdays in Lisbon and most Sundays nearby. Tuesdays and Saturdays are flea-market days in the Alfama. Most museums are free on Sunday until 14:00 and closed all day Monday.

LisboaCard: This card covers all public transportation (including the Metro), allowing free entrance to most museums (including Sintra sights) and discounts on others, plus discounts on city tours. If you plan to museum-hop, the card is a good value, particularly for a day in Belém (covers your transportation and sightseeing), but don't get the card for Monday, when virtually all sights are closed (24-hour card/2,100$; 48-hour card/3,500$; 72-hour card/4,500$; includes excellent explanatory guidebook). Buy it at the TI (Palacio Foz at Praça do Restauradores or at the airport). You choose the start date and time.

Pedestrian Warning: Sidewalks are narrow, and drivers are daring; cross streets with care. Lisbon has piles of people doing illegal business on the street. While it's generally safe, if you're looking for trouble, you could find it. For late-night strolling, choose your neighborhood wisely.

Language: Remember to try to start conversations in Portuguese (see "Survival Phrases," near the back of this book). Fortunately, many people in the tourist trade speak English. Otherwise, try Portuguese, French, or Spanish, in that order. Lisbon comes with some tricky pronunciations. Locals call their city Lisboa (LEEZH-bo-ah) and their river the Tejo (TAY-zhoo). Squares are major navigation points and are called *praça* (PRA-sah).

Time-Zone Change: Portuguese time is usually one hour earlier than Spanish time.

Banking: ATMs are the way to go, giving more escudos per dollar all over Lisbon. Banks offer fine rates but high fees to change checks or cash (bank hours are generally Mon–Fri 8:30–15:00). American Express cashes any kind of traveler's check at a decent rate without a commission, but the office is not central (Mon–Fri 9:30–13:00, 14:30–18:30, in Top Tours office at Avenida Duque de Loule 108, Metro: Rotunda, tel. 21-315-5885). Automatic bill-changing machines are available and seductive, offering fair rates but high fees.

Post Office and Telephones: The post office, at Praça dos Restauradores 58, has easy-to-use metered phones (Mon–Fri 8:00–22:00, Sat–Sun 9:00–18:00). The telephone center, on the northwest corner of Rossio Square, sells phone cards and also has metered phone booths (daily 8:00–23:00, accepts credit cards).

Internet Access: Ciber Ciado is at Largo de Picadero in the Baírro Alto (600$/hr).

Travel Agency: Agencies line the Avenida da Liberdade. Star Turismo at Praça dos Restauradores 14 is handy and helpful (tel. 21-346-0336).

Do-It-Yourself Walking Tours

The Baírro Alto and Chiado Stroll

For a walk worth ▲▲, leave the lower town on the funicular, called Elevator da Gloria, near the obelisk at Praça dos Restauradores. (Notice the plaque inside near the ceiling from the car's 100th birthday in 1985.) Leaving the funicular on top, turn right to enjoy the city view from Miradouro de São Pedro Alcantara (San Pedro Park belvedere). Wander over to the tile map, which helps guide you through the view, stretching from the castle birthplace of Lisbon on the right to the towers of the new city in the distance on the left. The centerpiece of the park is a statue honoring a 19th-century local journalist. This district is famous for its writers, poets, and bohemians.

If you're into port (the fortified wine that takes its name from Oporto, a city just north of here), you'll find the world's greatest selection directly across the street from the lift at **Solar do Vinho do Porto** (run by the Port Wine Institute, Mon–Sat 14:00–24:00, closed Sun, Rua São Pedro de Alcantara 45). In a plush, air-conditioned living room you can, for 200$ to 3,000$ per glass (poured by an English-speaking bartender), taste any of 300 different ports—though you may want to try only 150 or so and save the rest for the next night. Fans of port describe it as "a liquid symphony playing on the palate."

Follow the main street (Rua São Pedro de Alcantara) downhill a couple of blocks; it turns into the Rua Misericordia. The grid plan of streets to your right is 16th-century Renaissance town planning—predating the earthquake and grid plan of the lower town by two centuries.

Pombal's Lisbon

After the earthquake of 1755, Prime Minister Marques de Pombal rebuilt much of Lisbon. He had served as a diplomat in London where he picked up some city-planning ideas—considered pretty wild by 18th-century Lisbon.

Avenida da Liberdade is the tree-lined grand boulevard of Lisbon, connecting the old town near the river (where most of the sightseeing action is) with the newer upper town. Before the great earthquake this was a royal promenade. After 1755 it was the grand boulevard of Pombal's new Lisbon—originally limited to the aristocracy. The present street, built in the 1880s and inspired by Paris' Champs-Élysées, is lined with banks, airline offices, nondescript office buildings...and eight noisy lanes of traffic. The grand "rotunda"—as the roundabout formally known as Praça Marques de Pombal is called—tops off the Avenida da Liberdade with a commanding statue of Pombal, decorated with allegorical symbols of his impressive accomplishments. (A single-minded dictator can do a lot in 27 years.) Beyond that stretches the fine Edward VII Park. The 20-minute downhill walk from the Rotunda (Metro: Rotunda) along the mile-long avenue to the old town is enjoyable. The black-and-white cobbled sidewalks are a Lisbon tradition.

Praça dos Restauradores is the monumental square at the lower end of Avenida da Liberdade. Its centerpiece, an obelisk, celebrates the restoration of Portuguese independence from Spain in 1640. (In 1580 the Portuguese king died without a direct heir. The closest heir was Philip II of Spain—yuck. He became Philip I of Portugal, ushering in an unhappy 60 years when 3 Spanish Philips ruled Portugal.) Within a few meters of the obelisk is the neo-Manueline-style Rossio train station, Lisbon's oldest hotel (Avenida Palace, built to greet those

São Roque Church is on your left at Largo Trindade Coelho (8:30–17:00). Built in the 16th century, it's one of Portugal's first Jesuit churches. Wander slowly under its flat, painted ceiling and notice the rich side chapels. The highlight is the Chapel of St. John the Baptist (left of altar, gold and blue), which looks like it came right out of the Vatican. It did. Made in Rome out of the most precious materials, it was the site of one papal mass; then it was shipped to Lisbon—probably the most costly chapel per square inch ever constructed. Notice the beautiful mosaic floor and the three paintings that are actually intricate mosaics—a Vatican specialty (designed to avoid damage from candle smoke that would darken paintings). The São Roque Museum, with some old paintings and arriving by train), TI, bullfight ticket kiosk, a funicular which climbs to the high town, and a Metro station.

Baixa, between Avenida da Liberdade and the harbor, is the flat, lower city. The grid plan (with many streets named for the crafts and shops historically found there) and most of the five-story facades are Pombal's from just after 1755. Baixa's pedestrian streets, inviting cafés, bustling shops, and elegant old storefronts give the district a certain magnetism. I find myself doing laps in a people-watching stupor. The mosaic-decorated Rua Augusta (with the grand arch near the river framing the equestrian statue of King José I) has a delightful strolling ambience—reminding many of Barcelona's Ramblas. Notice the uniform and utilitarian Pombalan architecture with its decoration limited to wrought iron and tiles. In the years after the earthquake Lisbon did a lot of building without a lot of money.

Midway down the Baixa you'll see the 45-meter-tall **Santa Justa Elevator**. It was built in 1892 (a few years after, and inspired by, the Eiffel tower) to connect the lower town with the high town. While you can no longer enter the Bairro Alto from the skyway at the top, you can still ride the lift for a fine city view.

The Baixa has three great squares, each ornamented with a statue of a Portuguese king. **Rossio** and **Figueira** squares—congested with buses, subways, taxis, and pigeons leaving in all directions—stand side-by-side at the top. Rossio has been the center of Lisbon since medieval times.

Praça do Comércio, or Trade Square—where the ships used to stop and sell their goods—borders the Baixa at the riverfront. Nicknamed "Palace Square" by locals, for 200 pre-earthquake years it was the site of Portugal's royal palace. It's ringed by government ministries and is the departure point for city tours and the boat across the Tagus. The statue is of King José I, the man who put Pombal to work rebuilding the city.

church riches, is not as interesting as the church itself (200$, Tue–Sun 10:00–17:00, closed Mon).

After a visit with the poor pigeon-drenched man in the church square (WC), continue downhill along Rua Nova da Trindade (opposite McDonalds). At #20 you can pop into Cervejaria da Trindade, the famous "oldest beer hall in Lisbon," (see "Eating," below) for a look at the 19th-century tiles.

At the next intersection, signs point left to the ruined Convento do Carmo. Walk downhill to the square. The police guard the headquarters of the National Guard—famous among locals as the last refuge of the prime minister before the people won their democracy in the Revolution of 1974.

On Largo do Carmo, check out the ruins of the **Convento do Carmo**. Destroyed by the 1755 earthquake, its delicate Gothic arches stand as a permanent reminder of that disastrous event.

Next, leave Largo do Carmo walking a block uphill on Travessa do Carmo and take a left to Rua Garrett where (in the little pedestrian zone on the right) you'll find a new metro stop and an old café.

Coffeehouse aficionados enjoy the grand old **A Brasileira** café, which reeks with smoke and the 1930s (open daily). Drop in for a *bica* (Lisbon slang for an espresso) and a *pastel de Belém* (150$ cream cake—a local specialty). The statue outside is of the poet Fernando Pessoa—a regular at Brasileira.

This district, the **Chiado** (SHEE-ah-doo), is popular for its shopping and theaters. Rua Garrett, lined with fine shops, butts up against a new six-story shopping complex. Browse downhill, peeking into the classy shops such as the venerable Bertrand bookstore (at #73, English books and a good guidebook selection in Room 5). The lamps are decorated with the symbol of Lisbon: a ship—carrying the remains of St. Vincent—guarded by two ravens. Rue Garrett leads to Armazens do Chiado. To end this walk, catch the subway or rumble into Armazens (fourth floor) and out on the first floor back in the Baixa (lower city).

The Alfama Stroll

For another ▲▲ walk, explore this colorful sailors' quarter, which goes back to Visigothic days. It was a busy district during the Moorish period and finally the home of Lisbon's fisherfolk (and of the poet Luis de Camões, who wrote, "our lips meet easily high across the narrow street"). The tangled street plan is one of the few aspects of Lisbon to survive the 1755 earthquake, helping make the Alfama a cobbled playground of old-world color. A visit is best during the busy midmorning market time or in the late afternoon or early evening, when the streets teem with locals.

Consider riding a taxi or bus #37 from Praça Figueira to the castle—the highest point in town—and walking from there down to the Alfama viewpoint and into the Alfama.

Start at **Castle São Jorge**. Lisbon's castle is boring as far as castles go. But it's the birthplace of the city, it offers a fine view, and it's free (daily 9:00–21:00 or sunset). Straddle a cannon, enjoy the view and park, and wander the sterile ramparts if you like. Within the castle, **Olisiponia** (the Roman name for Lisbon) is a high-tech syrupy multimedia presentation offering a sweeping video overview of the city's history in English (600$, Thu–Tue 10:00–18:00, closed Wed).

It's a three-minute walk downhill (past 2 good recommended lunch restaurants; see "Eating," page 230) to another great Alfama viewpoint, at **Largo Santa Luzia**. (This square is a stop for trolleys #12 and #28; some prefer to start their Alfama exploration here and take the steep but worthwhile uphill hike to the castle.) Admire the panoramic view from the square's small terrace, Miradouro de Santa Luzia, where old-timers play cards in the shade of the bougainvillea amid lots of tiles. Find the set of 18th-century tiles that shows the Praça do Comercio before the earth-quake. The 16th-century Royal Palace (on the left) was completely destroyed in the quake. For a better view, hike around the church to the scenic catwalk. This is the place for the most scenic cup of coffee in town—at the Cerca Moura bar/café terrace (after 11:30, Largo das Portas do Sol 4).

The **Museum of Decorative Arts**, next to the Cerca Moura bar, offers a unique (but nearly meaningless, with its lack of decent English descriptions) stroll through aristocratic households richly decorated in 16th- to 19th-century styles (800$, Tue–Sun 10:00–17:00, closed Mon, Largo das Portas do Sol 2, tel. 21-886-2183).

From the Largo das Portas do Sol (Cerca Moura bar), follow the stairs (Rua Norberto de Araujo, between the church and the catwalk) into the Alfama. The old wall used to mark the end of Moorish Lisbon. When the stairs end (at the sports club) turn left...down more stairs.

Explore from here until you eventually end up on Rua de Sao Pedro, a main drag a few blocks below. The Alfama's urban-jungle roads are squeezed into tangled, confusing alleys; bent houses comfort each other in their romantic shabbiness; and the air drips with laundry and the smell of clams and raw fish. Get lost. Poke aimlessly, peek through windows, buy a fish. Locals hang plastic water bags from windows to try to keep away the flies. Favorite saints decorate doors protecting families. St. Peter is big in the Alfama—protector of the fishermen. Churches are generally closed since they share a roving priest. Rua de São Pedro, the fish market and liveliest street around, leads left to Largo do Chafariz de Dentro and the Fado museum.

The **House of Fado and Portuguese Guitar** tells the story of fado. Exhibits are in English and the small museum ends with an A-V show and a chance to hear some fado (450$, Wed–Mon 10:00–18:00, closed Tue; for more on fado, see "Nightlife," below).

Tours—Lisbon

▲▲**Ride a Trolley**—Lisbon's vintage trolleys, most from the 1920s, shake and shiver through the old parts of town, somehow safely weaving within inches of parked cars, climbing steep hills, and offering sightseers breezy views of the city. Line #28 is a Rice-A-Roni Lisbon joyride. Tram #28 stops from west to east include Estrela (the 18th-century late-Baroque Estrela Basilica and Estrela Park—cozy neighborhood scene with pond-side café and a "garden library kiosk"), the top of the Bica funicular (which drops steeply through a rough-and-tumble neighborhood to the river-front), Chiado square (Lisbon's café and "Latin Quarter"), Baixa (on Rua da Conceicão between Augusta and Prata), the cathedral (*sè*), the Alfama viewpoint (Santa Luzia belvedere), Portas do Sol, Santa Clara Church (flea market), and the pleasant and untouristy Graca district. Just pay the conductor as you board, sit down, and catch the pensioners as they lurch at each stop. For a quicker circular Alfama trolley ride, catch #12 on Praça da Figueira (departs every few minutes, 20-min circle, driver can tell you when to get out for the viewpoint near the castle—about three-quarters through the ride).

City Bus Tours—Two tours give tired tourists a lazy overview of the city. Neither is great, but both are handy, daily, and inexpensive. **Tagus Tour** lets you hop on and off their topless double-decker buses for 24 hours (2,000$, hrly, beginning at 11:00, May–Sept, 90-min tape-recorded tour covers the town and Belém). On the **Hills Tour** you follow the rails on turn-of-the-century trams through the Alfama and Baírro Alto (2,800$; live, bilingual guide; 2–5 departures daily, scenic ride . . . sparse information). Both leave from the Praça do Comércio (tel. 21-361-3060).

Sights—Lisbon

▲▲▲**Gulbenkian Museum**—This is the best of Lisbon's 40 museums. Gulbenkian, an Armenian oil tycoon, gave his art collection (or "harem," as he called it) to Portugal in gratitude for the hospitable asylum granted him during World War II. This great collection, spanning 2,000 years and housed in a classy modern building, offers the most purely enjoyable museum experience in Iberia. It's cool, uncrowded, gorgeously lit, and easy to grasp, displaying only a few select and exquisite works from each epoch.

Savor details as you stroll chronologically through the ages past the delicate Egyptian, vivid Greek (fascinating coins), and exotic Oriental sections and the well-furnished Louis land. There are masterpieces by Rembrandt, Rubens, Renoir, Rodin, and artists whose names start with other letters. The nubile finale is a dark room filled with Art Nouveau jewelry by the French designer Rene Lalique (600$, free Sun, Tue 14:00–18:00, Wed–Sun 10:00–18:00, closed Mon, pleasant gardens, good air-con cafeteria, take Metro from Rossio to São Sebastião and walk 200 meters, or 500$ taxi from downtown, Berna 45, tel. 21-793-5131).

▲▲**Museum of Ancient Art (Museu Nacional de Arte Antiga)**—This is the country's best for Portuguese paintings from her glory days, the 15th and 16th centuries. (Most of these works were gathered in Lisbon after the dissolution of the abbeys and convents in 1834.) You'll also find the great European masters—such as Bosch, Jan van Eyck, and Raphael—and rich furniture, all in a grand palace. Highlights include the *Temptations of*

St. Anthony (a 3-paneled altarpiece fantasy by Bosch, c. 1500);
St. Jerome (by Dürer); the *Adoration of St. Vincent* (a many-paneled
altarpiece by the late-15th-century Portuguese master Nuno
Goncalves, showing everyone from royalty to sailors and beggars
surrounding Portugal's patron saint); and the curious Namban
screens (16th-century Japanese depictions of Portuguese traders in
Japan). The museum has a good cafeteria with seating in a shaded
garden overlooking the river (600$, Tue 14:00–18:00, Wed–Sun
10:00–18:00, closed Mon, tram #15, bus #40, #49, #51, or #60
from Praça Figueira, Rua das Janeles Verdes 9, tel. 21-391-2800).

▲**National Tile Museum (Museu Nacional do Azulejo)**—
This museum, filling the Convento da Madre de Deus, features
piles of tiles, which, as you've probably noticed, are an art form in
Portugal. The presentation is very low-tech, but the church is
sumptuous, and the tile panorama of pre-earthquake Lisbon (upstairs) is fascinating (500$, Tue 14:00–18:00, Wed–Sun 10:00–
18:00, closed Mon, 10 min on bus #105 from Praça Figueira,
Rua da Madre de Deus 4, tel. 21-814-7747).

Lisbon's City Museum—This sounds good and is talked up by
the TI, but it's way out from the center, comes without a word in
English, and is a disappointment.

Cathedral (Sè)—Just a few blocks east of Praça do Comércio, it's
not much on the inside, but its fortress-like exterior is a textbook
example of a stark and powerful Romanesque fortress of God.
Started in 1150, after the Christians retook Lisbon from the Islamic
Moors, its crenelated towers made a powerful statement: The
Reconquista was here to stay. St. Anthony—another patron saint of
Portugal but best known as the saint in charge of helping you find
lost things—is buried in the church. In the 12th century his remains
were brought to Lisbon on a ship, as the legend goes, guarded by
two sacred black ravens...the symbol of the city. The **cloisters** are
peaceful and an archaeological work in progress—uncovering
Roman ruins (100$). The humble **treasury** shows off relics of St.
Anthony but is worthwhile only if you want to support the church
and climb some stairs (400$, Mon–Sat 10:00–17:00, closed Sun).

Parque das Nacoes—Lisbon celebrated the 500th anniversary of
Vasco da Gama's voyage to India by hosting Expo '98. The theme
was "The Ocean and the Seas," with an emphasis on the importance of healthy, clean waters in our environment. The riverside
fairgrounds are east of the Santa Apolonia train station in an area
suddenly revitalized with luxury condos and crowd-pleasing terraces and restaurants. Ride the Metro to the last stop (Oriente—
meaning east end of town) to join the riverside promenade. You
can go up the Vasco da Gama tower (500$, daily 10:00–22:00) or
visit Europe's biggest aquarium, the Oceanario, which simulates
four different ocean underwater and shoreline environments
(1,500$, daily 10:00–19:00).

Vasco da Gama Bridge—The second-longest bridge in Europe (14 km) was opened in 1998 to connect the Expo grounds with the south side of the Tagus and to alleviate the traffic jams on Lisbon's only other bridge over the river. As the 25th of April Bridge (see below) was modeled after the Golden Gate bridge in San Francisco (same company built it and was paid off by years of tolls), this new Vasco da Gama Bridge was designed with engineering help from the people building the new San Francisco Bay Bridge.

▲**25th of April Bridge**—At a mile long, this is one of the longest suspension bridges in the world. Built in 1966, it was originally named for the dictator Salazar but was renamed for the date of Portugal's 1974 revolution and freedom. For over 30 years locals could show their political colors by choosing what name to use. While conservatives called it the Salazar Bridge, liberals called it the 25th of April Bridge. Those who preferred to keep their politics private simply called it "the bridge over the river." Now, with the opening of the second bridge over the Tagus in 1998, people have to choose a name . . . and show their politics.

Cristo Rei—A huge statue of Christ (à la Rio de Janeiro)—with outstretched arms, symbolically blessing the city—overlooks Lisbon from across the Tagus River. It was built as a thanks to God, funded by Lisboetas grateful that Portugal stayed out of World War II. While it's designed to be seen from a distance, a lift takes visitors to the top for a great view (300$, daily 9:00–18:00). Catch the ferry from downtown Lisbon (6/hrly, from Praça do Comércio) to Cacilhas then take a bus marked "Cristo Rei" (4/hrly, from ferry dock). Because of bridge tolls, taxis to or from the site are expensive. For drivers, the most efficient visit is a quick stop on your way south to the Algarve.

Sights—Lisbon's Belém District

Three miles from downtown Lisbon, the Belém District is a stately pincushion of important sights from Portugal's Golden Age, when Vasco da Gama and company made it Europe's richest power. Belém was the send-off point for voyages from the Age of Discovery. Sailors would stay and pray here before embarking. The tower would welcome them home. For some reason, the grand buildings of Belém survived the great 1755 earthquake. Consequently, this is the only place to experience the grandeur of pre-earthquake Lisbon. After the earthquake, rattled and safety-conscious royalty choose to live here (in wooden rather than stone buildings). And the modern-day president of Portugal calls Belém home. To celebrate the 300th anniversary of independence from Spain, a grand exhibition was held here in 1940, resulting in the fine parks, fountains, and monument.

Get to Belém by taxi (800$ from downtown), bus (#27, #28, #29, #43, #49, and #51), or tram #15 from Praça da Figueira. The

Belém

first stop is the Coach Museum; the second is the monastery. Consider doing Belém in this order: the Coach Museum, pastry and coffee break, Monastery of Jerónimos, Maritime Museum (if interested), Monument to the Discoveries, Belém Tower. By taxi, start at Belém Tower. While there's a handy cafeteria at the Maritime Museum, Rua de Belém (between the Coach Museum and the monastery) is lined with inviting eateries. Remember, sights are closed on Monday.

▲▲**Coach Museum (Museu dos Coches)**—In 1905 the Queen of Portugal decided to use the palace's riding-school building to preserve this fine collection of royal coaches. Claiming to be the most visited sight in Portugal, it is impressive, with more than 70 dazzling carriages (well-described in English). The oldest is the crude and simple coach used by King (of Spain and Portugal) Philip II to shuttle between Madrid and Lisbon around 1600. Imagine how slow and rough the ride would be with bad roads and no suspension. Study the evolution of suspension—from the first coach, or "Kotze," made in a Hungarian town by that name in the 15th century—and the highly symbolic ornamentation of the coaches. The newly restored "Ocean Coach" stands shiny in the center with figures symbolizing the Atlantic and Indian Oceans holding hands, in recognition of Portugal's mastery of the sea (600$, free Sun until 14:00, Tue–Sun 10:00–17:30, closed Mon, tel. 21-361-0850).

Rua de Belém leads from the coach museum and the monastery past the guarded entry to Portugal's presidential palace, some fine pre-earthquake buildings, and a famous pastry shop. This shop, **Casa Pasteis de Belém** (Rua de Belém 88), is the birthplace of the wonderful cream tart called *pastel del Nata* throughout Portugal. Here they're called *pastel del Belém*. Since 1837 locals have come here to get them warm out of the oven. Sit down. Enjoy one with a *café com leite*. Sprinkle on the cinnamon and powdered sugar.

▲▲▲**Monastery of Jerónimos**—King Manuel (who ruled from 1495) had this giant church and its cloisters built (starting in 1505) with "pepper money"—a 5 percent tax on spices brought back from India—as a thanks for the discoveries. Sailors would spend their last night here in prayer before embarking on their frightening voyages. Here's a tour:

1. South portal: The ornate south portal, facing the street, is a great example of the Manueline style. Manueline—like Spain's Plateresque but with motifs from the sea—bridged Gothic and Renaissance. Henry the Navigator stands in the middle of the door with his patron saint, St. Jerome (above on the left, with the lion). This door is only used when Mass lets out.

2. Church interior: View the interior from the high altar looking back toward the entry. See how Manueline is a transition between Gothic and Renaissance. While in Gothic architecture huge columns break the interior into a nave with low-ceilinged ambulatories on either side, here the slender palm tree–like columns don't break the interior space, and the ceiling is all one height. Find some of the Manueline motifs from the sea: ropelike arches, the ships, and coral. Exotic new animals—another aspect of the "Age of Discovery"—hide in the capitals. It is, after all, the sea that brought Portugal 16th-century wealth and power and made this art possible.

3. Front of church: Now turn 180 degrees toward the front and see how the rest of the church is Renaissance. Everything but a cupola and the stained glass (replacement glass is from 1940) survived the earthquake. In the main chapel at the far front, elephants (who dethroned lions as the most powerful and kingly beasts) support two kings and two queens (King Manuel I is front-left). Walk back on the side with the seven wooden confessional doors. Notice the ornamental carving around the second one: a festival of faces from newly discovered corners of the world. Ahead of you (near the entry) is the tomb of Vasco da Gama.

4. Tombs: Vasco da Gama's tomb is decorated with richly symbolic carvings: The proud sailboat is a Portuguese caravel (a technological marvel in its day, with a triangular sail that could pivot quickly to catch the wind efficiently). The sphere is a common Manueline symbol. Some say the diagonal slash is symbolic of the unwritten pact and ambition of Spain and Portugal to split the world evenly. Even the ceiling—a Boy Scout handbook of rope and knots—comes with a whiff of the sea. The second tomb—with literary rather than maritime motifs—is a memorial (he's buried elsewhere) to Portugal's much-loved poet, Camões.

5. Cloisters: Leave the church (turn right, buy a ticket) and enter the cloisters. These cloisters are the architectural highlight of Belém. The lacy lower arcade is textbook Manueline; the simpler top floor is Renaissance. Study the carvings. Upstairs are better views of the church and the cloisters and the bookshop (church free, 600$ for cloisters, Tue–Sun 10:00–17:00, closed Mon; women's WC upstairs, men's downstairs).

Maritime Museum (Museu de Marinha)—If you're interested in the ships and navigational tools of Portugal's Age of Discovery, this museum, which fills the east wing of the monastery, comes with good English descriptions and is worth a look. Sailors love it (500$, Tue–Sun 10:00–18:00, closed Mon, Oct–May 10:00–17:00, Praça do Império).

▲Monument to the Discoveries—This giant riverside monument was built in 1960 to honor Prince Henry the Navigator on the 500th anniversary of his death. Huge statues of Henry, Magellan, Vasco da Gama, and other heroes of Portugal's Age of Discovery line the giant concrete prow of a caravel. Inside the monument, you can ride a lift to a tingly view (350$, Tue–Sun 9:00–17:00, closed Mon, tel. 21-362-0034). Notice the marble map chronicling Portugal's empire building (on the ground leading to the monument). Follow the years as Portuguese explorers gradually worked their way around Africa. Today, all that remains of Portugal's once huge empire is the Azores and Madeira (whose original inhabitants were Portuguese).

▲Belém Tower—The only purely Manueline building in Portugal (built 1515–1520), this tower protected Lisbon's harbor and today symbolizes the voyages that made Lisbon powerful. This was the last sight sailors saw as they left and the first when they returned, loaded with gold, spices, and social diseases. When the tower was built, the river went nearly to the walls of the monastery and the tower was mid-river. Its interior is pretty bare (600$, Tue–Sun 10:00–17:00, closed Mon, tel. 21-362-0034). The floatplane on a pedestal is a monument to the first flight across the South Atlantic (Portugal to Brazil) in 1922. The original plane is across the street in the Maritime Museum.

Popular Art Museum (Museu de Arte Popular)—This museum takes you through Portugal's folk art one province at a time, providing a sneak preview of what you'll see throughout the country (300$, Tue–Sun 10:00–12:30, 14:00–17:00, closed Mon, between the monument and the tower on Avenida Brasilia). Belém also has a cultural center, children's museum, and a planetarium.

Shopping
Flea Market—On Tuesday and Saturday, the Feira da Ladra flea market hops in the Alfama on Campo de Santa Clara.
Colombo Shopping Mall—While Lisbon offers decaying but

still-elegant department stores, a new shopping center (see below), classy specialty shops, and a teeming flea market, nothing is as impressive as the enormous Centro Colombo, the largest shopping center in Spain and Portugal. More than 400 shops—including the biggest FNAC department store, 10 cinemas, 60 restaurants, and a health club sit atop Europe's biggest underground car park and under a vast and entertaining play center. There's plenty to amuse children here and the place offers a fine look at work-a-day Lisbon (daily 10:00–24:00, pick up a map at info desk, Metro: Colegio Militar takes you right there, tel. 21-711-3636).

Armazens do Chiado—This grand new six-floor shopping center connects Lisbon's lower and upper towns with a world of ways to spend money. From the Baixa, Rua Assuncão leads into the mall. Escalators (and a less-obvious elevator) take you up past the fourth floor, which opens onto Rua Garrett, and to the sixth floor, which is a lively food circus.

Nightlife

Nightlife in the Baixa seems to be little more than loitering prostitutes and litter stirred by the wind. But head up into the Baírro Alto and you'll find plenty of action. The Jardím do São Pedro is normally festive and the Rua Diario de Noticias is lined with busy bars.

The trendy hot spot lately for young locals is the dock district under the 25th of April Bridge. The Docas (dock-ash) is a 400-meter-long strip of warehouses turned into restaurants and discos.

▲▲**Fado**—Fado—which means "fate"—is the folk music of Lisbon's backstreets. Since the mid-1800s it's been the Lisbon blues—mournfully beautiful, haunting ballads about lost sailors, broken hearts, and sad romance. To the lilting accompaniment of the Portuguese *guitarra* (like a 12-string mandolin), the singer longs for what's been lost.

These days, the fado songs come with a new casualty—a tourist's budget. Fado has become one of Lisbon's favorite late-night tourist traps, but it can still be a great experience. The Alfama has a few famous touristy fado bars, but the Baírro Alto is better (and safer late at night). Wander around Rua Diario de Noticias and neighboring streets either for a late dinner (after 22:00) or later for just drinks and music. Homemade "fado tonight" signs in Portuguese are good news, but even a restaurant filled with tourists can come with good food and fine fado. Prices for a fado performance vary greatly. Many have a steep cover charge, while others have a minimum purchase. Any place recommended by a hotel has a bloated price for the kickback.

Canto do Camões, run by friendly Gabriel, is my favorite. It's a great value with good food, music, and an honest style of business (open at 20:00, music from 21:00, 4,000$-or-more meal required, after 22:00 2,200$ minimum if seats are available, Travessa da Espera

38, call ahead to reserve, tel. 21-346-5464, e-mail: cantodocamoes @ip.pt). The meal is punctuated with sets of three fado songs with different singers. For a snack, a good vintage Porto goes nicely with a plate of *queijo di serra* (sheep cheese) and *pancetta* (salt-cured ham). Relax, spend some time, and close your eyes or make eye contact with the singer. Let the music and wine work together.

▲▲▲**Portuguese Bullfight**—If you always felt sorry for the bull, this is Toro's Revenge—in a Portuguese bullfight, the matador is brutalized along with the bull. After an exciting equestrian prelude in which the horseman (*cavaleiro*) skillfully plants barbs in the bull's back while trying to avoid the padded horns, a colorfully clad eight-man team (suicide squad called a *forcado*) enters the ring and lines up single file facing the bull. With testosterone sloshing everywhere, the leader prompts the bull to charge and then braces himself for a collision that can be heard all the way up in the cheap seats. As he hangs onto the bull's head, his buddies then pile on, trying to wrestle the bull to a standstill. Finally, one guy hangs on to el toro's tail and "water-skis" behind him. Unlike at the Spanish *corrida*, the bull is not killed in front of the crowd at the Portuguese *tourada* (but it is killed later).

You'll most likely see a bullfight in Lisbon or Cascais or on the Algarve (Easter–Oct, flyers at TI). In Lisbon's Campo Pequeno, fights are on Thursday at 22:00 mid-June through September (tickets 1,000–10,000$). The ring is small; there are no bad seats. To sit nearly at ringside, try the cheapest *bancada* seats, on the generally half-empty and unmonitored main floor.

Note: Half the fights are simply Spanish-type *corridas* without the killing. For the real slam-bam Portuguese-style fight, confirm that there will be *grupo de forcados*. Tickets are nearly always available at the door (no surcharge, tel. 21-793-2143 to confirm). For an 11 percent surcharge you can buy them at the green ABEP kiosk at the bottom of Praça dos Restauradores).

Movies—In Lisbon, unlike in Spain, most films are in the original language with subtitles. Many of Lisbon's theaters are classy, complete with assigned seats and ushers. Check the newspaper for what's playing.

Sleeping in Lisbon
(220$ = about $1, country code: 351)
Sleep Code: **S** = Single, **D** = Double/Twin, **T** = Triple, **Q** = Quad, **b** = bathroom, **t** = toilet only, **s** = shower only, **CC** = Credit Card (**V**isa, **M**asterCard, **A**mex), **SE** = Speaks English, **NSE** = No English. Breakfast is included unless otherwise noted.

With the exception of a few splurges, rooms downtown feel like Lisbon does downtown: tired and well-worn. While old Lisbon seems a little sleazy at night, with normal discretion, my listings are safe. See map on page 213.

Singles cost nearly the same as doubles. Addresses such as 26-3 stand for street #26, third floor (which is fourth floor in American terms). If the minibar is noisy, unplug it.

Sleeping Downtown in Baixa
(zip code: 1100)
Central as can be, this area bustles with lots of shops, traffic, people, buskers, pedestrian areas, and urban intensity.

Near Praça da Figueira: The **Lisboa Tejo** (leezh-boah tay-zhoo) is an oasis, with 58 comfortable rooms and an attentive and welcoming staff (Sb-14,000–16,000$, Db-16,000–18,000$, prices vary according to room size, 10 percent discount with this book, air-con, CC:VMA, Poço do Borratém 4, from southeast corner of Praça da Figueira, walk 1 block down Rua Dos Condes de Monsanto and turn left, tel. 21-886-6182, fax 21-886-5163, e-mail: hlt.reservas@mail.telepac.pt).

On Rua da Assuncão: The **Albergaria Residencial Insulana**, on a pedestrian street, is very professional, with 32 quiet and comfortable—if a bit smoky—rooms (Sb-10,000$, Db-11,000$, extra bed-2,000$, CC:VMA, elevator, air-con, Rua da Assuncão 52, tel. 21-342-3131, fax 21-342-8924, SE).

Pensão Aljubarrota is a fine value if you can handle the long climb up four floors, claustrophobic hallways, and the black-vinyl flooring. Once you're on top, it's a happy world of small and rustically furnished rooms with cute take-my-photo balconies from which to survey the Rua Augusta scene (2-night minimum stay, S-3,500–4,500$, D-5,800–7,000$, Ds-7,000–8,500$, T-8,400–10,800$, 10 percent discount with cash and this book, all but singles have balconies, CC:VM, Rua da Assuncão 53-4, tel. & fax 21-346-0112, Italian Pino and lovely Rita SE).

On or near Rossio Square: The well-located **Hotel Metropole**, which keeps its 1920s-style, is comfortable but somewhat overpriced. Its smaller back rooms are quieter (Sb-24,000$, Db-26,000$, CC:VMA, air-con, elevator, Rossio 30, tel. 21-346-9164, fax 21-346-9166).

Pensão Residencial Gerês, a good budget bet downtown, has bright, basic, cozy rooms with older plumbing. Recently remodeled, it lacks the dingy smokiness that pervades Lisbon's cheaper hotels (Sb-10,000$, Db-10,000–12,000$, Tb-15,000–18,000$, Qb-14,000$, high-end prices June–Oct, CC:VMA, no breakfast, Calçada do Garcia 6, uphill a block off the northeast corner of Rossio, tel. 21-881-0497, fax 21-888-2006, Nogueira family speaks some English).

Residencial Florescente rents 72 rooms on a thriving pedestrian street a block off Praça dos Restauradores. It's an old-world slumber mill, but rooms are clean, and some are nearly charming (S-4,000$, Ss-5,000$, Sb-7,000$, D-5,000$, Ds-6,000$,

Db-8,000$, Twin-b-10,000$, Tb-12,000$, no breakfast, most Db with air-con, CC:VMA, Rua Portas S. Antão 99, 1150 Lisbon, tel. 21-346-3517, fax 21-342-7733).

Sleeping Uptown along Avenida da Liberdade
These listings are a 10-minute walk or short Metro ride from the center.

Pensão Residencial 13 da Sorte is simple but cheery with 22 rooms and bright tiles throughout (Sb-7,000$, Db-8,500$, Tb-10,000$, no breakfast, CC:VM, elevator, just off Avenida da Liberdade near the Spanish Embassy at Rua do Salitre 13, 1250 Lisbon, 50 meters from Metro: Avenida, tel. 21-353-9746, fax 21-353-1851, Alexandra SE).

Hotel Lisboa Plaza, a four-star gem, is a spacious and plush mix of traditional style with bright-pastel modern elegance. It offers all the comforts, a warm welcome, and a free glass of port with this book (standard Db-23,500–27,500$, larger "superior" Db-30,000–35,000$, extra bed-6,000$, prices are highest in spring and fall, CC:VMA, air-con, nonsmoking floor, well-located on a quiet street off busy Avenida da Liberdade, a block from Metro: Avenida at Travessa do Salitre 7, 1250 Lisboa, tel. 21-321-8218, fax 21-347-1630, www.heritage.pt, e-mail: plaza.hotels@heritage.pt).

Hotel Britania maintains its 1940s-art-deco feel, offering a clean and professional haven on a quiet street one block off Avenida da Liberdade. Run by the Lisboa Plaza folks (above), it offers the same four-star standards—and a free glass of port (30 rooms, Db-20,000–27,500$, extra bed-6,000$, prices are highest in spring and fall, CC:VMA, air-con, elevator, nonsmoking floor, Rua Rodrigues Sampaio 17, 1150 Lisboa, tel. 21-315-5016, fax 21-315-5021, e-mail: britania.hotel@heritage.pt).

Hotel Avenida Palace—the most characteristic five-star splurge in town—was built with the Rossio Station in 1892 to greet big-shot travelers back when trains were new and this was the only station in town. The lounges are sumptuous, dripping with chandeliers, and the 82 rooms mix old-time elegance with modern comforts (Sb-32,000$, Db-36,000$, Db suite-75,000$, CC:VMA, air-con, elevator, Rua 1 December 123, 1200 Lisboa, tel. 21-346-0151, fax 21-342-2884). In keeping with its commitment to old-time charm, it has no e-mail address.

Orion Eden Citadines Apartment Hotel, a popular new concept, rents 120 slick and modern apartments by the day. Perfectly located at the Rossio end of Avenida da Liberdade and a clean, quiet pool of modernity amid the ramshackle charm of Lisbon, this is a particularly good value for groups or families of four (studio apartments with sofa beds that convert to double or twin beds—15,000–16,500$, apartments for 4 with bedrooms and sofa beds—18,000–19,500$, high prices April–Nov, kitchen, air-con, elevator, swimming pool, no breakfast, room cleaning once per week, CC:VMA, 24 Praça dos Restauradores, 1250 Lisboa, tel. 21-321-6600, fax 21-321-6666, e-mail: lisbon@citadines.com).

Residencia Roma, a sweet little place a block off busy Avenida da Liberdade and two blocks up the street from the Rossio Station, has 24 comfortable rooms and a secure feeling (Sb-7,500–9,000$, Db-9,400–11,000, extra bed-2,800$, high prices July–Oct, CC:VMA, air-con, back rooms quieter, Travessa da Gloria 22-A, tel. 21-346-0558, tel. & fax 21-346-0557, e-mail: res.roma@mail.telepac.pt).

Sleeping away from the Center
Hotel Ibis Lisboa-Centro is big, concrete, modern, and practical in a soulless area far from the center but near a Metro station. It offers plain, modern comforts and no stress for a good price (Sb-9,100$, Db-10,000$, no breakfast, CC:VMA, nonsmoking floors, air-con, next to Novotel and Metro: Praça de Espanha, Avenida Jose Malhoa, tel. 21-723-5700, fax 21-723-5701).

Eating in Lisbon

Eating between the Castle and the Alfama Viewpoint
(These are listed in order from the castle to the viewpoint.)
Arco Do Castello, an eight-table Indo-Portuguese restaurant, dishes up delicious fish and shrimp curries from Goa, a former Portuguese colony in India. A complete meal for two costs around 5,000$. Top it off with a shot of the Goan firewater, *feni*, made from cashews (Mon–Sat 12:30–24:00, closed Sun, just across from ramp leading into castle, tel. 21-887-6598).

Largo do Contador Mor is a whispy cobbled square a block above the Miradouro de Santa Luzia and a block below the castle with two good eateries: **A Tasquinha Restaurante**, with great outdoor seating at the top of the square, keeps locals and tourists happily fed with fine plates of grilled sardines (*sardinhas assadas*-1,300 ptas, daily 10:00–24:00, tel. 21-887-6899). Eat fast, cheap, and healthy at **Comidas de Santiago**, a little salad bar with great summer gazpacho (choose 2 salads on small plate for 530$ or 4 on big plate for 860$, daily 11:00–18:00, Largo do Contador Mor 21, tel. 21-887-5805).

For a seafood feast, consider dining high in the Alfama at the **Farol de Santa Luzia** restaurant (2,600$ fixed-price *menu turistico*, closed Sun, Largo Santa Luzia 5, across from Santa Luzia viewpoint terrace, no sign but many window decals, tel. 21-886-3884).

For cheap and colorful dinners, walk past Portas do Sol and follow the trolley tracks along Rua da São Tome to a square called

Largo Rodrigues Freitas, where **Nossa Churrasqueira** is busy feeding chicken to finger-lickin' locals on rickety tables with meager budgets (closed Mon).

This gritty chunk of pre-earthquake Lisbon is full of interesting eateries, especially along Rua San Pedro and on Largo de São Miguel. Brighten a few dark bars. Have an aperitif, taste the *branco seco* (local dry white wine). Make a friend, pet a chicken, ponder the graffiti, and pick at the humanity ground between the cobbles.

Eating in Baírro Alto

Lisbon's "high town" is full of small, fun, and cheap places. Just off São Roque's Square you'll find the very simple and cheap **Casa Trans-Montana** (closed Sun, down the steps of Calcada do Duque at #43). The bright and touristy **Cervejaría da Trindade**, a Portuguese-style beer hall, is full of historic tiles, seafood, and tourists. It's overpriced and in all the guidebooks but people enjoy the bright and boisterous old-time atmosphere (3,000$ meals, confirm prices, daily 12:00–24:00, CC:VMA, a block down from São Roque at Rua Nova da Trindade 20C, tel. 21-342-3506). You'll find many less-touched restaurants deeper into the Baírro Alto on the other (west) side of Rua Misericordia. See Fado (under "Nightlife") for the best option.

Eating in and near Rossio

For cod and vegetables prepared faster than a Big Mac and served with more energy than a soccer team, stand or sit at **Restaurant Beira-Gare** (a greasy spoon in front of Rossio train station at the end of Rua 1 de Dezembro, Mon–Sat 6:30–24:00, closed Sun). To get a house-special pork sandwich, ask for a *bifane no pão*.

The sixth floor of the new **Armazens do Chiado Shopping Center** is a food circus without a tourist in sight, offering a huge selection of fun eateries from traditional Portuguese to Chinese. **Chimarrao** offers an impressive self-serve pay-by-the-weight salad-and-meat buffet (all open daily until 23:30, between the low and high towns, between Rua Garrett and Rua Assuncão).

The Rossio's Rua dos Correeiros is lined with competitive local restaurants.

The "eating lane" is a galaxy of eateries with good seafood (opposite Rossio station, just off Praça dos Restauradores down Rua do Jardím do Regedor and Rua das Portas de St. Antão). **Restaurant da Casa do Alentejo** is upstairs in a cultural and social center for people from the traditional southern province of Portugal living in Lisbon. It fills an old ballroom and specializes in Alentejo cuisine (3-course 3,000$ *menu*, open from 19:00, Rua das Portas de St. Antão 58).

On Praça da Figueria: Casas Suissa is a bright, modern, air-conditioned place popular with locals because it's classy but affordable and free of riff-raff (cheap at the bar, reasonable at tables, good salads and fruit cups, daily 7:00–22:00, entries on both Praça da Figueria and Rossio squares).

Up Avenida da Liberdade: Cerevejaria Ribadouro is a popular splurge with locals for seafood. The menu is simple, with many items listed at per-kilo prices. The waiter will explain the price per portion (3,000$ meals, Avenida da Liberdade 155, at intersection with Rua do Salitre, Metro: Avenida, tel. 21-354-9411).

Drinks

Ginjinha (zheen-zheen-yah) is the diminutive name for a favorite Lisbon drink. *Ginjinha* is a sweet liquor made from the sour cherrylike *ginja* berry, sugar, and schnapps. It's sold for 150$ a shot in funky old hole-in-the-wall shops throughout town. The only choices are with or without berries (*com* or *sem fruta*) and *gelada* (if you want it from a chilled bottle out of the fridge—very nice). In Portugal, when someone is impressed by the taste of something, they say, "*Sabe melhor que nem ginjas*" ("It tastes even better than *ginja*"). The oldest *ginjinha* joint in town is a colorful hole in the wall at Largo de Sao Domingos #8 (just off Praça Pedro IV).

Transportation Connections—Lisbon

Remember to reserve ahead if your train requires a reservation.

By train to: Madrid (1/day, overnight 21:56–8:35, first class-11,000$, second class-8,000$, ticket and bed: 11,200$ in quad, 17,200$ in double, 22,500$ in single, about 7,000$ for a bed with a railpass, Rossio station can sell these), **Paris** (1/day, 17:56–15:00, 21 hrs), **Évora** (3/day, 2 hrs), **Lagos** (4/day, 3.5 hrs, likely transfer in Tunes), **Faro** (2 fast trains/day, 3.5 hrs), **Coimbra** (10/day, 2 hrs), **Nazaré Valado** (4/day, 2.5 hrs), **Sintra and Cascais** (4/hrly, 45 min). Train info: tel. 21-888-4025.

To Salema: Both bus and train take about five hours from Lisbon to Lagos. Trains from Lisbon to the south coast leave from the Barreiro station across the Tagus from downtown. Boats shuttle train travelers from Praça do Comércio to the Barreiro train station, with several departures hourly (175$, 30-min ride; note that schedule times listed are often when the boat sails, not when train departs). The 23:10-to-6:28 night train, while no fun, allows you to enjoy the entire day on the Algarve.

By bus to: Coimbra (12/day, 2.5 hrs, 1,450$), **Nazaré** (6/day, 2 hrs), **Fatima** (9/day, 1.5 hrs), **Alcobaça** (5/day, 2 hrs), **Évora** (12/day, 2 hrs), **Lagos** (8/day, 5 hrs, 2,400$, easier than train, must book ahead, get details at TI). Buses leave from Lisbon's Arco do Cego bus station (Metro: Saldanha, tel. 21-354-5439). Intercentro Lines' buses to Spain leave from the same station (tel. 21-315-9277).

Flying: You can generally buy a plane ticket to Madrid on

short notice for about 30,000$. Flying one way on a round-trip
is a little cheaper.

Driving in Lisbon
Driving in Lisbon is big-city crazy. If you enter from the north, a
series of boulevards takes you into the center. Navigate by following signs to Centro, Avenida da República, Praça dos Marques de
Pombal, Avenida da Liberdade, Praça dos Restauradores, Rossio,
and Praça do Comércio. Consider hiring a taxi (cheap) to lead you
to your hotel.

There are many safe underground pay parking lots (follow the
blue "P" signs), but they get more expensive by the hour and can
cost 6,000$ per day.

NEAR LISBON: SINTRA, CABO DA ROCA, CASCAIS, ESTORIL, AND ÉVORA
For centuries, Portugal's aristocracy considered Sintra the natural
escape from Lisbon. Now tourists do, too. Climb through the
Versailles of Portugal, the Pena Palace; romp along the ruined
ramparts of a deserted Moorish castle on a neighboring hilltop;
and explore the rugged and picturesque westernmost tip of Portugal at Cabo da Roca. You can also mix and mingle with the jet set
(or at least press your nose against their windows) at the resort
towns of Cascais or Estoril.

If you're heading south, you might venture inland to historic
Évora, exploring dusty droves of olive groves and scruffy seas of
peeled cork trees along the way.

Planning Your Time
While Évora is a stop on the way to Portugal's south coast, the
other sights combine to make a fine day trip from Lisbon.
Remember that there are two bullrings out here, and it's more
likely that your schedule will hit a fight here than in Lisbon.
Without a car I'd skip Cabo da Roca and do Sintra, Cascais, and
Belém as individual side trips from Lisbon.

By car, the 70-mile circular excursion (Lisbon–Belém–
Sintra–Cabo da Roca–Cascais–Lisbon) makes for a fine day.
Traffic congestion around Sintra can mess up your schedule. Fol-
low the coast from Praça do Comércio west, under the bridge to
Belém. Continue west to just before Cascais, where Sintra (11 km)
is signposted. Sintra itself is far easier by train than by car from
Lisbon. Consider not picking up your rental car until after Sintra.

Drivers who are eager for beach time can leave Lisbon, do the
Sintra circle, and drive directly to the Algarve that evening (4 hrs
from Lisbon). From Sintra/Cascais, get on the freeway heading for
Lisbon and exit at the Sul Ponte A2 sign, which takes you over the
25th of April Bridge and south on A2.

Sights near Lisbon

SINTRA

For centuries, Sintra—just 12 miles north of Lisbon—was the summer escape of Portugal's kings. Those with money and a desire to be close to royalty built their palaces in lush gardens in the same neighborhood. Byron called this bundle of royal fancies and aristocratic dreams a "glorious Eden," and today it's mobbed with tourists. You can easily spend a day in this lush playground of castles, palaces, sweeping coastal views, and exotic gardens.

Tourist Information: The helpful TI, a block off the town's main square, can provide a map and directions to the castles and can arrange *quartos* (rooms in private homes) for overnighters (daily 9:00–20:00, less off-season, tel. 21-923-1157). Their free map is a virtual Sintra guide packed with travel and sightseeing information. There is also a small TI at the train station (9:00–20:00).

Planning Your Time

A full day from Lisbon might go like this: Catch the early Lisbon-to-Sintra train (4/hrly from Rossio station, 45 min). Visit Sintra's new Museum of Modern Art (near train station). Catch the bus to the main square and TI, visit the National Palace, and buy a picnic lunch (fine ready-made "club" sandwiches at the bar 20 meters below the London-style phone booth on the main square). Catch the shuttle bus #434 (500$) up to Pena Palace. Lunch in Pena Gardens. Tour palace. Walk down to the Moorish castle and explore. Hike from the Moorish castle into town (30-min steep, wooded path; fork in path leads down from within the castle grounds—see map at entry turnstile). Catch train back to Lisbon (before or after dinner in Sintra). Note that the Pena Palace is closed Monday, the Sintra Museum of Modern Art is closed Monday and Tuesday, and the National Palace is closed Wednesday.

Getting around Sintra

Cars are the curse of Sintra. Traffic and parking can be terrible. But public transportation puts the "glorious" back into Byron's Eden. Across the street from Sintra's train station, bus #434 loops together all the important stops: old town/TI/National Palace; Moorish Ruins; Pena Palace; and back to the station (3/hrly, 2/hrly in winter, 500$ tickets good for 24 hours, buy from driver). It's a pleasant and level 10-minute walk from the station to the old town/TI/National Palace. Taxis don't use a meter but have set fares (e.g., from town center or train station to Pena Palace-1,500$). If you decide (probably regrettably) to drive to the sights, you'll take a one-way winding loop and be encouraged to park "as soon as you can" or risk having to drive the huge loop again.

Sights—Sintra

National Palace (Palacio Nacional)—While going back to Moorish times, most of what you'll see is from the 15th-century reign of João I and later Manueline work. Although it echoes with Portuguese history and intrigue, the castle is most interesting for Portugal's finest collection of 500-year-old *azulejos* (tiles), its armory, and its fine furnishings (400$, Thu–Tue 10:00–13:00, 14:00–17:00, closed Wed; it's the Madonna-bra building in the town center, a 10-min walk from the train station).

▲▲Pena Palace (Palacio de Pena)—This magical hilltop palace sits high above Sintra, a steep 15-minute hike above the ruined Moorish castle. Portugal's German-born Prince Ferdinand hired a German architect to build him a fantasy castle, mixing elements of German and Portuguese style. He got a crazy neo-fortified casserole of Gothic, Arabic, Moorish, Disney, Renaissance, and Manueline architectural bits and decorative pieces. (The statue on the nearby ridge is of the architect.) Built in the 1840s, the palace is so well-preserved that it feels as if it's the day after the royal family fled Portugal in 1910 (during a popular revolt making way for today's modern republic). This gives the place a charming intimacy rarely seen in palaces. English descriptions throughout give meaning to the rooms (400$, Tue–Sun 10:00–13:00, 14:00–18:30, closed Mon, closes at 17:00 off-season). For a spectacular view of Lisbon and the Tagus River, hike for 15 minutes from the palace to the Chapel of Santa Eufemia (the trail's closed but the determined and nimble can climb the fence).

Sintra

▲▲**Moorish Castle (Castelo dos Mouros)**—These 1,000-year-old Moorish castle ruins, lost in an enchanted forest and alive with winds of the past, are a castle lover's dream come true and a great place for a picnic with a panoramic Atlantic view. While built by the Moors, the castle was taken by Christian forces in 1147. What you'll climb on today, while dramatic, was much restored in the 19th century. To get from Sintra to the ruins, hike two miles, taxi, or ride bus #434—see "Getting around Sintra," above. The ruins are free (daily 10:00–19:30, closes at 17:00 off-season).

▲**Sintra Museum of Modern Art: The Berardo Collection**—Everyone's raving about Sintra's new private modern-art gallery, which is arguably the best in Iberia. The art is presented chronologically and grouped by style in hopes of giving the novice a better grip on post-1945 art (600$, Wed–Sun 10:00–18:00, closed Mon–Tue, 500 meters from train station, in Sintra's former casino on Avenida Heliodoro Salgado, tel. 21-924-8170).

Quinta da Regaleira—This neo-Manueline 1912 mansion and garden with mystical and masonic twists was designed by an Italian opera-set designer for a wealthy but disgruntled monarchist two years after the royal family was deposed (2,000$ for 90-min tour, by reservation only, 7 tours/day, tel. 21-910-6650, a 10-min walk from downtown Sintra).

Monserrate—Just outside of Sintra is the wonderful garden of Monserrate. If you like tropical plants and exotic landscaping, a visit is time and money well spent (free, daily 10:00–17:15, less in winter). Some say that the Pena Palace Park (below the palace) is just as good as the more famous Monserrate.

Sleeping and Eating in Sintra
(220$ = about $1, country code: 351)

Casa Miradouro is a beautifully restored mansion from 1890. With six spacious, stylish rooms, an elegant lounge, castle and sea views, and a wonderful garden, it's a worthy splurge. The place is graciously run by Frederic, who speaks English with a Swiss accent (Sb-14,630–19,650$, Db-17,050–22,450$, priciest mid-July–Sept, CC:VMA, non-smoking rooms, closed Jan–Feb, street parking, Rua Sotto Major 55, from National Palace go past Hotel Tivoli Sintra and 400 meters down hill, tel. 21-923-5900, fax 21-924-1836, www.casa-miradouro.com, e-mail: mail@casa-miradouro.com).

Vila Marques, another elegant old mansion, is funkier, with an eccentric-grandmotherly flair, fine rooms, and a great garden. It's 100 meters behind Hotel Tivoli and 200 meters from the National Palace (D-8,000$, D/twin-9,000$, no sinks in rooms, Rua Sotto Mayor 1, tel. 21-923-0027, Sra. Marques NSE and does not accept reservations).

In Sintra, the hardworking, tourist-friendly **Restaurant Regional de Sintra** feeds locals and tourists well (2,000$ dinners, daily 12:00–22:30, 200 meters from train station at Travessa do Municipio 2, tel. 21-923-4444).

Transportation Connections—Sintra

A slick commuter train connects **central Lisbon** (Rossio Station) with Sintra's new town, called **Estefania** (4/hrly, 45 min). Buses connecting Sintra and **Cascais** (1-hr trip, every 1.5 hours, bus stop is across street from Sintra train station) stop at Cabo da Roca.

CABO DA ROCA

Wind-beaten, tourist-infested Cabo da Roca is the westernmost point in Europe. It has a fun little shop, a café, and a tiny TI that sells a cool "proof of being here" diploma (500$, daily 9:00–20:00).

Nearby, on the road to Cascais, you'll pass a good beach for wind, waves, sand, and the chance to be the last person in Europe to see the sun set. If you crave a beach and have a car, Praia Adraga (north of Cabo da Roca) is desolate and beautiful.

CASCAIS AND ESTORIL

Before the rise of the Algarve, these towns were the haunt of Portugal's rich and beautiful. Today they are quietly elegant, with noble old buildings, beachfront promenades, a bullring, a casino, and more fame than they deserve. Cascais is the more enjoyable of the two; it's not as rich and stuffy and has a cozy touch of fishing village, great seafood, and a younger, less-pretentious atmosphere. Both are an easy day trip from Lisbon (4 trains/hrly, 40 min from Lisbon's Caís do Sodre station).

ÉVORA

Deep in the heart of Portugal, in the barren, arid plains of the southern province of Alentejo, Évora has been a cultural oasis for 2,000 years. With a beautifully untouched provincial atmosphere, fascinating whitewashed old town, plenty of museums, a cathedral, and even a Roman temple, Évora stands proudly amid groves of cork and olive trees.

The **major sights** (Roman temple of Diana, early Gothic cathedral, archbishop's palace, and a luxurious *pousada* in a former monastery) crowd close together at the town's highest point. Osteophiles bone up on their interest at the macabre "House of Bones" chapel at the Church of St. Francis, lined with the bones of 5,000 monks. A subtler but still-powerful charm is contained within the town's medieval wall. Find it by losing yourself in the quiet lanes of Évora's far corners.

The **TI** is on the central square, Praça do Giraldo 73 (Mon–Fri 9:00–19:00, Sat–Sun 9:00–12:30, 14:00–17:30, tel. 26-670-2671).

For budget sleeping and eating, look around the square. Évora has one of Portugal's most luxurious *pousadas* (the stuffy **Convento dos Loios**, Db-27,000–35,000$, includes breakfast, CC:VM, air-con, across from Roman temple, tel. 26-670-4051, fax 26-670-7248, www.pousadas.pt). **Residencia Riviera** is a better value (Db-10,500$, CC:VMA, air-con, Rue 5 di Octobro, tel. 26-670-3304, fax 26-670-0467). On the square, **Solar de Monfalim** is a fine traditional splurge (Db-14,000$, air-con, tel. 26-675-0000, fax 26-674-2367, e-mail: reservas@monfalimtur.pt). I ate well for a moderate price at **O Fialho** (closed Mon, Travessa Mascarhenas 14). For very local atmosphere, eat at the **"Restaurant"** just off the square at Rua Romano Romalha 11.

Three trains and three buses connect Évora daily with Lisbon (3 hrs). A daily bus and train connect Évora and Lagos/Algarve (5 hrs).

THE ALGARVE

The Algarve has long been known as Europe's last undiscovered tourist frontier. But that "jumbo shrimp" statement contradicts itself. The Algarve is well discovered, and if you go to the places featured in tour brochures, you'll find it much like Spain's Costa del Sol—paved, packed, and pretty stressful. But there are a few great beach towns left, mostly on the western tip, and this part of the Algarve is the south coast of any sun worshiper's dreams.

For some rigorous rest and intensive relaxation in a village where the tourists and the fishermen sport the same stubble, make sunny Salema your Algarve hideaway. It's just you, a beach full of garishly painted boats, your wrinkled landlady, and a few other globetrotting experts in lethargy. Nearby sights include Cape Sagres (Europe's "Land's End" and home of Henry the Navigator's famous navigation school) and the jet-setty resort of Lagos. Or you could just work on a tan and see how slow you can get your pulse in sleepy Salema. If not now, when? If not you, who?

Planning Your Time

The Algarve is your vacation from your vacation. How much time it deserves depends upon how much time you have and how much time you need to recharge your solar batteries. On a three-week Iberian blitz, I'd give it three nights and two days. After a full day of sightseeing in Lisbon, I'd push it by driving four hours around dinnertime to gain an entirely free beach day. With two days, I'd spend one enjoying side trips to Cape Sagres and Lagos and another just lingering in Salema. Plan on an entire day to get from Salema to Sevilla (with a break in Tavira). With more time, I'd spend it in Salema. Eat all dinners in Salema unless you're fighting bulls in Lagos. The only other Algarve stop to consider is Tavira.

The Algarve

Getting around the Algarve

Trains and buses connect the main towns along the south coast
(except on weekends, when service gets skimpy). Trains run nearly
hourly between Lagos and the Spanish border, and buses take you
west from Lagos, where trains don't go. A new highway makes
driving—barring traffic problems—quick and easy. (See "Route
Tips for Drivers in the Algarve" at the end of this chapter.)

SALEMA

One bit of old Algarve magic still glitters quietly in the sun—
Salema. It's at the end of a small road just off the main drag
between the big city of Lagos and the rugged southwest tip of
Europe, Cape Sagres. This simple fishing village, quietly discovered by British and German tourists, has a few hotels, time-share
condos up the road, some hippies' bars with rock music, English
and German menus, a classic beach, and endless sun.

Helpful Hints

Coastal Boat Tours: Local English-speaking guide Sebastian
offers a two-hour scenic cruise along the coast. He gives a light
commentary on the geology and the plant and bird life as he
motors halfway to Cape Sagres and back. Trips include nipping
into some cool blue natural caves. Morning trips are best for bird-
watching. Kicking back and watching the cliffs glide by, I felt like
I was scanning a super-relaxing gallery of natural art. Consider

being dropped at (nude) Figueira Beach just before returning to Salema (it's a 20-minute walk home to Salema—bring shoes, a picnic, and extra water). Easygoing and gentle Sebastian charges little more than what it costs to run his small boat (3,000\$ per person, daily 10:30 and 13:30 mid June–mid Sept, 2–5 passengers, tel. 28-269-5458 or ask for Sebastian at the beachside fishermen's hut or Pensión Mare).

Travel Agency: Horizonte Travel Agency changes money at fair rates; posts bus schedules; sells long-distance bus tickets (e.g., to Lisbon); rents cars, mopeds, and mountain bikes; books flights and hotels; offers apartment rentals in Salema; and runs all-day jeep tours to the nature park on the southwest coast (Mon–Sat 9:30–20:00, Sun 10:00–14:00; Oct–June Mon–Sat 9:30–19:00, closed Sun, CC:VMA, Largo de Liberdade 11, in town center across the stream from Hotel Residencial Salema, tel. 28-269-5855, fax 28-269-5920; e-mail: horizonte.passeios.turis@mail .telepac.pt, Andrea Fernandes SE).

Salema Beach Bum's Quickie Tour

Salema has a split personality: The whitewashed old town is for locals, the other half was built for tourists. Locals and tourists pursue a policy of peaceful coexistence. Tourists laze in the sun while locals grab the shade.

Market action: Salema's flatbed truck market rolls in most mornings—one truck each for fish, fruit, and vegetables and a five-and-dime truck for clothing and other odds and ends. The *1812 Overture* horn of the fish truck wakes you at 8:00. The bakery trailer sells delightful fresh bread and "store-bought" sweet rolls each morning (about 8:00–10:00). And afternoons around 14:30 the red mobile post office stops by.

Fishing scene: Salema is still a fishing village. While the fishermen's hut no longer hosts a fish auction, you'll still see the old-timers enjoying its shade, oblivious to the tourists, mending their nets and arm-wrestling the octopus. In the calm of summer, boats are left out on buoys. In the winter, the community-subsidized tractor earns its keep by hauling the boats ashore. (In pre-tractor days, such boat hauling was a 10-man chore.) The pottery jars stacked everywhere are octopus traps. These are tied about a meter apart in long lines and dropped offshore. Octopi, thinking these would make a cozy place to set an ambush, climb in and get ambushed. When the fishermen hoist them in, they hang on, unaware they've made their final mistake. Unwritten tradition allocates different chunks of undersea territory to each Salema family.

Beach scene: Locals, knowing their tourist-based economy sits on a foundation of sand, hope and pray that sand returns after being washed away each winter. Some winters turn the beach into a pile of rocks. In Portugal, restaurateurs are allowed to build a

Salema

temporary, summer-only, on-the-beach restaurant if they provide a lifeguard and run the green/yellow/red warning-flag system (red means dangerous). All over the country you'll see lonely beaches with solitary temporary structures housing such beach restaurants. The Atlantico Restaurant got permission to dominate Salema's beach by providing a lifeguard through the summer. And, as is often the case, they've quietly evolved from a temporary to a permanent business. Beach towns must also provide public showers and toilets, such as Salema's Balneario Municiple (daily 14:00–19:00, showers 150$, run by Manuela). The fountain in front of it is a reminder of the old days. When water to the village was cut off, this was always open.

On the west end of the beach, you can climb over the rocks past tiny tide pools to the secluded Figuera Beach. While the old days of black widows chasing topless Nordic women off the beach are gone, nudism is still risqué today. Over the rocks and beyond the view of prying eyes, Germans grin and bare it.

Community development: The whole peninsula has been declared a natural park, and further development is forbidden. Salema will live with past mistakes, such as the huge hotel in the town center that pulled some mysterious strings to go two stories over the height limit. Up the street is a huge community of Club Med–type vacationers who rarely leave their air-conditioned bars and swimming pools. Across the highway a mile or two inland is an even bigger golfing resort (worth exploring by car). Just off the beach is a tiny strip mall with a souvenir shop (Rosa's shop is silly with ceramics), a fine grocery store, and a pastry shop with the best coffee in town.

Salema after dark: Salema has three late-night bars, each worth a visit. Consider a Salema pub crawl. *Armarguinha* is a sweet and likeable almond drink you might try. The **Boia Bar** offers beachfront drinks and music. Guillerma Duarte's **Atabua Bar** is the liveliest, with the youngest crowd (20:00–02:00 or later, across the street, famous sangria). **A Aventura Bar and Creperie** offers a pleasant atmosphere for sipping drinks and sending e-mail (900\$/hr, 16:00–02:00, just past the Mini-Market).

Sleeping in Salema
(220\$ = about \$1, country code: 351, zip code: 8650)
Sleep Code: **S** = Single, **D** = Double/Twin, **T** = Triple, **Q** = Quad, **b** = bathroom, **t** = toilet only, **s** = shower only, **CC** = Credit Card (Visa, MasterCard, Amex), **SE** = Speaks English, **NSE** = No English. When a price range is given, the lowest is the winter rate and the highest is the peak-season summer rate.

Salema is crowded in July, August, and September. The town has three streets, five restaurants, several bars, a lane full of fisherfolk who happily rent out rooms to foreign guests, and a circle of modern condo-type hotels, apartments, and villas up the hillside. Parking is free and easy on the street (beware of the no-parking signs near the bus stop).

For maximum comfort there's no need to look beyond John's Pensión Mare. For economy and experience, go for the *quartos* (rooms rented out of private homes).

Pensiónes and Hotels
Pensión Mare, a blue-and-white building looking over the village above the main road into town, is the best good, normal hotel value in Salema (Sb-6,000–7,000\$, Db-9,000–10,000\$, Tb-10,000–12,000\$, includes good breakfast, 10 percent discount with this

book and cash if arranged in advance, CC:VMA, guests-only laundry service for 500$ per kilo, Praia de Salema, Budens 8650-194, Algarve, tel. 28-269-5165, fax 28-269-5846, www.algarve.co.uk). An easygoing Englishman, John, runs this place, offering six comfortable rooms, two fully equipped apartments, and a tidy paradise. He speaks English better than I do and will hold rooms with a phone call and a credit card. John also rents a gem of a fisherman's cottage on the "*quartos* street" for 14,000$.

Hotel Residencial Salema, the oversized hotel towering crudely above everything else in town, is a good value if you simply want a modern, comfortable room handy to the beach. Its 32 red-tiled rooms all have air-conditioning, balconies, and partial views (Sb-8,000–12,000$, Db-8,800–14,500$, 10 percent discount with this book, extra bed-30 percent more, includes breakfast, CC:VMA, elevator, changes money, rents cars and mopeds, closed Nov–March, tel. 28-269-5328, fax 28-269-5329, SE).

Estalagem Infante do Mar is a three-star hotel on top of the cliff. Its 30 rooms are plain but all have balconies, and the views are spectacular—ask for an upstairs room to get a full sea view (Sb-7,500–11,500$, Db-8,600–14,500$, CC:VMA, extra bed-30 percent more, includes small breakfast, pool, bar, restaurant, parking, changes money, has no address except its name, closed Nov–Feb, tel. 28-269-0100, fax 28-269-0109, SE). It's a stiff 10-minute walk uphill. From the Hotel Residencial Salema, cross the bridge and then head up.

Casa Saudade, a miniature parador, is a tastefully remodeled apartment for four with a kitchen, two bedrooms, and two terraces (15,000$ per day, 3-night minimum stay required, Rua Beco de 1 Maio #9; reserve by calling John of Pensión Mare at tel. 28-269-5165 or Wilfried at tel. & fax 28-269-5020). The same owner, Wilfried, rents **Casa Alegria**, a colorful apartment with a splash of Santa Fe and a fantastic view (at the top of the "*quartos* street").

Quartos *and Camping*

Quartos abound along the residential street (running left from the village center as you face the beach). Ask one of the locals at the waterfront or ask at the Boia Bar or Mini-Market. Prices vary with the season (doubles-3,000–6,000$), breakfast is not included, and credit cards are useless. Many places offer beachfront views. It's worth paying extra for *com vista* (view) rooms, since the rooms on the back tend to be dark and musty. Few *quartos*' landladies speak English, but they're used to dealing with visitors. Many will clean your laundry for a few hundred escudos. If you're settling in for a while or are on a tight budget, park your bags and partner at a beachside bar and survey several places. There are always rooms available for those dropping in. Especially outside of July and August, prices can be soft.

Casa Duarte has five pleasant rooms (4 with views), a communal kitchenette, and two terraces (D-4,000–6,500$, tel. 28-269-5206 or their English-speaking daughter Cristina at 28-269-5307; son Romeu, who works at the Mini-Market, also SE). From "*quartos* street," turn right at the Clube Recreativo and then left on the paved path. Duarte's is #7, the first building on the right. If you buy some *sardinhas fresquinhos* from the fish market in the morning (600$/kilo), Sra. Duarte will teach you how to cook them on her grill for lunch.

The friendly **Acacio family** rents a simple ground-floor Db on the beach and a fine upstairs apartment with kitchenette, balcony, and a great ocean view for two to four people (Db-4,000–6,000$, Tb/Qb in apartment-9,000–12,000$, on "*quartos* street" at #91, tel. 28-269-5473, Silvina NSE).

Maria Helena and **Jorge Ribeiro**, a helpful young couple, rent two small and humble doubles and a charming tree house–type apartment with a kitchen, fine terrace, and view toilet (D-4,500$, apartment-7,000$, Rua dos Pescadores 83, tel. 28-269-5289, SE).

Senhor and **Senhora Boto** rent two immaculate, comfortable rooms with hillside views (D-4,500–5,000$) and a spacious two-bedroom sea-view terrace apartment (Db-7,000–8,000$, Tb/Qb-9,000$, great value for up to 4 people). It's at the top of "*quartos* street" at Rua dos Pescadores 4 (walk 5 min up, on the left, tel. 28-269-5265, NSE).

Rosa rents a small double with a big terrace for 4,000$ and a comfortable apartment with balcony that can sleep two couples and a small child. This is a super value at 7,000$ to 8,000$, worth the hike and the two-night minimum stay (near top of hill, Rua dos Pescadoes 18, tel. 28-269-5255, NSE).

Campers (who don't underestimate the high tides) sleep free and easy on the **beach** (public showers available in the town center) or at a well-run **campground** with bungalows half a mile inland, back toward the main road.

Eating in Salema

Fresh seafood, eternally. Salema has six or eight places to eat. Happily, those that face the beach (the three listed below) are the most fun and have the best service, food, and atmosphere.

The **Boia Bar and Restaurant**, at the base of the residential street, has a classy beachfront setting, noteworthy service, and a knack for doing whitefish just right. Their vegetarian lasagna and salads are popular. And their hearty loss-leader breakfast gives you bacon, eggs, toast, coffee, and fresh-squeezed orange juice for the cost of two glasses of orange juice anywhere else in town (10:00–02:00, serving until 22:00; try to arrive for dinner by 19:00, tel 28-269-5382).

The **Atlantico** is noisier, big, busy, right on the beach, and especially atmospheric when the electricity goes out and faces flicker around candles. It's run by the Duarte clan, and the service is friendly. Consider taking your dessert wine or coffee to the beach for some stardust (12:00–24:00, serving until 22:00, tel. 28-269-5142).

The intimate **Mira Mar,** farther up the residential street, is run by gracious Florentine and Dieter, who serve Portuguese fare practically on the beach (12:00–24:00, serving until 23:00, tel. 28-269-5250).

If you'd rather share a tiny loft with the town bohemians than see the sea from your dinner table, hike three blocks inland to the **Carioca Restaurant** for a good selection of salads and seafood cooked on an open grill (Mon–Sat 17:00–24:00, closed Sun, walk 3 blocks inland, cross the stream, just above Carioca Bar—skip the bar).

Need a break from fish? **Carapou Frances**, in the middle of town, serves good pizzas for 800$ to 1,000$.

Romeu's **Mini-Market** has all the fixings for a great picnic (fresh fruits, veggies, bread, sheep's cheese, sausage, *vinho verde*) to take with you to a secluded beach or Cape Sagres. Romeu also changes money and gives travel advice.

Drivers who want a classy meal outside of town should consider the elegant **Restaurant Vila Velha** in Sagres or the romantic **Castelejo Restaurante** at Praia do Castelo (see "Cape Sagres," below).

CAPE SAGRES

This rugged southwestern tip of Portugal was the spot closest to the edge of our flat earth in the days before Columbus. Prince Henry the Navigator, determined to broaden Europe's horizons and spread Catholicism, sent sailors ever farther into the unknown. He lived here at his navigators' school, carefully debriefing shipwrecked and frustrated explorers as they washed ashore. (TI open Tue–Sat 9:30–13:00, 14:00–17:30, closed Sun–Mon, on main street Rua Comandante Matoso, tel. 28-262-4873.)

Portugal's "end of the road" is two distinct capes. Windy **Cabo St. Vincent** is actually the most southwestern tip. It has a desolate lighthouse that marks what was even in prehistoric times referred to as "the end of the world" (open to the public daily 10:00–17:00, snoop around, peek over the far edge, ask the attendant to spin the light for you). Outside the lighthouse, salt-of-the-earth merchants sell figs, fritters, and seaworthy sweaters (4,000$ average). **Cape Sagres**, with its old fort and Henry the Navigator lore, is the more historic cape (2 or 3 maritime history exhibits per year, old church, dramatic views). At either cape, look for daredevil windsurfers and fishermen casting off the cliffs.

Lashed tightly to the windswept landscape is the salty town of Sagres, above a harbor of fishing boats and the lavish **Pousada do Infante**. For a touch of local elegance, pop by the *pousada* for breakfast. For 1,500$ you can sip coffee and nibble on a still-warm croissant while gazing out to where, in the old days, the world dropped right off the table. The classy *pousada*, a reasonable splurge with a magnificent setting (Db-24,600$, 8650 Sagres, tel. 28-262-4222, fax 28-262-4225), offers a warm welcome to anyone ready to pay so much for a continental breakfast.

Restaurant Vila Velha in Sagres is the place to eat if you want to dine really well. Owner Luis speaks English and serves traditional cuisine with a candlelit and dressy ambience. While Vila Velha does fine fish, for some the meaty side of its menu offers a needed break from seafood (3,000$ meals, next to *pousada*, reservations smart, tel. 28-262-4788). Ask Luis for a glass of his homemade—and complimentary—*ginjinha* after dinner. A stop here makes sense after tripping out to Cape Sagres.

Sagres is a popular gathering place for the backpacking bunch, with plenty of private rooms in the center and a great beach and bar scene. From Salema, Sagres is a 20-minute drive or hitch, a half-hour bus trip (nearly hourly trips from Salema, check return times), or a taxi ride (3,500$ 2-hour round-trip includes 1 hour free in Sagres).

Many beaches are tucked away on the drive between Salema and Cape Sagres. Most of them require a short walk after you stop along N-125. In some cases you leave your car on access roads or cross private property to reach the beaches—please be considerate. Furnas beach is fully accessible by car. Ingrina and Zavial beaches are accessed by turning south in the village of Raposeira. Many beaches have bars. In Salema, ask at Pensión Mare or the Horizonte Travel Agency for directions to beaches before you head to Sagres.

The best secluded beach in the region is **Praia do Castelejo**, just north of Cape Sagres (from the town of Vila do Bispo, drive inland and follow the signs for 15 minutes). If you have a car and didn't grow up in Fiji, this really is worth the drive. Overlooking the deserted beach is **Castelejo Restaurante**, which specializes in seafood *cataplanas*, hearty stew that feeds two to three people (12 km from Salema at Praia do Castelo, tel. 28-263-9777).

LAGOS

The major town and high-rise resort on the west end of the Algarve was the capital of the Algarve in the 13th and 14th centuries. The first great Portuguese maritime expeditions embarked from here, and the first African slave market in Europe was held here (understandably not advertised by the local TI). The old town, defined by its medieval walls, stretches between Praça Gil

Eannes and the fort. It's a whitewashed jumble of pedestrian streets, bars, funky craft shops, outdoor restaurants, and sun-burned tourists. The church of San Antonio and the adjoining regional museum (Tue–Sun 9:00–12:30, 14:00–17:00, closed Mon) are worth a look, but the morning fish market at the harbor-front Mercado Municipal is more interesting (produce upstairs). The beaches with the exotic rock formations (of postcard fame) are near the fort.

Lagos has a small, for-tourists bullfight in its dinky ring from June through September on most Saturdays at 18:30. Seats are a steep 4,000$, but the show is a thriller. Signs all along this touristy coastline advertise this *stierkampf.*

Tourist Information: The TI is a six-minute walk from the train or bus stations; take the main road east in the direction of Portimão. The TI is near São João Church (Mon–Sat 9:30–12:30, 14:00–19:00, Fri–Mon until 17:30, tel. 28-276-3031). Neither the bus station nor the train station offers luggage storage. If you're continuing on to Sevilla by bus or train, read ahead and don't leave Lagos without schedules.

Coastal Boat Tours: Dutch-operated Bom Dia offers full- and half-day boat tours of nearby grottos, Cape Sagres, and dolphin "seafaris." Check out the possibilities at their ticket office (2-hour excursions start at 2,800$, marina at Lagos 10, tel. 28-276-4670).

Sleeping and Eating in Lagos
(220$ = about $1, country code: 351, zip code: 8600)
When a price range is given, the lowest is the winter rate, the highest is the peak-season summer rate. Lagos is enjoyable for a resort its size, but I must remind you that Salema is a village paradise and is only a 20-minute taxi ride (2,500–3,000$, no meter, settle price first) or 60-minute bus ride away.

Casa de São Goncalo de Lagos, a beautifully decorated 18th-century home with a garden, lovely tile work, parquet floors, and elegant furnishings, is a fine value. While the downstairs rooms are relatively plain, upstairs you'll find a plush Old World lounge, a dreamy garden, and 13 classy old rooms with all the comforts (Sb-8,000–12,000$, Db-10,000–14,000$, Qb-18,000–20,000$ depending on room and season, includes breakfast, closed Nov–mid-March, CC:A, Rua Candido dos Reis 73, on a pedestrian street 2 blocks from the TI, tel. 28-276-2171, fax 28-276-3927, SE).

If you missed the last bus to Salema (leaves Lagos around 20:30), these places are within 100 meters of the bus station.
Pensão Residencial Solar, a good budget bet, has 29 simple, clean rooms (Sb-5,000–9,000$, Db-8,000–15,000$, includes break-fast, CC:VMA, elevator, Rua Antonio Crisogono dos Santos 60, tel. 28-276-2477, fax 28-276-1784, SE). The big, slick, and sternly

run **Albergeria Marina Rio** faces the harbor front and the busy main street. Its modern, air-conditioned rooms come with all the amenities (Sb-7,000–16,500$, Db-8,000–17,000$, extra bed 2,250–5,100$, CC:VMA, swimming pool, elevator, Avenida dos Descobrimentos-Apartado 388, tel. 28-276-9859, fax 28-276-9960, e-mail: marinario@ip.pt, SE).

The Club Med–like **youth hostel** is a lively, social, and very cushy experience (dorm bed in quad-1,700–2,500$, some D-4,300–6,000$, includes breakfast, kitchen facilities, hostel card required, Rua Lancarote de Freitas 50, tel. 28-276-1970).

Transportation Connections—Lagos and Salema

Lagos to: Lisbon (5 trains/day, 5 hrs, possible transfer in Tunes; 5 buses/day, 5 hrs), **Évora** (1 bus/day, 5 hrs), **Vila Real St. Antonio** (4 trains/day, 4 hrs), **Tavira** (7 trains/day, 3.5 hrs, 2 daily express trains do it in 2 hrs). Bus info: tel. 28-276-2944.

Lagos and Salema: Lagos is your Algarve transportation hub and the closest train station to Salema (15 km). Buses go almost hourly between Lagos and Sagres (1-hr ride, last bus departs Lagos around 20:30, fewer buses on weekends); about half of them go right into the village of Salema—the others drop you at the top of the road into Salema (bus continues to Figueira). From here it's a 20-minute walk downhill into the village. From Lagos' train station (ignore the "*quartos* women" who tell you Salema is 60 km away), walk straight out, go through the marina, cross the bridge and then the main boulevard, and walk straight into the bright yellow EVA bus station. Before heading to Salema, pick up return bus schedules and train schedules for your next destination. If you venture into Lagos, buses to Salema (and Sagres) also stop on the waterfront. Allow 2,500$ to 3,000$ for a taxi from Lagos to Salema (settle price first).

Lagos and Sevilla: The direct bus between Lagos and Sevilla is worth every escudo (about 3,500$, 5 hrs, May–Sept 2/day except Mon; Oct–April 3–4/week, check ahead). The bus departs from the Lagos bus station and arrives at Sevilla's Plaza de Armas bus station, with stops at Algarve towns such as Tavira.

Unless you take the direct bus, getting to Sevilla is a very long day by bus or by bus and train. From Salema take an early bus to Lagos (I walk up to the main road to catch the Sagres–Lagos express bus). From Lagos you have two options: Take a bus or train to Faro (about 2 hrs either way) and catch the Faro–Sevilla bus (2 buses/day, 5 hrs), or take the train until the last stop in Vila Real de San Antonio (several morning departures, allow 4.5 hours, possible transfer in Tunes or Faro), which connects directly to Vila Real and the river-crossing ferry (300$, hrly, last ferry runs about 22:00) to the pleasant Spanish border town of Ayamonte (TI tel. 95-950-2121).

From the Ayamonte dock, walk through the town (angling slightly to the right) and find the bus stop next to the main square (shops take escudos; banks change coins). From Ayamonte to Sevilla, catch a direct bus to Sevilla (6/day, 2.5 hrs) or transfer at Huelva (frequent buses, easy transfer). From Huelva, buses run at least hourly to Sevilla (1 hr). The new Huelva bus station is heavenly: English information, ATMs, and a bank that changes Portuguese coins and sells phone cards (tel. 95-925-6900). From Huelva, you could take one of four daily trains to Sevilla (2 hrs), but I'd take the bus. Huelva's bus and train stations are connected by a 15-minute walk along Avenida Italia. Sunday schedules are limited and more frustrating. (See "Transportation Connections" near the end of the Sevilla chapter for more specifics.)

TAVIRA

Straddling a river, with a lively park, chatty locals, and boats sharing its waterfront center, Tavira is a low-rise, easygoing alternative to the other, more aggressive Algarve resorts. It's your best east Algarve stop. Because Tavira has handy bus connections to Sevilla (and other destinations) and good train service to the rest of Portugal (it's on the trans-Algarve train line, with hourly departures both east and west), many travelers find the town more accessible than Salema.

The many churches and fine bits of Renaissance architecture sprinkled through Tavira remind the wanderer that 500 years ago the town was the largest on the Algarve (with 1,500 dwellings according to a 1530 census) and an important base for Portuguese adventurers in Africa. The silting up of its harbor, a plague, the 1755 earthquake, and the shifting away of its once-upon-a-time lucrative tuna industry left Tavira in a long decline. Today the town relies on tourism.

Orientation

Tavira straddles the Rio Gilão three kilometers from the Atlantic. Everything of sightseeing and transportation importance is on the south bank. A clump of historic sights—the ruined castle and main church—fills its tiny fortified hill and tangled Moorish lanes. But today the action is outside the old fortifications along the riverside Praça da Republica and the adjacent shady, fountain- and bench-filled park. The old market hall is beyond the park. And beyond that is the boat to the beach island. The old pedestrian-only "Roman Bridge" leads from Praça da Republica to the north bank (2 recommended hotels and most of the evening and restaurant action).

Tourist Information: The TI is up the cobbled steps from the inland end of the Praça da Republica (daily 9:30–19:00, Sept–May 9:30–17:30, often closed for lunch and Sat and Sun during off season depending on staff availability, Rua Galeria 9, tel. 28-132-2511).

Tavira

The TI offers 500$ guided town walks (call for information and reservations).

Arrival in Tavira: The train station is a 10-minute walk from the town center: leave the station following the yellow "Turismo" sign and follow this road downhill to the river and Praça da Republica. The new riverside bus station is three blocks from the town center; simply follow the river into town.

Sights—Tavira

The TI's fine, free map describes a dozen churches with enthusiasm. But for most tourists, the town's sights can be seen in a few minutes. Uphill from the TI you'll find the ruined **castle**, offering only plush gardens and a fine city view (free, Mon–Sat 9:00–17:00). Just beyond the castle ruins is the town's most visit-worthy church, the **Church of Santa Maria**. From there I'd enjoy the riverside park at **Praça da Republica** and the fun architecture of the low-key 18th-century buildings facing the river. After dinner take a stroll along the fish-filled river, with a pause on the pedestrian bridge or in the park if there's any action in the bandstand.

Beaches—The big hit for travelers is Tavira's great beach island, **Ilha da Tavira**. The island is a long, almost treeless sandbar with a campground, several restaurants, and a sprawling beach. A summer-only boat takes bathers painlessly from downtown Tavira to the island (July–Sept 15 about hrly, timetable available at TI, 200$ round-trip, departs 200 meters downriver from the former market hall). It's an enjoyable ride even if you just go round-trip without getting out. Or you can bus, taxi, ride a rental bike, or bake during a shadeless three-kilometer walk out of town to Quatro Aguas, where the five-minute ferry shuttles sunbathers to Ilha da Tavira (runs constantly with demand, last trip near midnight in high season to accommodate diners).

Another fine beach, the **Barril Beach resort**, is four kilometers from Tavira. Walk, rent a bike, or take a city bus to Pedras del Rei and then catch the little train (runs April–Sept) or walk 10 minutes through Ria Formosa National Park to the resort. Get details at the TI.

Sleeping in Tavira
(220$ = about $1, country code: 351, zip code: 8800)
Residencial Lagoas is spotless, homey, and a block off the river. Friendly, English-speaking Maria offers a communal refrigerator, a rooftop patio with a view made for wine and candles, and laundry washboard privileges (S-3,500$, D-5,000$, Db-7,000$, Tb-8,500$, less off-season, no breakfast, Rua Almirante Candido dos Reis 24, tel. 28-132-2252). Maria also rents several apartments. Cross the Roman footbridge from Praça da República, follow the middle fork on the other side, and turn right where it ends.

The modern, hotelesque **Residencia Princesa do Gilão** offers bright, modern, riverfront rooms, some with balconies and a view (Db-7,000–8,000$, includes breakfast, Rua Borda de Agua de Aguiar 10, cross the Roman bridge and turn right along the river, tel. & fax 28-132-5171, SE).

Pensão-Residencial Bela Fria is a shiny eight-room place with a rooftop sun terrace overlooking the river. Its simple air-conditioned rooms are quiet, modern, and comfortable (Sb-4,000–6,000$, 10,000$ in Aug, Db-6,000–8,000$, 11,000$ in Aug, includes breakfast, Rua dos Pelames 1, directly across from the bus station, tel. 28-132-5375, fax 28-132-5375, e-mail: belafria @hotmail.com, some English spoken).

For quiet, spacious, comfort, **Rosa's Quartos** are tops. Rosa rents 14 big, new, shiny, marble-paved rooms on a quiet alley (Db-5,000–7,000$, over bridge and through Jardim da Alagoa square to Rua da Porta Nova 4, opposite St. Paul's church, tel. 28-132-1547, NSE).

For a splurge, consider **Hotel Mare**'s red-tiled and smartly appointed rooms, firm beds, sauna, restaurant, and rooftop terrace.

Some rooms on the second floor have balconies overlooking the river (Sb-4,000–9,000$, no singles in Aug, Db-7,000–13,000$, 16,000$ in Aug, includes breakfast, CC:VMA, air-con, Rua Jose Pires Padinha, on the TI side of the river just beyond the old market hall, tel. 28-132-5815, fax 28-132-5819, SE).

Eating in Tavira

Tavira is filled with reasonable restaurants. A couple of classy places face the riverbank just beyond the old market hall. A few blocks inland, hole-in-the-wall places offer more fish per dollar.

These places are all within two blocks of the pedestrian Roman bridge, just over the river from the town center. For seafood, I enjoyed the inexpensive and relaxed **Restaurant Bica**, below Residencial Lagoas (see first hotel listing, above). The **Patio**, on a classy rooftop, is worth the extra escudos. For Italian cuisine, consider **Patrick's** (good lasagna and curry dishes) and **Aquasul** (pasta, pizza, and more). From the bridge, if you turn left and go upstream through the tunnel you'll find the rickety riverside tables of the popular **Restaurant O Simão** (cheap, tasty grills). **Anazu Pasteleria** is the place to grab breakfast or nurse a late riverside drink (1 block to the right of the bridge).

Transportation Connections—Tavira

To: Lisbon (5 trains/day, 5 hrs; 10 buses/day, 5 hrs), **Lagos** (12 trains/day, sometimes a change in Faro, 2–3.5 hrs), **Sevilla by bus** (2/day, 3.5 hrs, easy transfer in Huelva; 1 direct bus, 2.5 hrs, Tue–Sun May–Oct, less off-season), **Sevilla by train** (go by bus instead). Train info: tel. 28-132-2354, bus info: tel. 28-132-2546.

CACELA VELHA

Just a few miles east of Tavira (1 kilometer off the main road), this tiny village sits happily ignored on a hill with its fort, church, one restaurant, a few *quartos*, and a beach, the open sea just over the sandbar, a short row across its lagoon. The restaurant serves a sausage-and-cheese specialty fried at your table. If you're driving, swing by, if only to enjoy the coastal view and imagine how nice the Algarve would be if people like you and me had never discovered it.

Route Tips for Drivers in the Algarve

Lisbon to Salema (150 miles, 4 hrs): Following the blue "Sul Ponte" signs, drive south over Lisbon's 25th of April Bridge. A short detour just over the bridge takes you to the giant concrete statue of *Cristo Rei* (Christ in Majesty). Continue south past Setubal to the south coast (following signs to Algarve, Vila do Bispo, Sagres, Lagos, and Salema). Just east of Vila do Bispo, you'll hit Figueira and the tiny road to the beach village of

Alentejo: Corks and Jokes

Driving from Lisbon to the Algarve, you'll pass through the Alentejo region, known for producing cork. Portugal, the world's leading producer of that wonderful tasteless, odorless seal for wine bottles, produces 30 million corks a day. Driving through the Alentejo region, you'll see vast fields of cork oaks. Every seven to nine years the bark is stripped, leaving a sore red underskin.

The Alentejo region is also known for being extraordinarily traditional. Throughout Europe, what a tourist might see as quaint is seen by city folk as backward. The people of Alentejo are the butt of local jokes. It's said you'll see them riding motorcycles in pajamas...so they can better lay into the corners. Many Portuguese call porno flicks "Alentejo karate." I met a sad old guy from Alentejo. When I asked him what was wrong, he explained that he was on the verge of teaching his burro how to live without food...but it died. The big event of the millennium in Lisbon was the arrival of the Alentejanos for Expo '98.

Salema. Decent roads, less traffic, and the glory of waking up on the Algarve make doing this drive at night a reasonable option.

Algarve to Sevilla (150 miles): Drive east along the Algarve. In Lagos, park along the waterfront by the fort and the Mobil gas station. From Lagos follow the signs to Faro and then, near Loule, hit the new freeway (direction: España) to Tavira. It's a two-hour drive from Salema to Tavira. Leaving Tavira, follow the signs to Vila Real and España. You'll cross over the new bridge into Spain (where it's 1 hour later) and glide effortlessly (90 minutes by freeway) into Sevilla. At Sevilla follow the signs to Centro Ciudad ("city center"), drive along the river, and park (at least to get set up) near the cathedral and tower.

CENTRAL PORTUGAL: COIMBRA AND NAZARÉ

While the far north of Portugal has considerable charm, those with limited time enjoy maximum travel thrills on or near the coast of central Portugal. This is an ideal stop if you're coming in from Salamanca or Madrid or are interested in a small-town side trip north from Lisbon.

The college town of Coimbra (3 hours north of Lisbon by train, bus, or car) is Portugal's Oxford and its easiest-to-enjoy city. Browse through the historic university, fortresslike cathedral, and lively Old Quarter of what was once Portugal's leading city.

Nazaré, an Atlantic-coast fishing-town-turned-resort, is black-shawl traditional and beach friendly. You'll be greeted by the energetic applause of the surf, widows with rooms to rent, and big plates of steamed shrimp. Have fun in the Portuguese sun in a land of cork groves, eucalyptus trees, ladies in seven petticoats, and men who stow cigarettes and fishhooks in their stocking caps.

Several other worthy sights are within easy day-trip distance of Nazaré. You can drop by the Batalha Monastery, the patriotic pride and architectural joy of Portugal. If the spirit moves you, the pilgrimage site at Fatima is nearby. Alcobaça has Portugal's largest church (and saddest romance). And Portugal's incredibly cute walled town of Óbidos is just down the road.

Planning Your Time
Few Americans give Portugal much time. Most do Lisbon and the south coast. On a three-week trip through Spain and Portugal, Coimbra and Nazaré each merit a day. There's another day's worth of sightseeing in Batalha, Alcobaça, and Fatima. If you're connecting Salamanca or Madrid with Lisbon, I'd do it this way (for specifics see Salamanca's and Coimbra's "Transportation Connections").

By Car
Day 1: Leave Salamanca early, breakfast in Ciudad Rodrigo, early afternoon arrival in Coimbra, tour university and old cathedral.
Day 2: Shop and browse the Old Quarter, lunch at Batalha, tour church, visit Fatima, evening in Nazaré.
Day 3: Make 10-mile side trip from Nazaré to Alcobaça (town, monastery, wine museum). Spend afternoon back in Nazaré with a look at Sitio and beach time. Seafood dinner.
Day 4: Visit Óbidos on your way to Lisbon. Arrive in Lisbon by noon.

By Train
Day 1: You have two miserably early alternatives: the 04:40-to-08:22 Salamanca–Coimbra train connection (5 hrs, 1 hr gained in Portugal) or the bus (7:00–10:30 on Mon–Tues and Sat–Sun, or worse, 02:15–6:15 on Fri; see Salamanca's "Transportation Connections" in Northwest of Madrid chapter). Spend the day seeing Coimbra.
Day 2: Catch morning bus (or train) from Coimbra to Nazaré. Set up and relax in Nazaré, Sitio, and on the beach. Seafood dinner.
Day 3: Do the triangular loop (Nazaré–Batalha–Alcobaça–Nazaré) by bus.
Day 4: Train into Lisbon.

COIMBRA
Don't be fooled by Coimbra's drab suburbs. Portugal's most important city for 200 years, Coimbra (KWEEM-bra) remains second only to Lisbon culturally and historically. It served as Portugal's leading city while the Moors controlled Lisbon. Only as Portugal's maritime fortunes rose was landlocked Coimbra surpassed by the ports of Lisbon and Porto. Today Coimbra is Portugal's third-largest city (pop. 100,000) and home to its oldest and most prestigious university (founded 1290). When school is in session, Coimbra bustles. During school holidays, it's sleepy. Coimbra's got a great Arab-flavored Old Quarter—a maze of people, narrow streets, and tiny *tascas* (restaurants with just a few tables).

Orientation
Coimbra is a mini-Lisbon—everything good about urban Portugal without the intensity of a big city. I couldn't design a more enjoyable city for a visit. There's a small-town feeling in the winding streets set on the side of the hill. The high point is the old university. From there, little lanes meander down like a Moroccan medina to the main pedestrian street. This street (named Visconde da Luz at the top, turning into Rua de Ferreira Borges halfway down)

Coimbra

runs from the square Praça 8 de Maio to the Mondego River,
dividing the old town into upper (Alta) and lower (Baixa) parts.

From the Largo da Portagem (main square by the river)
everything is within an easy walk. The Old Quarter spreads out
like an amphitheater—timeworn houses, shops, and stairways all
lead up to the university. The best views are looking up from the
far end of Santa Clara Bridge and looking down from the observation deck of the university or the arcade in the Machado de Castro
Museum. The TI and plenty of good budget rooms are along the
river, within four blocks of the train station.

Tourist Information

Pick up a map and the monthly cultural calendar at the TI at Largo
da Portagem (Mon–Fri 9:00–19:00, Sat–Sun 10:00–13:00, 14:30–
17:30; Oct–May 9:00–18:00, entrance on Navarro, tel. 23-985-
5930). Here you can get all bus schedules and information on sights
in central Portugal. Other TIs with similar hours are on Praça Dinis
and Praça da República (near the university). While there are no
regular walking tours, the TI has a list of private guides (such as
Cristina at tel. 23-983-5428, 15,000$ per half day).

Helpful Hints

The Abreu travel agency sells bus tickets to Salamanca and beyond (Rua da Sota 2, near train station A, tel. 23-985-5520, e-mail: jpeters.coimbra@abreu.pt, helpful James SE). ATMs and banks (Mon–Fri 8:30–15:00) are plentiful. Avis has an office in train station A (tel. & fax 23-983-4786) and Hertz is at Rua João de Ruão 1 (tel. & fax 23-983-4750).

Arrival in Coimbra

By Train: There are two Coimbra train stations, A and B. Major trains (e.g., from Lisbon and Salamanca) stop only at B (big). From there, simply hop the three-minute shuttle train to the very central A station (take the A train; free, included with ticket that got you to the B-train station). Local trains (e.g., to Nazaré) stop at both stations. Station A has a helpful English-speaking information office (*informações*) tucked away in a waiting room (daily 9:00–19:00, tel. 23-983-4998).

By Bus: The bus station, on Avenida Fernão de Magalhaes (tel. 23-985-5270), is a boring 15-minute walk from the center. Exit the bus station to the right and follow the busy street into town or take a taxi (500$). Local buses are expensive (210$), and by the time the #5 bus comes along, you could already have walked downtown. (If you need only bus schedules, the much more central TI has a folder with all the timetables.)

Do-It-Yourself Orientation Tour of Coimbra's Old Quarter

Coimbra is a delight on foot. You'll find yourself doing laps along the straight (formerly Roman) pedestrian-only main drag. Do it once following this quickie tour:

Start at **Santa Clara Bridge**. The bridge has been a key bridge over the Mondega River since Roman times. For centuries it had a tollgate (*portagem*). Cross the bridge for a fine Coimbra view, a lowbrow popular fairground, and free parking.

The square, **Largo da Portagem** (at the end of the bridge on the Coimbra side), is a great place for a coffee or a pastry. Pastelaria Briosa's pastries are best.

Strolling down the **pedestrian boulevard** you'll pass Pastelaria Arcadia on the left. Known as the "café of the old ladies," it's filled with local grandmothers enjoying English-style afternoon tea. Ignoring the illegal street vendors, find the Camera Municipal (on the right), with its free and interesting town photo exhibits. Wander in. Steps lead right under the ancient arched gateway—Arco de Almedina—into the old city and to the old cathedral and university. We'll go there later.

Farther along the pedestrian drag, stop at the picturesque corner just beyond the cafés (where the building comes to a triangular corner). The steep road climbs into Coimbra's historic ghetto (no Jewish community remains). On the left, stairs lead down into the pleasant **Praça do Comércio** (shaped like a Roman chariot racecourse—and likely to have been one 2,000 years ago) and the lower town. Look at your map. The circular street pattern outlines the wall used by Romans, Visigoths, Moors, and Christians to protect Coimbra. Historically the rich could afford to live within the protective city walls (the "Alta" or high town). Even today, the Baixa, or low town, remains a poorer section, with haggard women hurling buckets of dirty water into the streets, dirty children running barefoot, and drunk men peeing as if you don't exist.

Farther down (on the right) is a photography studio with a display case featuring graduation photos. Check out the students decked out in their traditional university capes (displaying rips on the hem for girlfriends) and color-coded sashes (yellow for medicine, red for law, and so on).

The pedestrian street ends at Praça 8 de Maio with the **Church of Santa Cruz** and its ornate facade. The shiny "necklace" on the angel behind the trumpeter is actually electrified to keep pigeons from dumping their corrosive load on the tender limestone.

People (and pigeons) watch from the terrace of **Café Santa Cruz** (to the right of church). Built as a church but abandoned with the dissolution of the monasteries in 1836 (the women's room is in a confessional), this was the 19th-century haunt of local intellectuals. (There's also a good self-service cafeteria behind the church at Jardim da Manga.)

Backtrack to **Arco de Almedina** (literally "gate to the *medina*") and climb into the old town. If you can't make it to Morocco, this dense jungle of shops and markets may be your next-best bet. Part of the old-town wall, this is a double gate with a 90-degree kink in the middle for easier defense. The two square holes in the ceiling, through which boiling oil would be poured, turned attacking Moors into fritters. Shops here show off the fine local blue and white ceramic work (*faianca*).

You're climbing the steep **Rua de Quebra Costas**—"Street of Broken Ribs." At one time this lane had no steps and literally was the street of broken ribs. During a strong rain this becomes a river. A few steps uphill is the old cathedral. Beyond that is the university.

Sights—Coimbra's Old University

Coimbra's 700-year-old university was modeled after Bologna's university (Europe's first, A.D. 1139). It's a stately, three-winged former royal palace (from when Coimbra was the capital), beautifully situated overlooking the city. At first, law, medicine, grammar, and logic were taught. Then, with Portugal's seafaring

Coimbra's Old University

orientation, astronomy and geometry were added. While Lisbon's
university is much larger, Coimbra's is still considered the country's most respected university. Combo tickets for all university
sites cost 500$ (daily 9:30–12:00, 14:00–17:00). Consider a taxi
ride to the Iron Gate and sightsee Coimbra downhill.

Iron Gate—Find the gate to the old university (on Praça da
Porta Ferrea). Before entering, stand with your back to the gate
(and the old university) and look across the stark modern square at
the fascist architecture of the new university. In what's considered
one of the worst cultural crimes in Portuguese history, the dictator
Salazar tore down half the old town of Coimbra to build these
university halls. Salazar, proud that Portugal was the last European
power to hang onto its global empire, wanted a fittingly monumental university here. After all, Salazar—and virtually all people
of political importance in Portugal—was educated in Coimbra. If
these bold buildings are reminiscent of Mussolini's EUR in Rome,
perhaps it's because they were built in part by Italian architects
for Portugal's little Mussolini.

OK, now turn and walk through the Iron Gate. Traditionally,

freshmen, proudly wearing their black capes for the first time, pass through the Iron Gate to enroll. But to get out they find an Iron Gate gauntlet of butt kicks from upperclassmen. Walk into the...

Old University Courtyard—The statue in the square is of King John III. While the university was established in 1290, it went back and forth between Lisbon and Coimbra (back then, university students were adults, privileged, and a pain to have in your town). In 1537 John III finally established the school permanently in Coimbra (away from Lisbon). Standing like a good humanist (posing much like England's Renaissance King Henry VIII), John modernized Portugal's education system Renaissance-style. But he also made the university the center of Portugal's Inquisition.

Survey the square with your back to the gate. The dreaded sound of the clock tower's bell—named the "baby goat" for its nagging—called the students to class. On several occasions the clapper has been stolen. No bell...no class. No class...big party. A larger bell (the "big goat") rings only on grand and formal occasions.

The university's three important stops all face this square: the Grand Hall (up the grand stairway on the right between you and the clock tower), St. Michael's Chapel (straight ahead, under the arch, then to the left), and King John's Library (across the square, farthest door on left).

The arcaded passageway between the Iron Gate and the clock tower is called Via Latina, from the days when only Latin was allowed in this part of the university. Purchase your tickets at the end of Via Latina immediately under the tower. See the following sights in any order you like.

The Grand Hall (Sala dos Capelos)—Enter from the middle of Via Latina. This is the site of the university's major academic ceremonies, such as exams and graduations. This was originally the throne room of the royal palace. Today the green rector's chair sits thronelike in front. While students in their formal outfits filled the benches, teachers sat along the perimeter, and gloomy portraits of Portuguese kings looked down. Since there is no clapping during these formal rituals, a brass band (on the platform in the back) would punctuate the ceremonies with solemn music. Tourists look down from balconies above the room.

View Catwalk: Continue around the Grand Hall and out onto the narrow observation deck for the best possible views of Coimbra. Scan the old town. Remember, before Salazar's extension of the university, this old town surrounded the university. The Baroque facade breaking the horizon is the "New" Cathedral—from the 16th century. Below that, with the fine arcade, is the Machado de Castro Museum, housed in the former bishop's palace and sitting on a Roman site (see below). And below that, like an armadillo, sits the old cathedral. The noisily painted yellow and blue windows above that are of a *republica*. Traditionally, Coimbra students (from the same distant town) lived together in groups of about a dozen in communal houses called *republicas*. Today *republicas* function as tiny fraternities—some are highly cultured, others are mini–Animal Houses. The Mondego River is the longest entirely Portuguese river. Over the bridge and above the popular fairgrounds is the 17th-century Santa Clara Convent—at 180 meters, the longest building in Coimbra. In 1836 Prime Minister Marquis de Pombal decreed that monasteries and convents were an obstacle to the modern development of Portugal and dissolved them all. Today these are generally museums or abandoned ruins. Pombal was a forceful figure. Not only did he rebuild Lisbon after the earthquake, but he also ended the Inquisition and expelled the Jesuits, who were the intellectual powers behind the Inquisition.

St. Michael's Chapel—This chapel is behind the 16th-century Manueline facade (enter through the next door—once inside, push the door on the left marked "capela"). The architecture of the church interior is Manueline (notice the golden "rope" trimming the arch before the altar). The decor is from a later time. I like the slinky 17th-century Adam and Eve tile paintings flanking the rope archway. The tiled walls are decked out in Persian carpet–type designs. The altar is 17th-century Mannerist, with steps unique to Portugal (and her South American colonies) symbolizing the steps the faithful take on their journey to heaven. The 2,100-pipe 18th-century German-built organ is notable for its horizontal "trumpet" pipes. Unique to Iberia, these help the organist perform the allegorical fight between good and evil—with the horizontal pipes trumpeting the arrival of the good guys. Finally, above the loft in the rear are the box seats for the royal family.

The **Museum of Sacred Art**, one glass door away, will likely be closed for renovation throughout 2001. In the museum's stairway, John the Baptist points the way to art that nuns and priests would find fascinating. The museum was created in 1910 to keep the art in Coimbra when the new republic wanted to move all the art to Lisbon.

King John's Library—This grand library displays 30,000 books in 18th-century splendor. The zealous doorkeeper locks the door at every opportunity to keep out humidity. Buzz to get into this temple of thinking. At the "high altar" stands its founder, the Divine Monarch John V. The reading tables inlaid with exotic South American woods (and ornamented with silver ink wells) and the precious wood shelves (with clever hide-away staircases) are reminders that Portugal's wealth was great—and imported. Built baroque, the interior is all wood. Even the marble is just painted wood. Look for the *trompe l'oeil* Baroque tricks on the painted ceiling. Gold leaf (from Brazil) is everywhere, and the Chinese themes are pleasantly reminiscent of Portugal's once-vast empire.

The books, all from before 1755, are in Latin, Greek, or Hebrew. Imagine being a student in Coimbra 500 years ago. As you leave, watch how the doorman uses the giant key as a hefty doorknob.

More Sights—Coimbra

Machado de Castro Museum—Housed in the old bishop's palace, this museum contains ceramics, 14th- to 16th-century religious sculpture (mostly taken from the dissolved monasteries), and a Roman excavation site. Upstairs, don't miss the impressive 14th-century *Cristo Negro* carved in wood. Until its restoration a decade ago, this was black from candle soot and considered to be a portrait of a black Christ. Enjoy the views from the top-floor arcade.

The Roman building in the basement provided a level foundation for an ancient Roman forum that stood where the museum does today. Notice the economical "plug-on" Roman busts (from the days when they'd keep the bodies but change the heads according to whoever the latest emperor was). At the entry read the Latin-inscribed Roman stone: bottom line—Aeminiens, referring to the people who lived in Roman Coimbra, then called Aeminium; fifth line—the 4th-century emperor of the day, Constantio; and the second line—a reference perhaps to an early alliance of barbarian tribes from the North Atlantic (250$, Tue–Sun 9:30–12:30, 14:00–17:30, closed Mon, free Sun morning, museum will close in 2002 for restoration). Visit this before or after the old university, since both are roughly at the same altitude.

Old Cathedral (Sè Velha)—Same old story: Christians push out Moors (1064), tear down their mosque, and build a church. The Arabic script on a few of the stones indicates that rubble from the mosque was used in the construction. The facade of the main entrance even feels Arabic. Notice the crenellations along the roof of this fortresslike Romanesque church; the Moors, though booted out, were still considered a risk.

The three front altars are each worth a look. The main altar is a fine example of Gothic. The 16th-century chapel to the right is one of the best Renaissance altars in the country. The apostles all look to Jesus as he talks, while musical angels flank the holy host. To the left of the high altar, the Chapel of St. Peter shows Peter being crucified upside down. The fine points of the carving were destroyed by Napoleon's soldiers.

The giant holy water font shells are a 19th-century gift from Ceylon, and the walls are lined with 16th-century tiles from Sevilla.

On the right just before the transept is a murky painting of a queen with a skirt full of roses. She's a local favorite with a sweet legend. Against the wishes of the king, she always gave bread to the poor. One day, when he came home early from a trip, she was busy doling out bread from her skirt. She pulled the material up to hide the bread. When the king asked her what was inside (suspecting bread for the poor), the queen—unable to lie—lowered the material and, miraculously, it was only roses.

The peaceful cloister (entrance near back of church) is the oldest Gothic cloister in Portugal. Its decaying walls, neglected courtyard, and overgrown roses offer a fine framed view of the cathedral's grassy dome (church is free, cloisters cost 100$, Mon–Fri 10:00–12:00, 14:00–19:30, may be closed Fri afternoons and off-season, but you're always welcome to drop by during Mass Mon–Sat 19:00 and Sun 11:00).

Little Portugal (Portugal dos Pequenitos)—This is a children's (or tourist's) look at the great buildings and monuments of Portugal in miniature, scattered through a park a couple of blocks south of town, across the Santa Clara Bridge (800$, daily 10:00–20:00, until 19:00 off-season).

Kayaks, Cruises, and Rapelling—O Pioneiro takes you from Coimbra to Penacova (25 kilometers away) by minibus and leaves you with a **kayak** and instructions on getting back. It's a three-hour paddle downstream on the Rio Mondego to Coimbra (3,000$, 10 percent discount with this book, daily April–mid-Oct, 1- and 2-person kayaks available, book by phone, meet at park near TI, tel. 23-947-8385 to reserve, best times to phone are 13:00–15:00 and 20:00–22:00, SE). Most people stop to swim or picnic on the way back, so it often turns into an all-day journey. For the first 20 kilometers you'll go with the flow, but you'll get your exercise paddling the last five flat kilometers.

If you'd rather let someone else do the work, O Basofia boats **cruise** up and down the river daily in summer (1,500$, 3/day, fewer off-season, 75 min, depart from dock across from TI, tel. 23-982-6815).

At your own risk, Capitao Dureza will take you **rappelling** and canyoneering (book by tel. & fax 23-342-7772).

Sights—Near Coimbra
▲**Conimbriga Roman Ruins**—Portugal's best Roman site is impressive...unless you've been to Rome. Little remains of the city, in part because its inhabitants tore down buildings to throw up a quick defensive wall against an expected barbarian attack. Today this wall cuts crudely through the site. Highlights are the fine mosaics of the Casa dos Fonts (under the protective modern roofing) and a delightful little museum (350$, daily 9:00–13:00, 14:00–20:00; museum opens 1 hr later, closes 2 hrs earlier, and is closed all day Mon; Sept–March ruins close at 18:00). The ruins are 15 kilometers south of Coimbra on the Lisbon road. On weekdays two buses leave for the ruins each morning from Coimbra's A Station and return late afternoon (255$). Normal buses run twice per hour to Condeixa but leave you a mile from the site. Check bus schedules at the Coimbra TI.

Sleeping in Coimbra
(220$ = about $1, country code: 351, zip code: 3000)

Sleep Code: **S** = Single, **D** = Double/Twin, **T** = Triple, **Q** = Quad, **b** = bathroom, **t** = toilet only, **s** = shower only, **CC** = Credit Card (Visa, MasterCard, Amex), **SE** = Speaks English, **NSE** = No English. Breakfast isn't included unless noted.

The listings are an easy walk from the central A station and Santa Clara Bridge. For the cheapest rooms, simply walk from the A station a block into the old town and choose one of countless *dormidas* (cheap pensions). River views come with traffic noise.

Hotel Astoria gives you the thrill of staying in the city's finest old hotel for a painless price (Sb-11,000–15,000$, Db-14,000–18,000$, depending on season, extra bed-5,000$, includes breakfast, 10 percent discount by showing this book at check-in, CC:VMA, air-con, elevator, fine art-deco lounges, plush breakfast room, public parking opposite hotel 1,000$/day, central as can be at Avenida Navarro 21, tel. 23-985-3020, fax 23-982-2057, SE). Rooms with river views cost nothing extra.

Hotel Oslo rents 33 good business-class rooms a block from the A station. Rooms are small but hint of Oslo (Sb-7,500–9,000$, Db-10,000–12,000$, third person-2,000$, CC:VMA, air-con, free parking, Avenida Fernão de Magalhaes 25, tel. 23-982-9071, fax 23-982-0614, SE).

Hotel Braganca's ugly lobby disguises 83 clean, comfortable, but often smoky rooms with modern bathrooms (Sb/shower-6,200$, Sb/tub-9,700$, Db/shower-9,700$, Db/tub-12,200$, save money by requesting a shower, or *chuveiro*, includes breakfast, 10 percent discount with this book, CC:VMA, air-con, elevator, parking next door 1,500$/day, Largo das Ameias 10, tel. 23-982-2171, fax 23-983-6135, e-mail: hbraganza@mail.telepac.pt, SE). Ask to sniff several rooms. (The manager believes that in 10 years the United States will grow out of its smoke-free-zones kick.)

Residencial Moderna hides 16 delightful little rooms in a shopping building overlooking a pedestrian street. Many rooms come with a balcony (ask *com varanda*) and parquet floors (Db-6,000–8,000$, 10 percent discount with this book, air-con, parking, a block from A station, Rua Adelino Veiga 49, third floor, tel. 23-982-5413, fax 23-982-9508, Fernandes family NSE).

Ibis Hotel is a modern high-rise. Its orderly little rooms come with all the comforts and American Motel 6 charm. Well-located on a riverside park, it's three blocks past the Santa Clara Bridge and the Old Quarter (Sb/Db-7,200–8,200$, breakfast extra, easy 520$/day parking in basement, elevator, some smoke-free rooms, Avenida Emidio Navarro, tel. 23-949-1559, fax 23-985-2140, e-mail: h1672@accor-hotels.com, SE).

Rivoli Pensão offers a fine location three blocks off the river on lovable Praça do Comércio. While a bit eccentric and minimal, it's friendly, super-clean, and a fine value (S-2,800$, D-5,500$, Ds-6,000$, Ts-7,800$, no rooms have toilets, Praça do Comércio 27, tel. 23-982-5550, NSE).

Pensão Santa Cruz overlooks the charming and traffic-free square called Praça 8 de Maio at the end of the pedestrian mall. It's a homey place, with 15 rooms van Gogh would paint. You'll find lots of stairs, dim lights, and some balconies worth requesting (D-2,500–4,000$, Db-3,500–5,500$, most expensive July–Aug, prices are soft so ask for relief if you need it, Praça 8 de Maio 21, third floor, tel. & fax 23-982-6197, www.interacesso.pt\~psantacruz, Walter and Anna SE).

Hospedaria Simões is buried in the heart of the old town, just below the old cathedral. Run by the Simões family, it offers 18 clean rooms, but only six have real windows; ask for a *quarto com janela* (Sb-3,000$, Db-3,500$, Tb-4,500$, Qb-5,600$, piles of stairs, fans, from Rua Ferreira Borges, go uphill through old gate toward cathedral, take first right, Rua Fernandes Tomas 69, tel. 23-983-4638).

On Largo da Portagem, in front of the bridge, **Residencial Larbelo** is run-down but mixes frumpiness and former elegance. The old-fashioned staircase, elegant breakfast room, and weary management take you to another age (Sb-4,000$, Db-5,000–6,000$, depending on season and plumbing—shower cheaper than bath, Largo da Portagem 33, tel. 23-982-9092, fax 23-982-9094, NSE).

The youth hostel, **Pousada de Juventude**, on the other side of town in the student area past the Praça da República, is friendly, clean, well run, and recently remodeled, but is no cheaper than a simple *pensão* (1,700–2,200$ beds in 4-bed rooms, closed 12:00–18:00, membership required, Rua Antonio Henriques Seco 14, tel. 23-982-2955, SE).

Eating in Coimbra

Restaurant Trovador, while a bit touristy, serves wonderful food in a classic and comfortable ambience, with entertaining fado performances nearly nightly after 21:00. It's the place for an old-town splurge (daily *menu* 2,500$, Mon–Sat 12:00–15:00, 19:30–22:30, closed Sun, CC:VM, facing the old cathedral, reservations necessary to eat with the music—ask for a seat with a music view, tel. 23-982-5475).

Boemia Bar, a happy student place, serves 1,000$ grilled-pork meals near the old cathedral, behind Restaurant Trovador (Mon–Sat 19:00–24:00, closed Sun).

Adega Paço do Conde knows how to grill. Choose your seafood or meat selection from the display case, and it's popped on the grill. Students, solo travelers, and families like this homey place (1,000$ meals, Mon–Sat 11:00–23:00, closed Sun,

Rua Paço do Conde 1, CC:VMA, take the last left off Praça do Comércio, opposite the church on Adelino Veiga, tel. 23-982-5605, Alfredo SE).

For a quick, easy, and cheap meal with locals next to a cool and peaceful fountain, slide a tray down the counter at **Self-Service Restaurant Jardim da Manga** (1,200$ meals, Sun–Fri 8:00–23:00, closed Sat, faces Jardim da Manga, behind Church of Santa Cruz on Rua Olimpio Nicolau Rui Fernandes, tel. 23-982-9156).

For an acceptable meal on a great square, eat at **Restaurant Praça Velha** (don't let the waiters con you, daily 8:00–01:00, Praça do Comércio 72).

The **Santa Cruz Café**, next to the Church of Santa Cruz, is Old World elegant, with outdoor tables offering great people-watching over the Praça 8 Maio.

Picnics: Shop at the municipal *mercado* behind the Church of Santa Cruz (Mon–Sat 8:00–14:00, closed Sun) or the supermarket **Minipreço** behind train station A. The well-maintained gardens along the river across from the TI are picnic-pleasant.

Transportation Connections—Coimbra

By bus to: Alcobaça (2/day, 90 min, 9:15 and 16:15, Sat–Sun 16:15 only), **Batalha** (3/day, 75 min), **Fatima** (9/day, 1 hr), **Nazaré** (5/day, 1.75 hrs, 1,300$), **Lisbon** (17/day, 2.5 hrs), **Évora** (8/day, 8.25 hrs), **Lagos** (7/day, 10 hrs with 1 change). Bus info: tel. 23-985-5270.

By train to: Nazaré/Valado (6/day, 3.5 hours, transfer in Figueira de la Foz, bus is better). Train info: tel. 23-983-4998.

To Salamanca: One train a day departs at 20:25 and drops you in Salamanca at 02:22 in the morning (5 hrs, 1-hr time difference). The better option is the direct bus (1/day Tue–Sat, 11:00–18:15, 6 hrs, 1-hr time difference, worth the 2,800–3,000$ even if you have a railpass; can buy ticket at bus station or at Abreu travel agency, Rua da Sota 2, near train station, tel. 23-982-7011).

NAZARÉ

I got hooked on Nazaré when colorful fishing boats littered its long, sandy beach. Now the boats motor comfortably into a new harbor a 30-minute walk south of town, the beach is littered with frolicking families, and it seems most of Nazaré's 10,000 inhabitants are in the tourist trade. But I still like the place.

Even with its summer crowds, Nazaré is a fun stop offering a surprisingly good look at old Portugal. Somehow the traditions survive, and the locals are able to go about their black-shawl ways. Wander the backstreets for a fine look at Portuguese family-in-the-street life. Laundry flaps in the wind, kids play soccer, and fish sizzle over tiny curbside hibachis. Squadrons of sun-dried and

Nazaré Area

salted fish are crucified on nets pulled tightly around wooden frames and left under the midday sun. Locals claim they are delightful—but I don't know. Off-season Nazaré is almost empty of tourists—inexpensive, colorful, and relaxed, with enough salty fishing-village atmosphere to make you pucker.

Nazaré doesn't have any blockbuster sights. The beach, tasty seafood, and funicular ride up to Sitio for a great coastal view are the bright lights of my lazy Nazaré memories.

Plan some beach time here. Sharing a bottle of *vinho verde* (new wine, a specialty of central Portugal) on the beach at sundown is a good way to wrap up the day.

Orientation

Nazaré faces its long beach, stretching from the new harbor north to the hill-capping old town of Sitio. Leaving the bus station, turn right and walk a block to the waterfront and survey the town. Scan the cliffs. The funicular climbs to Sitio (the hilltop part of town). Scan the road kinking toward the sea. The building (on the kink) with the yellow balconies is the Ribamir Hotel, next to the TI. Just beyond the Ribamir you'll find the main square (Praça Sousa Oliveira, with banks and ATMs) and most of my hotel listings.

Sitio, which feels like a totally separate village sitting quietly atop its cliff, is reached by a frequent funicular (110$). Go up at least for the spectacular view.

Tourist Information: The TI faces the beach (June–Aug daily 10:00–22:00; Oct–March daily 10:00–13:00, 15:00–18:00, tel. 26-256-1194). Ask about summer activities, bullfights in Sitio, and music on the beach (Sat–Sun 22:00).

Nazaré

❶ RIBAMAR HOTEL REST.
❷ ALBERGARIA MAR BRAVO
❸ RESIDENCIAL A CUBATA
❹ RESTAURANTE AQUARIO
❺ CASA DO FRANGOS REST.

Internet Access: Try the Cultural Center Library (on main road along beach on the way to the new harbor and fish market, Mon–Fri 9:30–13:00, 14:00–19:00).

Sights—Nazaré

Nazaré Fashions: Seven Petticoats and Black Widows—

Nazaré is famous for its women who wear skirts with seven petticoats. While this is mostly just a creation for the tourists, there is some basis of truth to the tradition. In the old days, women would sit on the beach waiting for their fishermen to sail home. To keep warm during a cold sea wind and stay modestly covered, they'd wear several dresses in order to fold layers over their heads, backs, and legs. Even today, older and more traditional women wear short skirts made bulky by several—but not seven—petticoats.

Black outfits are worn by a person in mourning. Traditionally, if your spouse died you wore black for the rest of your life.

This tradition is still observed, although in the last generation, widows began remarrying—considered quite racy at first.

The Beach—Since the new harbor was built in 1986, boats are no longer allowed on the beach. Before that they filled the squares in the winter and the beaches in the summer. Today it's the domain of the beach tents—a tradition in Portugal. In Nazaré, the tents are run as a cooperative by the old women you'll see sitting in the shade ready to collect 1,000$ a day. The beaches are groomed and guarded. Flags indicate danger level: red (no one in the water), yellow (wading is safe), green (no problem). If you see a mass of children parading through town down to the beach, they're likely from a huge dorm in town that provides poorer kids from this part of the country with a summer break.

Funicular to Sitio—Nazaré's funicular was built in 1889—the same year as the Eiffel Tower—by the same disciple of Eiffel who built the much-loved elevator in Lisbon. Ride up the lift; it goes every few minutes (110$ each way). Walk to the staggering Nazaré viewpoint behind the station at the top. Sitio feels different. Its people are farmers, not fishing folk.

Activities—Sitio stages Portuguese-style **bullfights** on Saturday nights from July through early September (tickets from 2,000$ at the kiosk in Praça Sousa Oliveira). Sitio's **NorParque** is a family-friendly **water park** with a pool, slides, and Jacuzzi (open June–Sept). Fish aficionados might enjoy the **auction** every weekday evening from 17:00 at the harbor (30-min walk, explain you're a *turista*, bidders have to pay an entrance fee).

A **flea market** pops up near Nazaré's town hall every Friday (9:00–13:00) and the colorful **produce market** bustles daily (8:00–13:00, off-season closed Mon, kitty-corner from the bus station).

Sleeping in Nazaré
(220$ = about $1, country code: 351, zip code: 2450)

You should have no problem finding a room, except in August, when the crowds, temperatures, and prices are all at their highest. You'll find plenty of hustlers meeting each bus and Valado train and waiting along the promenade. Even the normal hotels get into the act during the off-season. I've never arrived in town without a welcoming committee inviting me to sleep in their *quartos* (rooms in private homes).

I list a price range for each hotel: The lowest is for winter, the sky-highest for mid-July through August. In spring and fall expect to pay about midrange. You will save serious money if you arrive with no reservations and bargain. Even the big professional places are down on their knees for 10 months of the year.

Ribamar Hotel Restaurant has a prime location on the waterfront, with an Old World, hotelesque atmosphere, including 24 rooms with dark wood and four-poster beds (Sb-5,000–9,000$,

Db-6,500–12,500$, prices flexible, includes breakfast, parking-1,000$, 2,000$ in Aug, CC:VMA, some balconies, TV, good restaurant downstairs, Rua Gomes Freire 9, tel. 26-255-1158, fax 26-256-2224, some English spoken). Look for the yellow awnings and balconies.

Albergaria Mar Bravo is on the corner where the main square meets the waterfront next to Ribamar. Its 16 comfy rooms are modern, bright, and fresh, with air-conditioning and balconies (Sb-8,000–17,000$, Db-12,000–19,500$, depending on view and month, CC:VMA, elevator, Praça Sousa Oliveira 67-A, tel. 26-255-1180, fax 26-255-3979, SE).

Residencial A Cubata, a friendly place on the waterfront on the north end, has 22 small, comfortable rooms (Sb-5,000–10,000$, Db-6,500–15,000$, depends on view and season, includes breakfast, 10 percent discount with this book if you pay cash, CC:VMA, free parking, noisy bar below, Avenida da República 6, tel. 26-256-1706, fax 26-256-1700, not much English). For a peaceful night, forgo the private balcony, take a back room (saving some money), and enjoy the communal beachfront balcony.

Hotel Mare, just off the Praça Sousa Oliveira, is a big, modern, American-style hotel (Sb-6,000–11,500$, Db-8,000–14,500$, Tb-8,800–17,500$, includes breakfast, CC:VMA, all with air-con and balconies, elevator, free parking lot, Rua Mouzinho de Albuquerque 8, tel. 26-256-1122, fax 26-256-1750, SE).

Quartos: I list no dumpy hotels or cheap pensions because the best budget option is *quartos*. Like nowhere else in Iberia, locals renting spare rooms clamor for your business here. Except perhaps for weekends in August, you can stumble into town any day and find countless women hanging out on the street with fine modern rooms to rent. (I promise.) Their rooms are generally better than hotel rooms—for half the cost. Your room is likely to be large and homey, with old-time-elegant furnishings (with no plumbing but plenty of facilities down the hall) and in a quiet neighborhood, six short blocks off the beachfront action. I'd come into town and have fun looking at several places. Hem and haw and the price goes down. **Nazaré Amada** rents four fine rooms (average price for D-5,000$, 7,000$ July–Sept, Rua Adriao Batalha, garage, cellular 96-257-9371, SE).

Eating in Nazaré

In this fishing village even the snacks come from the sea. *Percebes* are local boiled barnacles, sold on the street like munchies. Merchants are happy to demonstrate how to eat them and let you sample one for free. They're great with beer in the bars.

Vinho verde, a northern Portugal specialty, is a very new wine—picked, made, and drunk within a year. It's refreshing and a bit like champagne without the bubbles, Generally white, cheap, and on every menu, it goes great with shellfish. *Amendoa amarga* is the local amaretto.

Nazaré is a fishing town, so don't order *hamburguesas*. Fresh seafood is great all over town, more expensive (but affordable) along the waterfront, and cheaper farther inland. Waiters will sometimes bring you food (such as olives or bread) that you didn't order. Just wave it away or else you'll pay for it.

A restaurant lane leads from the town square to the base of the funicular. Among the many hardworking places here, I like **Restaurante Aquario** (Largo das Caldeiras 14).

The family-run **Oficina** serves home-style seafood dishes, not fancy but filling, in a friendly setting that makes you feel like you're eating at someone's kitchen table (daily 12:00–15:00, 19:00–22:00, Rua das Flores 33, off Praça Dr. Manual Arriaga).

Chicken addicts can get roasted chickens to go at **Casa dos Frango** (Praça Dr. Manual Arriaga 20); picnic gatherers should head for the covered *mercado* across from the bus station.

Restaurante O Luis in Sitio serves excellent seafood and local cuisine to an enthusiastic crowd in a cheery atmosphere. While few tourists go here, friendly waiters make you feel very welcome. This place is worth the trouble if you want to eat well in Nazaré: Ride the lift up to Sitio and walk five minutes to Praça de Toros (2,000$ dinners, nightly 19:00–24:00, R. Teofilo Braga, tel. 26-256-1621).

Ta Mar bakery has a tempting selection of pastries and bread, including gingerbread and dense peasant bread (from bus station, take a left, then left onto the lively Rua Gil Vicente just opposite covered market, bakery is 100 meters down on the right).

Transportation Connections—Nazaré

Nazaré's train station is at Valado (3 miles toward Alcobaça, connected by semi-regular 200$ buses and reasonable, easy-to-share 1,000$ taxis). To avoid this headache, consider using intercity buses. If you're heading to Lisbon, trains and buses work equally well. While the train station is three miles from Nazaré and a trip to Lisbon requires a transfer in Cacem, you'll arrive at Lisbon's very central Rossio station (near recommended hotels). Lisbon's bus station is a Metro (or taxi) ride away from the center.

Nazaré/Valado by train to: Coimbra (6/day, 3.5 hrs, change at Foz da Figueira; see bus info below), **Lisbon** (7/day, 3 hrs). Train info: tel. 26-257-7331.

Nazaré by bus to: Alcobaça (stopping at Valado, 13/day, 20 min), **São Martinho** (9/day, 20 min), **Batalha** (8/day, 1 hr, some change at São Jorge), **Óbidos** (6/day, 1 hr; bus is better than train), **Fatima** (3/day, 90 min), **Coimbra** (6/day, 1.75 hrs; bus is better than train), **Lisbon** (5/day, 2 hrs). Buses are scarce on Sunday. Bus info: tel. 26-255-1172.

Day-tripping from Nazaré to: Alcobaça, Batalha, Fatima, or Óbidos: Traveling by bus you can see both Alcobaça and Batalha in one day (but not Sunday, when bus service is sparse). Alcobaça is easy to visit on the way to or from Batalha (and both are connected by bus with Óbidos). Ask at the bus station for schedule information and be flexible. Fatima has the fewest connections and is farthest away. Without a car, for most, Fatima is not worth the trouble. A taxi from Nazaré to Alcobaça costs about 2,000$.

BATALHA

The only reason to stop in the town of Batalha is to see its great monastery. Considered Portugal's greatest architectural achievement and a symbol of its national pride, the Batalha (which means "battle") Monastery was begun in 1388 to thank God for a Portuguese victory that kept it free from Spanish rule (600$, daily 9:00–18:00, Oct–March until 17:00, tel. 24-476-5497).

Tourist Information: The TI, located across from the monastery, has free maps and information on buses (daily 10:00–13:00, 15:00–19:00, Oct–March 14:00–18:00, tel. 24-476-5180). Batalha's market day is Monday morning.

Arrival in Batalha: If you take the bus to Batalha, you'll be dropped off within a block of the monastery and TI. There's no official luggage storage, but you can leave luggage at the monastery's ticket desk while you tour the cloisters.

Sights—Monastery of Santa María

Monastery Exterior—The equestrian statue outside the church is of Nuno Alvares Pereira, who commanded the Portuguese in the battle and masterminded the victory. Before entering the church, study the carving on the west portal (noticing the angels with their modesty wings).

Founder's Chapel—This chapel (near the church entrance) holds several royal tombs, including Henry the Navigator's. Tucked in the wall, Henry wears the church like a crown on his head.

Cloisters—Pay before entering. The greatness of Portugal's Age of Discovery shines brightly in the royal cloisters, which combine the simplicity of Gothic with the elaborate decoration of the Manueline style.

Chapter Room—This is famous for its fine and frighteningly broad vaults. The ceiling was considered so dangerous to build (it collapsed twice) that only prisoners condemned to death were allowed to work on it. Today unknowing tourists are allowed to wander under it. It's the home of Portugal's Tomb of the Unknown Soldier. The adjacent refectory holds a small museum of World War I memorabilia, and the long hall dotted with architectural scraps used to be the monks' dorm.

Keep your ticket, exit the first cloister to a square, follow signs to the right (WC is to the left), and you'll reach the...

Unfinished Chapels—The chapels were started for King Duarte around 1435 to house the tombs of his family and successors. Never finished, the building—with the best Manueline details you see here—is open to the sky. Across from the elaborate doorway are the tombs of King Duarte and his wife, their recumbent statues hand in hand, blissfully unaware of the work left undone.

Transportation Connections—Batalha
By bus to: Nazaré (5/day, 1 hr), **Alcobaça** (10/day, 30 min), **Fatima** (3/day, 30 min), and **Lisbon** (6/day, 2 hrs). Expect fewer buses on Sunday. By car, Batalha is an easy 10-mile drive from Fatima. You'll see signs from each site to the other.

FATIMA
On May 13, 1917, the Virgin Mary, "a lady brighter than the sun," visited three young shepherds and told them peace was needed. World War I raged on, so on the 13th day of each of the next five months Mary dropped in again to call for peace. On the 13th of October, 70,000 people witnessed the parting of dark storm clouds as the sun wrote "God's fiery signature" across the sky. Now, on the 13th of May, June, July, September, and October, and on the 19th of August, thousands of pilgrims gather at the huge neoclassical **basilica of Fatima** (evening torchlit processions for 2 nights, starting the night before, usually the 12th and 13th). In 1930 the Vatican recognized Fatima as legit, and in 1967, on the 50th anniversary, 1.5 million pilgrims—including the Pope—gathered here. Fatima welcomes guests. (TI tel. 24-953-1139).

The impressive **Basilica do Rosário** stands in front of a mammoth square lined with parks. (Dress modestly to enter the basilica.) Surrounding the square are a variety of hotels, restaurants, and tacky souvenir stands.

Visitors may want to check out two museums (both open daily 9:30–18:30). The **Museo de Cera de Fatima** is a series of rooms telling the story of Fatima one scene at a time with wax figures (700$, English leaflet describes each vignette). The **Museu-Vivo Aparicões**, a low-tech sound and light show, tells the same story (650$, worthless without English soundtrack playing). While the wax museum is better, both exhibits are pretty cheesy for those who are inclined not to take Fatima seriously.

Apart from the 12th and 13th of most months, cheap hotel rooms abound. Buses go from Fatima to **Batalha** (3/day, 30 min), **Leiria** (15/day 30 min), and **Lisbon** (15/day, 1.5–3 hrs, depending on route); service drops on Sunday.

ALCOBAÇA
This pleasant little town is famous for its church, the biggest in
Portugal and one of the most interesting. I find Alcobaça more
interesting than Batalha.

Tourist Information: The multilingual TI is across the
square from the church (daily 10:00–13:00, 15:00–19:00,
Nov–April closes at 18:00 and on Mon, tel. 26-258-2377).

Arrival in Alcobaça: If you arrive by bus, exit right from the
station (on Avenida Manuel da Silva Carolino), take the first right,
and continue straight (on Avenida dos Combatentes) to the town
center and monastery. It's a five-minute walk.

Sights—Alcobaça
▲▲**Cistercian Monastery of Santa María**—This abbey
church—the best Gothic building and the largest church in Portugal—is a clean and bright break from the heavier Iberian norm.
It was started in 1178 after this area was reconquered from the
Moors. It became one of the most powerful abbeys of the Cistercian
Order and a cultural center of 13th-century Portugal. The abbey,
clean and simple, is designed to be filled with hard work, prayer,
and total silence. The abbey and cloisters cost 600$ (worthwhile
200$ English leaflet, free info at TI, daily 9:00–19:00, until 17:00
off-season, tel. 26-258-3469).

Nave and Tombs of Dom Pedro and Ines: A long and
narrow nave leads to two finely carved Gothic tombs (from 1360) in
the transepts. These are of Portugal's most romantic and tragic couple, Dom Pedro (King Peter I) and Dona Inês de Castro. They rest
feet-to-feet in each transept so that on Judgment Day they'll rise and
immediately see each other again. Pedro, heir to the Portuguese
throne, was in love with the Spanish aristocrat Inês. Concerned
about Spanish influence, Pedro's father, Alfonso IV, forbade their
marriage. You guessed it—they were married secretly. The angry
father-in-law, in the interest of Portuguese independence, had Inês
murdered. When Pedro became king (1357), he ripped out and ate
the hearts of the murderers. And even more interesting, he had Inês'
rotten corpse exhumed, crowned it, and made the entire royal court
kiss what was left of her hand. Now that's *amore*. The carvings on
the tomb are just as special. Like religious alarm clocks, the attend-
ing angels are poised to wake the couple on Judgment Day. Study
the relief at the feet of Ines: Heaven, Hell, and jack-in-the-box
coffins on Judgment Day. Napoleon's troops vandalized the tombs.

More Tombs and Relics in the Sacristy: Near the king's
tomb, step into the Hall of Tombs for more deceased royalty.
Behind the high altar is the sacristy. In the round room decorated
with painted wooden sculptures, the little glassed-in hollows in the
statues and beams hold relics (tiny bits of bones or clothing) of the
monks who died in the monastery.

Cloisters: Pay before entering. Circle the cloister counter-clockwise. Cistercian monks built the abbey in 40 years, starting in 1178. They inhabited it until 1834 (when the Portuguese king disbanded all monasteries). Cistercian monks spent most of their lives in silence and were allowed to speak only when given permission by the abbot.

Kitchen: The 18th-century kitchen's giant three-part oven could roast seven oxen simultaneously. The industrious monks rerouted part of the River Alcoa to bring in running water. And how about those hard surfaces?

Refectory or Dining Hall: This is opposite the fountain in the cloister used by the monks to wash up before eating. Imagine the hall filled with monks eating in silence as one reads from the Bible atop the "Readers' Pulpit."

Hall of Kings: Located just before you reenter the nave, this hall features statues of most of Portugal's kings and tiled walls telling the story of the building of the monastery.

▲**Mercado Municipal**—The Old World is housed happily here under huge steel-and-fiberglass domes. Inside, black-clad, dried-apple-faced women choose fish, chicks, birds, and rabbits from their respective death rows. You'll also find figs, melons, bushels of grain, and nuts—it's a caveman's Safeway. Buying a picnic is a perfect excuse to drop in (Mon–Sat 9:00–13:00, closed Sun, best on Mon). It's a five-minute walk from the TI or bus station; ask a local, "*Mercado municipal?*"

▲▲**National Museum of Wine (Museu Nacional do Vinho)**—This museum, a half-mile outside Alcobaça (on the road to Batalha and Leiria, right-hand side), offers a fascinating look at the wine of Portugal (Tue–Sun 9:00–12:30, 14:00–17:30, opens 1 hr later Sat–Sun, closed Mon and off-season Sun, tel. 26-258-2222; your car is safer parked inside the gate). Run by a local cooperative winery, the museum teaches you everything you never wanted to know about Portuguese wine in a series of rooms that used to be fermenting vats. With some luck you can get a tour—much more hands-on than French winery tours—through the actual winery.

Eating in Alcobaça

Restaurante Coracoes Unidos is a fine, tourist-free restaurant in an old school (near the abbey and across the street from the post office).

Transportation Connections—Alcobaça

By bus to: Lisbon (5/day, 2 hrs), **Nazaré** (12/day, 30 min), **Batalha** (4/day, 30 min), **Fatima** (3/day, 75 min, more frequent with transfer in Batalha). Bus frequency drops on Sunday. A taxi to the Valado train station costs 800$; to Nazaré, 1,700$.

ÓBIDOS

This medieval walled town was Portugal's "wedding city"—the perfect gift for a king to give to a queen who has everything. (Beats a toaster.) Today it's preserved in its entirety as a national monument surviving on tourism. Óbidos is crowded all summer, especially in August. Filter out the tourists and see it as you would a beautiful painted tile. It's worth a quick visit.

Postcard perfect, the town sits atop a hill, its 40-foot-high 14th-century wall corralling a bouquet of narrow lanes and flower-bedecked, whitewashed houses. Óbidos is ideal for photographers who want to make Portugal look prettier than it is. Walk around the wall and peek into the castle (now an overly-impressed-with-itself *pousada*, Db-34,000$, CC:VMA, tel. 26-295-9105, fax 26-295-9148).

Wander the back lanes and lose yourself in this lived-in open-air museum of medieval town nonplanning. Study the centuries-old houses and drop by the churches. St. Mary's Church, on the town square, gleams with lovely 17th-century *azulejo* tiles. The small Municipal Museum, also on the square, is not worth the 300$ unless you enjoy stairs, religious art, and Portuguese inscriptions. Outside the town walls are a 16th-century aqueduct, a windmill, and a small produce market.

Óbidos is tough on the average tourist's budget. Pick up your picnic at the small grocery store just inside the main gate (on the street heading downhill), the larger grocery near the TI on Rua Direita, or the tiny market just outside the town wall.

Orientation

Tourist Information: There are two TIs almost next to each other in the middle of town on the main street, Rua Direita. The Região de Turismo do Oeste covers the region, and, a few doors down, the TI specializes in the town (Sun–Fri 9:30–19:00, Sat 10:00–13:00, 14:00–18:00, Oct–April 9:30–18:00, tel. 26-295-9231).

Arrival in Óbidos: Ideally take a bus to Óbidos and leave by either bus or train. If you arrive at the train station, you're faced with a 20-minute uphill hike into town (a killer with luggage). The bus drops you off much closer (go up the steps and through the archway on the right). While there's no official place to store luggage, the TI will let you leave your bag there.

Sleeping and Eating in Óbidos

To enjoy the town without tourists, spend the night. Two reasonable values in this overpriced toy of a town are the hotelesque **Albergaria Rainha Santa Isabel** (Sb-9,500–12,500$, Db-11,500–14,000$, third person-3,000$, includes breakfast, CC:VMA, air-con, elevator, on the main one-lane drag, Rua Direita, 2510 Óbidos, tel. 26-295-9323, fax 26-295-9115, e-mail: arsio@oeste .online.pt, SE) and **Casa do Poço**, with four dim, clean rooms around a bright courtyard (Db-9,000–14,500$, Tb-16,000$, includes breakfast, Travessa da Mouraria, 2510 Óbidos, in old center near castle, tel. 26-295-9358, fax 26-295-9282, SE).

For less-expensive intimacy, try a *quarto*. Signs advertise rooms for rent all over town. **Lelia** and **Joao Fonseca da Silva** rent two good rooms (D-5,000$, 100 meters in from the town gate on the low road, Rua Josefa d'Obidos, tel. 26-295-9113, NSE).

Eating: At **Restaurant O Barco**, professionals Mariana and Walter serve international and Portuguese cuisine with a French accent (2,500$, Tue–Sun 12:30–14:30, 19:30–22:00, closed Mon, walk down from St. Mary's Church, Largo Dr. Joao Lourenco, tel. 26-295-0925).

Transportation Connections—Óbidos
To: Nazaré (5 buses/day, 1 hr), **Lisbon** (3 buses/day, 75 min; 7 trains/day, 2 hrs, transfer in Cacem), **Alcobaça** (6 buses/day, 1 hr), **Batalha** (4 buses/day, 2 hrs). Fewer buses run on Sunday.

Route Tips for Drivers in Central Portugal
Lisbon to Coimbra: This is an easy 2.5-hour straight shot on the slick Auto-Estrada A1 (toll: 2,200$). You'll pass convenient exits for Fatima and the Roman ruins of Conimbriga along the way. Leave the freeway on the easy-to-miss first Coimbra exit and then follow the "centro" signs. Four kilometers after leaving the freeway you'll cross the Mondego River. You can go straight to the Ecovia park-and-ride (cheap parking, 2 blocks past the bridge, shuttle bus to the town center) or arc right, following Avenida Fernão de Magalhaes directly into town. Most hotels are near the train station and the next bridge—Ponte de Santa Clara. Free parking (safe during the day) is just over the Santa Clara Bridge.

Óbidos to Lisbon: Don't drive into tiny, cobbled Óbidos. Ample tourist parking is provided outside of town. From Óbidos, the slick tollway zips you directly into Lisbon. For arriving and parking in Lisbon, see that chapter. If going to Sintra, follow signs to Cascais as you approach Lisbon.

APPENDIX

Iberian History

The cultural landscape of modern Spain and Portugal was shaped by the various civilizations that settled on the peninsula. Iberia's sunny weather and fertile soil made it a popular place to call home.

The Greeks came to Cadiz around 1100 B.C., followed by the Romans, who occupied the country for almost 1,000 years, until A.D. 400. Long after the empire crumbled, the Roman influence remained and could be found in things like cultural values, materials, building techniques, and even Roman-style farming equipment, which was used well into the 19th century. And, of course, there was wine.

Moors (711–1492)

The Moors—North Africans of the Moslem faith who occupied Spain—had the greatest cultural influence on Spanish and Portuguese history. They arrived on the Rock of Gibraltar in A.D. 711 and moved north. In the incredibly short time of seven years, the Moors completely conquered the peninsula.

The Moors established their power and Moslem culture in a subtle way. Non-Moslems were tolerated and often rose to positions of wealth and power; Jewish culture flourished. Rather than brutal subjugation, the Moorish style of conquest was to employ their sophisticated culture to develop whatever they found. For example, they encouraged wine-making, although for religious reasons they themselves weren't allowed to drink alcohol.

The Moors ruled for more than 700 years. Throughout that time, pockets of Christianity remained. Local Christian kings fought against the Moors whenever they could, whittling away at the Moslem empire, gaining more and more land. The last Moorish stronghold, Granada, fell to the Christians in 1492.

The slow, piecemeal process of the Reconquista split the peninsula into the independent states of Portugal and Spain. In 1139 Alfonso Henriques conquered the Moors near present-day Beja in southern Portugal and proclaimed himself king of the area. By 1200 the Christian state of Portugal had the borders it does today, making it the oldest unchanged state in Europe. The rest of the peninsula was a loosely-knit collection of smaller kingdoms. Spain's major step toward unity was in 1469, when Fernando II of Aragon married Isabel of Castile. Known as the "Catholic Monarchs," they united the other kingdoms under their rule.

The Golden Age (1500–1700)

The expulsion of the Moors set the stage for the rise of Portugal and Spain as naval powers and colonial superpowers. The

Spaniards, fueled by the religious fervor of the Reconquista, were interested in spreading Christianity to the newly-discovered New World. Wherever they landed, they tried to Christianize the natives—with the sword, if necessary.

The Portuguese expansion was motivated more by economic concerns. Their excursions overseas were planned, cool, and rational. They colonized the nearby coasts of Africa first, progressing slowly around Africa to Asia and South America.

Through exploration (and exploitation) of the colonies, tremendous quantities of gold came into each country. The aristocracy and the clergy were swimming in money. It was only natural that art and courtly life flourished during this Golden Age.

Slow Decline

The fast money from the colonies kept Spain and Portugal from seeing the dangers at home. Great Britain and the Netherlands also were becoming naval powers, defeating the Spanish Armada in 1588. The Portuguese imported everything, stopped growing their own wheat, and neglected their fields.

During the centuries when science and technology in other European countries developed as never before, Spain and Portugal were preoccupied by their failed colonial politics. In the 18th century Spain was ruled by the French Bourbon family. (This explains the French Baroque architecture that you'll see, such as La Granja near Segovia and the Royal Palace in Madrid.) Endless battles, wars of succession, revolutions, and counterrevolutions weakened the countries. In this chaos there was no chance to develop democratic forms of government. Dictators in both countries made the rich richer and kept the masses underprivileged.

During World War I Portugal fought on the Allied side and Spain stayed neutral. In World War II both countries were neutral, uninterested in foreign policy as long as there was quiet in their own states. In the 1930s Spain suffered a bloody and bitter civil war between fascist and democratic forces. The fascist dictator Francisco Franco prevailed, ruling the country until his death in 1975.

Democracy in Spain and Portugal is still young. After a bloodless revolution, Portugal held democratic elections in 1975. After 41 years of a fascist dictatorship, Spain finally had elections in 1977.

Today socialists are in power in both countries. They've adopted a policy of balance to save the young democracies and fight problems such as unemployment and foreign debts—with moderate success. Spain recently joined the European Union. Today Spain's economy is among the fastest growing in Europe.

Art

The "Big Three" in Spanish painting are El Greco, Velázquez, and Goya.

El Greco (1541–1614) exemplifies the spiritual fervor of much Spanish art. The drama, the surreal colors, and the intentionally unnatural distortion have the intensity of a religious vision.

Diego Velázquez (1599–1660) went to the opposite extreme. His masterful court portraits are studies in realism and cool detachment from his subjects.

Goya (1746–1828) matched Velázquez's technique but not his detachment. He let his liberal tendencies shine through in unflattering portraits of royalty and in emotional scenes of abuse of power. He unleashed his inner passions in the eerie, nightmarish canvases of his last, "dark" stage.

Not quite in the league of the Big Three, Murillo (1617–1682) painted a dreamy world of religious visions. His pastel, soft-focus works of cute baby Jesuses and radiant Virgin Marys helped make Catholic doctrine palatable to the common folk at a time when many were defecting to Protestantism.

You'll also find plenty of foreign art in Spain's museums. During its Golden Age, Spain's wealthy aristocrats bought wagon-loads of the most popular art of the time—Italian Renaissance and Baroque works by Titian, Tintoretto, and others. They also loaded up on paintings by Rubens, Bosch, and Brueghel from the Low Countries, which were under Spanish rule.

In this century Pablo Picasso (don't miss his *Guernica* mural in Madrid), Joan Miró, and surrealist Salvador Dalí have made their marks (great museums featuring all three are in or near Barcelona).

Architecture

The two most fertile periods of architectural innovation in Spain and Portugal were during the Moorish occupation and in the Golden Age. Otherwise, Spanish architects have marched obediently behind the rest of Europe.

The Moors brought Middle Eastern styles with them, such as the horseshoe arch, minarets, and floor plans designed for mosques. Islam forbids the sculpting or painting of human or animal figures ("graven images"), so artists expressed their creativity with elaborate geometric patterns. The ornate stucco of Granada's Alhambra, the elaborate arches of Sevilla's Alcázar, and decorative colored tiles are evidence of the Moorish sense of beauty. Islamic and Christian elements were blended in the work of Mozarabic (Christians living under Moorish rule) and Mudejar (Moors living in Spain after the Christian reconquest) artists.

As the Christians slowly reconquered the country, they turned their fervor into stone, building churches both in the heavy, fortress-of-God Romanesque style (Lisbon's cathedral) and in the lighter, heaven-reaching, stained-glass Gothic style (Barcelona, Toledo, Sevilla). Gothic was an import from France, trickling into conservative Spain long after it swept through Europe.

The money reaped and raped from Spain's colonies in the Golden Age spurred new construction. Churches and palaces were built using the solid, geometric style of the Italian Renaissance (El Escorial) and the more ornamented Baroque. Ornamentation reached unprecedented heights in Spain, culminating in the Plateresque style of stonework, so called because it resembles intricate silver filigree work. Portugal's highly ornamented answer to Plateresque is called Manueline. Lisbon's Belém Tower is its best example.

In the 18th and 19th centuries, innovation in both countries died out. Spain's major contribution to modern architecture is the Art Nouveau work of Antonio Gaudí early in this century. Most of his "cake-left-out-in-the-rain" buildings, with asymmetrical designs and sinuous lines, can be found in Barcelona.

Bullfighting—Legitimate Slice of Spain or Cruel Spectacle?

The Spanish bullfight is as much a ritual as it is sport. Not to acknowledge the importance of the bullfight is to censor a venerable part of Spanish culture. But it also makes a spectacle out of the cruel killing of an animal. Should tourists boycott bullfights? I don't know.

Today bullfighting is less popular among locals. If this trend continues, bullfighting may survive more and more as a tourist event. When the day comes that bullfighting is kept alive by our tourist dollars rather than the local culture, then I'll agree with those who say bullfighting is immoral and that tourists shouldn't encourage it by buying tickets. Consider the morality of supporting this gruesome aspect of Spanish culture before buying a ticket. If you do decide to attend a bullfight, here is what you'll see.

While no two bullfights are the same, they unfold along a strict pattern. The ceremony begins punctually with a parade of participants around the ring. Then the trumpet sounds, the "Gate of Fear" opens, and the leading player—*el toro*—thunders in. An angry half-ton animal is an awesome sight, even from the cheap seats.

The fight is divided into three acts. Act 1 is designed to size up the bull and wear him down. The matador (literally "killer"), with help from his assistants, attracts the bull with the shake of the cape, then directs the animal past his body, as close as his bravery allows. The bull sees only things in motion and red. After a few passes the picadors enter, mounted on horseback, to spear the swollen lump of muscle at the back of the bull's neck. This lowers the bull's head and weakens the thrust of his horns. (In the 19th century horses had no protective pads and were often killed.)

In Act 2, the matador's assistants (banderilleros) continue to enrage and weaken the bull. The unarmed banderillero charges the charging bull and, leaping acrobatically across its path, plunges brightly-colored barbed sticks into the bull's vital neck muscle.

After a short intermission, during which the matador may, according to tradition, ask permission to kill the bull and dedicate the kill to someone in the crowd, the final, lethal act 3 begins.

The matador tries to dominate and tire the bull with hypnotic cape work. A good pass is when the matador stands completely still while the bull charges past. Then the matador thrusts a sword between the animal's shoulder blades for the kill. A quick kill is not always easy, and the matador may have to make several bloody thrusts before the sword stays in and the bull finally dies. Mules drag the bull out, and his meat is in the market *mañana*. *Rabo del toro* (bull-tail stew) is a delicacy.

Throughout the fight, the crowd shows its approval or impatience. Shouts of "*¡Olé!*" or "*¡Torero!*" mean they like what they see. Whistling or rhythmic hand-clapping greets cowardice and incompetence.

You're not likely to see much human blood spilled. In 200 years of bullfighting in Sevilla, only 30 fighters have died (and only one was actually a matador).

If a bull does kill a fighter, the next matador comes in to kill him. Even the bull's mother is killed, since the evil qualities are assumed to have come from the mother.

After an exceptional fight, the crowd may wave white handkerchiefs to ask that the matador be awarded the bull's ear or tail. A brave bull, though dead, gets a victory lap from the mule team on his way to the slaughterhouse. Then the trumpet sounds, and a new bull barges in to face a fresh matador.

A typical bullfight lasts about three hours and consists of six separate fights—three matadors (each with their own team of picadors and banderilleros) fighting two bulls each. For a closer look at bullfighting by an American aficionado, read Ernest Hemingway's classic *Death in the Afternoon*.

The Portuguese bullfight is different from the Spanish bullfight. For a description, see the Lisbon chapter. In Portugal, the bull is not killed in front of the crowd (but it is killed later).

Fiestas

Iberia has many regional and surprise holidays. Regular nationwide holidays are as follows:

Portugal: January 1, Easter, April 25, May 1, June 10, August 15, October 5, November 1, December 1, December 8, and December 25.

Spain: January 1, January 6, March 19, Good Friday, Easter, May 1, Corpus Christi (early June), June 24, June 29, July 18, July 25, August 15, October 12, November 1, December 8, and December 25.

Spain and Portugal erupt with fiestas and celebrations throughout the year. Semana Santa (Holy Week) fills the week before Easter with processions and festivities all over, but especially in Sevilla. To run with the bulls, be in Pamplona the second week in July. For more information, call or write to the Spanish or Portuguese National Tourist Offices (see page 8).

Numbers and Stumblers

- Europeans write a few of their numbers differently than we do: 1 = 1 , 4 = 4 , 7= 7. Learn the difference or miss your train.
- Europeans write dates as day/month/year (Christmas is 25/12/01).
- Commas are decimal points, and decimals are commas. A dollar and a half is 1,50. There are 5.280 feet in a mile.
- When pointing, use your whole hand, palm downward.
- When counting with fingers, start with your thumb. If you hold up your first finger to request one item, you'll probably get two.
- What we Americans call the second floor of a building is the first floor in Europe.
- Europeans keep the left "lane" open for passing on escalators and moving sidewalks. Keep to the right.

Let's Talk Telephones

This is a primer on telephoning in Europe. For specifics on Spain and Portugal, see "Telephones" in the Introduction.

Dialing Direct

Calling between Countries: Dial the international access code (of the country you're calling from), then the country code (of the country you're calling), the area code (if it starts with zero, drop the zero), and the local number. Note that Spain and Portugal don't use area codes (see "Europe's Exceptions," below). International access codes and country codes are listed on the next page.

Calling Long Distance within a Country: In most European countries, dial the area code (including its zero), then the local number. In Spain and Portugal all numbers have nine digits and are dialed direct throughout each country.

Europe's Exceptions: Some countries, such as Spain, Portugal, France, Italy, Norway, and Denmark, do not use area codes. To make an international call to these countries, dial the international access code (00 if you're calling from Europe, 011 from the United States or Canada), then the country code, then the local number in its entirety. (OK, so there's one exception—for France, drop the initial zero of the local number.) To make long-distance calls within any of these countries, simply dial the local number.

International Access Codes

When dialing direct, first dial the international access code of the country you're calling from. Virtually all European countries use "00" (the only exceptions are Finland, 990; Estonia, 800; and Lithuania, 810). For both the United States and Canada, it's "011."

Country Codes

After you've dialed the international access code, dial the code of the country you're calling.

Austria—43	Ireland—353
Belgium—32	Italy—39
Britain—44	Morocco—212
Canada—1	Netherlands—31
Czech Rep.—420	Norway—47
Denmark—45	Portugal—351
Estonia—372	Russia—7
Finland—358	Spain—34
France—33	Sweden—46
Germany—49	Switzerland—41
Greece—30	U.S.A.—1

Dial Away...

United States to Spain: 011/34/nine-digit number
United States to Portugal: 011/351/nine-digit number
Spain or Portugal to United States: 00/1/area code/number
Spain to Portugal: 00/351/nine-digit number
Portugal to Spain: 00/34/nine-digit number
Long Distance within Spain or within Portugal: Whether dialing across the street or across the country, use the same nine-digit number.
Directory Assistance: In Spain, dial 1004 for local numbers and 025 for international numbers (expensive). In Portugal, dial 13. (Note: In Spain a 608 or 609 area code indicates a mobile phone.)

Calling-Card Operators

It's cheaper to call direct, but some travelers prefer to use their calling cards (AT&T, MCI, or Sprint).

	AT&T	MCI	SPRINT
Spain	900-990-011	900-99-0014	900-99-0013
Portugal	05-017-1288	050-171-234	800-800-187
Morocco	002-110-011	002-110-012	———
Gibraltar	8800	———	———

Climate

First line, average daily low temperature; second line, average daily high; third line, days of no rain.

J	F	M	A	M	J	J	A	S	O	N	D

MOROCCO
Marrakesh

40°	43°	48°	52°	57°	62°	67°	68°	63°	57°	49°	42°
65°	68°	74°	79°	84°	92°	101°	100°	92°	83°	73°	66°
24	23	25	24	29	29	30	30	27	27	27	24

PORTUGAL
Lisbon

46°	47°	50°	53°	55°	60°	63°	63°	62°	58°	52°	47°
57°	59°	63°	67°	71°	77°	81°	82°	79°	72°	63°	58°
16	16	17	20	21	25	29	29	24	22	17	16

Faro (Algarve)

48°	49°	52°	55°	58°	64°	67°	68°	65°	60°	55°	50°
60°	61°	64°	67°	71°	77°	83°	83°	78°	72°	66°	61°
22	21	21	24	27	29	31	31	29	25	22	22

SPAIN
Madrid

35°	36°	41°	45°	50°	58°	63°	63°	57°	49°	42°	36°
47°	52°	59°	65°	70°	80°	87°	85°	77°	65°	55°	48°
23	21	21	21	21	25	29	28	24	23	21	21

Barcelona

43°	45°	48°	52°	57°	65°	69°	69°	66°	58°	51°	46°
55°	57°	60°	65°	71°	78°	82°	82°	77°	69°	62°	56°
26	23	23	21	23	24	27	25	23	22	24	25

Almeria (Costa del Sol)

46°	47°	51°	55°	59°	65°	70°	71°	68°	60°	54°	49°
60°	61°	64°	68°	72°	78°	83°	84°	81°	73°	67°	62°
25	24	26	25	28	29	31	30	27	26	26	26

Metric Conversion (approximate)

1 inch = 25 millimeters	32 degrees F = 0 degrees C
1 foot = 0.3 meter	82 degrees F = about 28 degrees C
1 yard = 0.9 meter	1 ounce = 28 grams
1 mile = 1.6 kilometers	1 kilogram = 2.2 pounds
1 centimeter = 0.4 inch	1 quart = 0.95 liter
1 meter = 39.4 inches	1 square yard = 0.8 square meter
1 kilometer = .62 mile	1 acre = 0.4 hectare

Basic Spanish Survival Phrases

Hello.	**Hola.**	**oh**-lah
Do you speak English?	**¿Habla usted inglés?**	**ah**-blah oo-**stehd** een-**glays**
Yes. / No.	**Sí. / No.**	see / noh
I don't speak Spanish.	**No hablo español.**	noh **ah**-bloh ay-spahn-**yohl**
I'm sorry.	**Lo siento.**	loh see-**ehn**-toh
Please.	**Por favor.**	por fah-**bor**
Thank you.	**Gracias.**	**grah**-thee-ahs
Goodbye.	**Adiós.**	ah-dee-**ohs**
Where is a...?	**¿Donde hay un...?**	**dohn**-day ī oon
...hotel	**...hotel**	oh-**tel**
...youth hostel	**...albergue de juventud**	ahl-**behr**-gay day *h*oo-behn-**tood**
...restaurant	**...restaurante**	ray-stoh-**rahn**-tay
...supermarket	**...supermercado**	soo-pehr-mehr-**kah**-doh
Where is the...?	**¿Dónde está la...?**	**dohn**-day ay-**stah** lah
...train station	**...estación de trenes**	ay-stah-thee-**ohn** day **tray**-nays
...tourist information office	**...Oficina de Turismo**	oh-fee-**thee**-nah day too-**rees**-moh
Where are the toilets?	**¿Dónde están los servicios?**	**dohn**-day ay-**stahn** lohs sehr-**bee**-thee-ohs
men / women	**hombres / mujeres**	**ohm**-brays / moo-*h*eh-rays
How much is it?	**¿Cuánto cuesta?**	**kwahn**-toh **kway**-stah
Write it?	**¿Me lo escribe?**	may loh ay-**skree**-bay
Cheap(er).	**(Más) barato.**	(mahs) bah-**rah**-toh
Is it included?	**¿Está incluido?**	ay-**stah** een-kloo-ee-**ee**-doh
I would like...	**Quería...**	keh-**ree**-ah
We would like...	**Queríamos...**	keh-**ree**-ah-mohs
...a ticket.	**...un billete.**	oon bee-**yeh**-tay
...a room.	**...una habitación.**	**oo**-nah ah-bee-tah-thee-**ohn**
...the bill.	**...la cuenta.**	lah **kwayn**-tah
one	**uno**	**oo**-noh
two	**dos**	dohs
three	**tres**	trays
four	**cuatro**	**kwah**-troh
five	**cinco**	**theen**-koh
six	**seis**	says
seven	**siete**	see-**eh**-tay
eight	**ocho**	**oh**-choh
nine	**nueve**	**nway**-bay
ten	**diez**	dee-**ayth**
At what time?	**¿A qué hora?**	ah kay **oh**-rah
now / later	**ahora / más tarde**	**ah-oh**-rah / mahs **tar**-day
today / tomorrow	**hoy / mañana**	oy / mahn-**yah**-nah

Basic Portuguese Survival Phrases

Hello.	**Olá.**	oh-**lah**
Do you speak English?	**Fala inglês?**	**fah**-lah een-**glaysh**
Yes. / No.	**Sim. / Não.**	seeng / now
I'm sorry.	**Desculpe.**	dish-**kool**-peh
Please.	**Por favor.**	poor fah-**vor**
Thank you.	**Obrigado[a].**	oh-bree-**gah**-doo
Goodbye.	**Adeus.**	ah-**deh**-oosh
Where is...?	**Onde é que é...?**	**ohn**-deh eh keh eh
...a hotel	**...um hotel**	oon oh-**tehl**
...a youth hostel	**...uma pousada de juventude**	**oo**-mah poh-**zah**-dah deh zhoo-vayn-**too**-deh
...a restaurant	**...um restaurante**	oon rish-toh-**rahn**-teh
...a supermarket	**...um supermercado**	oon soo-pehr-mehr-**kah**-doo
...the train station	**...a estação de comboio**	ah ish-tah-**sow** deh kohn-**boy**-yoo
...tourist information	**...a informação turistica**	ah een-for-mah-**sow** too-**reesh**-tee-kah
...the toilet	**...a casa de banho**	ah **kah**-zah deh **bahn**-yoo
men / women	**homens / mulheres**	**aw**-maynsh / mool-**yeh**-rish
How much is it?	**Quanto custa?**	**kwahn**-too **koosh**-tah
Cheap(er).	**(Mais) barato.**	(mīsh) bah-**rah**-too
Is it included?	**Está incluido?**	ish-**tah** een-kloo-**ee**-doo
I would like...	**Gostaria...**	goosh-tah-**ree**-ah
...a ticket.	**...um bilhete.**	oon beel-**yeh**-teh
...a room.	**...um quarto.**	oon **kwar**-too
...the bill.	**...a conta.**	ah **kohn**-tah
one	**um**	oon
two	**dois**	doysh
three	**três**	traysh
four	**quatro**	**kwah**-troo
five	**cinco**	**seeng**-koo
six	**seis**	saysh
seven	**sete**	**seh**-teh
eight	**oito**	**oy**-too
nine	**nove**	**naw**-veh
ten	**dez**	dehsh
At what time?	**A que horas?**	ah keh **aw**-rahsh
now / soon / later	**agora / em breve / mais tarde**	ah-**goh**-rah / ayn **bray**-veh / mīsh **tar**-deh
Today.	**Hoje.**	**oh**-zheh
Tomorrow.	**Amanhã.**	ah-ming-**yah**

For 336 more pages of survival phrases for your next trip to Iberia, check out *Rick Steves' Spanish & Portuguese Phrase Book and Dictionary*.

Road Scholar Feedback for
SPAIN & PORTUGAL 2001

We're all in the same travelers' school of hard knocks. Your feedback helps us improve this guidebook for future travelers. Please fill this out (or use the on-line version at www.ricksteves.com/feedback), attach more info or any tips/favorite discoveries if you like, and send it to us. As thanks for your help, we'll send you our quarterly travel newsletter free for one year. Thanks! **Rick**

Of the recommended accommodations/restaurants used, which was:

Best _____

      Why? _____

Worst _____

      Why? _____

Of the sights/experiences/destinations recommended by this book, which was:

Most overrated _____

      Why? _____

Most underrated _____

      Why? _____

Best ways to improve this book:

_____

_____

I'd like a free newsletter subscription:

_____ Yes   _____ No   _____ Already on list

_____
Name

_____
Address

_____
City, State, Zip

_____
E-mail Address

Please send to: ETBD, Box 2009, Edmonds, WA 98020

Faxing Your Hotel Reservation

Faxing is more accurate and cheaper than telephoning. Use this handy form for your fax (or find it online at www.ricksteves.com /reservation). Photocopy and fax away.

One-Page Fax

To: _____ @ _____
                    hotel   *fax*

From: _____ @ _____
                    name   *fax*

Today's date: ____ /_____ /____
                day   *month* *year*

Dear Hotel _____,

Please make this reservation for me:

Name: _____

Total # of people: _____   # of rooms: _____   # of nights: _____

Arriving: ____ /_____ /____ My time of arrival (24-hr clock): _____
            day *month* *year*   (I will telephone if I will be late)

Departing: ____ /_____ /____
            day *month* *year*

Room(s): Single___ Double___ Twin___ Triple___ Quad___

With: Toilet___ Shower___ Bath___ Sink only___

Special needs: View___ Quiet___ Cheap___ Ground Floor___

Credit card: Visa___ MasterCard___ American Express___

Card #: _____

Expiration date:_____

Name on card: _____

You may charge me for the first night as a deposit. Please fax, e-mail, or mail me confirmation of my reservation, along with the type of room reserved, the price, and whether the price includes breakfast. Thank you.

_____
Signature

_____
Name

_____
Address

_____
City   *State*   *Zip Code*   *Country*

_____
E-mail Address

INDEX

AVALON
TRAVEL
publishing

BECAUSE TRAVEL MATTERS.

AVALON TRAVEL PUBLISHING knows that travel is more than coming and going—travel is taking part in new experiences, new ideas, and a new outlook. Our goal is to bring you complete and up-to-date information to help you make informed travel decisions.

AVALON TRAVEL GUIDES feature a combination of practicality and spirit, offering a unique traveler-to-traveler perspective perfect for an afternoon hike, around-the-world journey, or anything in between.

WWW.TRAVELMATTERS.COM

Avalon Travel Publishing guides are available at your favorite book or travel store.